LOYALTY AND LOCALITY

POPULAR ALLEGIANCE IN DEVON
DURING THE ENGLISH
CIVIL WAR

LOYALTY AND LOCALITY

POPULAR ALLEGIANCE IN DEVON
DURING THE ENGLISH
CIVIL WAR

by
Mark Stoyle

UNIVERSITY
of
EXETER
PRESS

First published 1994 by
University of Exeter Press
Reed Hall, Streatham Drive
Exeter, Devon EX4 4QR
UK

© Mark Stoyle 1994
The right of Mark Stoyle to be identified as author
of this work has been asserted by him in accordance with
the Copyright, Designs & Patents Act 1988.

British Library Cataloguing in Publication Data
A catalogue record of this book is
available from the British Library

ISBN 0 85989 428 2

Typeset in 11/13pt Stempel Garamond
by Colin Bakké Typesetting, Exeter
Printed and bound in Great Britain
by Short Run Press Ltd, Exeter

For Lynn

Contents

PART III:
THE DETERMINANTS OF ALLEGIANCE, c.1600–1642

PART IV:
THE NATIONAL PICTURE

Illustrations

Abbreviations

APC	J.R. Dasent et al. (eds), *Acts of the Privy Council.*
BL	British Library, London.
Bod.	Bodleian Library, Oxford.
CCAM	M.A.E. Green (ed.), *Calendar of the Committee for Advance of Money, 1643–56,* (three volumes, 1881).
CCC	M.A.E. Green (ed.), *Calendar of the Committee for Compounding, 1643–60,* (five volumes, 1882–92).
CRO	Cornish Record Office, Truro.
CSPD	*Calendar of State Papers Domestic.*
CWA	Churchwardens' Accounts.
DCNG	*Devon and Cornwall Notes and Gleanings.*
DCNQ	Devon and Cornwall Notes and Queries.
DCRS	Devon and Cornwall Record Society.
DNB	*Dictionary of National Biography.*
DRO	Devon Record Office, Exeter.
E	Thomason Tracts, kept at the British Library.
ECAB	Exeter Chamber Act Book.
EHR	*English Historical Review.*
ECL	Exeter Cathedral Library.
EMAFU	Exeter Museums Archaeological Field Unit.
EQSOB	Quarter Sessions Order Books for the City of Exeter, kept at the Devon Record Office.
EQSR	Quarter Sessions Rolls for the City of Exeter, kept at the Devon Record Office.
HJ	*Historical Journal.*
HMC	*Historical Manuscripts Commission.*
JBS	*Journal of British Studies.*
JEH	*Journal of Ecclesiastical History.*
JHC	*Journal of the House of Commons.*
JHL	*Journal of the House of Lords.*

KAO   Kent Archives Office.
Nd   No date of publication.
NDRO   North Devon Record Office, Barnstaple.
P&P   *Past and Present.*
PRO   Public Record Office, London.
QSB   Quarter Sessions Rolls for the County of Devon, kept at the Devon Record Office.
QSOB   Quarter Sessions Order Books for the County of Devon, kept at the Devon Record Office.
RTPI   *Report and Transactions of the Plymouth Institution.*
SP   State Papers.
SRO   Somersetshire Record Office, Taunton.
TDA   *Report and Transactions of the Devonshire Association.*
TRHS   *Transactions of the Royal Historical Society.*
WA   *The Western Antiquary.*
WCSL   West Country Studies Library, Exeter.
WDRO   West Devon Record Office, Plymouth.

Acknowledgements

This book, which is a revised version of my Oxford D.Phil. thesis completed in October 1992, owes a great deal to a great many people. First, I should like to thank the bodies which have provided financial assistance: the British Academy for funding my initial research during 1988-91 and for electing me to a post-doctoral fellowship in 1993, the Institute of Historical Research for awarding me a Scouloudi Research Fellowship in 1991, and St Peter's College Oxford for presenting me with a graduate award in the same year. Second, I am grateful to the staff of the various record repositories which I have visited—the Bodleian Library, the British Museum, the Cornish Record Office, the Somerset Record Office, the Public Record Office and Dr Williams' Library—for the prompt and efficient service which they provide. I am especially indebted to Margery Rowe and her staff at the Devon Record Office and to Sheila Stirling and the librarians of the Devon and Exeter Institution for their unfailing helpfulness and courtesy throughout the course of my research. Third, I should like to thank Mike Rouillard of Exeter University's Archaeological Drawing Office for producing the maps which accompany this book, and Mike Dobson and Phil Semper of Project Pallas for helping to arrange the text.

Many generous scholars have helped me over the past six years. Richard Cust, Cliff Davies, Anne Duffin, Alastair Duke, Sean Goddard, Todd Gray, Tom Greeves, Chris Henderson, Jannine Juddery, Susan Lawrence, Stephen Porter, Ivan Roots, Dora Thornton, Nicholas Tyacke and Joyce Youings all provided information, assistance and advice. Simon Baker, Jonathan Barry, Martin Ingram, Marjorie McIntosh and Mary Wolffe read, and commented upon, my original thesis. Their comments have been invaluable. John Morrill and David Underdown—whose debate in the *Journal of British Studies* in 1985 first sparked off my interest in the subject of popular allegiance—have provided inspiration and encouragement ever since and I am deeply indebted to them both. My greatest intellectual debts are to Gerald Aylmer, George Bernard and Kevin Sharpe. Without them this book would have been immeasurably the poorer, indeed it would probably never have been written at all. I am more grateful to them than I can say. Most of all I would like to thank my parents, and my wife, Lynn.

Mark Stoyle
University of Exeter, May 1994.

Preface

Early one February morning in 1643 a body of horsemen swept down on the little moorland town of Chagford in Mid-Devon. The troopers were Cavaliers, or Royalists, supporters of King Charles I in his war against the Parliament, and they formed the advance guard of a much larger army which had recently crossed into Devon from Cornwall. At the troopers' head rode many gentlemen, including the poet Sidney Godolphin. The Cavaliers expected little opposition in Chagford, yet the town had recently been occupied by a body of Parliamentary militiamen and these men had been warned of the Royalist advance. When the King's horsemen rode into Chagford a volley of shots crashed out from the doors and windows. In the confused skirmish which followed many of the Cavaliers were wounded or killed. Amongst them was Sidney Godolphin who 'by too forward engaging himself . . . received a mortal shot by a musket, a little above the knee, of which he died in the instant', thus, the Royalist Earl of Clarendon lamented, 'leaving the ignominy of his death upon a place which could never otherwise have had a mention to the world'.[1]

Clarendon's comment set the tone for future accounts of the skirmish at Chagford. The story has since been told and re-told by legions of historians, and always in terms of the personal tragedy of a single Royalist gentlemen. Yet there were other sides to the engagement as well. It had an enduring impact on the local community, for instance. This sudden eruption of violence in a quiet, remote town took years to be forgotten. Tales of Godolphin's death were handed down from generation to generation and still circulated in Chagford during the last century. Even now the porch of the Three Crowns Inn is pointed out to visitors as the very spot where Godolphin expired. Local people were not only affected by Godolphin's death, moreover, they also helped to effect it.

xv

We will never know who shot Godolphin, but if his death can be attributed to any one person, that person is Richard Collyer of Okehampton, glove-maker. Newly-discovered evidence shows that it was Collyer, a Parliamentarian sympathizer, who warned the Roundhead soldiers of the Royalist advance. Two witnesses later deposed that 'the said Collyer went from Oakhampton to Chagford that nyght (when the Kinge's Armye laye in Oakhampton and were to goe to Chagford) and gave notice to the Parliament's Armye of the Kinge's Armye's comyng, and willed them to sett a stronge garde ... by which notice some worthye gents of the Kinge's Armye, as Mr Sidney Godolphin and others, were ... slayne'.[2] Collyer's midnight journey across the moorland roads had proved decisive. Thanks to his determination and initiative the Royalists had been worsted—but the glove-maker's name has been forgotten for three centuries. The Richard Collyers of the English Civil War—ordinary, unremarkable men who nevertheless felt a fierce attachment, to King or to Parliament— were every bit as important as the Sidney Godolphins. This book sets out to discover a little more about them.

PART I
THE CONTEXT

Introduction

This is not another attempt to explain the causes of the English Civil War. Rather, it is an endeavour to explain how and why that conflict divided the common people of a single English county. As this simple description suggests, this book deals largely (though not exclusively) with local issues and provincial affairs. It is not concerned with the doings of the great, but with husbandmen, seamen and spinsters. The bulk of the story is set in Devon, a county which, while rich and populous, was also somewhat isolated from the political centre, hardly in a position to determine national events. Accordingly, this book contains relatively little discussion of high politics or affairs of state. These issues are touched upon, of course, but only insofar as they affected the local populace, for it is the people of Devon who take centre stage here. They are the dramatis personae and it is their words and actions that will carry the story along. Yet as the focus of attention falls upon the players, the wider historical backdrop against which they perform should never be forgotten.

This study was not undertaken with the intention of illuminating events in Devon alone. Instead, it had its genesis in a desire to test and explore certain general theories about Civil War allegiance—and especially those put forward by David Underdown in his pioneering studies of popular behaviour and politics in the three western counties of Dorset, Somerset and Wiltshire. In a series of fascinating books and articles, culminating in *Revel, Riot and Rebellion*—surely one of the most important books on the English Civil War to appear in the last twenty years—Underdown has mapped out a cultural landscape whose very existence, let alone precise geographical boundaries and dimensions, had previously only been hinted at.[1]

3

Underdown's thesis is far too rich and complicated to be fully detailed here. Yet as far as wartime allegiances are concerned, his argument has three main components. First, he rejects the assumption that commoners were mere unthinking pawns, political neuters who took no interest in the arguments of the day. Instead, he claims that they, like their social superiors, had very definite political preferences, choosing to support one side or another in accordance with their own convictions and beliefs. Underdown's second argument is that these preferences operated on a regional as well as a personal basis, and that certain areas of the country were visibly more Royalist or Parliamentarian than others. His third and most contentious claim is that these regional variations reflected a fundamental split in English society. Drawing on the work of Joan Thirsk and others, Underdown has enlarged the concept of 'two rural peasant Englands'—that is to say, of two basic types of rural community, engaged in different types of agriculture and displaying different types of settlement pattern—into a more simple and dramatic one; that of 'two Englands'. Underdown claims that by 1600, as a result of population growth and economic change, England was divided into 'two quite different constellations of social, political and cultural forces, involving diametrically opposite responses to the problems of the time'. These two 'different constellations', he suggests, later went on to form the basis of the Royalist and Parliamentarian parties.[2]

Underdown's claims have received a somewhat mixed reception. Least controversial, perhaps, has been the emphasis which he has placed upon the political independence of the common people. Over the last fifteen years, scholars have become increasingly aware of the capacity of early modern commoners for independent action, and few would now portray them as biddable or supine.[3] In his contention that some parts of England were more Parliamentarian, some more Royalist, than others, Underdown again enjoys wide scholarly support.[4] By going one step further, however, and claiming that these regional divergences can be neatly mapped out and delineated on the ground, Underdown has unleashed a barrage of critical fire. Some have claimed that the boundaries between the different regions he has posited are amorphous and impossible to draw, others that the techniques used to define Royalist and Parliamentarian areas are flawed.[5] Still more hotly contested has been the argument that regional variations in the distribution of popular allegiance reflected differing patterns of agrarian practice.[6] Similar doubts have been cast upon the suggestion that agricultural practice affected cultural outlook.[7] More generally, scholars have accused Underdown of wanting 'to have things both ways', of tying himself in knots through self-contradictory arguments.[8] Pinned down and under fire, Underdown's thesis seems in danger of becoming sidelined.[9]

This book is an attempt to break the deadlock. By carrying out a broadly comparable study of popular allegiance in Devon, it subjects certain key aspects of the Underdownian thesis to a rigorous outside examination. Advancing from the positions which have already been consolidated, it seeks to capture further ground in the scholarly no-man's land across which the historical debate is currently raging. At the heart of this study are two overriding questions. First, is it really possible to discern sharply differentiated Royalist and Parliamentarian areas within individual English counties? And second, if this is indeed the case, to what should such striking variations in popular political behaviour be attributed?

In exploring these questions, this book ranges across a wide, and occasionally perhaps obscure, array of topics. Discussions of the arcane mysteries of Stannary Law, of subjects as diverse as racial identity, popular memory and village festivities, are mingled—though not, the author hopes, confused—in the following pages with investigations of agriculture and economics, of politics and religion. The study is equally extended in time, for it delves far back into the sixteenth century in order to show that events occurring long before 1642 helped to determine the form which the Civil War eventually took. Some of the topics discussed—neutralism, for example, and popular Parliamentarianism—have already received much scholarly attention.[10] Others, such as the question of allegiance patterns in cities, are subjects about which little is known.[11] Whether proceeding along well-trodden highways or comparatively lonely paths, though, this book always tries to keep its ultimate destination in mind. Brief diversions are occasionally made to examine some of the more fascinating distractions which glitter along the way, but such digressions are kept to a minimum. As a result, it is hoped that the study retains a structure and tightness of form, despite the diversity of the material upon which it is based.

The book is divided into four parts. The first paints a portrait of Devon as it was on the eve of the Civil War, demonstrating that the county's topography and size militated against its inhabitants possessing any true sense of common identity. The second examines patterns of popular allegiance within the county during the war itself—and it is this section which forms the core of the present study. As other writers have observed, Underdown's own discussion of allegiance patterns is 'the most important part' of *Revel, Riot and Rebellion*, the peg, so to speak, on which the whole book hangs. Yet it has also been claimed that Underdown's treatment of this vital subject is 'the least satisfactory' aspect of his work.[12] Clearly then, this subject above all others is worthy of detailed research. The third section of the book ranges rather more widely. It tries to explain why Devonians divided as they did during the Civil War—and in doing so uncovers many important links between patterns of popular behaviour during 1642–46 and those evinced during the pre-war period.[13] The final section of the book shifts the focus of attention away from Devon towards the country as a whole. Building upon the insights which have already emerged from the detailed case-study of a single county, it conducts a survey of nationwide allegiance patterns. During the course of this discussion, certain important trends in recent historiography are challenged and a number of new interpretations put forward. Throughout, the book seeks to elucidate the complicated internal rivalries which split the inhabitants of English towns and counties during the early modern period: rivalries which the Civil War fed off, exacerbated and, eventually, perpetuated.

Chapter 1

A Portrait of Early Stuart Devon

During the winter of 1645–46 a Londoner travelled to Devon in order to join the troops of the New Model Army in their billets before Exeter. He was not impressed by what he found. Writing to a friend in the capital a few days later, the reluctant exile noted that 'I found the West country indeed craggy and the people and entertainment for the most part crabbed', adding that 'if ever I return to London again, I shall … indeavour to have an higher esteem of the precious opportunities that are there'.[1] His comments remind us that the laudatory encomiums lavished upon the shire by local chroniclers like Hooker and Risdon owed a great deal to their own sense of proprietorial pride. As far as the majority of seventeenth-century Englishmen were concerned, Devon was no Garden of Eden but a wild, remote and somewhat rugged county, whose inhabitants were dull and backward. Such attitudes have persisted into the twentieth century and are reflected in the jesting references of present-day tourists to the simple Devonshire farmer, trundling about his execrable country roads on a battered tractor.

Such bucolic detachment is singularly hard to discern amongst Devonshire folk nowadays, and even during the seventeenth century the backwardness and isolation of local people may well have been exaggerated. The county's inhospitable terrain is still with us, however, and can still present the traveller with difficulties from time to time. Of all the counties of southern England, Devon and Cornwall are the most rugged and mountainous. Indeed the geographical feature which is generally agreed to separate the highland zone of England from the more gentle lands to the east is the River Exe—the waterway which divides Devon from north to south and upon which Exeter, the regional capital, is situated. Because so much of the county was hilly, and because the local road system was so bad, wheeled traffic was rarely seen in early Stuart Devon, while in Cornwall it was practically unheard of. As late as 1628 heavy wagons were unable to proceed west of Plymouth. Even heavily-laden horsemen had some difficulty in getting about and in 1642 it was noted that Devon was unfit for the movement of armoured cavalry, it being a 'fast and craggy country'.[2] As a result of the difficult terrain goods and commodities were commonly transported on pack-horses, or on primitive wooden sleds.[3]

The problems caused by the county's rugged topography were alleviated to some extent by the ready availability of water-borne transport. Devon is bounded by the sea on two sides and local people have always taken full advantage of this. Hundreds of craft—some very large, some mere skiffs—plied a busy trade in Devon's coastal waters during the early seventeenth century, carrying goods and passengers on short local trips as well as on longer hauls to other parts of the realm and to countries beyond the seas. Extensive use was also made of Devon's navigable rivers. Cargoes could be ferried up and down the Exe in the east, the Dart, Plym and Tamar in the south and the Taw and Torridge in the north.[4] The one disadvantage of Devon's extensive coastline was that it made the county as a whole uncomfortably vulnerable to pirates. Such raiders were extremely active off South-west England during the Caroline period and they caused continual alarums and excursions along the South Devon coast. During the 1620s and 1630s many local seamen were carried off as prisoners by the corsairs, prompting anguished cries for help from the inhabitants of the South Devon ports.[5]

Fortunately, most Devonians dwelt far enough from the sea to feel relatively secure from piratical attack. Devon was a huge county, stretching seventy-five miles from north to south and seventy-three from east to west, and many local people must have lived out their lives without ever having visited the coast. (Even in the 1850s one elderly inhabitant of Lustleigh in Mid-Devon had never travelled to the sea-coast just thirty miles away.[6]) Within this vast area of land there was much topographical diversity. Devon has been well-described as 'a county of contrasts' and the shire is indeed a bewildering hotchpotch of differing terrains. In addition to pasture and arable land, it is possible to find chalk downs, woodlands and salt marsh here. Nor should one forget the extensive tracts of moorland which cover the centre of the county and parts of the north-east. In 1808 Charles Vancouver was able to identify no fewer than eight separate 'districts' of Devon on the basis of underlying soil type.[7] For the purposes of this book the county can be more conveniently divided into four main regions.[8]

The four regions

The first of these is East Devon, roughly defined as that part of the county which lies to the east of the River Exe (see Map 1 and—for a full list of the region's parishes—Appendix 1). Topographically, this region has more in common with Dorset than with the rest of Devon.[9] This is particularly true of the eastern corner of the region, which contains extensive downlands. Sheep were grazed here during the early modern period, and corn was also grown. As one moves westwards the hills give way to a more gentle land of rich, red earth, which extends up to and a little beyond the valley of the Exe. Arable farming was carried out here during the 1600s and local villages tended to be large and tightly nucleated. Higher up the Exe Valley land was more commonly used for pasture and there was a good deal of woodland. Many communities in this area were heavily industrialized, their inhabitants having been involved in the cloth trade since the late medieval period.[10] Partly as a result of this early industrialization, partly as a result of the local soil's fertility, East Devon was the most densely populated region of the county in 1642.

East Devon contained several urban communities and the most important of these was Exeter, the 'capital' of South-west England. One of the largest cities in the kingdom, a contemporary termed it 'the only emporium and principal ornament of the west'.[11] Exeter possessed a castle, a cathedral and nineteen parish churches, and acted as an administrative and economic centre for the surrounding countryside. The city could boast over 3,000 adult males in 1642.[12] The sheer size and importance of Exeter, together with the fact that it was a county in its own right, mean that it cannot be considered as just another East Devon town. Accordingly, Exeter will be treated as a separate entity throughout this book. Exeter aside, the chief towns of East Devon were Cullompton, Honiton and Tiverton. Tiverton was the largest of these, and was, indeed, the second most populous community in the county. Almost 2,000 adult males lived here in 1642, and Risdon described the town as 'full of people and inhabited with

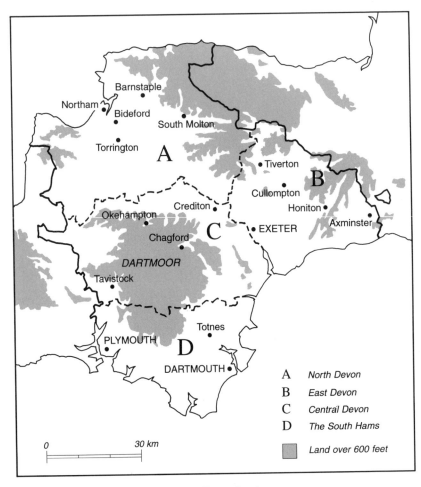

A   North Devon
B   East Devon
C   Central Devon
D   The South Hams

Land over 600 feet

Map 1.   Devon in 1642.

rich clothiers, the chief commodity of the place being the trade of clothing'.[13]

The East Devon countryside is relatively flat, especially in the vicinity of Exeter. West of the Exe lies the highland zone which makes up the rest of Devon. As soon as the traveller crosses the Exe at Exeter, he finds the countryside to the west rising steeply before him. A forbidding escarpment stretches across the landscape from north to south, presenting a daunting obstacle to further progress. This natural feature effectively marks the boundary between highland and lowland Devon and, even today, the villages which lie in the hills just a few miles to the west of Exeter seem curiously remote from the city. At the southern end of this escarpment are the Haldon Hills. These were described as 'high and barren' during the seventeenth century, and the heathland which covered them was reported to 'take up a large circuit of land'.[14] After the traveller has clambered over Haldon he will find himself amongst the scattered villages of the Teign valley, which remained isolated and little frequented until quite recent times.[15] Beyond the Teign the land begins to rise steeply once more and, should the traveller persevere in his journey, he will eventually arrive at Dartmoor, the core of the highland zone, parts of which are more than 1,500 feet above sea level. Dartmoor and its 'skirts'—that is to say the central part of the county, which stretches westward from Exeter to the Cornish border—will be referred to throughout this book as Central or Mid-Devon.

Dartmoor was considered extremely wild and remote during the early modern period and even today it retains many of the characteristics of a true wilderness. It is an area of rocky outcrops and moorland, a series of high granite plateaux, interspersed with peat bogs and deep, winding valleys. The region is exposed and snow is common; a seventeenth-century writer observed that Dartmoor's 'tops and torres are ... often covered with a white cap'.[16] The high moor itself was simply too inhospitable to live on. Around its skirts, however, lay a surprising number of homesteads and hamlets, villages and small towns.[17] Many of the people who dwelt in these communities made their living from the moor. Effective arable farming on Dartmoor itself was impossible, but many types of crop could be grown upon its fringes and even the high moorlands themselves were by no means useless. The region was an important centre for pastoral transhumance. A contemporary observed that, every summer, 'the bordering neighbours bring great herds of cattle, and flocks of sheep to pasture there'.[18] Moreover the area was 'richer in its bowels than in the face thereof'. Tin was mined on Dartmoor, and turves were cut from the heathlands and used by the 'by-dwellers' for winter fuel. In 1610 it was claimed that some '100,000 horse loads of turf [are] annually carried from Dartmoor Forest'.[19]

Not all of Central Devon is moorland of course. As one moves away from Dartmoor itself the landscape gradually becomes more gentle and, in some parts of the region, pockets of very fertile soil exist. In such areas population was high. Crediton, which stands on the same rich red 'mould' as the villages of the Exe Valley, was a busy, populous town during the seventeenth century. Tavistock, an extensive parish on the western side of the moor, possessed many acres of arable land and 750 adult male inhabitants in 1642.[20] Yet in most parts of the region the poor nature of the soil was reflected in the small size of local communities. Central Devon was the most thinly populated region of the county during the seventeenth century.

To the south of Mid-Devon lay the region known as the South Hams.[21] This area was extremely fertile and contemporaries termed it the garden of Devonshire. The region was less heavily wooded than other parts of the shire and contained both pasture and arable land of the highest quality. The soil of the South Hams was said to produce 'plenty of corn, and a sweet nourishing grass'. Cider was made here too. Risdon, in his *Survey of Devon*, noted at least three South Hams parishes which were remarkable for the fertility of their soil. Thus Staverton was 'a place passing fruitful', Paignton 'one of the fruitfullest lordships in all this county' and Modbury 'a place for ... fertility of soil inferior to few in this county'.[22] The region's chief towns were Plymouth and Dartmouth. Both were major ports, Plymouth specializing in commerce while Dartmouth served as the centre of the local fishing industry.[23] Plymouth boasted 1,440 adult males in 1642, Dartmouth around half as many. The region as a whole was thickly populated, containing almost a quarter of the county's population despite its relatively small size.

The last region to consider is North Devon, which stretches from the northern fringes of Dartmoor to the shores of the Bristol Channel. Risdon considered this part of the county to be 'lean and barren, except about [the] towns, where the husbandman, by improvement, hath inforced fertility'. Owing to the barren nature of the soil much of North Devon was given over to pasture. Near the coast, however, crops were more commonly grown. Risdon attributed this to the proximity of the sea, 'from whose shore sand is carried to better [the] grounds'. North Devon's most productive area of arable land lay around the estuary of the River Taw, where the parish of Northam was particularly noted for its fertility.[24] In addition to arable land and pasture North Devon contained a good deal of moorland, particularly on its eastern side, where the region was separated from Somerset by the forest of Exmoor and from East Devon by the moors around Rackenford and Witheridge.

The chief town of North Devon was Barnstaple, a community containing some 750 adult males, which lay upon the River Taw. Barnstaple was in decline during the 1600s but its inhabitants continued to dominate local affairs. In 1644 Barnstaple was said to 'rule the rest of the neighbouring towns, viz: Torrington, Biddiford and [South] Moulton'.[25] These three places, together with Northam, formed the second rank of North Devon towns. Bideford, like Barnstaple, was a port or haven town and was expanding very rapidly. It contained 662 adult males in 1642. South Molton, broadly similar in size, was the centre of the north-east Devon cloth trade. Northam, somewhat larger, was situated at the mouth of the Taw/Torridge estuary and many seamen lived here. Finally Torrington was the chief town of north-west Devon and 'flourishe[d] with merchants and men of trade ... being the most convenient place for ... a general meeting in those parts'.[26] North Devon was a well-populated region. Although the pattern of settlement was somewhat scattered in the north-west, many people lived in the tract of land between the Taw and the Torridge. North Devon contained almost a third of the county's population in 1642.

Fishing and the cloth trade

In all four regions of Devon husbandry of one sort or another was the chief occupation of the common people. Yet agriculture was by no means the only way to earn a living. In 1631 the Devon JPs noted that many of 'their commons [were] engaged as fishermen and in the manufacture of wool' and there can be no doubt that these two occupations provided employment for thousands of

Devonians during the early modern period.[27] That fishing should have been a major industry comes as little surprise. The county's intimate relationship with the sea has already been noted, and in 1627 it was observed that '[this] county … yields the King more seamen than any part of the Kingdom'.[28] Detailed contemporary records confirm the importance of seamen in local society. A survey of 1619 reveals that 3,653 mariners dwelt along the South Devon coast, and Todd Gray has estimated that perhaps half as many men were similarly employed in North Devon.[29] The county as a whole must have contained at least 5,000 mariners during the early 1620s. This figure represents well over 5 per cent of the county's adult male population.[30] Nor did the numbers engaged in fishing decline much during the next twenty years. In 1636 it was claimed that the chief Devon ports, together with Weymouth, Melcombe and Lyme in Dorset, had sent out no fewer than 7,000 men in the fishing fleets to Newfoundland.[31]

Of all the Devon regions the South Hams contained the largest number of mariners.[32] This was chiefly because the numerous creeks and inlets of the South Devon coast made the area hospitable to shipping. The same could not be said of North Devon, where the shoreline was rocky and dangerous.[33] Yet, as has been shown, many hundreds of mariners dwelt here too. The fishermen of North and South Devon concentrated their attentions upon different types of fish. Pilchards were the staple catch in the south, while herrings were more commonly taken in the north.[34] Some fishing was carried out in East Devon too. Risdon described Sidmouth as 'one of the especialest fisher towns of this shire' and many neighbouring communities were also involved in the trade.[35] Central Devon possessed fewest seamen. The short stretch of coast between Teignmouth and Dawlish constituted Mid-Devon's only seaboard, and while many fishermen dwelt here, they did not form a large proportion of the region's total population.

Fishing was integral to Devon's economy. Yet more important still was the second occupation referred to by the JPs in 1631, the manufacture of wool. Reference has already been made to the long history of the cloth trade in Devon, and to the fact that the chief centres of the industry lay in the north and east of the county. What has not yet been made sufficiently clear is the scale of the industry. Thomas Westcote, a local gentleman, claimed that, as far as the manufacture of cloth went, 'this province for quantity, quality and variety … may compare with, if not exceed, most countries'. Indeed he termed Devon 'the drapery of the western parts'.[36]

Westcote sketched a valuable portrait of the Devon cloth industry. Tiverton, he observed, 'hath ... such store in kersies [a kind of coarse, narrow cloth] as ... will not be believed' while Crediton 'yields many of the finest sorts of kersies, for which, and for fine spinning it hath the pre-eminence'. From North Devon, 'Barnstaple and Torrington furnish us with bays [i.e. baize] and such like: and Pilton, adjoining, vents cotton for lining' while at Tavistock, in Mid-Devon, 'there is also a good market for cloth'. Turning to East Devon, Westcote noted that 'at Axminster you may be furnished with fine flax thread', that Honiton and Bradninch produced bone lace, that Ottery St Mary, 'with divers other places' manufactured 'mixed coloured kersies' and that Cullompton produced 'kersey stockings'. Westcote concluded his account by commenting that 'this might be enlarged with other petty commodities belonging to other towns'.[37]

Westcote's account demonstrates that cloth-making was carried out in every region of Devon. Other sources confirm this. Woollen manufacture was concentrated particularly heavily in the north and east of the county, but was widespread in Mid-Devon and the South Hams too.[38] It is hard to say exactly how many people were employed in the cloth industry, but the numbers involved must have been huge. A document of 1628 mentions 'the many thousand poor artisans, as weavers, fullers, spinsters, dyers, and such like, wherewith the western parts abound' and in 1631 it was claimed that 'many thousands in these western parts [are] interested in the [cloth] trade'[39]. Westcote believed that too many local men were involved in woollen manufacture, and that the very success of the industry was threatening the county's wellbeing. He observed that 'the meanest sort of people ... will now rather place their children to ... these mechanical trades than to husbandry ... whereby husbandry labourers are more scarce ... than in former times'. He also noted that those involved in the cloth trade were vulnerable to sudden economic fluctuations and that 'every rumour of war or contagious sickness (hindering the sale of these commodities) makes a multitude of the poorer sort chargeable to their neighbours'.[40] This last comment was undoubtedly true. Walter Yonge noted in 1622 that, in Exeter, 'there are 300 poor weavers ... which go about the streets to crave relief by begging, because they can get no work, for trades are so bad'. Unemployment amongst the cloth-workers was considered extremely dangerous and Yonge himself feared a popular insurrection if the weavers were not speedily 'set ... on to work'.[41]

Mining and the stannaries

Devon's third major industry was tin-mining. The granite of Dartmoor yields an exceptionally fine variety of tin and from the very earliest times this valuable resource has been periodically exploited by those who dwell nearby.[42] During the Middle Ages tin-mining in Devon and Cornwall enjoyed a period of expansion. Accordingly, special administrative institutions were set up to ensure that the Crown received the maximum benefit from these valuable mineral deposits. The tin-bearing areas in each county were divided up into four districts. Each district was known as a 'Stannary', and each Stannary had its administrative headquarters in a different town. In Devon the four Stannary Towns were Tavistock, Chagford, Ashburton and Plympton. At the head of the Stannaries stood the Lord Warden, usually a prominent noble, who was answerable to no one but the monarch. He was assisted in his duties by two Vice-Wardens, drawn from the ranks of the local gentry.[43]

The main task of the Warden and his deputies was to regulate the activities of the tin-miners themselves, the 'tinners' as they were known. These miners were an uncommonly tough breed of men. They had to be, for excavating tin from the inhospitable soil of Dartmoor was dangerous and back-breaking work. Accidents were frequent and injuries often fatal. It was observed of the Devon tin-miner by an early modern writer that 'there is no labourer in hardness of life to be compared; for his apparel is coarse, his diet slender, his lodging hard, his drink water, and for lack of a cup he commonly drinketh out of his spade or shovel'.[44] No doubt this description is exaggerated, but it does convey the impression which the miners made upon their contemporaries. Everyone agreed that a tinner's life was extremely hard. One writer who knew the miners well stated that they were 'the most Herculean and stoutest men upon earth'.[45]

Harsh and demanding though it was, a tinner's lot had considerable compensations. The miners risked their lives to supply the King with tin, but in return he granted them important favours. As a result of this intimate partnership with royalty the tinners enjoyed a status and prestige that was unique. The tin-miners, a contemporary observed, 'for their most faithful and loyal services, have the greatest privileges ... of any people in the kingdom'.[46] This was undoubtedly true. Tinners were exempt from national and county taxes, had the right to be mustered in their own militia units and could not be tried by the county courts for any crimes except wounding and murder.[47] If accused of any other offence, a tinner had the right to be tried by his own Stannary court. The miners possessed their own representative assembly too. Each of the Devon Stannaries sent delegates to the Great Court, or Tinners' Parliament, which legislated upon all matters concerning the miners.[48]

The Dartmoor Stannary was, therefore, virtually a self-governing state within the state; an organisation with its own laws, courts and military forces. The county authorities had no jurisdiction over the Stannaries and the tinners emphasized their independence from local society by referring to all other men as 'foreigners'.[49] The tinners stood out in other ways, too. They were famed for their enthusiastic adherence to the old festive culture, and for drinking and general debauchery. In 1614 an inhabitant of Buckfastleigh described the local Stannary bailiffs as 'poore men, of smale creditt or estimacion' adding that they 'have spent theyre whole estate in boowsing and drincking and other lewde vices and more they would spend if they had it'.[50] The tinners also possessed common customs and symbols, which helped to bind them together as a separate, and very distinct, community. The 'Tinners Rabbits', those intricately carved designs which occur upon the roof bosses of several moorland churches, are a good example.[51] According to nineteenth-century antiquarians, the rabbits were the tinners' badge and their presence in a church commemorates building work funded by local miners. Several Dartmoor churches, including 'the Cathedral of the Moor' at Widecombe, were built or restored with the profits of the tin trade.[52]

How many tinners lived in Devon? Precise figures cannot be given, for no detailed census exists and one must rely, therefore, upon guesses and approximations. During the 1590s the total number of tinners in Devon and Cornwall was estimated at 10–12,000 men.[53] As Devon accounted for a fifth of total tin production at this time, it seems reasonable to assume that the county would also have supplied around a fifth of the miners.[54]

This in turn would suggest that some 2,000 men were employed either full-time or part-time in the Devon tin-works. Such a figure accords well with Hooker's statement that the Devon Stannary maintained 'great nombres of householders, famylies and inhabitants ... of the said countie'.[55] The miners' numbers must have fallen considerably during the 1620s and 1630s, when the industry suffered a serious decline.[56] Even so, it is clear that the tinners remained an important group in Devon society right up to the Civil War.[57]

The Stannaries were not the only parts of Devon to lie under Royal protection. This was also true of several other areas. The entire 'forest of Dartmoor', for example, together with the borough of Lydford and the manors of Bradford, Bradninch and South Teign, formed part of the Duchy of Cornwall and therefore belonged to the Crown. Other Royal estates included the manors of Shebbear and West Ashford and the local holdings of the Duchy of Lancaster (most of which lay in East and Central Devon). The inhabitants of these areas were tenants of the Crown and were therefore expected to perform military service for the King. They also enjoyed unusual privileges and liberties. Tenants of the Duchies of Cornwall and Lancaster could not be fined or arrested without the prior consent of the Duchy bailiff, nor could they be constrained to attend the assizes or county sessions as jurymen. They did not have to pay the usual tolls and taxes, and had the right to be tried by the Duchy courts. Both Duchies could appoint tithingmen and other petty officials, and the Duchy of Lancaster even possessed its own head constables.[58]

Nobility, gentry and county government

Overall supervision of those parts of Devon which lay outside the Royal demesne was vested in the local nobility and the higher gentry. During the seventeenth century the chief noble families resident in Devon were the Bourchiers, Earls of Bath, and the Russells, Earls (and later Dukes) of Bedford. The Bourchiers had the deepest local roots. The family had been established at their mansion house of Tawstock, near Barnstaple, since the fifteenth century.[59] By comparison the Russells were relative newcomers to Devon, having been 'planted' in the shire by Henry VIII during the 1530s.[60] Nevertheless it was the Russells who were the more important of the two families and from their base at Tavistock they wielded an immense amount of power. Following the 2nd Earl's death in 1585, however, the Russells' influence became somewhat diminished. This was chiefly because the 2nd Earl's successors spent most of their time in London, rather than on their Devon estates. In the Russells' absence William Bourchier, 3rd Earl of Bath, became the leading local magnate.

From 1587 to 1623 Bath held the position of Lord Lieutenant and was perhaps the most important man in Devon. By virtue of his Lieutenancy, Bath commanded the county militia or 'trained bands'. On paper, at least, this was a force to be reckoned with. It was remarked in 1627 that '[this] county ... has in it more trained soldiers ... than any part of the kingdom' and surviving muster lists reveal that Devon possessed 7–8,000 militiamen.[61] Most of these part-time soldiers served in the county's six main militia regiments, each of which was around 1,000 strong. Yet there were several additional units as well. Prominent among them was the Trained Tinners regiment, consisting of 400 miners drawn from the Devon Stannaries (these men were generally mustered alongside the tenants of the Duchy of Cornwall).[62] South Devon, too, maintained an auxiliary regiment of 400 men, presumably because it was felt to be particularly vulnerable to attack. Several of the larger towns boasted their own town band or civic militia. Barnstaple, Dartmouth and Totnes all mustered one such unit during the 1630s, while Exeter and Plymouth possessed four town bands apiece.[63] As Lord Lieutenant, Bath commanded all these units and also appointed the Deputy Lieutenants who oversaw the minutiae of military affairs. All the available evidence suggests that Bath took his military duties seriously and that he was prompt and efficient in carrying them out. Nor did he forget his other local responsibilities. Between 1600 and 1623 Bath worked hard to maintain peace and good order in his county, often in the face of considerable local difficulties.[64] The Crown lost a valued servant when he died in 1623.[65]

Following Earl William's death the Lord Lieutenancy reverted to the Russell family. Between 1623 and 1642 the post was held successively by the 4th and 5th Earls of Bedford. Neither man spent much time in Devon, preferring to leave the ordering of the militia to the Deputy Lieutenants and the day-to-day running of the shire to the JPs. The 4th Earl of Bath, Earl William's son, was equally detached from county affairs. His successor, Henry Bourchier, the 5th Earl, was a little more effective, but, like the

Russells, spent a good deal of his time in London.[66] As Henry only succeeded to the Earldom in 1637, moreover, his knowledge of his 'country' (the term which seventeenth-century Englishmen used in rather the same sense as manor or patch is used in London slang today) cannot have been very deep.[67]

With the noblemen who were supposed to oversee local affairs generally rather inactive between 1623 and 1642, the role of the higher gentry, baronets, knights and esquires, became even more important than usual in the government of the county. Almost 400 such individuals are known to have lived in Caroline Devon. They formed the elite of local society and dominated county affairs. The Deputy Lieutenants, the sheriffs, the militia colonels and the knights of the shire were all chosen from this group.[68] So were the Justices of the Peace, or JPs, with Devon having around sixty of these indispensable local magistrates during the early Stuart period.[69]

Beneath the higher gentry stood the lower gentry, individuals whose influence was largely confined to the parochial and hundredal level. There were over 1,500 men of this rank in Caroline Devon.[70] Minor gentlemen could not aspire to the most prestigious local offices, but nevertheless, many important posts were open to them. The office of head constable, for example, was often held by lesser gentlemen, and yeomen, too, had a part to play in local government. They served as constables and were frequently summoned to appear on juries. Westcote observed that, like the minor gentry, 'the better sort' of yeomen were often 'returned to pass upon trials of matters of fact'.[71] Both yeomen and lesser gentry regularly attended the half-yearly assizes and, of course, the quarter sessions, at which the Devon JPs sat in solemn judgement upon all sorts of malefactors.

The county bench was the chief engine of local government but it was not omnipotent. Within the sea of quarter sessions jurisdiction lay several islands of special privilege. As we have seen, the tin-miners possessed their own courts, and many of Devon's urban communities also lay outside the jurisdiction of the bench. Exeter had its own sessions court, as befitted a separate county and city. In consequence, the lives of the citizens were dominated by a small mercantile elite.[72] The situation was broadly similar in Barnstaple, Dartmouth, Okehampton, Plymouth, Tiverton and Totnes. Here, too, local affairs were strictly regulated and controlled by small groups of the most wealthy inhabitants.[73]

Religious affairs

Religious affairs in the diocese of Exeter (which embraced both Devon and Cornwall) were controlled by a powerful group of clerical administrators, who dwelt in Exeter's Cathedral Close. As Westcote observed, 'it is ... unnecessary to particularize the several degrees of ecclesiastical dignities and offices, [they] being in every diocese alike'.[74] The character of the three men who stood at the head of the hierarchy between 1600 and 1642 deserves a little more attention.[75] William Cotton, appointed to the bishopric in 1598, was a generally effective prelate who remained active in the diocese until his death in 1621. His successor, Valentine Carey, spent less time in Devon and made little impression upon local affairs. Joseph Hall, who succeeded Carey in 1627, possessed religious beliefs which were rather less conservative than those of his predecessors. Hall's scholarship and tact won him many local admirers, and he remained popular in Devon until his removal in 1642.[76]

All three diocesans had to cope with religious dissent. Devon contained two distinct groups of religious nonconformists at this time. Least important were the catholics (or papists), those who refused to abandon the doctrines of the Church of Rome. Devon's catholic population was very small. Between 1600 and 1610 only fifty-one persons were presented at the sessions for recusancy and the numbers did not rise much over the next thirty years.[77] The Protestation Returns record the names of only forty-four definite recusants. Even if these individuals are combined with the thirty-eight other persons who refused the oath for unspecified reasons, some of whom were probably catholics as well, one is still left with a total of fewer than one hundred recusants. The county's adult male population at this time was around 72,000.[78] Clearly, then, the proportion of catholics to conformists was minuscule, with only ten Devon parishes known to have had catholic families continually resident between 1600 and 1642.[79] Outside these recusant strongholds, the direct influence of catholicism upon local people must have been extremely limited.

If popular catholicism was negligible, recusancy was much stronger in the upper echelons of county society. Many of the most important Devon families—the Bassets, Careys, Chichesters, Courtenays and Giffords, for example—had catholic connections.[80] Possibly encouraged by the presence of these powerful sympathizers, catholic priests made frequent incursions into Devon, and seminary priests were apprehended near Lyme in 1608, at Barnstaple in 1609, at Exeter in 1621 and 1625, and at Plymouth in 1633.[81] These incidents sparked off a series of temporary alarms. Similar anxieties were occasionally aroused by the belligerent words of local catholics, like the Exeter woman who forecast in 1628 that 'err longe she should see [many] come to St Peters to confession', adding that 'two or three catholicks would bee hard enough' for the entire city militia.[82] Sometimes comments like these resulted in the temporary stepping-up of pressure on the recusant community.[83]

Far more numerous and important than the catholics were the radical protestants, or puritans, those who wished to see further reformation of the church's liturgy and ceremonies. Puritans were active in many Devon parishes by 1600, prompting Bishop Cotton to launch a determined drive for conformity.[84] Yet despite Cotton's best efforts local puritanism continued to thrive and the presentation of Joseph Hall in 1627 greatly strengthened the puritan position. Although Hall harried out-and-out separatists, the vast majority of Devon puritans were able to follow their consciences with relative impunity under the benevolent eye of their new diocesan. The attitude of many local gentlemen, meanwhile, was positively favourable to advanced protestant ideas. Many of the county elite were themselves puritans and this group probably had the upper hand on the county bench.[85] Hall's toleration and the support of the local gentry meant that Devonshire puritanism was able to thrive, even in the hostile religious climate of the 1630s. One historian has estimated that puritans formed 5 per cent of the county's population by 1642, others have suggested that this figure should be put higher still.[86] Most, in any case, would agree with J.T. Cliffe that Devon was 'one of the most puritan counties in England'.[87]

This chapter has touched upon some of the threads which served to bind early Stuart Devon together, enabling the county to act, in some respects at least, as a coherent and united community. We have seen that the majority of Devonians were governed by the same ruling elite, and that the more prosperous inhabitants participated in common institutions, like the assizes, quarter sessions and musters. Yet we have also seen that in many other ways, and particularly at the popular level, Devon was a deeply fractured society. The competing ideologies of catholicism and puritanism (not to mention anglican conformism), the conflicting jurisdictions of town, county and duchy, the diversity of agricultural and industrial practice, the jealousies between tinner and 'foreigner', all these things served to divide local people and cement their affections and allegiances to units below, or sometimes above, the level of the county.

Most importantly of all, perhaps, Devonians were divided by distance. As late as 1794 it was observed that 'so great is the extent of the county, and so little intercourse is there between the people in different districts, that it is very rare to find a man who is acquainted with any part of the county, except ... his immediate neighbourhood, and [scarcely any] possess a general knowledge of the whole county'.[88] What was true in the 1790s was still more true in the 1640s. Seventeenth-century Devonians rarely equated their 'country' with their county. Even the Earl of Bath clearly identified himself with his own home region, rather than with Devon as a whole, and it is hard to imagine that those of less exalted social status would have taken a wider view. Distance and poor communications ensured that it was the immediate neighbourhood, not the county, which had the first claim on local allegiances.[89] And when the institutions which had hitherto served to hold the county together were either abandoned or weakened during 1642–43, Devon split apart along essentially parochial lines.

PART II

Patterns of Allegiance, 1642–1646

Introduction

It is beyond the scope of this book to explain how conflict between King and Parliament first came to break out. Nor is a detailed account of the war's events necessary, for this is a subject which has already been dealt with elsewhere. There are two military histories of the Civil War in Devon, together with narrative accounts of the sieges of Plymouth and Exeter and articles on the local Royalist war effort.[1] As these works make clear, Devon was thrown into utter chaos between 1642 and 1646. Rival armies marched and counter-marched across the countryside and not even the most remote and isolated villages were able to escape the hot breath of war. Minor skirmishes took place everywhere and full-scale battles occurred at Modbury, Torrington and Sourton. Exeter and Dartmouth were each besieged and taken on two separate occasions, and Barnstaple on three, while Plymouth endured intermittent siege throughout the period 1642–46. The chronology on the following pages gives a brief summary of events. What it cannot convey is the immense burden which the war placed on the civilian population. Taxation and plundering reduced many local people to miserable poverty, while the widespread demolition of property made matters even worse. Nor was this all. Terrible epidemics scoured the county in 1643 and 1645, carrying off thousands of local people, while recruitment and impressment carried off many thousands more. The Civil War was perhaps the most devastating episode in Devon's recorded history. It is with the behaviour of the county's ordinary inhabitants as the old, familiar world crumbled around them that the second part of this book is chiefly concerned.

Chronology

1642 AUGUST, King Charles I raises his standard at Nottingham. Beginning of the Civil War.

SUMMER, local adherents of King and Parliament struggle for control of Devon.

SEPTEMBER, capture of the Royalist Earl of Bath brings Devon firmly into the Parliamentarian camp.

NOVEMBER, Devon invaded by Royalist army from Cornwall.

DECEMBER, Royalist invasion repulsed.

1643 JANUARY, Devon again invaded by the Cornish Royalists.

FEBRUARY, local risings in favour of Parliament. Skirmish at Chagford. Royalists defeated at Modbury. Temporary cessation (or truce) between the Parliamentarians in Devon and the Royalists in Cornwall.

APRIL, cessation expires.

MAY, Parliamentarian army invades Cornwall, but is routed at Stratton.

JUNE, Royalists occupy much of Devon and lay siege to Exeter.

JULY–AUGUST, Parliamentarian garrisons of Plymouth and Dartmouth try to relieve Exeter, but without success.

SEPTEMBER, Prince Maurice arrives in Devon with a large Royalist army. Exeter and Barnstaple surrender to the King.

OCTOBER, Maurice takes Dartmouth and besieges Plymouth.

DECEMBER, Maurice abandons the siege of Plymouth, having suffered heavy losses.

1644 MARCH–APRIL, pro-Parliamentarian risings in East Devon.

APRIL, Maurice besieges Lyme.

JUNE, Earl of Essex marches into the South-West with a large Parliamentary army. Maurice abandons the siege of Lyme.

JUNE–JULY, pro-Parliamentarian risings in North and South Devon.

JULY, Essex marches into Cornwall, followed by the main Royalist army under Charles I.

SEPTEMBER, Essex defeated in Cornwall. Devon restored to the Royal allegiance, but Plymouth remains defiant.

SEPTEMBER–DECEMBER, Royalist commander Sir Richard Grenville besieges Plymouth.

1645 JANUARY–FEBRUARY, Grenville launches a series of un-successful assaults on Plymouth.

MARCH, Grenville abandons the siege of Plymouth.

JUNE, Battle of Naseby in Northamptonshire. King's main field army is defeated by Parliament's New Model Army.

JULY, Battle of Langport in Somerset. Royalist Western army, under Lord George Goring, is defeated by the New Model Army. Goring's rapacious cavalry fall back into Devon. 'Clubman' risings begin.

AUGUST–SEPTEMBER, Goring battles with the Devon Clubmen.

OCTOBER, New Model Army invades and occupies East Devon.

1646 JANUARY, New Model Army advances into South Devon, storms Dartmouth and relieves Plymouth.

FEBRUARY, New Model Army advances into North Devon, and defeats the Royalists at Torrington.

MARCH, Royalist Western army surrenders in Cornwall.

APRIL, Barnstaple and Exeter surrendered to Parliament.

MAY, Charles I surrenders. End of the First Civil War.

Chapter 2

'The Well-affected Corner': Popular Parliamentarianism in Devon, 1642–1646

> Accordingly this flameing sword of God is fourbished, and glitters to make a great slaughter, and in execution of its commission rides in circuit throughout the whole land, keeping its assizes in every corner and quarter of the Kingdom, slaying and destroying sinners by hundreds and by thousands, from one end of the nation unto another.[1]

The words of John Quick, the Devon nonconformist, vividly convey the murderousness and destructiveness of the conflict which wrought such havoc upon his native county between 1642 and 1646. Yet Quick's portrayal of the Civil War as a divine judgement upon sinners, a ruthless slaughter of hapless and helpless victims, tells us nothing about what contemporaries actually thought of the conflict, about the decisions which they made and the sides which they took. Fortunately other sources reveal a great deal more about the political allegiances of mid-seventeenth-century Devonians. In September 1645 a petition was presented to the House of Commons by one hundred gentlemen and ministers of Devon. The petitioners were at pains to stress their county's affection to the Parliament. Devon, they averred, contained '[as] many ... well affected persons as any county in England', and later historians have found little reason to doubt this claim.[2] Throughout the war the majority of Devonians displayed an abiding attachment to the Parliamentary cause.

The Course of the War

Devon's affection to Parliament first became apparent in summer 1642. Attempts to raise the county for the King at this time met with a uniformly hostile response. The Royalist Commission of Array was regarded with distrust and those who promoted it were seen as dangerous incendiaries. Riots occurred in several towns when the Earl of Bath tried to publish the commission and, although he managed to gain the support of some local gentlemen, his appeals to the commons were contemptuously rebuffed. Spurning the Array men, local people responded instead to Parliament's militia ordinance. In August it was reported from Devon that 'the militia is put in execution among us, and the whole county come in cheerfully unto it, notwithstanding the opposition of the Earl of Bath'.[3] Bath's popular appeal was so limited, indeed, that his opponents felt able virtually to ignore him. While the Earl dithered, Parliamentary supporters turned their attention to Sherborne Castle in Dorset, which had been occupied by a force of Royalists. Many Devonian volunteers marched out of the county in August 1642 to help eject the King's men. An Exeter merchant noted in his private chronicle that 'there rose in Devonshire a thousand horse and foot' at this time 'that voluntarily went in service against Sherborne'.[4] A few weeks later Bath himself was arrested and Royalist activity in Devon came to a halt.

By October 1642 Parliamentary dominance of Devon seemed absolute. Yet Cornwall had been secured for the King, and in November Sir Ralph Hopton led a Royalist army across the Tamar. Over the next few weeks the Royalists made determined efforts to raise men in Devon. They met with success in some areas but most of the countryfolk remained 'well-affected to the Parliament'.[5] As a result Hopton was unable to gain control of the county and in January 1643 he suddenly withdrew, having learnt that the Earl of Stamford was approaching with a large Parliamentary army.[6]

Next month Hopton advanced into Devon again and laid siege to Plymouth. Stung into action the Parliamentarians summoned the county to oppose him, an initiative which met with an overwhelming response. Parliamentary news pamphlets were soon reporting that, in Devon, 'the whole country do unanimously join together against ... [the] Cavaliers'.[7] One pamphlet claimed that 9,000 men had been raised, a second that 'the volunteers and the

Trayned Bands of those parts are about ten thousand strong'.[8] So great were the numbers who flocked to Parliament's banner that many could not be supplied with weapons. A third pamphlet reported that the 'Devon men ... [did] come in in great multitudes ... and those that wanted arms came with clubs and staves'. Some reports spoke of the Parliamentarians having raised 13,000 or even as many as 14,000 men.[9]

These claims are clearly exaggerated. In recent years historians have become increasingly aware of the propagandist bias of Civil War news pamphlets, or 'diurnals', the vast majority of which were designed to push a partisan point of view. Thus Roundhead publications stressed Cavalier defeats and vice versa, while Parliamentarian writers consistently overstated popular hostility to the King. In some cases reports were simply fabricated, but there is no need to conclude from this that all the pamphlets are equally useless, containing 'nothing but falsehoods and chimeraes'.[10] Most of the pamphleteers did not publish out-and-out lies, rather, they bent the truth. Used with caution, the pamphlets can still provide valuable evidence, especially when the general tenor of what they say is supported by other, more reliable, sources.

This is certainly true of the events of February 1643. On this occasion, news reports that thousands of Devon men had turned out for Parliament were fully confirmed by other sources. Thus the Royalist Bevill Grenville noted in a letter to his wife that the Devon militia were 'many thousand [strong] as the report goes' and estimated the Parliamentary strength at 5,000 men.[11] Even the Royalist journal *Mercurius Aulicus* acknowledged the Roundheads' success, admitting that 'the leaders of the Rebels in Devonshire had raised a great power in that county, consisting partly of the trained bands thereof, and partly of such others of the country people, whom they had seduced unto their party, the whole amounting to ... 6,000 men'.[12] Financial records show that Parliament's supporters laid out large sums of money on billeting 'the countie forces of trained bands' and supplying 'the great armie' at this time, while a private journal reveals that one Roundhead infantry company doubled in size through the addition of 'unarmed [country]men'.[13] The Parliamentarians' success in drumming up support can hardly be doubted. All the evidence suggests that February 1643 saw a huge popular rising against the Royalists, very similar to that which had occurred in Somerset during August 1642.[14]

On 21 February the countrymen launched themselves upon the Cornish troops at Modbury, forcing the Royalists to retreat. Soon afterwards a truce was agreed and Hopton retired to Cornwall. For a second time, Royalist attempts to take control of Devon had foundered on the rock of popular hostility. The temporary cessation which followed lasted for two months, prompted partly by a genuine desire for peace, partly by the pressing need of both sides to reorganise and regroup. Intensive negotiations took place during March and many hoped that some sort of compromise would be reached. Parliament was opposed to the idea of a truce, however, and—encouraged by the existence of 'a strong party [in Devon] that will readily observe the orders of Parliament to the uttermost of their lives and fortunes'—local MPs succeeded in scuppering the talks.[15] As a result both sides began to build up their forces again during April.

The cessation expired on 22 April and conflict was immediately resumed. On 14 May Stamford advanced to Stratton in Cornwall with a large Parliamentary army and ordered his men to dig in, confident that his superior numbers would deter any assault. Two days later his army was attacked and utterly broken by the Royalists. Over 300 Parliamentarians were killed and 1,700 captured. The battle of Stratton brought Parliamentary dominance of Devon to an end. With Stamford's army destroyed, the Royalists were able to march into the county unopposed and the whole of Devon now lay open to the King's forces. Hopton was anxious to move further east, however, and on 2 June he marched into Somerset with the bulk of his army, leaving a curious power-vacuum behind him. Royalist supporters now controlled Central Devon, but the North, the South and most of the major towns were still held for Parliament. During the ensuing months the county was riven in two as the rival factions struggled for control.

In the aftermath of Stratton local behaviour underwent something of a sea-change and for the first time the Parliamentarians found it hard to raise men in Devon. Several contemporary comments illustrate this. Late in May an Exeter man lamented that 'the hearts of Parliament friends are down, and many daily drop off from us'.[16] A month later a Parliamentary mariner reported that 'this county is so fallen off ... that the very fisher boats are as cautious to come near us, as though we were Turks'.[17] The change in popular behaviour is clear, but how had it come about? I.R. Palfrey has suggested that the alteration was the result of a skilful Royalist propaganda campaign. By paying careful attention to local sensibilities, he contends, the Royalists were able to bring the populace round to their point of view during mid-1643.[18] Palfrey's claims are important because they suggest that Devon, far from being an intrinsically Parliamentarian county, was one which could, with the exercise of a modicum of tact, be persuaded to support the King.

How convincing are these claims? There can be little doubt that the Royalist propaganda campaign was well conceived and executed. It is clear too that certain areas of the county did indeed lend considerable assistance to the King's forces during mid-1643. But to conclude from this that the Royalists had persuaded the entire local community to support the King and oppose the Parliament would be unwarranted. Despite the propaganda campaign, large areas of Devon continued to hold out for Parliament throughout summer 1643, only surrendering when overwhelming force was brought to bear against them. In these areas, at least, Royalist propaganda does not seem to have taken effect. Different regions of the county reacted in very different ways to the Royalist overtures.

All this is not to deny that there had been a considerable shift in allegiances during April–May 1643. Stamford himself admitted as much, conceding that the Parliamentarians' 'extraordinary (though necessary)' demands for money had alienated many local people.[19] Support for this statement is provided by the comment of a disgruntled Devonian 'that it was pyttie the Parliament were not pluckt out by the eares … [for] they sate there for nothing but to bribe and pole the country'.[20] The Parliamentarians' intransigence over the matter of the peace talks almost certainly lessened their credit still further. Even so it is tempting to conclude that it was the result of the battle of Stratton, rather than anything which took place before it, which chiefly explained the change in local behaviour.

After Stratton many Devonians must have felt that Parliament had lost the war and this impression can only have been reinforced by Hopton's subsequent victories. By late July conviction that Parliament's cause was doomed was widespread. Indeed it led the most calculating of Parliament's supporters to change sides. Several individuals were later castigated for joining 'that knot of *utrusques* [i.e. turncoats] who look only to their own preferment and estates' after Waller's defeat at Roundway Down.[21] Yet most of Parliament's supporters did not turn their coats. Instead they simply 'fell away', as the expressive contemporary phrase had it, laying down their arms and going home. A simple desire for self-preservation could explain these actions as well as any sudden conversion to Royalism. However great a man's commitment to the Parliamentary cause, he could hardly be expected to fight on when all the evidence suggested that the 'rebellion' was about to be crushed and condign punishment meted out to the 'traitors' who had taken part in it.

Whether one ascribes the withdrawal of popular support from Parliament at this time to a genuine change in local opinion, or to coercion and fear of punishment, there can be little doubt that the Royalist cause was now reaching its zenith. In August the balance of power shifted decisively to the King when the Cornish army, now under Prince Maurice, marched back into Devon. Maurice's arrival prompted Barnstaple and Exeter to surrender almost at once, and Dartmouth fell a month later. Maurice could now concentrate all his attentions upon Plymouth and for a time it seemed that Royalist victory was assured. Yet Maurice had underestimated the determination of Plymouth's defenders. The Royalists suffered a humiliating series of reverses before the town and on Christmas Day 1643 the King's dispirited army withdrew. The siege of Plymouth had been an unmitigated disaster for the Royalists. Hundreds of their men had been killed and wounded and many more were 'desperately sick'.[22] Worse still, the defeat had shown that the war was not yet lost to Parliament.

Encouraged by Maurice's failure, Parliamentary supporters became active again and in March 1644 a revolt broke out in East Devon.[23] The rebels had been encouraged by the Roundhead garrison of Lyme in Dorset and the Royalists decided to punish the town for its temerity. In April Maurice brought the full weight of his army to bear upon Lyme. The ensuing siege proved as unfortunate for the Prince as the earlier attempt upon Plymouth. The Royalists were unable to penetrate the town defences and again lost hundreds of men. Meanwhile popular hostility to the King was resurfacing. It was reported in May that, should the Parliamentarians march into Devon, they would 'find the country very ready and willing to join with them'.[24] This statement was amply confirmed in the summer, when Essex arrived on the scene with a Parliamentary army. Having forced Maurice to abandon the siege of Lyme, Essex entered East Devon early in July, where local people greeted him with joy. At the same time full-scale anti-Royalist revolts broke out in North Devon and the South Hams.

By mid-July the Royalist position seemed on the verge of collapse, yet the arrival of reinforcements and the misjudgements of the Parliamentarians quickly transformed the situation. On 20 July Essex took the unwise decision to march still further into the west. Meanwhile Charles I had arrived in Devon with the main Royalist army. The combined forces of the King and Prince Maurice eventually proved strong enough to defeat the Parliamentary invasion. Essex was trapped in Cornwall and his army destroyed. Following this signal victory Charles marched back through Devon in triumph, while his troops subdued the areas which had revolted during July. But despite these important successes, the King was unable to achieve complete local dominance. Both Plymouth and Lyme continued to hold out—and both were to become increasingly troublesome during the ensuing months.

Throughout late 1644 the siege of Plymouth was vigorously maintained by the Royalists. Yet in March 1645 the main blockading forces were called away. Henceforth it became all the besiegers could do simply to contain the Parliamentary garrison. Similar problems beset the Royalists in East Devon where the defenders of Lyme were tightening their grip upon the surrounding countryside. Local stability disintegrated altogether in July when thousands of demoralized Royalist horsemen arrived in the shire. The Royalist cavalry (whose commander, Lord Goring, either would not or could not control them) committed such terrible depredations that, in many areas, the countryfolk rose *en masse* to drive them away (see Chapter Six, pp. 111–132). By September Devon was in a state of chaos, as countrymen fought Royalists in the north, Royalists fought Plymothians in the south and everyone—Roundhead and Cavalier alike—did their best to protect themselves from Lord Goring's cavalry. These anarchic conditions did nothing to endear the Royalists to the populace. It was reported in July 1645 that 'in the whole countie of Devon there is scarce one of a hundred that relish the King's cause now'.[25] Fortunately for the people of Devon, relief was at hand. As the King's cause faltered elsewhere, Parliament at last felt able to turn its attention to the South-West and in October the New Model Army advanced into Devon. Fairfax's men met with an enthusiastic welcome, one correspondent noting that 'there are very many of the inhabitants of Devonshire come in to the assistance of his Excellency'.[26]

Devon folk continued to support Parliament throughout the final campaign of 1646. A Parliamentary officer later recalled that 'all the country was generally affected to our party'.[27] When Fairfax advanced across Devon, he met with overwhelming popular support. When he pursued the Royalists into Cornwall, local auxiliaries helped to guard his rear, blocking up the remaining Royalist garrisons. Parliamentary sources commented that the Devon auxiliaries were 'very active' in this service and the final reduction of the county undoubtedly owed much to local troops.[28] In 1646, as in 1644–45 and 1642, support for Parliament was overwhelming. Throughout the whole course of the war, in fact, Devon's commitment to the Parliamentary cause faltered only once, during mid-1643, when Parliament's fortunes were at their nadir. And even this temporary lapse probably owed more to conviction that Parliament's cause was lost than to anything else.

Parliamentarianism in North Devon

Devon was a broadly Parliamentarian county then, but hints have already appeared that some parts of the county were more Parliamentarian than others. Whereabouts was enthusiasm for the Parliamentary cause strongest? As long ago as 1792 John Watkins opined that Charles I had 'had no greater enemies in any part of his dominions than in the chief towns in the north of Devonshire'.[29] Watkins' judgement is fully confirmed by the surviving evidence. Contemporary observers all agreed that North Devon was a hotbed of Parliamentarianism. Thus Clarendon described the area as 'notoriously disaffected' while Fairfax eulogised it as 'that well-affected corner'. Similar comments were made by many other individuals.[30] Throughout the Civil War North Devon supported Parliament on every conceivable occasion. During 1642–43 the region supplied many men to the Parliamentary armies. After Stratton North Devon continued to hold out for Parliament when other regions of the county had submitted. In June 1644 the people of North Devon took advantage of Essex's invasion to rebel against the King and when Fairfax occupied the region in 1646 local men again flocked in to assist the Parliamentary forces.

The Parliamentarianism of North Devon as a whole can hardly be doubted. And within this fervently Parliamentarian region, Barnstaple was the most fervently Parliamentarian community of them all. Barnstaple's sympathies were clear from the very outset of the troubles. When Bath tried to raise the townsfolk for the King in August 1642 his advances were ignored.[31] Instead of rallying to Bath, the inhabitants raised their own Parliamentary garrison and encouraged other local towns to do the same. Five hundred Parliamentarian volunteers were soon assembled at Barnstaple and later that year it was reported that 'that town is fortifying itself, and resolves to spend the last drop of their bloods before they ... [the Royalists] shall have it'.[32]

When Royalist troops advanced into North Devon in December 1642 the inhabitants of Barnstaple attacked them and drove them away. Local records make it clear that, around the same time, a large group of men—many of them 'Barumites', as the townsfolk were known—marched off to Tawstock and pulled down the bridge there, presumably to prevent it from being used by future attackers.[33] Not content with defending their own 'country', the townsfolk also assisted Parliament's forces in South Devon and Cornwall, and throughout the campaigns of 1642–43, Barnstaple men formed the core of the Parliamentary forces in North Devon.[34]

Following the defeat at Stratton, Barnstaple continued to defy the King. Though cut off from the main Parliamentary armies, the town held out for several months, only surrendering when its own local troops had been vanquished by a force of Royalist veterans, and even now the townsfolk refused to accept a Royalist garrison. Remarkably, Prince Maurice acceded to their wishes and Barnstaple remained unoccupied by Royalist troops. But despite the Prince's leniency the townsmen continued to cause trouble. In early 1644 they raised great objections to the Oath of Association which the Royalists were then promoting throughout the western counties.[35] On this occasion an attempted insurrection was quelled by Royalist troops, but six months later the townsmen revolted again. This second revolt was prompted partly by rumours that Irish soldiers were about to be billeted in the town and partly by the news that Essex's Parliamentary army was approaching.[36] In June 1644 the inhabitants took to the streets and ejected the King's supporters. Soon afterwards they repulsed a powerful force of Royalist soldiers, subsequently holding their ground until Essex sent a cavalry brigade to relieve them.[37]

During the summer of 1644 the inhabitants of Barnstaple worked hard to strengthen their defences. Again, this seems to have been a truly popular initiative, with financial accounts recording the purchase of large quantities of beer and bread 'for workmen that tooke noe wages'.[38] Sadly for the townsfolk, there was insufficient time to complete the work. After Essex's defeat Barnstaple was forcibly restored to the Royal allegiance and a powerful garrison was imposed upon the town.[39] The ensuing months were miserable indeed for the townsfolk. The King's men had little sympathy for those who, as one loyalist commented sourly, 'could never keep their fingers out of a rebellion', and they made determined efforts to break the inhabitants' spirit.[40] The townsmen were said to be suffering greatly at the hands of the King's men in March 1645 and later that year it was reported that the Royalists had 'infinitely wronged' many 'honest people in the town'.[41] The inhabitants' Parliamentary zeal was by no means extinguished during this period of repression, however. After Barnstaple had finally been wrested from the Royalists in 1646, it was noted that 'the whole country hereabouts [is] of solid well-affected persons to the Parliament'.[42]

Second only to Barnstaple in its commitment to the Parliamentary cause was Bideford. The townsmen assisted Parliament in many engagements; at Torrington in 1642, at Modbury, Holsworthy and Launceston in early 1643, and at the second battle of Torrington in August 1643.[43] After the Parliamentarians' defeat in this latter engagement, strong Royalist forces laid siege to Bideford. The townsmen remained defiant for several more weeks, however, not surrendering until Parliament's cause seemed lost. Next year, a Royalist garrison was placed in the town, making further displays of Parliamentary sentiment extremely dangerous. Nevertheless in late 1645 the townsmen attacked a band of Royalist troopers.[44] Northam was similarly well-disposed towards Parliament. Like Bideford, it supplied large numbers of men to the Parliamentary armies during 1642–43, and like Bideford, it held out against the Royalists during summer 1643 until subdued by force of arms.[45]

The people of South Molton were also bitterly opposed to the Royalists. The eye-witness account of the riot which occurred

there when Bath tried to publish the Commission of Array is
deservedly well known:

> the common sort of the town ... fell in a great rage ... and
> swore that if ... [the Royalists] did attempt any thing there,
> or read their Commission ... they would beat them all
> downe and kill them, aye, if they were all hanged for it; and
> thereupon betooke themselves to arms, both men, women,
> and children.

The crowd was estimated to contain at least 1,000 people and it
was observed that 'amongst this crew there were both men and
women ... which do daily beg from door to door'.[46] This description may well be exaggerated, coming as it does from a Parliamentarian news pamphlet. But local records show that passive
resistance to the King continued to manifest itself in South
Molton even after the Royalist conquest. In November 1643 a
number of the inhabitants refused to appear on the posse comitatus (the county gathering, or muster of able bodied men, which
the Royalist sheriff periodically summoned in order to raise
troops).[47] In April 1644 the town constables purposely mis-
directed a group of Royalist soldiers, an offence for which they
were afterwards presented at the county sessions.[48] Most remarkable of all is the fact that, in 1645, an entire company of South
Molton men left their homes under Royalist occupation and
marched off to join the Parliamentary garrison at Taunton.[49] This
action speaks volumes for their commitment to the Parliamentary
cause.

Considerable affection for Parliament was also displayed by the
people of Torrington. A company of Parliamentarian soldiers was
mustered here in January 1643. Next month 250 men marched
away from the town to take part in the Parliamentary attack upon
Modbury.[50] After Stratton, Torrington—like its neighbours—
continued to resist the King. The townsmen maintained this
defiant stance throughout July 1643, but by 5 August Torrington
had been occupied by Royalist troops.[51] Curiously, Torrington,
unlike the other North Devon towns, does not seem to have
offered any resistance to the Royalists at this time, nor did it
display any further signs of Parliamentarianism. These anomalies,
together with other pieces of evidence (which are discussed in

Chapter Three, pp. 56–59), suggest that Torrington, though broadly Parliamentarian, was less fervently attached to the cause than were its neighbours.

Parliamentarianism was strong in the smaller towns of North Devon too. This can be seen most clearly in the case of Ilfracombe, which declared for Parliament during the July 1644 uprising. Soon afterwards a Royalist cavalry brigade appeared before the town. When the inhabitants refused to admit them the Royalists set light to their houses. A bloody fight ensued, in which ten of the townsmen and one townswoman were killed. Despite these heavy losses the 'townsmen and sailors' kept up the fight until the Royalists had been 'beaten out'. Ilfracombe remained defiant until September, when it was finally recaptured by the King's troops. From this time onwards a permanent Royalist garrison had to be stationed in the town, presumably to keep an eye on the inhabitants.[52] Holsworthy was another Parliamentarian town. Roundhead soldiers were mustered here in August 1642 and during the subsequent Royalist occupation many of the townsfolk set off to Plymouth to join the Parliamentary garrison. When Fairfax marched into Holsworthy in 1646 it was reported that 'the townsmen showed much cheerfulness' at his arrival.[53] In Chulmleigh, too, Parliamentarianism was strong. The town constables were described as 'ill-affected' to the King in early 1646 and, a month later, Parliamentary sources noted that the Royalists had 'threatened ... to plunder the town, which is generally well-affected'.[54]

Evidence for popular allegiances in the rural parishes of North Devon is scarcer than for the towns, but what information does survive suggests that the countrymen were every bit as Parliamentarian as their urban neighbours. Individual local villages were described as 'well-affected' to the Parliamentary cause, and throughout the war the inhabitants of rural North Devon repeatedly opposed the King's forces.[55] When Royalist fugitives passed through the region in 1642 the local countrymen 'would hardly relieve them, though they carried themselves very peaceably, and paid to a mite for what they took'.[56] In 1643 the inhabitants of many local parishes failed to attend the Royalist posse. Most of the defaulters lived in the rural parishes of the north-east (the five communities which produced the largest numbers of defaulters were Witheridge, Bishops Nympton, West Down, East Down and Sandford). Throughout the Royalist occupation, inhabitants of the countryside around South Molton consistently failed to appear on the posse.[57]

During the July 1644 uprising the inhabitants of North Devon flocked to serve the Parliament. Over forty north-east Devon parishes contributed money to the fortifications of Barnstaple at this time and when a foot regiment was ordered to be raised 'in Molton hundreds', the requisite number of men was swiftly found.[58] The countrymen of North Devon continued to assist the Parliamentarians even after Essex's defeat. In September a Royalist noted that 'the rabble are still bold that command the country to store them [i.e. the Parliamentary garrison of Barnstaple] with all manner of provisions'.[59] Further signs of rural Parliamentarianism emerged during January 1646, when the constables of Cheldon, King's Nympton, Worlington, Thelbridge and Woolfardisworthy were all noted to be 'ill-affected to his Majestie's service'.[60] On Fairfax's subsequent advance to Chulmleigh, Parliamentary sources reported that the country people round about 'showed themselves very joyful at his Excellency's approach, and brought in much provision to our army'.[61]

Parliamentarianism in South Devon

South Devon presents a broadly similar picture. Here too the ports and the larger towns were strongly Parliamentarian. Plymouth's protracted resistance to the King is well known. Between 1642 and 1646 Plymouth endured continual Royalist attacks, but was never subdued. That this was so was chiefly because of the Parliamentary zeal of the townsfolk. Financial records make it clear that the inhabitants contributed large sums of money towards Plymouth's defence, as well as working on the fortifications and serving as soldiers.[62] Contemporaries frequently commented upon Plymouth's attachment to the Parliamentary cause. In 1642 the town was described as 'very hearty for ... Parliament' and its inhabitants as 'zealous in the public cause', while two years later it was noted that 'the townsmen are very courage[ous] and make the garrison, which is one thousand, four thousand ... they are unanimous, have shut up shops, betaken them to the works, and do bravely'.[63] The Royalist point of view is aptly summed up in a document which refers with obvious distaste 'to the disloyal and rebellious town of Plymouth'.[64] The depth of Parliamentarian feeling in Plymouth is vividly illustrated

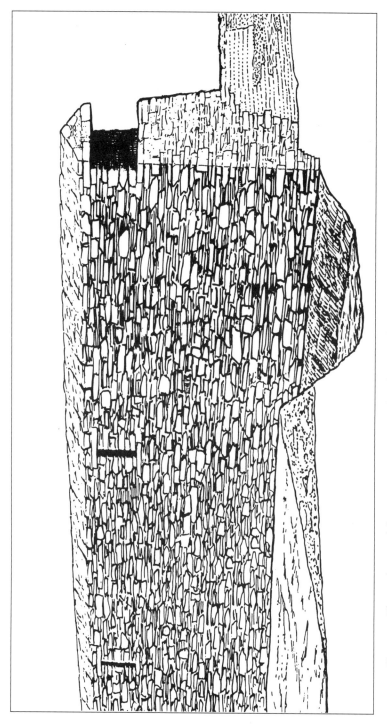

Figure 1. Plymouth town defences, 1643: a reconstruction drawing of the massive stone wall which was built by the citizens of Plymouth in order to keep out the King's forces. (By permission of Exeter Museums Archaeological Field Unit)

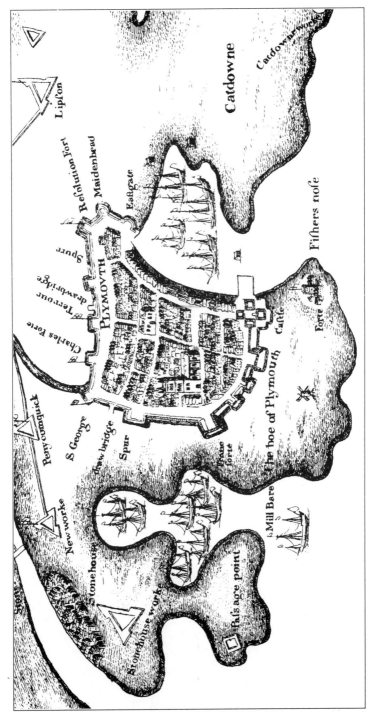

Figure 2. Plymouth town defences, 1644: this contemporary plan shows the full extent of the inner-wall at Plymouth. The names of the forts which stood along the circuit are significant, for they help to indicate the defenders' motivation: patriotism (St George), purity (Maidenhead) and, supposedly, loyalty (Charles). Terrour and Resolution stand for courage and resolve.

by the fact that, when Sir Alexander Carew tried to betray the garrison, the townswomen 'were very hardly intreated to forbear the hanging of him'.[65]

Equally attached to the Parliamentary cause was Dartmouth. Financial records show that over one hundred inhabitants of Dartmouth gave money to Parliament, that soldiers from Dartmouth assisted the Parliamentary armies at Sherborne, Braddock Down and Modbury, and that at least two companies of pro-Parliamentary volunteers were raised in the town.[66] When Royalist forces advanced into South Devon in 1642 the people of Dartmouth refused to admit them. This recalcitrance angered the King's supporters, and soon afterwards the town governors sent an anxious letter to Parliament, complaining that the neighbouring Royalist gentry 'begin to threaten the ruin of this poor town'. In the course of the letter the townsmen repeatedly stressed their support for Parliament, referring to their 'hearty desires to the service' and to the large sums of money which they had raised for Parliament's use.[67] Soon afterwards several Royalist gentlemen were brought into Dartmouth as prisoners and this sight was described as '[much] gladding … the hearts of the good people there'.[68] Around the same time a Parliamentary observer referred to Dartmouth as this 'faithful town'.[69]

Like Plymouth and Barnstaple, Dartmouth remained constant in its allegiance after Stratton. In July 1643 Plymouth and Dartmouth combined to send an army to the relief of Exeter.[70] After Exeter fell, a pamphleteer reported that 'Dartmouth men have to my knowledge sworn to fight it out to the last man rather then they will endure such thraldome as Exeter … [does] now endure, and if the Cavaliers enter there, it shall be by the sword'.[71] The townsfolk were as good as their word. When Prince Maurice moved into South Devon, his advance guards were attacked by Dartmouth men. When he summoned the town, the inhabitants refused to listen. When he instituted a full-scale siege, the townsmen merely strengthened their defences. It eventually took a bloody assault to wrest the town from its Parliamentary defenders.

After its capture Dartmouth remained sullen and restive. It was reported in late 1643 that 'the townsmen in Dartmouth are very weary of the Cavaliers' and by June 1644 the inhabitants were plotting to eject them.[72] When this scheme failed, sixty of the townsmen left their homes and went to Plymouth. Despite the departure of these men (who were presumably Parliament's most committed local supporters) the town remained constant in its allegiance. In August 1645 a sea-captain cruising off the South Devon coast observed that the people of Dartmouth were generally well-affected to Parliament. When Fairfax arrived in the South Hams in 1646 he found that many of the Plymouth garrison were Dartmouth men.[73] Dartmouth's intrinsic Parliamentarianism can hardly be doubted. A loyalist minister, condemning disobedience and rebellion in a sermon, referred with disapproval to Dartmouth as a place 'where ... there were many too much disposed to those sins'.[74]

Did the inhabitants of South Devon's smaller towns and villages share the Parliamentary sentiments of Plymouth and Dartmouth? A good deal of evidence suggests that they did. Several local communities are known to have demonstrated support for Parliament. At Ugborough 'a great bonfire' was made by the parishioners to celebrate 'the news of a victory obtained over the King's army'.[75] At Totnes in 1643 the townsfolk refused to tell a Royalist officer which way a group of Parliamentary troops had fled, later sending a company of soldiers to join the Plymouth garrison.[76] Throughout the war South Devon men continually came in to Plymouth.[77] Pamphlets stressed again and again that the garrison enjoyed the support of the surrounding countryfolk.[78]

Perhaps the most impressive evidence for the Parliamentarianism of the South Hams is the insurrection which occurred there during summer 1644. This major disturbance, like those which occurred in North Devon at the same time, was sparked off by the advance of Essex's army. The first sign that trouble was brewing appeared on 24 June, when John Berkley, the Royalist Governor of Exeter, wrote to Edward Seymour, his opposite number at Dartmouth, warning him to strengthen his garrison. Berkley also advised Seymour to 'secure all that refuse the Protestation', a clear sign that trouble was expected from the local populace. Berkley was particularly anxious to secure a certain Mr Roope, who had been released at Seymour's request while on his way to Exeter as a prisoner. Berkley clearly considered this action to have been most unwise; 'God grant you have no cause to regret it' he muttered darkly.[79] These words were prophetic, for Roope later played a leading part in the South Hams insurrection.

Seymour received a second warning on 29 June, this time

informing him that the people of Dartmouth were planning to rise against him.[80] This plot was foiled, but soon afterwards disturbances broke out to the north of the town. Maurice was informed on 11 July that 'divers persons disaffected to his Majesties service ... do associate and meet together about Torbay in a hostile and warlike manner, to the great terror and distraction of his Majesties loyal subjects'.[81] Accordingly, the Prince wrote to Seymour, ordering him to suppress the rebels. Seymour's response is unknown, but it is clear that trouble was now breaking out across the whole of South Devon. Sixty men from Dartmouth came in to the Parliamentarians at Plymouth on 11 July.[82] Two days later Parliamentary troops marched out to Kingsbridge and, soon afterwards, the town was occupied by insurrectionary forces.[83]

Over the ensuing weeks the rebellion gathered pace. The Royalist presence in South Devon was soon restricted to Dartmouth and Salcombe Castle alone. Charles I himself wrote to Seymour on 15 August, noting that 'divers persons in the South Hams and other parts thereabouts, being very ill-affected to us ... do endeavour to raise the posse comitatus and thereby disturb the peace and security of those parts'.[84] The King ordered Seymour to suppress the disturbances at once, but he failed to comply, probably because his forces were too weak. Soon afterwards Seymour sent to Exeter for reinforcements, but Berkley was unable to help and appeals to the Royalist field army met with no more success. Edmund Fortescue wrote to Seymour from Cornwall on 23 August, explaining that, although he had requested the King to send some horse to the South Hams 'for the redemption of those parts from those devils that now are in them', Charles had been unwilling to weaken his cavalry force while Essex remained at large.[85]

Not until the end of August, by which time it had become clear that Essex's army was doomed, did Royalist troops at last become available to march to Seymour's relief. On 1 September Berkley ordered several officers to assist Seymour at once 'with all the force possible you can, both horse and foot'. He wrote to Seymour again two days later, requesting him to arrange a place at which their forces could meet in order to 'do what may be convenient against those of Kingsbridge'.[86] The need to pursue Essex's fleeing horsemen eventually prevented Berkley from attending this rendezvous, but there can be little doubt that the disturbances in the South Hams were brought to an end within the next few days. By 11 September persons who had participated in the risings were being rounded up and imprisoned.[87] The Royalist county commissioners later 'convented divers persons' to appear before them at Kingsbridge, inquiring 'what men had aided and assisted the Parlyament' and who had 'acted ... for the Parlyament in or nere Kingsbridge'.[88]

The commissioners' assumption—that the South Hams rebellion had been Parliamentarian in its motivation, rather than simply neutralist—is borne out by other evidence. Of the three prominent individuals known to have taken part, two (Nicholas Roope and Arthur Upton) had previously served as Parliamentary officers, while the third (Adrian Swete) made his dislike for the King's cause manifestly clear in his own private journal.[89] Moreover the attempt of the South Devon rebels to raise the posse comitatus mirrors the use of exactly the same tactic during the pro-Parliamentary disturbances in the north of the county.[90] The risings almost certainly formed part of a coherent grand plan, devised by Parliamentary sympathizers upon Essex's approach.

The South Devon rising covered a wide area. Kingsbridge and Torbay were the main centres of the revolt but individual participants are also known to have come from Slapton, Stokenham, Modbury and Dartmouth. That so many communities were involved in the insurrection suggests that the rebels enjoyed considerable popular support. Other scraps of evidence (Seymour's inability to suppress the disturbances without outside assistance, for example) point the same way. A list compiled in the aftermath of the rising reveals that Brixham, Churston Ferrers and Kingswear alone had produced thirty-three 'rebellious persons'.[91] There is no way of knowing if these villages were typical, but if the insurrection received a similar degree of support from parishes right across the region, the rebel forces must have been extremely numerous.

The risings of 1644 provide clear evidence that the people of the South Hams were prepared to rise in support of Parliament. Their willingness to do so was demonstrated again in 1646, when the New Model Army met with an enthusiastic response from the region. When Fairfax summoned 1,000 local men to assemble at Totnes in January, over three times as many appeared, amply confirming 'the readiness of the country to do service'.[92] These volunteers were clearly South Devon men, for they 'came all out of the four next hundreds to Totnes'.[93] Nor were these the only

South Devonians to assist Parliament. In February it was reported that 'the country people nere Salcombe are risen, and offer to keep in the [Royalist] Fort' there.[94] That local people did indeed participate in these operations is confirmed by the parish registers of Malborough, which record the death of Roger Hingston, an inhabitant of the village, 'slain against the fort of Salcombe'.[95]

Parliamentarianism in East and Central Devon

In East Devon, too, Parliamentarian sentiment was widespread, especially in the larger towns. Tiverton, the region's most populous community, was especially forward in the Parliamentary cause. Volunteers set off from here for Sherborne in 1642.[96] After Parliament's defeat at Stratton, Tiverton's inhabitants prepared to resist the advancing Royalists and barricades were erected in the streets. Local countrymen showed their support for the townsfolk by promising to come in and assist them, but, owing to treachery, the plan failed and the Royalists were able to march in unopposed. Soon afterwards the townsmen were fined £1,000, presumably because they were known to have assisted Parliament.[97] Tiverton continued to defy the King, however, and when the men of East Devon were summoned to appear on the posse in June 1643, no fewer than forty-three Tivertonians failed to attend.[98]

Further evidence of local Parliamentarianism appeared in 1644, when Essex's army met with an enthusiastic reception at Tiverton. Writing from here on 15 July Essex observed that local countrymen were very willing to enlist in his army. Royalist sources confirmed this, acknowledging that Essex had won the affections 'of the common people' during his stay at Tiverton.[99] Even after Essex had marched away, the townsfolk continued to defy the King. When Royalist troops attempted to reoccupy the town in August 'they were resisted by the inhabitants [for] some time, by throwing stones &c'. Eventually the King's soldiers fired upon the crowd. The townsmen then scattered and were pursued through the town by the Royalist horse. Once the resistance had been crushed, a local miller, who had presumably been prominent in the disturbances, was hanged from a sign-post by the vengeful troopers.[100] This can have done little to reconcile the inhabitants of Tiverton to the Royalist cause. Towards the end of 1644 the Royalists set up a permanent garrison there, probably as much to overawe the inhabitants as to defend the town from enemy attack. Nevertheless Tiverton Castle was briefly siezed from the Royalists in September 1645, presumably by the townsmen.[101] During the campaigns of 1645–46 Parliament again received much support in this district, pamphleteers reporting that 'the country ... rise in great numbers about Tiverton, and much love us'.[102]

Similar commitment to the Parliamentary cause was displayed by the nearby cloth-towns of Halberton and Cullompton. In August 1642 the constable of Cullompton refused to publish the Royalist Sheriff's warrants. When it was thought that Bath's adherents might try to enter the town, the inhabitants 'showed a great deal of undaunted courage, and opposed them very much'. It was noted at this time that the Parliamentarians were 'likely to have many volunteers out of this parish' to march against Sherborne.[103] In the event, not only volunteers, but three companies of the trained bands as well, marched into Dorset. Later that year men from Halberton came in to assist the Parliamentarians at Exeter. Local people turned out for Parliament again in February 1643, when John Weare (himself a Halberton man) led 'a considerable number' of his neighbours to Modbury.[104] When Essex's army advanced into this area in 1644 his requests for men resulted in a 'great appearance'. Two whole regiments were raised here and, writing from Cullompton in July, Essex observed that 'I find a great affection in the country to the Parliament'.[105] After Essex had been defeated, 'divers' inhabitants of the countryside around Halberton left their homes and joined the Roundhead garrison at Taunton.[106]

These were not the only local communities to come out in support of Parliament. Uffculme was later described by one of its inhabitants as a wholly well-affected parish, while in August 1642 'the whole country' around Hembury mounted guard on the fort there, in order to prevent the Royalists from siezing it.[107] Hostility to the King manifested itself again in this district in May 1643, when one John Searle persuaded the constable of Buckerell 'to put himself and others of the parishioners in arms ... to withstand the King's army from coming that way'.[108] When Henry Carey, the Royalist Sheriff, summoned East Devon to appear on the posse in June, twenty-four inhabitants of Buckerell failed to appear. Nor was this an isolated pocket of resistance. Searle had assured his auditors 'that neighbouring parishes would join with them' in resisting the Royalists and they do indeed seem to have done so. Fifty-eight men from nearby Awliscombe also refused to turn out on the posse.[109]

The rural parishes in the north-east of the region were similarly reluctant to assist the King. Carey's officials later noted that fifty-three inhabitants of Culmstock, twenty-nine of Hemyock and thirty-four of Clayhidon had refused to appear on the posse.[110] As the war progressed these three communities continued to display a fierce hostility to the Royalists, prompting the constable of Culmstock to complain that 'none in the parish were right for the King'.[111] The spirit of defiance prevalent in this area was most clearly demonstrated in March 1644, when a full-scale insurrection broke out against the Royalists. According to a local gentleman, this revolt was prompted by a Parliamentary victory near Lyme, which 'so heartened Devonshire as that the inhabitants of Hemyock presently rose for the freeing of their country'.[112]

The insurrectionaries' first step was to sieze Hemyock castle in the hope of 'the country's general aid and assistance'. They also asked for help from the Parliamentary garrison of Lyme. The rising was clearly a positive demonstration of support for Parliament, one Roundhead officer claiming that '[we have] the hearts of the country', another that 'the country befriends us'. Assisted by forces from Lyme, the rebels seemed on the verge of success, yet the Royalists reacted swiftly. Marching on Hemyock they surrounded the castle and forced out its defenders. Two hundred prisoners were taken, most being 'country men'. These unfortunate captives were 'bound up like rogues' and carried off to Exeter. The ringleaders were even less fortunate; three of them were hanged on the spot by the Royalists, who forbade the victims' relatives to cut the bodies down.[113] This ruthless action can only have confirmed the hostility which local people felt towards the King.

Thorncombe, in the extreme north-east of the region, was also very well-affected to Parliament. Fortunately, a Royalist presentment (or constable's report), probably dating to 1643–44, has survived for the parish. This shows that no fewer than twenty-three of the villagers had served as volunteers in the Parliamentary garrisons of Exeter, Dorchester and Lyme. In addition nine local men had lent money to the Parliament or had encouraged others to do so, six had shown themselves to be disaffected to the King 'by giving of ill words' and one more was languishing in a

Royalist gaol, having been captured 'in arms'.[114] A total of thirty-nine men from this one small parish are known to have aided Parliament. This seems conclusive proof of Thorncombe's Parliamentarianism, the presentment also showing just how many people were involved in the political divisions of the day.

A great deal of evidence survives for popular Parliamentarianism in East Devon. Yet support for Parliament was much more impressive in some areas than in others. All the communities dealt with so far lie in the north-east of the region. In other parts of East Devon not a single community is known to have demonstrated clear support for Parliament's cause.[115] East Devon presents something of a contrast to the regions surveyed above, therefore. While communities throughout North Devon and the South Hams are known to have favoured Parliament, in East Devon, such communities were concentrated in one particular area.

In Mid-Devon the situation was different yet again. There were very few signs of popular Parliamentarianism here. Only two Mid-Devon communities can be attributed to the Parliamentary camp with any degree of confidence. The first is Crediton, which in early 1643 was plundered by Hopton's army. Later that year Crediton people helped to loot Fulford House, the seat of a local Royalist, perhaps in a spirit of revenge. In 1643 twenty-nine of the townsmen failed to appear on the Royalist posse.[116] In 1646, finally, the King's troops threatened to burn Crediton down, again suggesting that the inhabitants were seen as hostile to the Royalist cause.[117] The second Mid-Devon community for which firm evidence of popular Parliamentarianism survives is Moretonhampstead. The inhabitants of Moreton joined the people of Crediton in the sack of Fulford House, and forty-six of the townsmen later refused to serve on the posse. As Moreton's adult male population was only around 400 at this time, this is a most impressive figure. During the latter stages of the war, moreover, the Plymouth garrison sent scouts to Moreton 'for intelligence', again suggesting that the townsfolk sympathized with Parliament.[118] Moreton and Crediton aside, Mid-Devon was apparently bare of Parliamentarian communities.

This chapter has revealed that, while the traditional view of Devon as a broadly Parliamentarian shire is correct, there were distinct regional variations in the strength of popular support for Parliament. Pro-Parliamentary communities were most heavily

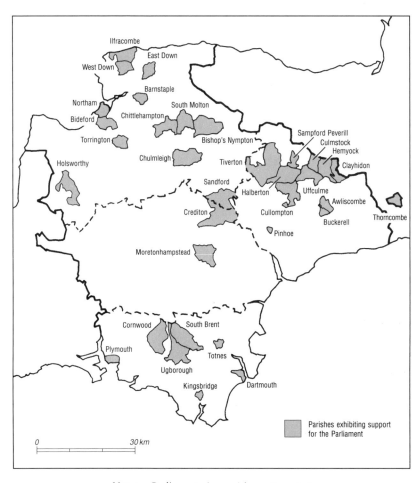

Map 2. Parliamentarian parishes, 1642–1646.

concentrated in the north, the north-east and the south of Devon. In Mid-Devon and the countryside to the east of Exeter such communities were few and far between (see Map 2). Why should this have been so? Was Mid-Devon more insulated from the war's events? Hardly, for taxation, billeting and recruitment affected the entire county. A host of recent studies have demonstrated that it was simply not possible for people in most parts of England to escape the war's effects.[119] Were the inhabitants of this area peculiarly apathetic and uninterested, then? It is hard to see why this should have been so. Instead it is tempting to suggest that majority opinion in these particular areas favoured the King.

Chapter 3

'Our Ill-affected Country Parishes': The Strongholds of Popular Royalism

Across the country as a whole Royalist communities are much harder to identify than Parliamentarian ones. There are several good reasons for this. Most important is the fact that the Parliamentarian news pamphlets—which still serve as a vital source of information about the war's events—were reluctant to admit that any community outside the Celtic fringe wholeheartedly supported the King. Roundhead propagandists tended to suppress, or at least to play down, evidence which contradicted this theory, while the equivalent Cavalier literature did little to redress the balance. The Royalists produced far fewer news pamphlets than the Parliamentarians did. In addition the style of Royalist propaganda was very different from that of their rivals, preferring to stress the social status of the King's chief supporters, rather than the affection which existed for him among more humble folk.[1] As a result the extent of popular Royalism in England has been seriously underplayed. Taking the evidence of the pamphlet literature at face value, some historians have concluded that lower-class support for the King was minimal, indeed practically non-existent outside Cornwall, Wales and the catholic areas of Lancashire.[2]

To take such a view is to go too far; as John Morrill has observed Parliamentary pamphlets simply cannot be relied upon to give an accurate assessment of the strength of popular Royalism.[3] But this is not to say that their evidence is altogether useless. The very fact of the pamphlets' habitual bias means that, whenever they do refer to a particular town or village as 'malignant' (or ill-affected), their testimony can be relied upon. In this chapter such scraps of evidence as emerge from the pamphlets will be combined with the testimony of contemporary letters, legal records and financial accounts in order to plot the distribution of popular Royalism in Devon. The pattern of recruitment to the King's local infantry regiments will also be studied. This should indicate the regions from which the King found it relatively easy to obtain men, and those which proved more unwilling.[4]

Popular Royalism in North Devon

Unsurprisingly, in view of the discoveries made in Chapter Two, the region of the county in which evidence for popular Royalism is hardest to find is North Devon. While individual supporters of the King were relatively numerous, local communities as a whole displayed not the slightest sign of enthusiasm for the Royalist cause. Throughout the whole of North Devon, in fact, only one community is known to have exhibited definite pro-Royalism. This was the market town of Torrington. Torrington's Royalist sympathies were first displayed in December 1642 when Colonel John Acland led a force of Royalist cavalry into North Devon. Acland's advance was prompted by a desire to raise men and Royalist sources later observed that the colonel had come to North Devon with the express intention of 'settling the posse comitatus there'.[5] By 25 December Acland's men had established themselves in Torrington, where they were 'entertained by consent of the Maior'.[6] Other sources make it clear that the Royalists had been invited to come to Torrington by the inhabitants.[7] The cordial reception which Torrington accorded Acland stirred up intense resentment in the neighbouring towns of Barnstaple, Bideford and Northam. One pamphlet reported that the Barumites were 'much offended at the Towne of Torrington for quartering [the Royalist] Horse', while another stated that 'the fury of the Barnstaple men [was] such that they vowed to plunder and pillage Torrington for harbouring such guests'.[8] The hostility felt towards the people of Torrington by their neighbours is clearly apparent in a contemporary letter written by a Barnstaple man, which contains frequent angry references to the 'base townsmen' of Torrington and to the treacherousness of their behaviour.[9]

While their opponents raged, the Royalists attempted to raise the surrounding countryside for the King and these efforts met with some success. A Parliamentary pamphlet later put the Royalist strength in Torrington at '13 or 14 hundred at least'. The same source admitted that, in addition to the original occupying force, many local gentlemen and a number of 'trained souldiers' were now present in the town as well.[10] That members of the local militia had joined Acland's party is significant, for it suggests that a certain degree of Royalism existed in the countryside around Torrington, as well as in the town itself.[11] Alarmed by these developments the inhabitants of Barnstaple, Bideford and Northam decided to attack Torrington at once, before the Royalist interlopers could receive any further accretions of strength.

On the afternoon of 31 December some 600 Parliamentary troops advanced upon Torrington, determined to eject their enemies from the town in which they 'nestled'. The Royalists, apparently deciding that discretion was the better part of valour, made hasty preparations to escape. Soon afterwards Acland's troops departed, having 'left the townesmen to make good the workes, and charged them not to let ... [the Parliamentarians] know they were gone'. According to Parliamentary sources, the inhabitants faithfully obeyed these instructions, holding the fortifications on the town's edge for five more hours while the Royalists made good their escape. During this time the townsmen fired upon the Parliamentarians, inhibiting them from any further advance. Early next morning the attackers finally managed to enter the town. Having won the day, the Parliamentary soldiers set about plundering the houses of the '3 or 4 malignants' who had 'invited the Cavaliers to Torrington' in the first place.[12]

The events of late 1642 make it clear that Torrington contained a sizeable Royalist element. While the initial invitation to the King's forces might conceivably have emanated from a small clique of individuals, the resistance which the townsfolk offered to the Parliamentary troops after Acland had gone provides evidence that at least a modicum of popular Royalism existed in the town. The Parliamentary threat to pillage the town similarly suggests that many of the inhabitants were regarded as Royalist. Events which took place later in the war strongly support this view. As noted in Chapter Two, pp. 40–41, Torrington was the first of the major North Devon towns to surrender to the King's forces during summer 1643. Significantly, this action again seems to have been regarded as the rankest treachery by the inhabitants of Barnstaple, Bideford and Northam. In August, they sent out a second army against Torrington, this time with orders to 'put all to the sword, both old and young, and then to plunder the towne, and at length to fire it'.[13] The Barnstaple forces were beaten off in the end, but the depth of hatred exhibited between one Devon town and its closest neighbours during this bloody affair is quite remarkable.

Another curious incident savouring of inter-town hostility occurred during the North Devon uprising of summer 1644, when one Humfrey Vanstone was buried in Torrington after having been 'shott by one of the Barnstaple troopers, as he was comming to church on Sunday at forenoone prayer'.[14] It is also worth pointing out that Torrington is one of the few places in North Devon from which the Royalists are definitely known to have recruited men.[15] Yet with all this said, Torrington can hardly be portrayed as a stronghold of fanatical loyalism. As we have seen, the town provided large numbers of men for the Parliamentary armies, too, and was referred to approvingly in several Parliamentarian sources. It seems fairest to conclude that, unlike the other North Devon towns, Torrington was deeply divided in its allegiance.

No other North Devon community is known to have assisted the King. A few cases in which small loyalist groups tried to betray otherwise Parliamentarian communities are documented. A group of 'malevolent townsmen' allegedly plotted to hand Bideford over to the King in April 1643, for example, while five months later the Mayor of Barnstaple was reported to have 'betrayed' his fellow citizens by entering into negotiations with Prince Maurice.[16] In neither case was the evidence for local Royalism very impressive. At Bideford the Royalist conspirators were swiftly arrested by their fellow citizens, while the charges laid against the Mayor of Barnstaple seem to have been largely unfounded.[17]

What of Royalist recruitment efforts in North Devon? Did attempts to raise soldiers here meet with success, or did they founder amidst a sea of local hostility? It must be admitted at once that, in the 1640s as today, no community was happy to see its menfolk marched away to war and possible death. Military impressment was deeply unpopular and some historians have claimed that the Royalists, in particular, found it difficult to raise men.[18] Yet even when such considerations are borne in mind, all the evidence suggests that the King's recruiters met with a peculiarly negative response from the inhabitants of North Devon.

During the first months of the war, few local men were induced to fight for the King. A report of September 1642 did claim that the Earl of Bath had 500 footmen at Tawstock, but there was no sign of these troops when Bath was arrested a few days later.[19] The Royalists were no more successful during early 1643. Particularly significant was their failure to raise an appreciable number of men in North Devon during May–July 1643, when recruits from other parts of the county were flocking to the King's army. Not until the Royalists seemed on the verge of outright victory, in fact, did men from North Devon at last begin to turn out for the King. In August 1643 a company of Royalist soldiers was raised in Torrington and during the following month recruits were procured from all over the region.[20] By mid-September over 2,000 North Devon infantrymen had been raised.[21] This was an impressive figure, but the recruiters' success seems unlikely to have been a result of genuine popular enthusiasm for the King. It probably owed more to conviction that Parliament's cause was doomed.

Maurice's failure to take Plymouth in late 1643 swiftly disabused local people of the notion that the war in the South-West was over. Significantly, most of the North Devon men who had taken up arms during August and September now melted away.[22] The Royalists were never again able to raise a respectable number of recruits from North Devon. This was not for want of trying as many Royalist commanders made determined efforts to raise soldiers here. In 1645, for instance, Colonel Alan Apsley embarked upon a recruitment drive in the countryside around Barnstaple. Initially his plans were most ambitious. A surviving muster list indicates that Apsley intended to raise 500 men from a score of North Devon parishes alone.[23] Yet these high expectations were never met. Apsley never managed to collect more than 500 men in total and even this figure included the 'foreign' troops whom he had originally brought with him and the Barnstaple trained band, which had little choice but to turn out for the King.[24] Once one has discounted these men (and also considered the fact that Apsley had the whole of North Devon to recruit from) it becomes clear that the numbers actually raised were derisory.

There were other similar episodes, all bearing witness to the dismal failure of Royalist recruitment in North Devon. Between 1642 and 1646 a succession of Royalist officers, local worthies and 'foreigners', good men and bad, made repeated attempts to raise local troops for the King. Yet despite the cruellest of threats and penalties, the men of the region consistently failed to appear. The loyalist gentry of North Devon were unable to raise a single volunteer infantry regiment from among their tenants and neighbours. Even the trained bands of the region were unwilling to turn out for the Royalists, and were never employed by them to any considerable purpose. The failure of the Royalist recruiters was complete.

Popular Royalism in South Devon

What was the situation in the South Hams? This area has traditionally been considered the stronghold of Devon Royalism, yet as we saw in Chapter Two, pp. 42–49, many South Devon parishes demonstrated considerable enthusiasm for the Parliamentary cause, suggesting that the loyalty of the South Hams may well have been exaggerated. The most striking display of Royalism to occur in South Devon during the Civil War was undoubtedly the gathering of the posse comitatus at Modbury in December 1642. This meeting attracted much local support. Hopton claimed that 'a great concourse of people' appeared, while Parliamentary sources admitted that 2–4,000 'trained souldiers and voluntiers' had turned out.[25] These figures are impressive, especially when one considers that most parts of Devon, (including all the larger towns) were still under the direct control of the Parliament. Large numbers of Devonians were clearly prepared to come out for the King when conditions seemed favourable.

It is tempting to see this episode as conclusive proof of South Devon's Royalism. Yet the gathering at Modbury was intended to be a muster of the posse for the entire county, not just a meeting for the Royalists of the South Hams. Analysis of the places of residence of those who attended the muster reveals that people had travelled to Modbury from all over Devon. Of the twenty-four Devonians definitely known to have attended, only nine were from the South Hams. Six came from Mid-Devon, three more from the North and two from the East (the residences of the other four are unknown).[26] Most of these individuals were gentlemen and therefore unusually mobile, but it seems probable that many of the commoners who attended the posse had also travelled from outside the South Hams. The success of the Modbury gathering was not necessarily indicative of overwhelming popular Royalism in South Devon, then. The fact that many South Devon communities exhibited open hostility to the King should also warn us against making too hasty a pronouncement on the underlying allegiance of the region. And indeed, when one comes to look for hard evidence of Royalist communities in the South Hams it is simply not to be found.

Modbury apart, only one other South Devon community showed any support for the King. This was Totnes. Here, as in North Devon, pro-Royalism first raised its head during the Cornish advance of 1642. Hopton held a muster in the town in December, apparently with some success. A newsbook later alleged that Hopton had 'entertained' over 1,000 'tailors, weavers and shoemakers'.[27] Presumably these men were potential recruits and presumably many of them were Totnesians. A few days later fifty-six inhabitants of Totnes combined to lend Hopton £239.[28] Again this suggests that a considerable number of Royalists dwelt within the town. It should be noted too that the Totnes archives contain two petitions, one dated 1644, the other dated 1665, both of which stress the Corporation's affection to Charles I.[29] According to these petitions, the inhabitants of Totnes had constantly demonstrated their loyalty by 'ayding and assisting his Majestie's forces with powder, amunnicion and money upon all occasions'. Documents were annexed to show that, in September 1644, only fourteen of the townsfolk had been 'in actual rebellion' against the King, and that even they were 'of low and meane quality'.[30] These are important pieces of evidence. Yet it should not be forgotten that the petitions were composed with the specific aim of currying Royal favour. There is no doubt that some Totnesians were Royalists, but claims that there was near universal support for the King in the town must be regarded with suspicion. As Chapter Two has shown, p. 46, Totnes assisted Parliament too. It seems safest to assume that allegiances within the town were divided.

The shortage of Royalist communities in the South Hams was counterbalanced, to some extent, by the success of the King's recruiters here. The musters at Modbury and Totnes in 1642 have already been noted, and during 1643–45 local men continued to turn out for the King. South Devon was, throughout the war, the region which maintained the largest number of infantry units in the Royal army. Two volunteer regiments (those of Colonel

Henry Champernowne and Colonel Edmond Fortescue) were recruited almost exclusively from the South Hams, while a third (that of Colonel Edward Seymour) derived much of its strength from the same region. These units mustered some 2,000 men in 1643–44.[31] In addition the local trained bands supported the King's army on numerous occasions, lying in garrison at Dartmouth, guarding the coasts against Parliamentary shipping, and assisting in the siege of Plymouth.[32] While the quantity of the South Devon recruits was impressive, however, their quality was rather more doubtful. Parliamentary sources claimed that the local militia only served the King under duress, and this may well have been true.[33] Certainly the behaviour of the South Devon units was somewhat craven at times. At Dartmouth in 1646 two South Devon infantry regiments capitulated very quickly despite having the benefit of prepared positions.[34] Soon afterwards another local regiment defected en masse.[35] So while many recruits were procured from the South Hams, their commitment to the King's cause was hardly unswerving.

Popular Royalism in Mid-Devon

In Mid-Devon evidence for popular Royalism is relatively widespread, much more so than in any other part of the county. This was the only region of Devon in which hints of popular Royalism are known to have appeared before the Cornish advance of November 1642. During the preceding summer, militiamen from the countryside west of Exeter had refused to attend a Parliamentary muster at Haldon, one of a series which the Roundheads were holding across the county.[36] As far as is known, the muster at Haldon was the only one to be disrupted in this way. This suggests that, as early as August 1642, the people of Mid-Devon were dissenting from the pro-Parliamentary views of their neighbours. Clear-cut Royalism first became apparent in the region during November 1642, when Hopton's army occupied Tavistock. A posse was called and, on the next day, 400 local recruits appeared in the town.[37] Hopton was disappointed with this response, the turnout being lower than expected. Nevertheless, this was the first time that the Royalists had managed to raise more than a handful of men in Devon. That this should have occurred in the central region of the county is significant (though the example of Modbury warns us against assuming that all those who attended the meeting had necessarily come from Mid-Devon).

The muster at Tavistock was only a beginning. In late 1642 Royalist activity became evident in the hill country to the west of Exeter. The constable's accounts for Tedburn St Mary provide some precious scraps of evidence concerning the behaviour of local people at this time. They reveal, for instance, that prior to December 1642, Tedburn's village militia had taken part in several military exercises at Exeter.[38] This is significant for it demonstrates that the inhabitants of Tedburn were continuing to obey the commands of the Parliamentary authorities in the city. During December this situation seems to have changed. The first sign that something unusual was afoot was the payment made to two local men for the expenses of their journey 'to Madbery'.[39] As we have seen, a Royalist muster was held at Modbury on 7 December. It seems very probable that the individuals referred to in the accounts had attended this meeting, despite the fact that Modbury was so many miles away and the Parliamentary garrison at Exeter so close. Already, signs of a nascent pro-Royalism were surfacing in Tedburn, and similar sentiments were about to emerge in other local communities.

In early December the inhabitants of several Mid-Devon parishes gathered their 'militia-arms' at Dunsford and 'there stood upon their guard' against the Parliamentarians.[40] The decision to assemble the parish weapons probably reflected local hopes of an imminent Royalist advance and it seems certain that the countrymen intended to assist Hopton's army. Parliamentarian sources later claimed that the arms belonged to 'malignants' and were 'designed for the assistance of rebellious forces against King and Parliament'.[41] Most of the villages which took part in the exercise are unidentified, but it is clear that Tedburn contributed to the store of weapons. The constable's accounts for Tedburn record the payment of 2s. 6d. to a certain 'Mistres Turner ... for one hors [to] carry the [parish] armes to Dunsford'.[42]

Receiving word of these developments, the Exeter Parliamentarians sent out a troop of horse to seize the weapons at Dunsford. Some sort of attempt was made upon the village on 11 December. During the course of this fracas Captain Vaughan, the commander of the troop, 'was killed with a musket-shot' from 'out of a window'.[43] Perhaps thrown into a panic by the death of their leader, perhaps outnumbered by the assembled countrymen, the Parliamentary troopers fled from the scene, leaving the countrymen in possession of Vaughan's body. The treatment which the villagers subsequently accorded the corpse suggests that they felt little sympathy for the Parliamentary officer. Two village constables and another local man, 'a sergeant to Captain Prouze', were later accused of having stripped Vaughan's body, removing his clothes and a ring.[44] All three individuals were men of some local importance, and that they, rather than some village ne'er-do-well, should have treated Vaughan's corpse in this way suggests that the community as a whole had approved of the captain's murder.

Some of the dead man's clothes were taken up by the bystanders, perhaps to serve as trophies. Humfrey Southcombe, the man alleged to have shot Vaughan, acquired a pair of gloves and some spurs. Vaughan's horse was also appropriated. A witness later deposed that, on the day after the killing, Anthony Turner, Vicar of Tedburn, and Mark Woodley, husbandman, had returned from Dunsford with 'one of the troop horses of Exeter'. Partly on the strength of this testimony, Turner was later committed by the Parliamentary authorities in Exeter as an accessory to Vaughan's murder.[45] Turner's story is an interesting one. He was initially apprehended on 14 December, at an inn in the City suburbs. On being searched, he was found to possess two gloves and a spur, which Vaughan had been wearing on the day of his death. When asked to explain how he had come by these items, Turner claimed that, earlier that day, he had visited Dunsford 'to speake with Mr Garnett, the parson of that parishe'. Garnett being away from home, Turner had gone to an alehouse instead. Here he met with 'James Cornishe, & Humfrey Southcombe & others, with whome ... [he] did then drinke some beare'. While they were drinking Southcombe told Turner that he had 'a commoditie for hym', Cornish adding that 'it was a good paire of gloves'. Turner claimed not to have paid much attention to this at the time, but later admitted that he had paid Southcombe a shilling for the gloves and some spurs.[46]

It might be argued that Turner had had no way of knowing to whom the gloves belonged. Yet, as he afterwards confessed, Cornish had frankly told him in the alehouse 'that the foresaid Southcome had killed the said Nicholas Vaughan'.[47] It is hard to believe that Turner could really have had no suspicions as to the ownership of the gloves after this. In fact the vicar seems to have been far more deeply involved in the affair at Dunsford than he cared to admit. It is significant that Mr Garnett, the minister whom Turner confessed to having come to see, was a prominent Royalist sympathizer.[48] Most damning of all is the fact that one 'Mistris Turner' had helped to transport the parish arms of Tedburn to Dunsford in the first place. This woman was almost certainly Anthony Turner's wife, and her involvement again suggests that the vicar had been a leading protagonist in the whole affair.

The area around Dunsford was clearly strongly Royalist in its sympathies. The initial gathering of the arms, the defiance offered to the Parliamentarians and the killing of Vaughan all confirm this. Perhaps most striking of all is the image which Anthony Turner's evidence presents; of a group of local men sitting calmly in the village alehouse, frankly admitting that one of their number had just slain a Parliamentary officer. That this was something to boast of in Dunsford surely confirms that the village was a Royalist stronghold.

Significantly, the repulse of the Parliamentarians at Dunsford acted as a signal for other local loyalists to rise. A witness later recalled that on 'the same day Captayne Vaughan was slayne at Dunsford', three men gathered arms together in the village of Ide 'to resist such [Parliamentary] forces ... as should come foorth [from Exeter] for the apprehending of Mr Satterlie, Minister of Eede'.[49] Like Garnett and Turner, Satterlie was a Royalist clergyman, and his parishioners obviously feared that he would be arrested by the Parliamentarians. The few additional pieces of evidence which survive give the distinct impression that other parishes between Exeter and Dartmoor had now risen up in favour of the King. On 24 December an Exeter brewer who dwelt in the city's western suburbs was 'complayned of for sending of beere and ale into the countrie, unto those places that give intertaynement to the Cavalliers and their adherents, whereby they are incouraged to persiste in those wayes'.[50] This again confirms that certain local communities were assisting the Royalists, and it is clear that the communities referred to lay to the west of Exeter.[51]

The main Royalist army began to advance upon Exeter a day or two later. As Hopton approached the city he received valuable assistance from local activists. On 26 December the individuals who had previously collected arms at Ide ordered two local men 'to goe foorth upon Long Downe to see if they could there discover any troopes of horse comyng from ... [Exeter]'.[52] Presumably this was done in order to provide the advancing Royalists with intelligence. A few days later the constable of Tedburn gave a small sum of money to 'tenn soldiers of the King's Army'.[53] Despite such local assistance, the Cornish army was unable to maintain itself before Exeter and on 1 January 1643, Hopton ordered his men to retreat.

Hopton's retreat spelt disaster for those who had helped him during his initial advance. As soon as the Parliamentarians regained control, they dismissed the head constables of the two hundreds which lie immediately to the west of Exeter, replacing them with men they could trust. Presumably this was done because the constables had assisted in, or at the very least failed to prevent, the Royalist rising of December 1642. Nor were they the only ones to suffer. *Mercurius Aulicus* gloomily admitted that, upon Hopton's departure, 'such of the Devonshire gentry as had shewne any testimony of their fidelity unto his Majesty' were arrested.[54] One such individual was Francis Fulford. Captured at his mansion of Great Fulford near Dunsford at the beginning of January, Fulford was sent to prison in Exeter.[55] Around the same time, his house was looted by a mob of local people. Interestingly enough, the places from which these individuals are recorded to have come (Crediton, Sandford, Newton St Cyres, Exeter and Moreton) all lie some miles away from Great Fulford. The inhabitants of the neighbouring villages apparently took no part in the looting. This suggests that local people were sympathetic towards Fulford, and may well be further evidence of the innate Royalism of this particular district.[56]

Information about Royalism in Mid-Devon after 1643 is scarcer, but it is clear that many local communities continued to support the King. Pre-eminent amongst them was Tavistock. It has already been shown that men turned out to join the Cornish army here in November 1642. Further evidence of Royalism appeared in July 1644, when Essex's army occupied the town. While they were in Tavistock, the Parliamentarians destroyed monuments and furniture in the Church and pillaged the town itself. From this one can infer that they saw the townsfolk as hostile. Local tradition, surviving into the nineteenth century, recalled with apparent glee that several of the marauding Roundhead troopers had been terrified and forced to flee by a townswoman masquerading as a ghost.[57] This story, too, suggests that local opinion was against the Parliamentarians.

Following Essex's defeat many Parliamentary captives were brought to Tavistock town hall, where they were imprisoned and treated abominably. A writer of the 1650s charged Tavistock's inhabitants with revelling in the misfortune of these luckless captives, lamenting that 'I fear the blood of those that starved in this town in the late troubles, will be laid to the charge of some of you, that did not pity them nor relieve them; but rather rejoyced in their misery (as many of you did) and helped to make it greater'.[58] Royalism continued to be a powerful force in Tavistock even after the war was over. The most recent historian of mid-seventeenth-century Devon has noted that Tavistock was 'a centre of ... hostility to Interregnum governments'.[59] Some time after Charles I's execution, one Tavistock man said that he hoped 'to have a Kinge again and that ... he should have the carrying [of] the roundheaded rogues to gaol', and one suspects that this statement represented majority opinion in the town.[60]

Popular Royalism was also discernible in several other Mid-Devon communities. At Spreyton, the minister of the parish, who had reported the pro-Royalist constable to the Parliamentarians, was later forced to flee as a result of the local opprobium which his action had aroused.[61] At Powderham the Royalists were able to persuade 120 local 'countrymen' to garrison the castle against Fairfax.[62] Further evidence of Royalism appeared at Tedburn, the villagers sending supplies to Hopton's army before Exeter in the summer of 1643.[63] At Germansweek it was later recalled that while many of the parishioners had fought for the King, not one had fought against him.[64] The market town of Chagford was another Royalist stronghold (those who killed Godolphin here in February 1643 were not local men, but Parliamentary troops from North Devon). A large Parliamentary force entered the town in April and arrested several of the inhabitants. Later that year, the townsmen lodged angry complaints against the soldiers.[65] Towards the end of the war a store of Royalist arms was hidden in the town, not being given up until 1647.[66]

The attitude of Crediton is more difficult to ascertain. Two Royalist meetings were held here; in July 1643 and June 1645.[67] Both attracted a great deal of support, and much of it may well have come from the townsfolk. Yet as in the case of Modbury, the fact that a popular meeting was held in a town did not necessarily mean that all those who attended it came from there. That Royalist meetings were held at Crediton, in other words, does not prove that Crediton itself was Royalist. Indeed, a good deal of evidence suggests quite the reverse, and therefore Crediton cannot safely be classed as a Royalist community.

Predictably enough, Mid-Devon provided the Royalist army with many recruits. Local men turned out for the King at Tavistock in 1642 and at Okehampton in July 1644.[68] The local trained bands were active in the Royal service, fighting at Exeter in 1643 and at Plymouth during 1643–45.[69] Two volunteer regiments were also raised here: Colonel Henry Carey's foot—chiefly recruited from Haytor, Tavistock, Teignbridge, Exminster and Wonford hundreds—and the 'Tinners Regiment', which was made up of miners from the Dartmoor Stannaries. Even so, the Royalists raised fewer men in Central Devon than they did in the South Hams and it could be argued that the South Hams, not Mid-Devon, was the most Royalist of the two regions. Yet this would be to ignore the very different calibre of the troops raised from each area. The Mid-Devon regiments were much more enthusiastic than those of the South Hams. Certainly they are the only Devon units known to have been picked out for special praise by contemporaries, one being described as a gallant, the other as a brave regiment.[70]

The Tinners Regiment, in particular, stood head and shoulders above all other Devon units in its devotion to the King. When the unit was first raised, there was unusual competion amongst local Royalist officers to command it, presumably because it was felt that the miners would perform particularly well in battle.[71] In 1643 the regiment took part in the successful storm of Mount Stamford fort near Plymouth and in 1644 the unit was lauded by *Mercurius Aulicus* as the 'brave regiment of Tinners'.[72] In April 1645 the Tinners were chosen to form the nucleus of Prince Charles's Foot, the best infantry regiment in the King's Western Army. A Royalist officer noted at this time that the Tinners were 'right good men'.[73] Following the defeats of January–February 1646 the Tinners did not simply disperse, as most of the King's other Devon infantry regiments did, but retired into Cornwall instead. Even after the shattered Royalist field army had finally surrendered, some of the Tinners retired into Pendennis Castle, where they, together with other Royalist die-hards, held out for another five months. After the Restoration the captain who had led the Tinners throughout the war was knighted in recognition of the service which he and his men had performed.[74] The Royalist fervour of the Tinners contrasts very markedly with the reluctance displayed by many other Devon units, and draws attention to an important split within county society.

Popular Royalism in East Devon

East Devon remained under firm Parliamentary control for much of 1642. As a result few signs of popular Royalism were visible here during the early months of the conflict. In December 1642, however, Royalist troops occupied Topsham on the east bank of the River Exe. Soon afterwards the Parliamentarians in Exeter threatened to burn the place to the ground.[75] This suggests that they had little affection for the inhabitants of Topsham, and may even have suspected them of helping the Royalists. The inhabitants were apparently punished once the Parliamentarians regained control of the town. In January 1643 a local loyalist wrote a despairing letter to Hopton, in which he lamented that 'we [the Royalist party] here all over the country give ourselves up for lost', and added that 'Topsham ... hath already suffered'.[76]

When the Royalist army returned to the region in mid-1643, signs of popular Royalism surfaced once again. During June and July the posse was summoned throughout East Devon, meeting with a good response in the western part of the region. Only a handful of men from this area were presented for not appearing on the posse, compared with over 300 from the north-east.[77] When Admiral Warwick landed a force of Roundhead troops at Exmouth in July, local people hastened to oppose him. A Parliamentary source admitted that 'the countrey people ... fired their beacons and in great numbers came down upon them [Warwick's men] and drove them out of the town'.[78] Many East Devon communities, including Bradninch and Ottery, sent contingents of men to Topsham to help the King's commanders repel this attack.[79] In August 1643 a Parliamentary commander made angry reference to a recent engagement 'at Topisham, when my men were betrayed by the towne', a comment which again suggests that Topsham's inhabitants had been assisting the Royalists.[80]

Further evidence of local Royalism appeared in 1644, when the inhabitants of Axminster sent Charles I a petition asking that their town should be garrisoned by Royalist troops.[81] It is not known how many people subscribed to this petition, so it may well have been unrepresentative of majority opinion, but the fact that it was drawn up at all clearly implies that there was a sizeable Royalist party in Axminster. It is significant, too, that the Lyme garrison made determined, and ultimately successful, attempts to raze the town to the ground during 1644–45.[82] Such action would scarcely have been taken if Axminster had been considered sympathetic to the Parliamentary cause.

Axminster, Topsham and Bradninch are all known to have shown signs of Royalism, yet of all the East Devon towns, Ottery St Mary was the most fervently Royalist. Ottery not only helped to repulse the naval attack of 1643, but also continued to exhibit hostility to Parliament during the final campaign of 1645–46, thus joining that select band of local communities which remained loyal to the King even when his cause was plainly lost. Following the New Model Army's advance into Devon, several Parliamentary units were quartered at Ottery. The soldiers did not meet with a friendly reception for, according to local tradition, the townsmen exhibited considerable hostility towards them. The eighteenth-century historian Polwhele states that the inhabitants resisted Parliamentary attempts to raise men and money from their town. He also claims to have seen a contemporary 'remonstrance', in which the townsmen fulminated against the Parliamentarians' activities.[83] Sources independent of Polwhele make it clear that the Parliamentarians repaid the townsmens' hostility with interest. Having burst into the parish church, Fairfax's soldiers 'broke down a curious organ, beheaded every statue in ye isles ... where loyal families had peculiar burying places, cract ... ye 5th commandment and broke off ye head of ye eagle on which the Bible lay'. They also rifled the church library.[84]

The devastation of Ottery St Mary church by the Parliamentary soldiers was no random act of destruction. Many years later an octogenarian resident of Ottery attested 'that the great abuses done to this Church was occasioned by the Parliament Army's malice against that loyal Town, which had 500 in the King's service and but 8 in the Parliament Army'.[85] This comment again stresses the fact that, even in 'Parliamentary' Devon, certain towns and villages were perceived to be much more loyal (or malignant) than others. The point is occasionally made in other surviving sources. In April 1643 an Exeter Parliamentarian made scathing reference to 'our ill affected ... countrey parishes', while the Exe

Valley village of Thorverton was later described by its Parliament-arian minister as an inherently malignant place.[86]

Two further incidents remain to be examined, both of which suggest that the inhabitants of the rural parishes between Exeter and Ottery St Mary had Royalist sympathies. The first occurred in June 1645, when the Royalist commander Sir Richard Grenville was 'importuned by many of the Gentry and inhabitants of Devon, to give them leave to procure ... [arms] to defend them-selves therewith against the Lyme forces [the Parliamentary garrison of Lyme] and free plunderers'.[87] Grenville was quartered in Ottery at this time and it seems probable, particularly in view of the reference to Lyme, that those who had asked him for permission to arm themselves also lived in this area.[88] Grenville recommended the scheme to the Royalist commissioners and 'a meeting was ... appointed at Broad-clyst to speak with the country thereabouts concerning the same'. Owing to squabbles amongst the King's commanders the meeting never took place. Nevertheless, the affair had shown that the countrymen of the Ottery/Broadclyst area were prepared to work with the Royalists, something which was to be demonstrated again a few months later.[89]

The second incident suggestive of Royalist sympathies in this area occurred in February 1646, when a Parliamentary news-book reported a pro-Royalist rising near Exeter.[90] This report is important, as it is the one piece of evidence to suggest that popular uprisings against the New Model Army took place in Devon. The pamphlet began by claiming that the Royalists in Exeter had 'animated' the people of the surrounding countryside to make 'some bold attempts ... on Major Generall Massey's Brigade' (i.e. on the Parliamentary troops who were blockading the eastern side of the city). The pamphlet then went on to describe one such attempt in detail. The disturbance in question involved a party of Royalist troopers, who had arrived in Exeter on 20 January.[91] Finding that supplies in the city were short, the horsemen resolved to break out. Over the next few days, the would-be escapers were 'drawn up' on several occasions and at last, 'through long watching opportunity', managed to break through the Parlia-mentary lines.[92] According to the pamphlet, the Royalists were helped to escape by a group of local countrymen.

If this source is to be believed, the Exeter Royalists had persuaded the nearby countryfolk to rise up and 'joyne togeather' with the troopers when they finally made their escape from the city. Accordingly, when the Royalist cavalry sallied out, 'the poore countrymen very ignorantly appeared and made a shew of fighting, thinking to be seconded by their friends'. The country folk had been duped, however. Far from assisting the peasantry, the Royalists 'made use of them only to facilitate their escape, and left them to shift for themselves'. Despite this ignoble desertion, the countrymen remained determined to fight the Parliamentarians, but eventually 'came off by Weeping-Crosse for a hundred of them were killed and taken'.[93]

It must be recognized at once that the veracity of this report cannot be guaranteed. The escape of the Royalist horse is well documented, but the involvement of local irregulars is only referred to in the pamphlet quoted above. It may well be that the clash between Massey's soldiers and the countrymen has been exaggerated. Yet the story seems unlikely to have been mere fabrication. Parliamentary propagandists had little incentive to make up stories about 'poore country men' attacking Fairfax's soldiers. Rather, they would have tended to play such incidents down. It is much more likely that other writers had purposely refrained from mentioning the skirmish, therefore, than that the diurnalist mentioned above had simply invented it. This being the case, one would probably be justified in regarding the episode as further evidence of Royalist sentiment amongst the inhabitants of the countryside immediately to the east of Exeter.

Patterns of Royalist recruitment tend to confirm that support for the King was particularly strong here. Between 1643 and 1646 two volunteer regiments, those of Colonel Cholmley (later Colonel Walker) and Colonel Berkley, were continually maintained by the communities of East Devon. A further regiment was raised by Colonel John Acland in 1643. All three units performed well in the King's service and, significantly enough, most of the men who served in them were drawn from the countryside between Exeter and Ottery. By contrast, Colonel Francis Bluett's regiment, which was largely recruited from the north-east of the region, proved mutinous and unwilling and did not endure for long.[94] The differing behaviour of the four units reflects the differing political sentiments of the areas from which they were drawn.

This chapter has confirmed the general impressions about allegiance patterns in Devon which emerged from Chapter Two.

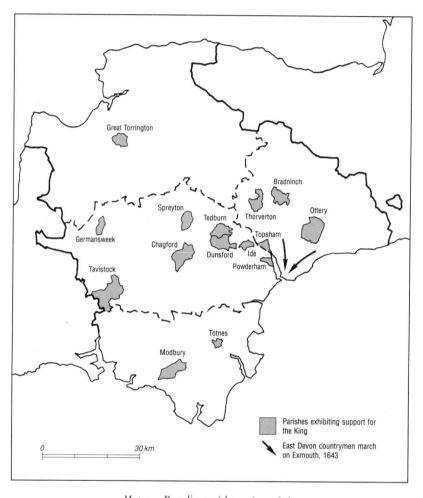

Map 3. Royalist parishes, 1642–1646.

North Devon, previously identified as the most Parliamentarian region of the county, now turns out to be the region in which pro-Royalist communities were rarest and in which the King's recruiters achieved least success. South Devon, too, was very bare of Royalist communities, bearing out the suggestion that the region had supported Parliament. The situation in Mid-Devon was similar to that in the South Hams and the North, in so far as an absence of support for one side was reflected in an abundance of support for the other. In this region, however, it was Royalist communities which were the rule, Parliamentary ones the exceptions (see Map 3). The situation in East Devon was more complicated. Chapter Two showed that many towns and villages here supported the Parliament, yet several other local communities supported the King. Similarly, East Devon produced some Royalist infantry units which were forward in the King's service, but others which were mutinous and unwilling. One is forced to conclude that, unlike the other three regions of the county, East Devon was seriously divided within itself.

What is particularly striking, both in East Devon and elsewhere, is the clear dichotomy between those communities which supported Parliament and those which supported the King. Almost every parish contained both Royalists and Parliamentarians, of course, yet in very few places do the contending parties seem to have been anything like evenly balanced. Only three Devon towns—Exeter, Totnes and Torrington—exhibited significant support for both King and Parliament. Most communities, by contrast, seem to have overwhelmingly supported one side or the other. Moreover, few towns and villages are known to have shifted their underlying allegiance in response to changing circumstances (a point which is examined in more detail in Chapter Six, pp. 111–132). Thus most of Barnstaple's inhabitants continued to support Parliament throughout the war, just as most of Ottery's inhabitants continued to favour the King. This is not to say that local communities were impervious to shifts in military fortune. Even the larger towns had, perforce, to submit themselves to the party which was locally dominant. Nevertheless, as soon as they got the chance, or as soon as the situation became too much to bear, most communities would revert to their true allegiance.

Chapter 4

Refining the Picture:
Further Light on Allegiance
Patterns

Examining the behaviour of local communities between 1642 and 1646 has permitted a provisional picture of wartime allegiance patterns in Devon to be sketched out. Is there any way of adding to this information and gaining a fuller picture? Folklore supplies some fascinating hints. During the last century the soubriquet 'Moreton Roundheads' was commonly applied to the people of Moretonhampstead by the inhabitants of the neighbouring parishes.[1] As Moreton lies in the middle of Central Devon, this at first seems to contradict the theory that the region favoured the King. Yet the surrounding countrymen would only have used the opprobrious term Roundheads to describe the inhabitants of the town if they themselves had been enemies of the Parliament. The nickname thus provides striking confirmation of the Royalist outlook of the district as a whole. Oral tradition claimed that Moreton and Chagford had supported different sides during the Civil War and as late as the 1950s a strong sense of rivalry persisted between the two towns: Chagford children greeting their contemporaries from Moreton with cries of 'Here come the little Roundheads!'.[2] In East Devon too traditions of rival allegiance lingered on. Within the past fifty years, a suggestion that Buckerell and Feniton parishes should be combined was resisted on the grounds that the two villages had been on opposite sides during the Civil War.[3]

Delinquents and suspects

Intriguing as these folk memories are they can hardly be relied on for a closely-detailed picture of wartime allegiance patterns. A more scientific approach was adopted by S.K. Roberts in his study of Interregnum Devon. Using the records of the Parliamentary Committee for Compounding, Roberts found that, of 300 Devonians fined after the Civil War for their 'delinquency' (or Royalism), 'three quarters hailed from Exeter and the south and east of the county'.[4] This statement is undoubtedly correct. But the distribution of this particular group of individuals cannot be taken as proof that South and East Devon were the regions of the county in which Royalism was most firmly rooted. Many of the delinquents had only come to the committee's attention because their neighbours had denounced them. Obviously ex-Royalists who dwelt in Parliamentary areas were far more likely to be informed against than those who lived in communities which favoured the King. So the preponderance of delinquents from the south and east of the county may well reflect the strength of Parliamentarianism in these areas, rather than that of Royalism. In any case, the vast majority of those whose names appear in the records of the Committee for Compounding were gentlemen rather than commoners. The same is true, albeit to a slightly lesser degree, of the delinquents who were pursued by the Committee for Advance of Money. Of the 220 Devonians investigated by this latter body, at least 104 were gentlemen, professionals or merchants, while only thirteen can be positively identified as yeomen, husbandmen, or artisans (the status of the remaining 103 is unknown).[5]

At first sight, the enormous list of suspects compiled at the direction of Major-General Desborough in 1655–56 seems a much more promising source of information. This document contains the names of almost 1,000 Devonians who were suspected of being disaffected to the state and it lists commoners as well as gentlemen.[6] John Morrill has pointed out that the circumstances under which the list was drawn up remain obscure, and that 'we do not know that the suspects were … primarily ex-Royalists'.[7] This is undoubtedly true, but the evidence from Devon is suggestive. Of the 963 Devon men who appear on the list, 184 (19 per cent) are definitely known to have supported the King during the Civil War. In Exeter, for which more additional information survives than for other places, the picture is clearer still. Of the eighty-four Exeter residents who appear on Desborough's list, twenty-seven (32 per cent) can be positively identified as Royalists from independent sources.[8] One cannot prove that all the suspects were Royalists, of course—most of them were simply too obscure for details of their allegiance to be recorded elsewhere—but the fact that so many can be identified as supporters of the King does suggest that the list's primary function was to serve as a roll-call of malignants.[9]

Unfortunately, even with this point established, identifying local allegiance patterns from Desborough's list remains problematic. There are several reasons for this. To begin with, the list reflects only what the central authorities were told by their local informants. As a result it may well have become distorted by the political preferences of the various Devon communities, some of which would have been keener than others to denounce supporters of the King. Another, much more serious, weakness is the fact that the list covers only certain parts of the county. While East Devon, Central Devon and Exeter are dealt with at length and provide the names of many hundreds of individuals, no returns at all are made for the greater part of North Devon and the South Hams, nor indeed for many of the larger towns. This is interesting in itself, of course. A survey designed to list Royalist sympathizers would hardly have concentrated upon the very areas where such persons were known to be least numerous. That Desborough focused his attentions upon Central and East Devon and largely ignored the North and South tends to confirm that it was the former regions which were regarded as the most pro-Royalist.

The distribution of the suspects from East Devon and Mid-Devon is also intriguing. Of the 351 East Devon men who appear on Desborough's list, 226 (65 per cent) lived in the arable district between Exeter and Ottery, while only 125 (35 per cent) lived in the densely populated north and east of the region. This supports the theory that East Devon was divided into a Parliamentarian north-east and a Royalist south-west.[10] In Mid-Devon Royalist suspects were common everywhere except, significantly enough, in Crediton and Moretonhampstead. These two large towns produced only three suspects between them, tending to confirm that the inhabitants' sympathies lay with Parliament. Desborough's list is useful for identifying patterns of popular behaviour in certain limited areas then. Unfortunately it cannot be used to identify county-wide allegiance patterns because of the lack of names from North Devon and the South Hams.

Maimed Soldiers: Royalists

Is there no way of gaining really detailed insights into allegiance patterns across the county as a whole? Fortunately there is. The Devon sessions records contain a mass of material relating to the county's 'maimed soldiers', men who had been wounded in the state's service and had fallen into destitution as a result. Throughout the early-Stuart period such individuals were eligible for a pension. In order to obtain it, they had first to send a petition to the county JPs. This petition usually stated the claimant's name and place of residence, and often included a description of his wounds and the service in which he had received them. During the Civil War the Royalist authorities began to issue such pensions to men who had been maimed while fighting against Parliament. The position was reversed after 1646 and it was ex-Parliamentarians who were compensated by the county authorities. Following the Restoration the wheel of fortune turned yet again. Pensions formerly awarded to Parliamentarians were now withdrawn, and old Royalist soldiers began to send in petitions once more. The names, residences and sometimes the entire petitions of hundreds of maimed soldiers, both Roundhead and Royalist, still survive in the sessions rolls.

These petitions illustrate the experience of the common soldier during the English Civil War as no other source can. The petition of Nathaniel Jefford, a Royalist husbandman from Dunsford in Mid-Devon, is especially vivid. Jefford's petition relates how he had served as 'a souldier in his Majestie's service, under the command of Major Fulford . . . from the very begginning of the late Rebellion untill the end thereof, and was for severall yeares a corporall in the said company, and in the said service received many woundes, and first at Weymouth was shot in the shoulder, and at [Taunton] was shot in the neck and knockt in the back of the head with a stocke of a musket and was left for dead . . . and was also engaged with the said Major . . . at his house at Fulford, and was . . . taken and brought prisoner to the city of Exeter and was kept a close prisoner [for] 17 weeks . . . and by the wound in his neck . . . lost the liberty of his speech, which has been imperfect ever since'.[11] There are scores of similar petitions, all bearing witness to the suffering caused by the war. Some of the petitions show the deep commitment which was felt by many soldiers of both sides. An Okehampton man noted that he had been sold into slavery by the Roundheads for refusing to renounce the Royal cause.[12]

The maimed soldiers' petitions can shed crucial light upon patterns of popular allegiance. In his study of Dorset, Somerset and Wiltshire David Underdown has analysed the distribution of wartime pensioners in an attempt to work out where support for the King was strongest.[13] Yet his methods and conclusions have attracted considerable criticism.[14] In conducting a similar exercise for Devon, it is necessary to proceed with caution. The obvious starting-point for any analysis of the Devon maimed soldiers' petitions is the collection of transcripts from the sessions rolls and order books made by O.M. Moger during the 1960s. These transcripts list the names of 446 Royalist and 106 Roundhead petitioners.[15] Certain points should be borne in mind when dealing with the material relating to the Royalist pensioners (i.e. those who were awarded pensions in the period 1643–46 and from 1660 onwards). First, the handful of gentry claimants must be excluded from any study of popular allegiances. So must those individuals who are known to have served as senior officers, for military rank in the Royalist army was generally concomitant with social status.[16] It is also necessary to winnow out many other irrelevant claimants; for example, old soldiers who had served under Elizabeth I and James, those who had fought for Charles I in wars abroad and, from 1660 onwards, casualties of Charles II's foreign wars.

Thus the nature of the evidence presents certain problems. How can one separate the relevant petitioners, those who were both commoners and veterans of the Civil War, from the irrelevant ones? In the absence of the petitions themselves, such a task is impossible, and this has been siezed upon as the chief flaw in Underdown's argument. Because the petitions for Dorset, Somerset and Wiltshire do not survive, Underdown is unable to differentiate between Civil War and non-Civil War petitioners and this, it has been claimed, casts doubt upon his conclusions.[17] Fortunately, no such problem exists for Devon. Not only were many of the Devon petitions copied into the sessions rolls in full, but a quite separate collection of petitions has also survived.[18]

These hitherto unnoted documents (together with other stray petitions), not only provide many new names, but also make it possible to dismiss irrelevant claimants. Having eliminated these individuals, and also those for whom no place of residence is recorded, one is left with a grand total of 199 men who definitely served in the Royalist army and an additional 234 who probably did so.[19]

These figures make it possible to gain further important insights into Devon allegiance patterns. By adding up the total number of petitioners from each region one can locate the districts in which Royalist recruitment efforts met with most success and thus, by inference, the districts in which the King enjoyed the greatest amount of popular support. Such calculations reveal that, just as the discussion in preceding chapters had indicated one might expect, the largest number of Royalist petitioners came from Central Devon. Of the 433 definite and probable Royalist veterans identified from the county as a whole, 171 (40 per cent of the total) were Mid-Devon men. East Devon, too, provided over a third of the petitioners, 139 altogether. In striking contrast, North and South Devon could only muster 108 Royalist petitioners between them, fifty-four men from each region (see Table 1).[20]

These results are extremely suggestive, but before placing too much weight on them, we must ensure that the picture has not been unduly distorted by the inclusion of so many probable Royalist soldiers in the figures. Despite the efforts which have been made to exclude non-Civil War petitioners, some will inevitably have slipped through. If too many such individuals become included in samples of probable Royalist soldiers, then analysis of the soldiers' places of residence will not provide an accurate picture of the county-wide provenance of genuine Civil War

Table 1: *Regional origins of all Royalist petitioners whose place of residence is known.*

Central Devon	171	(40% of total)
East Devon	139	(32% of total)
South Devon	54	(12% of total)
North Devon	54	(12% of total)
Exeter	15	(4% of total)
Total	433	

petitioners.[21] To guard against this, and to check that the general trends outlined in the figures quoted above are correct, one must examine the geographical distribution of the 199 petitioners who are definitely known to have served in the Royalist army. The results of such an examination are reassuring. If one takes into account only these men, the preponderance of petitioners from Central Devon becomes even more overwhelming. Of the 199 definite Royalist veterans, no fewer than eighty-four (44 per cent of the county total) came from Mid-Devon. A further fifty-two veterans (27 per cent of the county total) were East Devon men, whilst twenty-nine (15 per cent of the county total) came from the South Hams. Only twenty-two such individuals (a mere 11 per cent of the county total) came from the North (see Table 2).

These figures become even more instructive when local population is taken into account. Although Mid-Devon provided the largest number of Royalist petitioners it was not the most densely populated region of the county. Exactly the opposite was the case. Devon contained 72,000 adult males in 1642[22] and, of these, only 13,000 were residents of the central region. This figure represents a mere 18 per cent of the county's adult males, but the same region supplied almost 40 per cent of Devon's definite and probable Royalist petitioners. The contrast with the other regions is striking. North Devon boasted 29 per cent of the county's adult males but only 13 per cent of the Royalist petitioners. A similar picture emerges in the South Hams, which contained 22 per cent of the county's adult males but only 13 per cent of the Royalist petitioners. In East Devon there is no such disparity, 139 maimed

Table 2: *Regional origins of Royalist petitioners who are definitely known to have served as foot soldiers in the Civil War.*

Central Devon	84	(44% of total)
East Devon	52	(27% of total)
South Devon	29	(15% of total)
North Devon	22	(11% of total)
Exeter	5	(3% of total)
Unknown	7*	
Total	199	

* Not included in percentages above.

soldiers, 32 per cent of the total, being produced from a region which contained approximately 31 per cent of Devon's adult male population. If it is assumed that the total number of petitioners produced by any one region is roughly in proportion with the total number of men which that region supplied to the Royalist Army, the importance of the figures set out above becomes clear. The suggested pro-Royalism of Central Devon is confirmed, as is the anti-Royalism of North Devon, while the lack of petitioners from the South Hams casts doubt on claims that this area was a bastion of popular Royalism. East Devon's rather ambivalent position is also confirmed, the region producing petitioners roughly in proportion to its population.

Comparisons at the parochial level reveal further interesting statistics. The ten parishes with the largest number of petitioners in proportion to adult male population are set out below. First are Lustleigh and Christow (one Royalist petitioner for every thirteen adult males), followed by Bridford (1:14), Bondleigh (1:21), Chudleigh (1:22), Bradninch (1:24), Spreyton (1:25), Drewsteignton (1:30), Chagford (1:32) and Trusham (1:32). Nine of these ten parishes are situated in Mid-Devon, in a small area north-east of Dartmoor. The next twenty-three parishes are; Dunterton, South Tawton, Throwleigh, Doddiscombsleigh, Oakford, Sampford Peverill, Zeal Monachorum, Gidleigh, Lydford, Upton Pyne, Broadclyst, Mary Tavey, Holne, Tavistock, Whitchurch, Topsham, Stoke Gabriel, Newton Abbot, Dunchideock, Silverton, Morchard Bishop, Sampford Courtenay and Okehampton. Of these, fifteen are situated in Mid-Devon, five in the east of the county, two in the north and one in the south. Map 4 illustrates these findings, and makes clear the existence of a solid bloc of Royalist parishes around the northern fringes of Dartmoor. These thirty-three parishes aside, one should also note the large number of petitioners recorded from Axminster and Ottery St Mary. The protestation returns for these two towns have not survived, but neither was very large. The number of petitioners they produced is therefore especially impressive. Ottery, with twenty, provides the largest concentration of ex-Royalist soldiers in the entire county. Axminster, with nine, is also well represented. It seems fair to include these towns amongst the places indicated to be pro-Royalist by the evidence of the petitions.

Ottery, Axminster, Bradninch, Chagford, Tavistock and Topsham were all identified in Chapter Three as places which

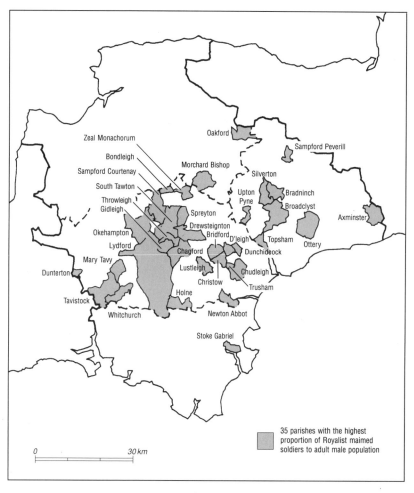

Zeal Monachorum
Bondleigh
Sampford Courtenay
South Tawton
Throwleigh
Gidleigh
Okehampton
Lydford
Mary Tavy
Dunterton
Tavistock
Whitchurch
Oakford
Sampford Peverill
Morchard Bishop
Silverton
Upton Pyne
Bradninch
Broadclyst
Axminster
Spreyton
Drewsteignton
Bridford
D'leigh
Topsham
Ottery
Chagford
Dunchideock
Lustleigh
Christow
Chudleigh
Trusham
Holne
Newton Abbot
Stoke Gabriel

35 parishes with the highest proportion of Royalist maimed soldiers to adult male population

0   30 km

Map 4. Royalist maimed soldiers.

displayed Royalist behaviour in the years 1642–46. Suggestions that these communities favoured the King are now confirmed by the statistics gleaned from the maimed soldiers' petitions.[23] The negative evidence is also of the utmost importance: towns producing few Royalist petitioners seem likely to have favoured Parliament. The figures for the Royalist towns can be put into perspective by examining the ratios for the towns which have been identified as Parliamentarian. Thus Tiverton produced only one petitioner for every 294 adult males, South Molton 1:304, Bideford 1:331, Dartmouth 1:404, Northam 1:617, Plymouth 1:1440 and Barnstaple 0:731. The disparity between these figures and those for such parishes as Lustleigh and Christow (1:13) is striking, and must surely be indicative of deep divisions within Devonshire society.

The statistics derived from the petitions also cast fascinating light upon the ancient hostility between Moretonhampstead and the surrounding villages. Of the ten Devon parishes with the highest proportion of Royalist petitioners to population (of the ten most Royalist parishes in the entire county, in other words), no fewer than four were immediate neighbours of Moretonhampstead. In striking contrast, Moreton itself possessed only two Royalist petitioners—and this from a population of over 400 adult males. Moreton's position as a Parliamentarian town in a fiercely Royalist area is thus confirmed and the quaint rivalries of the nineteenth century are revealed in their true light, as pale descendants of the bloody feuds and conflicts of Civil War England.

Maimed Soldiers: Parliamentarians

Before supportive conclusions can be sought from an examination of the Parliamentarian petitions, it must be stressed that these are much less satisfactory than their Royalist counterparts. To start with, the size of the sample is much smaller; the names and residences of only 154 Roundhead petitioners are known. It would be perilous to draw firm conclusions from such slender evidence, yet the information need not be dismissed out of hand. Other historians have had to make do with less, for example, Underdown was able to identify the names and residences of only 102 Roundhead soldiers from the whole of Dorset, Somerset and Wiltshire.[24] The Devon evidence permits the identification of half as many men again and this for only one county. Used with caution, the Parliamentary petitions can act as a valuable supplement to those of the Royalists. A cursory examination of the evidence shows that sixty-nine of the Parliamentary veterans, 44 per cent of the total, lived in South Devon (see Table 3). This suggests that Parliamentarianism was particularly strong in the South Hams. To take such a view would be too simplistic, however, for the figures have become distorted by the peculiar circumstances of Plymouth. Throughout the Civil War, Plymouth remained under intermittent Royalist siege. Virtually all male inhabitants were therefore constrained, *nolens volens*, to fight for Parliament at one time or another, and after four years of incessant conflict, Plymothian casualties were uniquely high.[25] This is reflected in the fact that no fewer than fifty-four of the Parliamentarian maimed soldiers identified from South Devon were inhabitants of the town.

As this example demonstrates, patterns of recruitment owed a great deal to military realities. When discussing the recruitment of soldiers in Devon, one should remember that the Royalists controlled most of the county most of the time. North and Central Devon were occupied by them continuously between 1643 and 1646. In the South, they kept up a constant and reasonably effective siege of Plymouth, preventing the Parliamentary garrison from having much contact with the communities which lay beyond the port's immediate hinterland.[26] As a result, Parliamentary recruiters were denied access to North, South and Central Devon throughout much of the war. The effect of the continued Royalist occupation on Parliamentary recruitment is shown by the scantiness of Roundhead petitioners from these areas. Only forty-five petitioners, less than a third of the county total, can be identified from North, South and Mid-Devon

Table 3: *Regional origins of all Parliamentary petitioners whose place of residence is known.*

South Devon	69	(44% of total)
East Devon	48	(32% of total)
North Devon	18	(12% of total)
Central Devon	12	(8% of total)
Exeter	7	(4% of total)
Total	154	

(Plymouth excluded). It would be unwise to place too much trust in such a small sample, but some tentative conclusions can be drawn. First, it is notable that Mid-Devon produced the smallest number of Parliamentary petitioners, lending support to the theory that the area favoured the King. Only twelve petitioners, just 8 per cent of the county total, came from this region (and half of these were residents of Moretonhampstead and Crediton). South Devon provided only a few more petitioners, scattered about in no particular pattern.

The figures for North Devon are more useful. Of the three regions under discussion, North Devon provided the largest number of Roundhead petitioners, eighteen in all. This supports the view that the region was pro-Parliamentarian. Yet, possibly, the figure is still rather low in view of the vociferous anti-Royalism exhibited here. The discrepancy is probably explained by the fact that, during the Royalist occupation, North Devon was particularly remote from the centres of continued Parliamentary resistance. Any North Devon commoner wishing to enlist in the Parliamentary army would have had to tramp right across the county, to Lyme or to Plymouth. This in itself doubtless did much to deter potential volunteers. Only the most ardent would have been willing to leave their homes and families so far behind.

From mid-1643 onwards Parliamentary recruiters were generally denied access to most regions of Devon. The exception was the eastern part of the county which was seldom under entirely effective Royalist control owing to the proximity of Lyme. Like Plymouth, Lyme held out for Parliament throughout the war, but it was never so successfully blockaded by the Royalists. As a result Lyme's defenders were able to make frequent incursions into East Devon, levying supplies from the surrounding villages and raiding as far west as Honiton.[27] The region thus became something of a debatable ground between the two parties. This permitted much Parliamentary recruitment to take place, and there are more Roundhead petitioners from this region than from any other (forty-eight names in all, 32 per cent of the county total).

Which local communities provided the greatest number of soldiers? Since the easternmost part of the region was closest to Lyme and hence to Parliamentary protection, one might expect that most of the petitioners would have dwelt in this area. Yet this was not the case as hardly a single petitioner came from here. Instead, the majority were clustered further to the west, in a broad band of countryside stretching from Somerset to the sea. The three parishes of Culmstock, Hemyock and Clayhidon alone supplied eleven petitioners. Further to the south and east lay the cloth towns of Tiverton (three petitioners), Uffculme (one petitioner), Halberton (five petitioners), Cullompton (eight petitioners), Broadhembury (two petitioners) and Honiton (three petitioners). Further south still was the fishing village of Sidbury, which produced two more Parliamentary soldiers. Almost all the other petitioners were scattered about in this same central band. Eight petitioners were recorded from Exeter and its immediate vicinity, but otherwise the western part of the region was even barer than the east. Map 5 (p. 88) plots the distribution of the Roundhead petitioners, and shows that most of them came from parishes already identified as Parliamentarian in Chapter Two.

How do the Royalist petitions for the region compare with the Roundhead ones? East Devon contained 32 per cent of all Roundhead petitioners, 32 per cent of all Royalist petitioners, and 31 per cent of the county's total population. At first sight these figures seem agreeably consistent, suggesting that the recruitment efforts of the two sides enjoyed a similar rate of success in this region. The figures also seem to support Roberts's contention that 'loyalties followed the spread of population'; that is, that the greater the population of an area, the greater the number of both Parliamentarians and Royalists to be found there.[28] Yet it has already been noted that it was precisely the least populous region of Devon which supplied the largest number of Royalist petitioners. This at once casts doubt on Roberts's thesis and, returning to the figures for East Devon, it again becomes clear that the bare statistics are very misleading. That such a high percentage of Roundhead petitioners were from East Devon was attributable not to population figures but to the fact that the Parliamentarians were usually unable to recruit elsewhere. In fact, a detailed examination of the relative numbers of Royalist and Roundhead petitioners in the separate East Devon communities would appear to disprove Roberts's thesis.

Eleven Roundhead petitioners were recorded from the three north-eastern parishes of Culmstock, Hemyock and Clayhidon. Yet despite the fact that, county-wide, over three times as many Royalist as Parliamentarian petitions survive, not a single Royalist

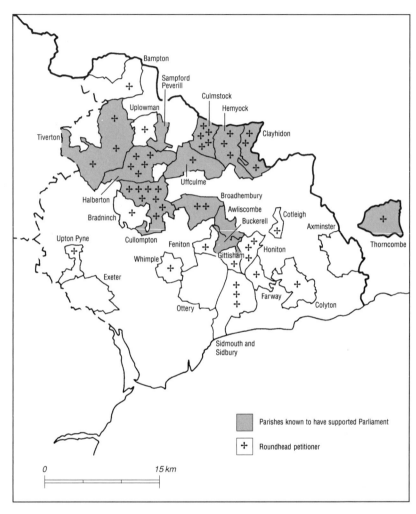

Map 5. Parliamentarian petitioners in East Devon.

petitioner came from these parishes. Little sign of equal loyalties here. To take another example, the three East Devon cloth towns of Axminster, Bradninch and Ottery produced nine, fourteen and twenty Royalist petitioners respectively. Yet the equivalent figures for Roundhead petitioners were zero, one and zero. The idea that Royalism and Parliamentarianism were both rooted equally strongly in the same areas is, in fact, quite erroneous. A fairly clear dichotomy existed between the villages and towns in which the rival sets of petitioners lived.

This discovery disposes of the argument that the distribution of petitioners simply reflects the incidence of post-war poverty.[29] Had this been the case, then most of the Royalist and Parliamentarian petitioners would surely have come from the same, economically-depressed, places. In Devon it can be shown that they do not. A related claim, that post-Restoration petitions are unreliable as a guide to wartime allegiance patterns because many of the petitioners might have moved to different parishes after 1646, has been effectively refuted by Underdown, who notes that 'the act under which the pensions was granted states very clearly that each qualified person was to "repair to the place where he was last settled before he took up arms" and to put in his claim there'.[30] In the end, it seems hard to doubt that the maimed soldiers petitions provide the best possible means of gauging local allegiance patterns. And in Devon, as in Dorset and Wiltshire, the evidence of the petitions suggests that different towns and villages supported different sides.

Occupation and allegiance

Was this geographical divide matched by a vocational one? Before bringing this statistical investigation to a close, the pre-war occupations of those who fought for King or Parliament should be examined. It has already been suggested that the members of at least one occupational group, the tin-miners, favoured the King. Local seamen, by contrast, seem to have supported the Parliament. One pamphlet stressed that Parliament's soldiers in Devon were 'all seamen and volunteers', and financial records reveal that mariners were absolutely central to the defence of Dartmouth, Plymouth and Barnstaple.[31] Assertions that pre-war occupations significantly affected wartime allegiances are not new, of course. Historians have frequently made such claims, and the assertion that clothworkers, in particular, were fiercely attached to the Parliamentary cause is a historical commonplace.[32] Can the maimed soldiers' petitions cast any light upon the connections between pre-war occupation and wartime allegiance?

Evidence for the Parliamentarian petitioners is very limited. The occupations of only nine are known. Obviously firm conclusions cannot be drawn from such a tiny sample, but it is worth pointing out that a third of the individuals whose trades are recorded were mariners, whilst another third were clothworkers. Surprisingly, only one of the Parliamentary veterans was a husbandman. Of the other two, one had worked as a miller and the other as a servant. If these figures are at all representative, they lend support to the theory that the Parliamentary army derived much of its strength from seamen and clothworkers.

Turning to those who had fought for the King, the picture becomes much clearer. The occupations of seventy-seven Royalist petitioners are definitely known (see Table 4). Of these, no fewer than thirty-four (44 per cent of the total) were husbandmen. Seven others were described as labourers, and the majority of these men too would probably have worked on the land. The next most well-represented group was that of the artisans and small traders: carpenters, barbers, blacksmiths, butchers, masons, tailors and the like. Nineteen of the Royalist petitioners (25 per cent of the total) belonged to this latter group. Less numerous, but still forming a respectable proportion of the sample as a whole, were the clothworkers. Almost a fifth of the Royalist petitioners were employed in dyeing, weaving and worsted combing. Of all the occupational groups, seamen were the least well represented, with only 3 per cent of the sample being described as mariners.

Table 4:   Occupations of Royalist petitioners.

Husbandmen	34	[44%]
Artisans/Small Traders	19	[25%]
Clothworkers	14	[18%]
Labourers	7	[9%]
Mariners	2	[3%]
Others	1	[1%]
Total	77	

Are these figures truly representative of the occupations of lower class Royalists in Devon? Independent evidence strongly suggests that they are. Desborough's list includes the names of 640 Devon commoners.[33] Of these 228 (36 per cent of the total) were described as husbandmen and seventy-nine (12 per cent of the total) as labourers (see Table 5). These figures are very similar to those obtained from the maimed soldiers' petitions. Labourers and husbandmen comprised 53 per cent of the ex-soldiers whose occupations are known, and 48 per cent of Desborough's lower-class suspects. A comparison of the figures for other occupations produces equally striking results. Artisans and small traders supplied 27 per cent of Desborough's suspects, for instance, and 25 per cent of the Royalist maimed soldiers, while clothworkers provided 20 per cent of the suspects and 19 per cent of the maimed soldiers. These statistics surely clinch Underdown's argument that the two sources—list and petitions—'reinforce each other'.[34] Seamen were even less well represented on the list than they were amongst the petitioners. Only seven of the Devon suspects, just 1 per cent of the total, were involved in trades connected with the sea.

Suspicions that Devon seamen were overwhelmingly hostile to the King are thus confirmed. The discovery that around 20 per cent of the Royalist petitioners and suspects were clothworkers, on the other hand, warns us against assuming that all clothworkers were committed Parliamentary activists. Several historians have pointed out that the link between cloth manufacture and Parliamentarianism was by no means absolute, and the evidence from Devon suggests that they are right to do so.[35] Most clearly of all, the evidence of both the petitions and the list demonstrates

Table 5: Occupations of non-gentle Royalist suspects.

Husbandmen	228	[36%]
Artisans/Small Traders	172	[27%]
Clothworkers	129	[20%]
Labourers	79	[12%]
Mariners	7	[1%]
Others	25	[4%]
Total	640	

that the King's most important lower-class supporters were husbandmen and labourers. Such men comprised 40–50 per cent of all the Royalist foot soldiers whose occupations are known, and clearly formed the backbone of Charles I's Devon infantry regiments.

What of the tin-miners? Although the tinners are known to have fought bravely for the King, not a single Royalist petitioner described his occupation as that of tin-miner, nor did the title appear on Desborough's list. At first sight, this discrepancy suggests that the miners' Royalism may have been exaggerated. Yet there is a simple explanation for their lack of representation in the statistics. Tinning had been in steep decline throughout the 1630s and the Civil War came as a body-blow to an ailing industry. The interruption of trade caused by the war, together with the impressment and death of many of the miners, caused most local mines to be abandoned in 1642–43.[36] The workings quickly fell into decay, and by 1646 the Devon tinning industry had effectively collapsed.[37] As a result, those who had once been tinners now had to turn their hands to other trades. It is this, rather than any lack of loyalty to the Crown, which explains the absence of tin-miners from the post-Civil War petitions and from Desborough's list of suspects.

Chapter 5

A Fractured Polity:
Allegiances in Exeter

Most of Devon's largest towns have been discussed, at least summarily, in the preceding chapters. Yet one vitally important urban community, the city of Exeter, has been reserved for special attention. Exeter's size and importance make it an obvious candidate for detailed investigation, as does the fact that it is the community about which the greatest amount of relevant information has survived. In this chapter political attitudes in Exeter will be examined in some depth, in order to see how patterns of urban allegiance compared with those which existed in the countryside and the smaller towns.

The city's experiences during the Civil War can be briefly summarized. In summer 1642 Exeter, like Devon as a whole, was secured without bloodshed by local supporters of Parliament. Over the next few months the city's fortifications were strengthened, and regular Parliamentary troops were admitted towards the end of the year. As a result the citizens were able to withstand a Royalist assault in December 1642. (An earlier attack, alleged to have occurred in November, was a fabrication of the London pamphleteers.[1]) During early 1643 Exeter served as the headquarters of the Parliamentary forces in the West. Following the defeat at Stratton, however, the city's position became increasingly exposed. In June Royalist forces began a full-scale siege of Exeter which continued throughout the summer of 1643 until, early in September, the garrison was forced to surrender. For the next two-and-a-half years Exeter remained firmly in Royalist hands. Work on the defences continued to be carried out and by late 1645 the city had become a veritable fortress. As a result Exeter was able to hold out for the King until early 1646, by which time the defeat of the Royalist armies elsewhere had made further resistance hopeless. The city was finally given up to Fairfax on 13 April 1646.[2]

How did the citizens of Exeter view these events? Did most of the townsfolk support the Parliament's cause, or did Exeter become a Parliamentary garrison against the wishes of the majority of its inhabitants? Was the Royalist capture of the city regarded as an act of liberation or as one of subjugation? Did the urban community react to the events of 1642–46 as a unified body or was local consensus shattered by the pressures of the war? To what extent, finally, did Exonians themselves participate in the conflict? Were committed partisans of King and Parliament only to be found amongst the urban elite or were even the most humble townsfolk capable of principled political commitment? One way of tackling these questions is to study the reports of the London pamphleteers.

'Outside looking in': The view of the diurnalists

Throughout the war it was regularly asserted in the London press that the inhabitants of Exeter were fervent supporters of the Parliamentary cause. In November 1642 'the good city of Exceter' was reported to be 'very odious [to the Royalists] for its fidelity to Parliament'.[3] A month later it was reported that 'the city of Excester stands well affected to the Parliament'.[4] One pamphleteer stated in 1643 that Exeter was both as rich and 'as right' as Gloucester, while another styled it that 'most constant, most faithfull' city.[5] In 1644 Queen Henrietta Maria herself was alleged to have complained that the majority of the inhabitants were Roundheads.[6] Soon afterwards a pamphleteer asserted that 'the greater part of the city of Exeter are well-affected to the Parliament'.[7] Similar comments were made during 1645–46. It was claimed in September 1645 that if Fairfax should besiege the city '[not] a fifth man of the town will ... draw a sword to oppose him'.[8] By February 1646 even this low estimate had been considerably reduced, and it was asserted that 'of citizens, besides townsmen, there are not ... [a tenth] that will fight [for the king].'[9]

These reports, and the many others like them, seem to provide firm evidence of the citizens' Parliamentarianism. Yet things are not as clear-cut as they at first appear. While some pamphleteers had no doubts about Exeter's commitment to 'the Cause', others were much less confident. One diurnalist lamented in November 1642 that the citizens had 'many malignants among them that assist the cavallires'.[10] Soon afterwards it was reported of the Exeter Parliamentarians that 'their greatest fear is the malignants amongst them, of which there is too great store'.[11] The 'Excestrian Malignants' continued to be referred to throughout early 1643 and anxiety about Royalist sympathizers in Exeter became particularly acute after the defeat at Stratton.[12] In June 1643 a correspondent reported that the city could still withstand the King's forces, but only 'if there bee not treachery amongst ourselves'.[13] Parliamentarians in Exeter were by now openly admitting that there are 'malignants amongst us that are of strength and ability'.[14]

Disdainful comments about the people of Exeter continued to appear in the London diurnals throughout the rest of the war. After Maurice's capture of the city a pamphleteer sneered that the King's troops had 'wanted no tale-bearers to informe them which were for or against them during the siege'.[15] It was several times observed in 1645 that the townsmen were 'active' in defending Exeter against the New Model Army.[16] When Fairfax's troops finally marched into the city, one correspondent noted that the inhabitants 'are generally (for ought I can yet perceive) as malignant as may be'.[17] He later observed that 'there are some in the town that are exceeding malignant' and later still commented disapprovingly that 'the citizens have learned like the Cavaliers to sweare God damne them &c', adding that 'they need good ministers to teach them better'.[18]

The picture which emerges from a study of the diurnals is thus a confusing and contradictory one. On the one hand the city was praised as a bulwark of the Parliamentary cause, on the other it was depicted as a hotbed of malignancy. This confusing mixture is perfectly illustrated by a report of 1646 which, having first observed that 'there are in Exeter many notable sticklers that have acted much for the King', added that 'there are also many precious men there that have suffered too much by them [the Royalists]'.[19] No other Devon community is known to have had such wildly contradictory statements made about its allegiance. This suggests that the situation in Exeter was much more complicated than elsewhere. It is clearly necessary to go beyond the assertions of the pamphleteers and examine the course of events in detail. The following discussion concentrates upon 1642–43, partly because this is the period for which the greatest amount of information survives and partly because it was during these years that the citizens exercised the greatest amount of control over their own affairs.

The course of events

During the early months of 1642 the inhabitants of Exeter, like the inhabitants of every other English town, gradually came to recognize that armed struggle between King and Parliament was inevitable. Amongst the civic elite fears of a potential conflict had been circulating for some time.[20] This is not the place to discuss Exeter politics during the pre-war years, but it is important to note that, from 1640 onwards, a powerful puritan faction had been busily engaged in strengthening its position on the City Council, or Chamber.[21] By early 1642 Exeter's governing body was dominated by individuals who were favourably disposed towards Parliament's cause. Of the twenty-four men who belonged to the Council at this time, three-quarters later went on to support the Parliament.[22] Attitudes may have changed during the six months before the war began. Nevertheless it seems probable that, by January 1642, the Chamber's ultimate allegiance had—to all intents and purposes—already been decided.

Signs of the way the wind was blowing appeared as early as March 1642, when a man was reported to the city sessions court for speaking 'daungerous wordes touching the Parliament'.[23] Still clearer evidence of the position being adopted by the authorities emerged on 30 June, when a weaver was bound over 'for speaking seditious words against Puritans and Rowndheadds'.[24] Two weeks later John Laurence, a mason, was bound over, for 'speaking of seditious words against the peace'.[25] What Laurence had said is unknown, but one suspects that he was a supporter of the King. Certainly an offender who appeared before the sessions court later that month was punished for abusing Parliament. The judges were informed on 29 July that Richard Bennet, goldsmith, had spoken 'some scandalous words of the Parliament as that they kept back the monie from the souldiers in Ireland'. He was also alleged to have said that 'Mr Pym was a traytor as the Kinge had soe called him'.[26] For these misdemeanours, Bennet was committed to gaol; the first Exonian known to have been imprisoned solely for expressing his opposition to Parliament's proceedings.[27]

By July 1642 it was readily apparent to all that the city authorities were lining up on the side of Parliament. Yet it was also becoming clear that a significant number of the citizens opposed the Council's stance. Further evidence of local division emerged in August 1642, when the pro-Parliamentarian faction faced the first real challenge to its authority. This was occasioned by the arrival of the Earl of Bath, who had been sent to Devon by Charles I with orders to rally the local community to the Royal cause. In order to convey his message to as wide an audience as possible, Bath planned to attend the summer Assizes at Exeter.[28] This news cannot have pleased the city authorities. The prospect of Bath himself, a large number of county gentlemen and the usual crowds of onlookers all flocking into Exeter at once was an alarming one. Indeed it was feared that Bath might try to seize control of the city. On 9 August, the very day that the Earl was expected to arrive, the Chamber ordered that the town magazine should 'not be delivered up unto any person ... without the consent of this house'. Soon afterwards four councillors were despatched to meet Bath, with a message that he would only be admitted to the city if he came 'in an ordinarie way unarmed'.[29] In the event the Earl's demeanour appears to have satisfied the city authorities, for later that day he rode into Exeter without incident.

Bath's presence clearly had a heartening effect upon the local Royalists and tentative efforts were made to halt Exeter's slide into the Parliamentary camp. On the very day of Bath's arrival a man was brought before the sessions court and charged with speaking 'verie seditious and traiterous words of the King ... [namely] that the Kings majestie had given his broade seale to the rebells in Ireland against the protestants. And that the King should mayntayne papists about him against the protestants'.[30] The man was promptly committed to prison for this speech, his punishment showing that, for the moment at least, such open hostility to the King would not be tolerated. During this same period attempts were made to disseminate Royalist propaganda in Exeter. On 11 August a 'musitian' named John Gollopp sang a 'scandalous songe ... concerning severall Lords and other Parliament men' at a public house. Further investigations revealed that he had sung another 'scandalous songe ... touching ... the five members of the House of Commons' at the Bear Inn earlier that week.[31] Gollop later admitted that 'manie gentlemen' had been present at the Bear while he was singing. Indeed he claimed that it was one of them who had initiated the singing in the first place, when 'he delivered unto this examinant a song written in paper and willed this examinate to sing the same'.[32]

This episode provides a rare insight into the methods used to influence popular opinion in the months immediately before the Civil War. It also gives an idea of the frenzied 'politicking' which must have been going on in Exeter at this time. On the surface the activities of those gathered at the Assizes were studiously moderate. Petitions were sent to both King and Parliament requesting a 'happie accomodation' and Bath as a man of 'eminency and known interest in his Majesty's favour' was requested to use his good offices to secure amity 'between his Majesty and Parliament'.[33] The general tone of the meeting was pro-Parliamentarian, but there was no hint of extremism as yet. Two men were ordered to be examined for speaking 'scandalous wordes ... of the Book of Common Prayer' and the Assizes finally broke up with no ugly incidents having occurred.[34]

Nevertheless, for Bath the meeting had been a wretched failure. He had proved completely unable to rally the county's representatives behind the King. On 12 August he rode out of Exeter having achieved nothing. Most of the pro-Royalist county gentry probably went with him. Bath's departure effectively handed Exeter over to the King's enemies. Hitherto fears that Royal control might somehow be re-imposed upon the city had ensured that open support for Parliament remained muted. Yet now the King's local representative had shown that he was unable to influence affairs in the city. Indeed his precipitate departure appeared an admission of weakness. With the fear of immediate repercussions removed the Parliamentarian faction on the Chamber could now throw off its neutralist mask. The King's few supporters on the Council began to cease attending meetings, leaving the field wide open to their opponents.[35] Henceforth no more royal officials were to enter the town, no more individuals were to be prosecuted in the city courts for abusing the King, no more measures were to be taken to protect the rites and ceremonies of the established Church. Exeter was now, in fact if not in name, a city held for Parliament.

Over the next two months the Parliamentarian grip on the city was inexorably tightened. Individuals speaking in favour of the King or against the Parliament were arrested, while officials of

doubtful allegiance were removed from their posts[36]. The Dean
and Chapter (widely suspected of favouring the King) were forced
to admit the city watchmen to the Cathedral Close.[37] On 30
August, moreover, the Mayor and 'some of the Aldermen' (presumably the pro-Parliamentarian ones) elected a 'Committee for
the Safetie of the Cittie'.[38] This body was henceforth to be of great
importance in Exeter, and of the fifteen men who sat on it, all but
three later went on to support the Parliament. In September the
crucial mayoral elections were held, resulting in the return of
Christopher Clarke, a moderate Parliamentarian.[39] Soon afterwards, Parliament authorized the Chamber to raise men, set
watches and erect fortifications.[40]

Many Exonians must have approved of these developments.
The pro-Parliamentarian councillors could hardly have pushed
their programme through in the face of unanimous local hostility
and indeed there is a good deal of evidence of popular enthusiasm
for Parliament's cause. One hundred and fifty Parliamentary
volunteers turned out at a muster held in the city in mid-August.
Later that month an unknown number of Exonians marched off
to join the Roundhead forces at Sherborne.[41] That Christopher
Clarke was elected Mayor suggests that the Parliamentarian
faction had the largest number of voices amongst the city
freemen.[42] Yet once again support for Parliament was by no
means universal. Dissident voices continued to be heard, the
volunteers were abused, Clarke's election disturbed and the
expedition to Sherborne condemned.[43] So great was local resistance to the Chamber's policies, indeed, that the Commons
ordered a Parliamentary garrison to be placed in Exeter 'in case of
any opposition'.[44]

The final assertion of Parliamentary dominance over Exeter
took place on 2 November, when the Mayor ordered that the
town gates should be opened to a troop of Parliamentary horsemen.[45] This was the first time that an armed force of 'foreigners'
had been permitted to enter the city and the Chamber's order thus
signalled an end to any pretensions of neutrality. Disturbances at
once broke out in the city streets, disturbances in which known
Royalists were prominent. Yet the protesters were unable to
prevail, the rioting was quelled, the horsemen were admitted and
those who had opposed their entry were hunted down and
jailed.[46] The riots marked the Royalists' last chance to regain
control of the city without outside assistance. Hereafter Exeter

was to remain firmly in Parliamentary hands until it was captured by force of arms.

Despite the imposition of a Parliamentary garrison, support for the King continued to be voiced. On 15 November Thomas Warner, a fuller, told another local man 'that he had byn to drinke a health to the King and the Cavaliers and to the confusion . . . of the Roundheads'.[47] Two weeks later a shopkeeper advised a group of Parliamentary soldiers setting out against Hopton's army in Cornwall 'to retourne home again to their wives for the Cornish would sett wyldfire in their tayles'.[48] Hostility to Parliament was also expressed by dissident members of the civic elite. In December 1642 it was reported from Exeter that 'last yeares mayor ... Master Lyn[n]' had written 'a letter to the King to invite him to come to that city'. Unfortunately for Lynn the 'letter was intercepted and brought to Parliament', prompting the Commons to send for its author and for 'two other of the Malignant aldermen there [in Exeter].'[49]

Royalist sympathizers were treated with increasing severity as Hopton's army drew closer to the city. During December 1642 many loyalists were arrested and imprisoned.[50] But it was not until Hopton's forces had been repulsed that the floodgates of repression really opened. In the wake of Hopton's retreat the Parliamentarians and their local supporters embarked on an orgy of plunder, intimidation and imprisonment, focused chiefly on the inhabitants of the Cathedral Close. Property was seized, the Cathedral itself was pillaged and defiled, and clergymen and other suspected Royalists were carried away to prison-ships moored at Topsham. According to one source, Archdeacon Helliar was dragged from his bed at midnight and hurried away to prison 'and from thence to the ship[s] because he refused to contribute such sums as they demanded'. A similar fate befell Canon Hutchenson.[51]

Parliamentary sources confirm these reports. One pamphleteer commented that 'the malignants in the city of Excester, because they would not contribute any moneys for the safety of the commonwealth, were put into divers ships, and sent out to sea, which hath made them to yield, and to submit themselves to a reasonable assessment'.[52] A letter written from Exeter on 7 January 1643 observed that 'this week we had many great delinquents apprehended', specifically mentioning Helliar and Hutchenson.[53] Many Exeter people clearly approved of the rough treatment which was meted out to the Royalists. It was later recalled that, as Hutchenson was dragged through the streets by the Roundhead soldiers, 'he ... was abused and hooted at by the boys and exposed to the affronts and revilings of the base, insolent multitude'.[54] Other people evinced more sympathy for the captives, however, and Helliar was said to have been 'pitied by all his neighbours'.[55] Once again the evidence suggests that the civic community was divided in its allegiance.

The events of March 1643 point the same way. In that month negotiations for a local truce began between the Parliamentarians in Devon and the Royalists in Cornwall.[56] Soon afterwards it was agreed that representatives of both sides should meet at Exeter. This decision was bitterly opposed by the city authorities and by local Parliamentarians. Royalist sources observed that 'some of the factious people of that cittye' had written to Parliament, informing the Speaker 'that the treatye was without their consent'.[57] Meanwhile a group of 'zealous' local women organized a petition against the treaty and presented it to the Earl of Stamford.[58] When the Royalist delegates finally appeared before the gates they were refused admittance. Indeed they had to be guarded by Parliamentary troops for their own safety. The Royalists soon hastened away, complaining that 'wee thought it no honour, nor safety to stay longer at the foote of the citty that refused to receive us'.[59]

One might well conclude from this that Exonians were united in their hostility to the King's commissioners. Yet, once again, the true position was more complicated. A contemporary letter reveals that fears of an internal revolt underlay the city authorities' opposition to the talks. On 9 March Richard Saunders (the major of Exeter's Parliamentarian trained bands) sent an anxious missive to the House of Commons, voicing the fears of the city authorities. There was a distinct possibility, he said, that the Royalist delegates would incite the 'considerable number of malignant inhabitants' to rise up in revolt and free the 'daring, violent and desperate ... [Royalist] prisoners ... wherewith two prisons are full'. Once this had been effected, Saunders went on, it would be easy for the Royalists to seize control of the city. He therefore requested the Commons to send 'such orders as they see fit' to enable him to deal with the situation.[60] This letter is important, for it demonstrates that—even after the arrests and imprisonments of January 1643—the Royalist faction continued to be regarded as both powerful and dangerous.

The situation remained broadly the same throughout the summer of 1643. Hundreds of local people assisted the Parliamentary forces during this period. They built fortifications, served in the city trained bands and joined the volunteer companies which had been raised by Parliamentary activists.[61] City crowds also demonstrated violent hostility to captured Royalists. When Dr William Coxe was committed to prison on suspicion of being a spy, 'many of the townspeople came to see him, as if he had been a publike show, who, instead of pitying, revile[d] and reproach[ed] him'.[62] Yet at the same time pro-Royalist sentiments continued to circulate. Several more individuals were charged with having made seditious speeches in May, while in June and August, Parliamentary correspondents referred with anxiety to malignants within the walls.[63] As the net tightened around Exeter the King's supporters grew increasingly bold. An abortive Royalist insurrection occurred on 22 August when, during an engagement between the garrison and the besiegers, ten men seized possession of St Martin's church tower and refused to come down. Eventually they were forced out and arrested by Parliamentary officers.[64] These were the last inhabitants of Exeter to suffer for their Royalism, however, and on 5 September the city was surrendered to the King.

Did this capitulation reflect the wishes of the inhabitants? Both sides later claimed that the people of Exeter had shown little commitment to the city's defence. A Roundhead pamphleteer railed against the citizens, complaining that they did not 'well stomach ... their soldiers, not paying them, nor quartering them like men, suffering hundreds of them to lye upon [market] stalls'. He also alleged that it was the citizens who had persuaded Stamford to surrender and referred to them contemptuously as 'those that hope only to be quiet in this world, and wish for peace and pardon at any rate'.[65] Clarendon made similarly disparaging comments, claiming that Exeter was surrendered 'after ... [the inhabitants] had suffered no other distress ... than the being kept from taking the air without their own walls, and from being supplied from the country markets'.[66]

These accusations are patently unjust. The defenders of Exeter had endured a long siege, suffered many casualties and repulsed a series of major attacks. They had laid out vast sums of money in Parliament's service.[67] Their final surrender was only brought about by a full-blown assault, which captured a vital section of the city defences.[68] To accuse Exeter's Parliamentary defenders of half-heartedness or lack of resolve would be unfair, yet Clarendon and many other contemporaries obviously felt that the city was given up too easily. Why did the city authorities decide to surrender when they did? It is tempting to concur with Eugene Andriette, who suggests that the strength of the Royalists in Exeter may well have played a vital part in persuading the Parliamentary commanders to capitulate.[69] This was certainly the view of one local Parliamentarian, who later complained that Exeter had been betrayed and that the city had only surrendered because 'Chudlie's side' [Royalist sympathizers within the walls] had 'treacherously prevailed'.[70]

It is clear that the city remained badly divided throughout the period of the Royalist occupation. Many of the citizens served the King with enthusiasm during these years, fighting in the Royalist armies and helping to improve the city fortifications. Yet others continued to speak out for Parliament. In March 1644 a tanner's wife asserted that 'the Roundheads were better than the Cavalliers and that she did hope to see the tymes [change] againe', while later in that same year, three men were apprehended 'for speaking of scandalous words of the King's army'.[71] Many other instances of popular support for Parliament during this period could be cited.[72] Following the surrender of the city in 1643, for example, many of the townsmen are known to have left their homes and journeyed to the Parliament's quarters. Five hundred 'exiles from Devon and Exon' were later noted to be living in London.[73]

This chapter began by noting that wartime pamphleteers had been uncharacteristically vague about the political preferences of the inhabitants of Exeter, some portraying the city as a Parliamentarian stronghold, others depicting it as a hotbed of malignancy. Detailed examination of events has now helped to show why this confusion arose. There were, in fact, considerable parties in favour of both sides at Exeter. Indeed, the existence of these two competing groups was freely acknowledged by the citizens themselves, several of whom specifically referred to 'the Parliament[s] partie in this Cittie' or to 'such as were held [to be] for the king'.[74]

The make-up of the rival parties

It is impossible to be sure which of the two factions possessed the greatest amount of support. The fact that the city authorities managed to secure Exeter for Parliament in 1642 tempts one to assume that it was the Roundhead party which was the largest. This has certainly been the conclusion of several recent authorities, who agree that, while the loyalists were reasonably numerous, they remained very much in the minority.[75] By contrast, earlier historians tended to portray the Royalists as the stronger party. Thus Jenkins, writing in 1806, claimed that 'the major part of the citizens ... were firmly attached to the Royal cause', while Karkeek, writing in 1876, agreed that the rebel party in Exeter was 'not of sufficient influence to defy [its] opponents'.[76] One is reminded very much of the conflicting assessments of the pamphleteers!

The impressionistic judgements quoted above are of little real help. It seems best to abandon the unprofitable question of which side was the strongest and examine the composition of the rival parties instead. (Because social stratification in the larger towns was so much more complex than it was in the countryside, all social classes will be included in the discussion which follows.) Fortunately, it has proved possible to determine the allegiance of a surprising number of Exonians and this is particularly true for the Royalist party. Desborough's list names eighty-four Exeter men who were suspected of favouring the King. The records of the city sessions court supply the names of around fifty more (and of five Royalist women as well). In addition, a number of individuals are known to have served in the King's army, or to have been fined for their delinquency after the war. Drawing on all available sources, it is possible to identify 185 Exeter men who supported Charles I.[77]

At first sight, this figure does not seem particularly impressive. After all, there were well over 3,000 adult males in Exeter in 1642. Only 6 per cent of the city's adult males can positively be identified as Royalists, therefore. In absolute terms this is a small percentage, yet in relative terms it is not. Most of the other large Devon towns contained far fewer Royalists. For example, in Barnstaple, the two known Royalists comprised just 0.3 per cent of the total adult male population! The situation was very similar in the other big towns: the equivalent figures for Bideford, Plymouth, Crediton and Tiverton are 0.5 per cent, 0.8 per cent, 1 per cent and 2 per cent respectively. The disparity between these figures and the one for Exeter means that the relative strength of Royalism in the city can hardly be doubted.

Owing to the nature of the evidence it is much harder to identify committed supporters of Parliament. No lists of Parliamentary suspects were compiled by the Royalists or, if they were, none have survived. Those sources which do exist are difficult to use. Thus the muster books dating to the period of the first siege provide the names of almost 300 Exeter men who served under Parliamentary officers, and one suspects that the majority of these individuals sympathized with Parliament's cause.[78] Yet it is impossible to be sure, for many could have been forced into service. At least one of those named on the muster lists—Phillip Job, a brewer's apprentice—is known to have spoken out forcefully against the Roundheads, opining that 'the Parliament's lawes were not worth a turde'.[79] Similarly, although the names of 200 people who worked on the city fortifications during 1643 are known, it is impossible to be sure of their motivation.[80]

One Exeter loyalist regarded the decision to work on the defences as an open avowal of support for Parliament, expressing the hope that 'all those that had made those workes in Exeter for the defence of the cittie to keep out the King and his companye would be hanged for their labour'.[81] Yet several of the workmen are later known to have supported the King. Compulsion, or a simple desire for profit, may well have been as important as zeal for the Parliamentary cause in persuading people to participate in the work.[82] Setting aside the men named in the muster books and fortifications accounts, how many Parliamentary supporters can be positively identified in Exeter? From the sources examined so far a total of 108 Roundheads have been identified; ninety-nine men and nine women.[83] How do these individuals compare with their Royalist counterparts?

More information survives about the socio-economic status of the Royalists than the Parliamentarians. From a variety of sources, the occupations of 137 male Exeter Royalists can be recovered. Of these, twenty-one (roughly 15 per cent of the total) were gentlemen or esquires. A further seventeen (12 per cent of the total) were innkeepers, while seventeen more were merchants. The cloth trade was similarly well represented as eighteen of the Royalists worked as fullers, weavers and combers. Also numerous are shopkeepers, for example, chandlers, grocers, goldsmiths, mercers, stationers, haberdashers and woollen-drapers. Thirteen such men (9 per cent of the total) are known to have supported the King. Eight of the Royalists were vintners or brewers, six were employed in the building trade, five were purveyors of foodstuffs and five more worked as tailors and embroiderers. Four earned their livelihoods from trades connected with horses, three worked as barbers and three were described as apothecaries. The professional classes were represented by six clerics, three attorneys and a doctor-at-law. None of the city loyalists are known to have worked in agriculture but there are three yeomen, who may well have farmed land in the suburbs.[84]

Turning to the Parliamentarians, a rather different picture appears. Here, gentlemen and esquires are not so well represented as they were amongst the Royalists. Of the fifty-seven Exeter Parliamentarians whose occupations are known, only two (4 per cent of the total) were gentlemen. Not one is known to have been an innkeeper, an occupation which accounted for 13 per cent of the known city loyalists. Conversely, the Parliamentarian faction contained a higher proportion of merchants, shopkeepers and clerics than did the King's party. These three occupations account for 21 per cent, 14 per cent and 7 per cent of the total sample respectively. Most well represented of all are the clothworkers, who make up 25 per cent of those whose occupations are known.[85] These findings suggest that, while both parties possessed a considerable amount of support amongst the civic elite and the middling sort, the Royalist faction—with its many gentlemen and esquires—was weighted more heavily towards the top end of local society than was the Parliamentarian group.[86]

The geographical spread of allegiances

Where did the members of the rival factions live? Were Royalists and Parliamentarians scattered all over Exeter, or did each side draw its supporters from distinct areas of the city? The events of the war itself provide some clues. The pro-Royalist disturbance at St Martins Church in August 1643 has already been noted. So has the care which the Parliamentarians took to impose their authority over the Cathedral Close. The behaviour of the local Roundheads in January 1643 clearly demonstrates the bitter animosity which they felt towards the inhabitants of the Close. One correspondent crowed that 'the cathedrall men look like ghosts, now their mouths are stopt that they can sing no longer'.[87] Another source relates that, having ripped out the Cathedral organ-pipes, a crowd marched past the crestfallen choristers, jeering, 'Boys, we have spoilt your trade, you must go sing hot pudding pies!'.[88]

The Parliamentarians clearly saw the Cathedral Close as the centre of disaffection to their regime and the places of residence of the known Exeter Royalists suggests that they were right to do so. As many as one in four of the adult male inhabitants of the Close and St Martins can be shown to have supported the King. For the neighbouring parishes of St Stephens, St Pancras and All-Hallows Goldsmith Street the equivalent figures are 1:8, 1:11 and 1:13, while for St Mary Major, (just to the south of the Close) the figure is 1:15. Only one other parish produced such a high proportion of Royalists. This was St Olaves, with one known Royalist for every eight adult males. Elsewhere in the city, the proportion of known Royalists to adult male population was much lower; 1:25 in St Kerrian and St Petrock, for instance, 1:30 in St Paul, 1:50 in St Mary Steps and 1:116 in St Mary Arches.[89] There can be little doubt that Royalism in Exeter was centred upon the Cathedral Close (see Map 6, p. 108).

An examination of the geographical distribution of Parliamentarian supporters reveals a very different picture. The Roundheads were strongest in precisely those areas where the Royalists were weak. Thus of the adult male inhabitants of St Kerrian, one in six are known to have supported the Parliament. The same was true of one in eight of the adult male inhabitants of St Mary Arches and St Petrock. The Parliamentarian faction was also comparatively well represented in the parishes of St George, St Mary Steps, St Lawrence, and St Pancras; where the equivalent figures were 1:20, 1:30, 1:36 and 1:39 respectively. Conversely, in many of the parishes where the Royalists were most numerous, the Parliamentarians were very poorly represented. Thus the Cathedral Close and the parishes of All Hallows Goldsmith Street and St Martin produced zero, zero and one Parliamentarian supporter respectively.[90] Compare this with the Royalist figures of seven, six and fifteen.[91]

The analysis conducted so far suggests that, in the wealthy intra-mural areas of Exeter, Parliamentarianism and Royalism were rooted in quite different parishes. Thus the King's supporters were strongest in St Stephens, St Martins and the Close, while the Parliamentarians were strongest in St Kerrian, St Petrock and St Mary Arches. Only one intra-mural parish is known to have contained an appreciable number of partisans of both

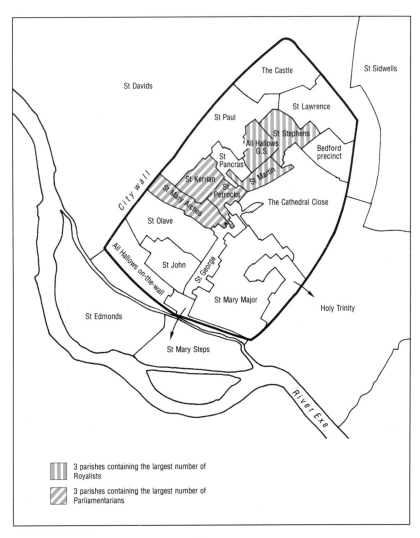

Map 6. Allegiance in Exeter.

sides. This was St Olaves, in the west quarter, which produced five Parliamentarians and eight Royalists.[92]

In the suburban parishes, known supporters of either side are more difficult to find. Does this reflect political apathy amongst the poorest sections of local society? It probably does, in part, yet one should not forget the limitations of the evidence. The poverty of those who dwelt in the suburbs meant that they were unlikely to become prominent in either faction. This in turn meant that they were unlikely to appear in the surviving records. And there are scraps of evidence to suggest that, even in these areas, some people did make political choices. After the Restoration, Richard Cooke, an indigent weaver of St Sidwells, petitioned the Chamber for the gift of a gown and a shirt, claiming that he had been 'ever a loyall subject [and soldier of] his majestie King Charles the first'.[93] When one looks at the relative proportions of known Royalists to Parliamentarians in each of the suburban parishes, moreover, some interesting figures emerge. Thus, in St Sidwells, one in every forty-three adult male inhabitants is known to have supported the King, but only one in 237 the Parliament. For Trinity the equivalent figures are 1 : 26 and 1 : 145, for St Edmunds 1 : 76 and 1 : 77, and for St Davids 1 : 97 and 1 : 50.[94] If one takes these figures as indicative of the feelings of the concealed majority, St Davids emerges as a Parliamentarian parish, with St Sidwells and Trinity as pro-Royalist.

Is it really credible to suggest that a close-knit city like Exeter could have been divided into sharply differentiated Royalist and Parliamentarian zones? The findings of other historians tend to support such an idea.[95] W.G. Hoskins demonstrated long ago that the city parishes were graded in a strict economic hierarchy, with the richest citizens living in the centre of town and the poorest in the suburbs.[96] If the parishes were divided along economic lines is it not likely that they were divided along political lines too? Individual parishes certainly possessed very definite identities. The inhabitants of St Sidwells were referred to as 'the Grecians' during the 1690s while those who dwelt in the western suburbs were termed 'the Algerines'.[97] Evidence from later periods shows that Exeter people were proud of their parishes, and prepared to fight for them. During the 1820s 'boys would meet in the evening, armed with sticks, to uphold the honour of their parish, which was called "parish fighting"'. Several of these contests were fought in deadly earnest, and there is no reason to suppose that things

were very different in the early modern period.[98] It seems perfectly probable that rivalries had existed between the various city
parishes long before 1642, and that these divisions were merely
widened and exacerbated by the conflicts of the 1640s. This
intriguing subject must await further examination elsewhere. For
the moment it is enough to note that the civic community of
Exeter, like the county community of Devon as a whole, divided
along parochial lines during the English Civil War.

Chapter 6

Neutralism:
The Case of the Clubmen

So far attention has been focused almost entirely upon the committed activists, upon Royalists and Parliamentarians, Round-heads and Cavaliers. Yet, as recent scholars have stressed, there were other currents of opinion too, those of neutralism and indifference.[1] Many English men and women were enemies of the war itself rather than of each other. It seems likely that this was particularly so amongst the poor, who knew from bitter experience that it was they, rather than their social superiors, who would be expected to bear the brunt of any fighting. In Devon, as in other counties, the popular dread of war was often made explicit. In Mid-Devon in 1641 'hedgers at the hedg, plowmen at the plow [and] threshers in the barnes' explained their decision to sign a petition in favour of episcopacy by claiming that it would ensure 'they should have peace for evermore, for thes not[e]s were to conclude peace'.[2] A similar desire for peace was frequently displayed during the war itself. A pamphleteer noted with scorn in 1644 that words of peace 'are often bandied from the mouths of ignorant people ... especially in the more remote western parts'.[3] Nor were the commoners alone in their desire to halt the fighting. From the county elite, too, continual pleas for peace went out between 1642 and 1646.[4]

Throughout Devonshire society there clearly existed a deep-seated antipathy to the war. To claim that Devonians were posit-ively itching to fight, to fall upon their neighbours' throats, would be wrong. Most people were dragged into the conflict with immense reluctance and this basic hatred of the war undoubtedly contributed, in some cases at least, to a lack of commitment. In Devon, as elsewhere, changing sides was commonplace, and at least 10 per cent of the county's knights and peers were turn-coats.[5] Similar shifts in allegiance took place further down the social scale. Several Parliamentary field officers went over to the King after Stratton, including Major James Chudleigh.[6] Similar defections occurred amongst less senior officers, for example, Lieutenant Thomas Winston of Brixton, Ensign John Loveys of Lewtrenchard and Ensign George Battishill of Plymstock all deserted the Parliamentary garrison at Plymouth and joined the Royalists.[7] Many defections are known to have occurred amongst the common people too. John Dintch of Diptford, a Royalist foot soldier, 'left the [King's] service and went into [the Parliamentary garrison at] Plymouth'.[8] The continual incidence of defection, combined with the general abhorrence of the war itself, presents something of a problem. How can such behaviour be squared with the claims made in Chapters Two, Three and Four, that indi-vidual communities displayed a real and enduring commitment to one side or the other?

The first thing to note is that, while side-changing was relatively common, it was still regarded with distaste. The special venom which Parliamentary pamphleteers reserved for 'Skellum' Gren-ville and James Chudleigh is proof of this, as is the contempt which local people expressed towards those who had turned their coats.[9] Nor was scorn the worst that 'renegadoes' had to fear. George Battishill was executed when his former comrades re-captured him, as were many other defectors; Lieutenant Abel Hyward at Barnstaple in 1644, Captain George Sadler at Exeter in 1645 and a whole string of unfortunates at Plymouth.[10] These executions were intended to act as a deterrent, of course, but the wide sanction given to such punishments reinforces the impres-sion that changing sides was seen as mean and contemptible. This in turn suggests that turncoats were the exception rather than the rule.

Admittedly, many contemporary comments give the impression of a world of shifting sand, one in which the 'base' and 'cowardly' common people ceaselessly switched their allegiance in order to stay in favour with the winning side. During the dark days of 1643 such behaviour was frequently attributed to the people of Devon by embittered Parliamentary pamphleteers, one diurnalist claiming that Stamford was being besieged in Exeter 'by the same popularity as ran away before' (i.e. by the Devonian militiamen who had fled at Stratton).[11] Such claims undoubtedly had a basis in truth. Many local people had deserted the Parliament and joined the King. Yet it is arguable that as many had changed sides owing to fear and coercion as had been converted by the force of Royalist propaganda. And even at the Royalist high-tide, many areas of Devon remained true to their Parliamentary allegiance.

This—together with the evidence for principled popular involvement advanced in Chapters Two and Three—surely demonstrates that the view of the common people as an uninterested mass, a mere insensate cargo, shifting from side to side of the heaving ship of state, is far too simplistic. Instead, one could perhaps draw a more useful analogy with the political situation of today. Yes, there were people who were uncommitted to either side, people whose minds could be changed, people who were open to persuasion or simply did not care—'floating voters' in today's parlance. Yet, then as now, there were also rock-solid constituencies, villages, towns or regions in which one side or the other possessed an inherent, inbuilt advantage. As a result, individual defections did little to alter the underlying pattern of allegiance. Not even the most inspired propaganda campaign, it seems, could change Parliamentarian strongholds into Royalist ones, or vice versa.

The Clubmen

The model put forward above is, perhaps, somewhat contentious. Many would no doubt argue that it underestimates the true strength of neutralism as a positive force. The best way to deal with such criticisms is to tackle the subject head-on and carry out a detailed case study of popular neutralism in Devon. Real or apparent neutralism surfaced in the county on two main occasions between 1642 and 1646; during the negotiations for a local truce in 1643 and during the Club risings of 1645–46. The 1643 negotiations have recently received a good deal of attention, and sprang, in any case, from an elite initiative rather than a truly popular one.[12] They can be put to one side. Much more relevant are the Clubmen, those rural insurrectionaries who rose in huge numbers across Western England during 1645, determined to protect themselves, their homes and families from the ill-disciplined soldiers of both sides.[13]

Some of the most impressive and well-documented Club risings took place in Somerset and Dorset. Resistance to plundering soldiers first began to manifest itself here in February 1645, and in June rustic protest swelled to a crescendo as Clubmen rose 'in great numbers in several parts of the country'.[14] Royalist and Parliamentarian commanders alike were quick to appreciate the military potential of these gatherings and, for a time, the Clubmen were assiduously courted by both sides. By the end of 1645, however, Club activity had largely ceased, partly as a result of judicious Parliamentarian repression, but mainly because the seat of war (and thus most of the plundering soldiers themselves) had moved on elsewhere.

The Clubmen have often been regarded as genuine neutrals, equally prepared to resist robbers of either side. Yet several historians have noted marked differences in the behaviour and attitudes of the various Club groups. As long ago as 1904 G.M. Trevelyan contrasted the fiercely anti-Royalist Clubmen of Somerset and Devon with those of Dorset, Wiltshire and Hampshire, who, he suggested, 'were more under the influence of the Cavalier gentry'.[15] More recently David Underdown has carefully explored and defined these contrasts, coming to the conclusion that clear variations in the political preferences of the different Club groups can indeed be discerned. These variations, he suggests, were regionally based and reflected pre-existent patterns of allegiance, with basically pro-Parliamentary communities producing basically anti-Royalist Clubmen and vice versa.[16] Can these ideas be applied to the Clubmen of Devonshire?

First Stirrings?

Underdown excludes the Devon Club risings from his study because, he claims, they all took place after 10 September 1645 'the date after which it was obvious that Parliament was going to win'.[17] Yet, in fact, Clubmen had been active in Devon since July, while the first hints of Club activism probably occurred earlier still. The narrative of the Royalist commander Sir Richard Grenville suggests that the wave of discontent which was sweeping the western counties during June 1645 caused considerable ripples in Devon too. In that month Grenville was 'very much importuned by many of the gentry and inhabitants of Devon, to give them leave to procure ... arms upon their own charges to defend themselves ... against the Lyme forces [the Parliamentary garrison of Lyme] and free plunderers'. Grenville was quartered at Ottery at this time, and there can be little doubt—particularly in view of the reference to Lyme—that those who had asked him for permission to arm themselves were East Devon folk. (One of those involved, John Duke, definitely dwelt near Ottery.[18]) The inhabitants of this region had suffered greatly through the war as the area was continually being fought over by the rival garrisons of Ottery and Lyme, and widespread devastation had been caused. It seems unlikely to be mere coincidence that Grenville was asked to sanction an irregular defence force here just as Club disturbances were becoming widespread in the counties to the east. Almost certainly, the request was initiated by the same fears and resentments which had already resulted in Club activity taking place elsewhere.

Grenville clearly felt that the suggestions of the East Devon petitioners had merit and he recommended the scheme to the Royalist commissioners. Accordingly 'a meeting was ... appointed at Broad-clyst to speak with the country thereabouts concerning the same'. The Governor of Exeter was jealous of Grenville's activities and prevented the meeting from going ahead. As a result 'the country was discouraged and the hopes of those forces lost'.[19] The failure of this scheme should not conceal its importance, however. That Broadclyst was chosen as a meeting place is significant, for this village lies at the heart of the rich tract of arable land between Exeter and Ottery, the very part of East Devon which has already been identified as pro-Royalist. Nor should it be forgotten that it was in precisely this same area that local countrymen would rise against the New Model Army in 1646.[20] In this district, at least, there is clear evidence of a continuity between popular Royalism and something closely approximating to anti-Parliamentarian Club activity. The fact that this was an arable area perhaps lends support to Underdown's claim that pro-Royalist Club groups were most commonly found in the fielden districts.[21]

Enthusiasm for an irregular defence force did not end with the abortive Broadclyst meeting. Grenville was approached again later in June, this time by 'many of the gentry of Devon', and requested to 'command a general meeting of all the inhabitants of Devon at Crediton ... to advise of speedy means to raise a powerful army in the county for the defence and security of the same'. Grenville readily agreed, but he was unable to attend the meeting in person and had to send some of the Royalist commissioners in his stead. When the commissioners arrived at Crediton, they 'found there present above 5,000 of the chief inhabitants of that county; whose propositions were, that if they might have Sir R. Grenville for their commander, and that none of their arms should be taken ... from them, nor they carried out of their county without their own consents; that they would generally provide themselves of arms and munitions ... towards the defence of their county against the enemy'. The commissioners were not impressed by these suggestions and, according to Grenville, they not only denied the countrymen permission to choose a commander, but also 'by words giving the country great distaste, made them to depart very much discontented [so that] the hopeful meeting to raise a great army became desperately lost'.[22]

It is easy to see why the commissioners should have poured cold water on the Crediton propositions. Raising irregular forces was a risky business at the best of times, for troops raised in this way might always turn against those who had armed them.[23] Nor can the prospect of such a force being led by the truculent, unpredictable Grenville have helped to recommend the scheme. The Prince's counsellors evidently shared the commissioners' doubts, for they later reprimanded Grenville for assembling men without proper authority.[24] In the absence of any further evidence, the significance of the Crediton meeting must remain debatable. The prominence of local gentlemen in the affair hardly suggests that it was a manifestation of truly popular sentiment. Nor was the choice of Crediton as a meeting-place necessarily significant; the town often served as a county rendezvous because of its central location. It should not be forgotten that Crediton lay on the edge of Royalist Mid-Devon, however. Many of those who attended the rendezvous may well have come from this region.

The first Club risings

The gathering of June 1645 was the Royalists' last real chance to raise a substantial force of irregulars in Devon. Within weeks of the meeting's collapse, the relative calm which had hitherto prevailed in the county was irretrievably shattered—by the arrival of thousands of Royalist cavalrymen. On 10 July Lord Goring's Royalist army was comprehensively defeated at Langport in Somerset. Unable to face the Parliamentarians again, Goring fled westwards into Devon. As his demoralized forces retreated across

West Somerset they were harrassed and attacked by local Clubmen.[25] Significantly, these attacks continued even after the Royalists had crossed the Devon border. It was reported on 15 July that Club groups were hindering Goring's retreat 'giving him alarms and disarming his men' and similar reports appeared throughout the next week. The Devon Clubmen were said to be over 500 strong and firmly behind the Parliament. These are the earliest reports of full-blown Club activity in the county and it is significant that the insurgents were already being described as strongly pro-Parliamentarian.[26]

Upon arriving in Devon, Goring initially tried to strike up some sort of deal with the Clubmen (as he had managed to do before in Somerset). It was reported on 15 July that 'Goring hath yet some hopes of the Devonshire Clubmen' and there can be little doubt that he was trying to drum up support amongst the country people.[27] In a declaration of 20 July Goring summoned 'all such as are able to beare arms for the defence of [their] owne country-mens estates and lives and to oppose all thieves, plunderers and rebels ... to appear at a general rendezvous to be appointed by me, where they shall be mustered and receive arms ... that so [they] may be the more able to defend [them] selves and [their] country'.[28] Goring was clearly hoping to encourage pro-Royalist meetings of the type which had occurred in June. Little evidence about the impact of this particular initiative survives, but a Parliamentary report of 18 July—which noted that the Prince of Wales had 'sent to the Devonshire men to rise as one man for him (which some begin to do in the southern parts thereof)'—indicates that the Royalist campaign had achieved some modest successes, at least in its initial stages.[29]

Even the writer quoted above was quick to point out that these pro-Royalist areas were exceptional, however, stressing that 'the northern parts of that county and the general part of it' had risen against the King and in favour of Parliament. Club groups in North Devon reportedly cried out 'a Fairfax, a Fairfax ... to shew their testimonies of fidelity to the Parliament' and it was claimed that the countrymen 'begin to rise in so many places for the Parliament, as promiseth a general rising against the Cavaliers'.[30] Claims that North Devon was proving particularly hostile to the Royalists were confirmed by a letter from Somerset, which noted that Goring was trying to raise men between Tiverton and Barnstaple but that 'the people are disaffected to him [and] rise as hereabouts'.[31] Later reports confirmed that hostility to the Royalists was strongest along the Somerset border. Royalist troopers fought with Clubmen in the woods at Dulverton on 20 July, while four days later the Devon Clubmen had a rendezvous 'near Martinstone' (probably Martinhoe in the extreme northeast of the county).[32] Another party of Clubmen gathered 'at Goosmoore' in Halberton parish on 23 July.[33]

The Royalists apparently tried to win this latter group over, for, on the same day, Hopton 'kept his rendezvous' at nearby Clyst Hydon, 'endeavouring what may be to get the Clubmen to him'.[34] How Hopton's overtures were received is unknown, but the Royalists still seem to have retained a tenuous hold over some of the Devon Club groups at this time. It was reported on 24 July that 'Gorings horse and dragoons do march with some parties of the Clubmen, and quarter amongst them'.[35] Yet once again the pro-Royalist groups were exceptional. Pamphleteers stressed that only a few parties of Clubmen had come out in support of the King, noting that other groups had rejected the Royalist overtures and were refusing to be 'misled'. It was repeatedly alleged in the London diurnals that the Royalists wished to exploit the Clubmen for their own ends. One pamphlet claimed that Goring intended to betray the Clubmen by calling them together and forcing 'all … that appear … to serve … the King whether they will or no'.[36] Such reports probably reflected local fears. By late July Devonians were becoming increasingly disillusioned with the Royalists.

Goring's Crew

This was hardly surprising. Even as Goring urged local people to take up arms against 'thieves [and] plunderers', Royalist troops were indulging in 'unheard of rapine' across vast stretches of the countryside. Diurnalists made frequent references to the outrages of Goring's cavalry and claimed that their dreadful behaviour was inclining the populace to Parliament's side. One pamphleteer reported that 'the inhumanity of … Goring's men in Devonshire … not only makes him detestable to the people, but also puts them upon inviting us to be their deliverer'.[37] Another claimed that 'Goring is so barbarous about Devonshire, that they long for Sir Thomas Fairfax's coming thither to relieve them', while a third asserted that the countrymen were 'at perfect hatred' with the

Royalists.[38] Loyalist writers were equally damning, for example, Clarendon denounced Goring's troopers as 'dissolute, wicked and ill disciplined', claiming that they had 'alienated the hearts of those who were best affected to the King's service' by their 'intolerable insolences and disorders'.[39] As a result of such statements, Goring's army is invariably portrayed in modern textbooks as the Civil War equivalent of a barbarian horde. But the sources quoted above are deeply prejudiced against Goring and his men. Parliamentary pamphleteers were bound to present the activities of the Royalist troopers in the worst possible light, while Clarendon was Goring's personal enemy. On several occasions Clarendon deliberately distorted pieces of evidence in order to drag Goring's name through the mire.[40] Have partisan sources confused the issue? Were Goring's men really as black as they have been painted?

Unfortunately, detailed examination of the local evidence suggests that they were. The municipal records of Exeter and Totnes reveal that both communities were desperate to keep Goring's troops outside their walls. Totnes actually paid the troopers to keep away. On 6 November the Mayor handed over £7 (in part-payment of a larger sum) to 'the quarter master of my Lord Goring's horse for the keeping them out of the town'.[41] At Exeter the citizens joined forces with the Royalist garrison in order to present a united front against Goring. In October the city council gave the governor £100 as a reward for barring the gates to Goring's men, and soldiers and townsfolk worked together to deny the troopers admittance.[42] (This is reminiscent of the situation in Cornwall, where countrymen helped Grenville's soldiers to barricade the Tamar bridges against Goring.[43])

Those communities which were too small or too poor to keep Goring's troopers at bay suffered devastating financial loss. A surviving set of constable's accounts for the little parish of Charles, in North Devon, throws considerable light upon their character and appetite. This document lists the provisions which were consumed by one troop of Royalist horse during the winter of 1645. Although there were only thirty-four men in the troop, and they only remained in the village for six days, they and their horses nevertheless managed to consume fifty-one bushels of oats, fourteen loads of hay, four bushels of wheat, half a bushel of peas, eighteen chickens, three sheep, large amounts of beef, bacon, pork, butter and cheese, and 'one fat goose'. The total cost to the parish eventually came to £19 18s. 10d. This sum included a payment of twenty shillings to the troopers 'to shoe their horses and to keep them from plundering'. Even so, when the unwelcome guests finally came to leave they took with them 'two horses, with money, clothes and other things'.[44] One only has to imagine this sort of thing happening time after time, in village after village, for month after month, to understand the anger and despair of the country people. Nor was plundering the worst which Devonians had to fear. Soon after Goring's men arrived in Devon parish registers began to record the killing of local people by soldiers, clear evidence that the war had entered a new and more brutal phase. On 1 October Jankey Cadwin was buried at Crediton, having been 'killed by a soldier'.[45] Eleven days later Grace Vicarie was interred at Moretonhampstead, she too having been 'slain by a soldier'.[46] Both places were under Royalist occupation at the time.

The savagery of Goring's men was not confined to the King's enemies. Some of the most telling evidence against the troopers is provided by former Royalists. John Davey, a loyalist of Burrington, claimed that he had 'suffered very much ... both by the imprisonment of his person as also the destruction of his estate, by burning of his house, plundering of his goods and most unsufferable payments exacted from him to his utter undoing' by a group of Goring's horse during the summer of 1645.[47] Ambrose Potter of Silverton, another Royalist, later recalled that during the same miserable summer he had been forced to move his family to Exeter 'to avoide the common injuries and abuses of troopers and soldiers of the King's army then fallen down into the West Country'.[48] A petition also survives from eighty-five residents of the South Hams, testifying that two Captains in a locally-raised Royalist infantry regiment had 'rescued divers goods of ours which the General Goring's licentious horse had plundered and [also] stopped divers others from misusing and plundering of us ... to the great hazard and danger of their persons and lives'.[49] Clearly, even serving Royalist officers faced great personal danger if they dared to resist 'Goring's Crew'.[50]

The immense difficulties which the Royalist recruiters were labouring under during the summer of 1645 are now plain to see. The King's commanders could promise local people the moon, but as long as Goring's horsemen continued to ravage the countryside, the chances of local men turning out for the King were non-existent. Instead popular risings against the Royalists became more and more likely.

The risings escalate

At the beginning of August several reports appeared in the London press concerning the Devon town of 'Walton'. According to the pamphleteers Goring had recently threatened to plunder this community. As a result the inhabitants of the town, and of fourteen neighbouring parishes besides, had risen up against him.[51] The initial reports are garbled, but they were clearly correct in the essentials. Subsequent information makes it plain that 'Walton' was, in fact, North Molton (or Molton), a populous parish in north-east Devon. A major insurrection was soon underway in this area. Parliamentary sources noted on 7 August that 'the well-affected in Moulton stand in their own defence against Goring' and a week later 400 countrymen were said to be gathered in the town, commanded by a certain 'Squire Courtenay'.[52]

The North Molton rising was not only anti-Royalist, it was manifestly pro-Parliamentarian as well. The description of the Clubmen as well-affected suggests as much, as do reports that the insurgents were eagerly awaiting, indeed urgently requesting, Fairfax's advance. The Royalists could not afford to let such open defiance continue and by 15 August Goring's horse were massing around the town. Soon afterwards a fierce engagement took place. One report claimed that the Clubmen themselves had initiated the battle, being 'so valiant as to advance' against the Royalists.[53] But the countrymen were no match for Goring's experienced troopers, and a bloody rout ensued. Reports began to appear on 19 August that Goring had defeated the Devon Clubmen, slaying twenty of the insurgents and capturing eighty more.[54] These claims are confirmed by the Charles constable's accounts, which record payments made to Royalist soldiers 'when the Club men were routed at North Molton'.[55] According to some diurnals Goring subsequently put his prisoners to the sword, thus causing 'multitudes [to] rise against him'.[56] It may be doubted whether even Goring's men would have been quite as ruthless as this, but the reports seem grimly consistent. Whatever the case the Royalist success was only temporary. By the end of August local people were again 'stirring against Goring'.[57]

Following their defeat at North Molton the Clubmen decided to co-operate more closely with the Parliament. (A diurnal hinted at this change in strategy, noting that the Devon men 'are as angry as they were, only they intend to be wiser'.[58]) The nearest regular Parliamentary force at this time was General Massey's Brigade in West Somerset. On 2 September the Devon Clubmen sent a delegation to Massey, pleading for assistance 'against the enemy which do seek to destroy them'. Massey must have been favourably impressed, for he rode into Devon that same day 'to treat with the country concerning the same'. By this time the market town of Bampton had become one of the main Devon Club centres and it was here that Massey and his men were conducted. The Parliamentary forces were 'made very welcome' by the inhabitants and 'entertained with much freedom and alacrity'. Massey quickly discerned the potential of the burgeoning Devon Club movement and when he returned to Somerset he left sixty troopers in Bampton, 'to secure the town' against the Royalists.[59]

Encouraged by Massey's support the Clubmen recommenced their activities with a vengeance. Following the Bampton meeting Club insurrections broke out right across north-east Devon. At Tiverton the castle was briefly occupied by pro-Parliamentary elements and had to be recaptured by Goring's troops.[60] Near Barnstaple, meanwhile, Club groups were actively harrassing the Royalist garrison. The countrymen were drawn from many local parishes (though only Ashford, South Molton and Charles are specifically referred to) and were well enough organized to issue a formal declaration in mid-September.[61] No copies of this document have survived, but it was clearly anti-Royalist in tone.

According to one diurnal the North Devon Clubmen's declaration was very similar to those which had been drawn up by the inhabitants of Somerset and Wiltshire, 'and in most things do[th] agree with theirs'. The North Devon Clubmen had several additional grievances though. First there was the question of plundering. The declaration claimed that Charles I himself had promised to protect local people from unruly soldiers. Even so, the situation had worsened until plundering and robbery were everyday occurrences and now the Clubmen sought redress. Their other main grievance centred upon Barnstaple, for by the terms of a previous treaty Barnstaple was to have been left ungarrisoned. Nevertheless Royalist soldiers had quickly occupied the town. The Clubmen complained that these soldiers had not only 'plundered the Country round about' but had also 'infinitely wronged many honest people in the town'.[62] The inclusion of Barnstaple's grievances in the declaration is significant, demonstrating that the insurgents felt a positive identification with the townsfolk.

While they waited for their declaration to take effect the North Devon Clubmen continued to harass the Royalists. A diurnal reported on 16 September that 'very many of the inhabitants of Devon' had joined forces with Massey and that 'they hate Goring and that crew'. Next day it was claimed that the Clubmen had defeated and killed Sir Alan Apsley, the Governor of Barnstaple, and were even now blockading the town.[63] These reports were clearly exaggerated as Apsley was certainly not killed in this engagement.[64] Reports that the Clubmen had 'blocked Barnstaple up' are more plausible, however. The Clubmen were clearly very strong around Barnstaple and the small Royalist garrison may well have been unable to clear the surrounding countryside of insurgents. Apsley's task was made still harder by the Clubmen's decision to fortify the local villages.[65] (A 'barracado' set up in Braunton at this time was probably erected by Clubmen.[66])

By mid-September the Royalist grip on north-east Devon had become extremely tenuous. Pro-Parliamentary Club groups were now holding Bampton, South Molton and much of the country around Barnstaple. Aided by similar groups in west Somerset, the Devon Clubmen had freed large areas of their county from Royalist control. Pamphleteers gleefully reported that the Clubmen 'on the hither [eastern] side of Devon offer to be made formidable' and that Massey was 'listing the Clubmen under several [Parliamentary] officers'.[67] Disaffection was spreading to other regions too. A letter of 18 September reported that 'at Ashburne the Clubmen under Colonel Foord, well-affected to the Parliament, took 100 of ... [Sir John Berkley's] horse'.[68] 'Ashburne' was probably Ashburton and 'Colonel Foord' was probably William Ford of Ilsington, a prominent local gentleman. Ford had previously served as a Royalist officer, as had two of his sons.[69]

The Royalist response

With north-east Devon in open revolt and signs of discontent beginning to appear in other areas, too, the Royalist commanders resolved upon vigorous countermeasures. Goring was given the task of bringing the disturbances to an end. He hoped to achieve this by unleashing his men upon the communities of the Devon/ Somerset border, the district in which the Clubmen were strongest. On 20 September Goring issued a proclamation from Exeter, noting that 'divers inhabitants of this county and Somerset under pretence of securing themselves from the plundering of the soldiers, have assembled in a tumultuous manner', and ordering 'all persons that lately under the name of Clubmen have taken up arms or assisted the enemy, or opposed His Majesty's forces' to submit. If the Clubmen failed to obey, the proclamation concluded ominously, they would be 'proceeded against'.[70] The Clubmen must have taken this threat seriously and appealed to Parliament for help, for the House of Commons informed Fairfax on 22 October that 'there are 2,500 well affected Clubmen in ... [Devon], who will be ruined for declaring themselves and their good affection to the Parliament unless some help is speedily sent them'.[71]

Fairfax was still many miles to the east, however, and in late September Goring marched out of Tiverton with a powerful force, determined to crush the Clubmen once and for all. Moving up the Exe valley, Goring's men arrived at Bampton 'in which town', a pamphleteer noted, 'there was no defence but the inhabitants'. The beleaguered townsfolk 'stood in their defence as they were able' but were quickly overpowered. A vicious sack of the town ensued. Goring was determined to punish the inhabitants for their rebelliousness and 'the towne was [therefore] plundered, and a great part of it ... burnt'.[72] Having disposed of all resistance here, the Royalists proceeded up the valley to Minehead. Another fight with the Clubmen ensued and Goring's men were again victorious. Minehead, too, was sacked, as was nearby Watchet.[73] Having quelled West Somerset the Royalists marched back into Devon, finally halting at Ilfracombe.[74]

Goring's punitive expedition temporarily subdued the North Devon Clubmen, but discontent continued to smoulder. A few weeks later the New Model Army arrived in Devon, triggering off yet another outburst of Club activity, this time in the South Hams. On 12 October Sir Hugh Pollard, the Royalist Governor of Dartmouth, learnt that some Clubmen had gathered in Harberton parish and sent out 'a party of 200 foot & 20 horse to surprise them'. The Royalist plan went badly wrong and, as Pollard himself admitted, his men 'not only failed' but were 'sufficiently beaten'. Next day Pollard urgently requested reinforcements, stressing that 'we ... [must] recover this affront & prevent a growing mischief'.[75] Assembling a scratch force of troops took the Royalists several days. Meanwhile negotiations of some sort took place at the house of one 'Widdow Oliver' near Totnes. On 14 October Mrs Oliver was paid two shillings 'for quarter of 3 soldiers of Sir Hugh Pollards taken by the Clubmen and sent thither', and a week later she was paid again, this time 'for 2 Trumpeters & 1 Captaine of the Reformadoes with a soldier, divers meals with the Clubmen'. A day or two before this Pollard's men had finally marched out. The Mayor of Totnes provided '8 dozen of bread' for Pollard's soldiers 'to carry with them against the Clubmen'.[76]

The results of this expedition are unknown, but Club activity in the area probably ceased soon afterwards. Fairfax decided on 20 October that he would not, after all, march any further west that year.[77] This decision must have dashed the Clubmen's hopes and accordingly they began to disperse. The more determined of them sought shelter in the nearest Parliamentary garrison, rather than simply returning to their homes. On the very day of Fairfax's decision, (something which hints at the close links between the insurgents and the Parliamentarians) 152 Clubmen were paid two shillings apiece for coming into Plymouth.[78] These men are presumably identifiable with the 250 Clubmen later reported to have joined the garrison.[79]

Continued disturbances

The cessation of the Parliamentary advance brought Club activity to a halt throughout much of Devon. But there are hints that the situation in the North remained unsettled. Prince Charles informed Goring on 25 October that, in consequence of 'the distressed state of the garrison of Barnstaple', the contribution due to the garrison from the neighbouring parishes was to be 'suspended for the present'. As Cotton observes, it seems rather odd that the garrison's distressed condition should have been cited as a reason for supplying it with fewer provisions! The only reasonable inference is that the Royalists were unwilling to antagonize local people by ordering them to bring in supplies. This in turn suggests that the Clubmen remained a threat in this particular region.

Indeed, it may well have been their activities which had distressed the garrison in the first place.[80]

November 1645 saw Goring leave for France. Unfortunately for the people of Devon his horsemen remained behind, now under the nominal command of Lord Wentworth but as ill-disciplined and unruly as ever. By this time the Royalist troopers had spread themselves out across the entire county and nowhere was safe from their depredations. Nevertheless Devon remained quiescent throughout much of November and December. The only Club activity known to have taken place during this period was the continued exodus of Clubmen from the South Hams into Plymouth. Some seamen who had been wrecked on the south coast arrived in Plymouth on 20 November, having travelled there 'from about Kingsbridge, with some Clubbamen'. Over the next few days several more groups of South Devon Clubmen came in to the garrison.[81]

In mid-November Club activity broke out in Cornwall, as countrymen and locally-raised Royalist infantry regiments joined together to prevent Wentworth's horse from crossing the Tamar. A particularly impressive insurrection took place in December, when inhabitants of Stratton, Poundstock, Marhanchurch and Bridgerule in north-east Cornwall began 'to body against the enemy'. The villagers of East Bridgerule in Devon may well have assisted their Cornish neighbours at this time.[82] The last major outbreak of Club activity in Devon occurred a month later. Once again a rising broke out in the north of the county and, once again, the trouble was prompted by the Royalist horse.

The Hartland Rising

On 9 January 1646 the New Model Army at last resumed its westward march. Three days later the King's troops evacuated their billets in the South Hams.[83] Unable to cross the Tamar (which was still being held against them by the Cornish) the Royalist horse now had nowhere to go to but the remote north-west corner of Devon. By 21 January Wentworth had established his headquarters at Holsworthy. Thousands of horsemen were soon spread out across the surrounding countryside, pillaging and plundering the local people and Holsworthy itself was later reported to have been ruined by the troopers' excesses.[84] Presumably spurred on by hopes of an imminent Parliamentary advance, the countrymen again rose against their tormentors. It was reported late in January that 700 Clubmen had gathered in north-west Devon. Hartland, Woolfardisworthy, Parkham, Clovelly, Morwenstow and Kilkhampton (the last two being Cornish parishes) were all said to have contributed men to the revolt.[85] This particular insurrection is not only the last Club rising known to have occurred in Devon, it is also the best documented. A hitherto unnoted set of borough accounts has survived for Hartland. This account book contains several entries relating to the January 1646 rising and provides an extremely rare insight into the way in which Club groups actually operated on the ground.

The accounts show that the Hartland Clubmen's overriding concern was to ensure the safety of their own community. Watchmen were stationed on the approach roads and guards posted at the edge of the town. The watch was kept up night and day in these places and candles were bought to provide the watchmen with light. Money was also spent on beer, bread and tobacco for 'them that watcht'. To deter potential attackers, turnpikes were erected and a chain strung across the main road. Having secured their position, the townsmen next called in reinforcements from the surrounding hamlets. Four men were given a penny each for going to the nearby settlement of Prathuish 'to give them notice to bring in their muskets', while another man was paid 4d. for travelling to the neighbouring parish of Welcombe, presumably on a similar mission. Money was also laid out on 'drink bestowed on Clovelly men', confirming that the Hartlanders were co-operating with other local communities in their resistance to the Royalists.[86]

Who were the leaders of the Hartland Clubmen? According to one diurnal, the insurrection had been encouraged and led by 'Colonel Cary of Clovelly, a Cavalier'.[87] This can only be a reference to Robert Carey, former governor of the Royalist garrison at Bideford. That he, of all people, should have led the insurgents is significant, demonstrating once again that Goring's troopers had alienated even the most prominent loyalists. Nor was Carey the only local notable to support the Clubmen. The Hartland accounts reveal that two other gentlemen participated in the rising. The first was named only as 'Mr Velly'. This must surely be John Velly of Hartland, another ex-Royalist, who had served under Carey in the Bideford garrison.[88] The third gentry participant was Mr John Lutterell, also of Hartland but, sadly, his political allegiances are unknown. The Velleys and the Lutterells were the two most important families in Hartland so, clearly, the local community was firmly united against the Royalist troopers.

The January revolt was short-lived. The Hartland accounts only record payments being made for the town's defence over a period of six days. No further mention of Club activity in north-west Devon appears in the diurnals either, so it must be presumed that the rising either fizzled out or was crushed before the end of January. (That a Royalist officer was killed near Hartland at this time strongly suggests that some sort of encounter did take place between the Clubmen and Goring's troops, as does the tradition that several Clovelly men were killed by soldiers 'during the Civil Wars'.[89]) Two weeks later, the Royalists were finally driven out of Devon, and Club activity ceased for good.

Several time-honoured assumptions about the Devon Club movement have received ample confirmation from the evidence presented above. The overwhelmingly pro-Parliamentarian nature of the disturbances, the fact that they were mostly sparked off by the activities of Goring's troopers, the fact that those troopers behaved appallingly badly, none of these things can now be seriously doubted. It has also become apparent that the Devon Club risings had much in common with those which occurred elsewhere. At Barnstaple hints have been found of the co-operation between town and country which Underdown traced at Salisbury.[90] In North Devon, as in Somerset and Dorset, evidence has been found of a readiness to co-operate with the Clubmen of neighbouring counties.[91] In the risings centred upon Exmoor, the Blackdowns and Hartland, support has been found for Ronald Hutton's contention that Clubmen were commonest in poor and rugged areas (though the South Hams risings do not fit this pattern). More generally the self-contained nature of the Devon risings reminds one of Hutton's observation that Club groups represented separate, and very distinct, 'portions ... of their respective county communities'.[92] It is clear, too, that most of the ordinary Devon Clubmen were drawn from the same social strata as those of Dorset and Somerset, that is to say, from amongst the yeomanry and respectable husbandmen.[93] One pamphleteer made this point explicit, noting that the Molton Clubmen were 'farmers and sufficient men many of them'.[94]

Most of the leaders of the Devon Club groups were men of considerable local importance. Admittedly, Mr Bulhead of

Ashreigney, later described as 'a Captain of the Clubmen', does not seem to have been of a particularly elevated social status.[95] But of the other five leaders whose names are known, at least four—Carey, Ford, Lutterell and Velly—were prominent local gentlemen, and Carey had served as a JP.[96] Identifying 'Squire Courtenay' is more difficult, but it seems probable that he was John Courtenay of Molland, esquire, another JP.[97] The political allegiances of these men are intriguing. At least four had previously served in, or assisted, the King's army, Carey as a colonel, Ford as a captain, Velly as a lieutenant and Courtenay as a commissioner. Why should ex-Royalists have been so prominent in the markedly pro-Parliamentarian Devon Club movement? The explanation may well be that the Clubmen felt they would receive a fairer hearing from the Royalist authorities if their grievances were presented by known loyalists. By rising under such men, the Clubmen could legitimize their protest to some exent, could even claim that they were obeying Goring's orders to rise *en masse* against plunderers. The participation of the gentry themselves can best be explained by assuming that they had put their country's good above their own political preferences.

Where do these discoveries leave the question of popular allegiances? Can the Club risings cast any light at all upon the subject or does the fact that Goring's men had turned the entire county against them by mid-1645 mean that the incidence of Club risings after this date is useless as a means of gauging popular allegiances? The behaviour of Carey, Courtenay and Ford points towards the latter conclusion. That these former loyalists should have deserted the King and joined the anti-Royalist Clubmen suggests that, amongst the gentry at least, changing sides was the order of the day. Yet this does not tell the whole story. As the previous discussion has shown, certain areas of Devon were much more prone to Club activism than others (see Map 7, p. 130), and the distribution of Club activity reflected the underlying pattern of popular allegiance, with many Club groups appearing in Parliamentarian areas, but very few in Royalist ones.

In Royalist Mid-Devon only one Club disturbance is known to have occurred; the incident at 'Ashburne' in September 1645. The Ashburton affair is the least well documented of the Devon risings.[98] Arguably at least, this suggests that it was also the least important. From the other Royalist district, lower Exe Vale, no Club disturbances at all are recorded (unless one counts the

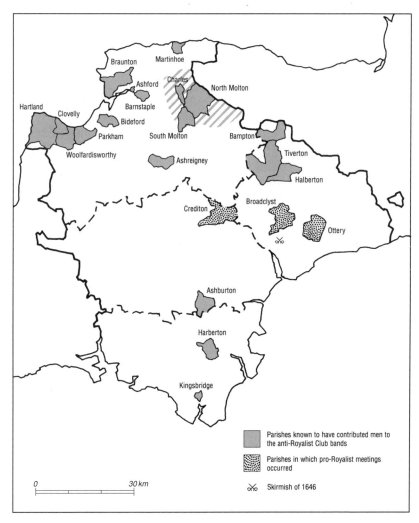

Map 7. The Clubmen, 1645–1646.

pro-Royalist rising of 1646). In the northern corner of East Devon, by contrast—the area in which popular Parliamentarianism was strongest—Club activity was widespread. There was an anti-Royalist rising at Bampton, a meeting at Halberton and a disturbance of sorts at Tiverton.[99] South Devon also saw several Club risings. In this broadly Parliamentarian area, anti-Royalist revolts occurred at Harberton and Kingsbridge, and the frequent references to the South Devon Clubmen suggest that they were a force to be reckoned with.[100] In North Devon pro-Parliamentary Club activity was endemic, and three major insurrections occurred here; at North Molton, at Hartland and around Barnstaple. A Club meeting also took place at Martinhoe. At least fifteen North Devon communities are known to have contributed men to the Club groups, whilst fourteen more parishes, sadly unnamed, rose up against the Royalists around North Molton.[101] North Devon was clearly the stronghold of the Devon Club movement. Can it be mere coincidence that it was also the most fiercely Parliamentarian region of the county?

How else might these regional contrasts be explained? One could, of course, suggest that north-east Devon was particularly prone to Club activity because it had reason to expect swift relief from Fairfax. Yet this was also true of south-east Devon, which lay almost as close to the Parliamentary forces but nevertheless remained quiescent. Alternatively, one could claim that North Devon saw the most Club activity simply because Goring's troopers were billeted there for longer than anywhere else. At first sight this seems a plausible line of argument. North Devon was certainly the first local region to suffer at the hands of Goring's men. By September 1645, however, the troopers had begun to disperse themselves across the entire county.[102] From this time onwards, the burden was fairly evenly spread. Even so, trouble continued in North Devon while other areas remained quiet. Clearly, peculiar local factors were at work, helping to prolong the disturbances in North Devon when they had subsided elsewhere. It is hard to avoid the conclusion that it was the fervent Parliamentarianism of this particular region which had set it apart.

Pre-existent allegiance patterns, rather than an automatic response to military depredations, were what chiefly determined the stance of the Devon Clubmen. Pro-Parliamentary Club groups only flourished in pro-Parliamentary areas with little sign of Club activity in Royalist districts. Sullen and unhappy though the

Royalist communities undoubtedly were, they could not bring themselves to rise in support of Parliament. Indeed, on at least one occasion they actually rose against the New Model Army! We must conclude with Underdown that the Clubmen were not true neutrals and, indeed, to regard the Clubmen as belonging to a distinct movement of any sort, let alone a truly neutralist one, may well be a mistake. The word 'Clubmen' was used by Devonians both before and after 1645–46 simply to denote a group of armed peasants.[103] If the Clubmen of 1645–46 are regarded in this light, rather than as members of a particular movement, it becomes easy to see why they should have behaved as they did. Throughout 1642–44 large numbers of men, armed with clubs and described as Clubmen, rose in North and north-east Devon to resist the Royalists.[104] In 1645–46, exactly the same thing occurred. It is surely misleading to divorce the second group of risings from the first and treat them as a phenomenon which was altogether new.

PART III

The Determinants of Allegiance, c.1600–1642

Introduction

The second part of this book has shown that Devon split apart along internal lines during the Civil War. Certain areas of the county were demonstrably more Parliamentarian or Royalist than others: so much is clear. Yet why should this have been so? What was it that persuaded the inhabitants of some local communities to support the Parliament, while others supported the King? Several historians have suggested that popular allegiances were chiefly determined by purely fortuitous military manoeuvres, that the common people simply obeyed the orders of whichever side was locally dominant. Yet, again and again, we have seen that—in Devon at least—this was not the case. Other explanations must be sought, therefore, explanations which take into account the county's social, topographical and ecological make-up, its cultural divergences and its politico-religious history. In the following chapters, each of these subjects is examined in depth.

Chapter 7

Deference or Defiance?
The Role of the Gentry

When one comes to look for the determinants of popular allegiance the role of the gentry cannot be ignored. For centuries it has been claimed that Civil War armies in general, and the King's army in particular, were semi-feudal, that contemporary gentlemen were able to raise large numbers of soldiers simply by ordering their tenants and neighbours to turn out for whichever side they themselves espoused.[1] Several previous historians have applied these theories to Devon, for example, P.Q. Karkeek claimed in 1876 that 'the majority of the [county's] great land-owners were Royalists; and from sheer necessity their tenants and followers were on the same side'.[2] Such opinions are now coming under fierce assault. Recent studies have placed increasing emphasis upon the political independence of the commoners and many would now agree with Wrightson that the middling sort 'fought not simply as dutiful tenants, but often as their own men defending their own cause'.[3] As Morrill has observed, 'the idea that the labourers, cottagers and others blindly followed their ... masters' lead needs important qualification'.[4] This chapter explores the question of just how important gentry influence was in determining the allegiance of lower-class Devonians.

The Devon Gentry

On the eve of the Civil War noble influence in Devon was relatively weak. The county was governed instead by a ruling elite of greater gentry families. Clearly it was these men, the leaders of the county community in peacetime, who would expect to wield the greatest influence over the common people during the war. Yet below this elite group lay many hundreds of lesser gentlemen, and they too exerted a great deal of power within their own, more localized, spheres of influence. How many gentlemen were there altogether in 1642? This question is difficult to answer because contemporary definitions of gentility varied widely and many individuals claimed to be of gentle birth on grounds that were flimsy, to say the least. Nevertheless, the protestation returns give at least a rough idea of the number of gentry families living in Devon at this time. The returns for the county list twelve knights and baronets, ninety esquires, 570 gentlemen and 103 'misters' (the latter a somewhat indeterminate title which encompasses varying degrees of local eminence).[5] The equivalent returns for Exeter record two esquires, thirteen gentlemen and eighty misters (many of the latter being rich city merchants). Altogether 870 gentlemen and quasi-gentlemen are recorded. This is an impressive figure. Nevertheless it underestimates the gentry's true strength (and particularly that of the knights), for the returns for some fifty county parishes have not survived. In addition many of the returns which do survive make no reference to social title. Bearing these points in mind—and also the fact that a recent study has identified no fewer than 2,006 individual gentlemen who were active in Devon at some time between 1625 and 1640—it seems safest to conclude that the county contained at least 1,500 gentlemen on the eve of the Civil War.[6]

In Devon, as in other counties, the richest gentlemen tended to live in 'the most pleasant and economically attractive areas'.[7] Some parts of the county—the rich arable lands of the Exe Valley, for example, the South Hams and the Taw/Torridge basin—fairly teemed with prosperous gentry families. In the bleak uplands of Central and north-west Devon there were few such families.[8] Here the leaders of local society tended to be members of the 'squirearchy' or 'hedge gentry', individuals of ancient lineage but small means. This continued to be the case for many hundreds of years. During the 1820s an observer wrote disparagingly of 'that dreary and sterile tract between Lifton and the Irish Channel', commenting that 'a country gentleman is not to be found between Lifton and Clovelly'.[9] The protestation returns provide a less impressionistic picture of the regional distribution of the Devon gentry. Of the 870 named gentlemen, 12 per cent lived in East Devon (an area for which, it should be remembered, many returns do not survive), 11 per cent in Exeter, 19 per cent in the South

Hams, 19 per cent in Mid-Devon and no fewer than 39 per cent in North Devon. It is instructive to compare these figures with the general spread of population. East Devon and North Devon each contained around 27 per cent of the county's total population in 1642, while South Devon contained 22 per cent, Mid-Devon 19 per cent and Exeter 5 per cent.

Even allowing for the under-representation of East Devon, it is clear that North Devon, Mid-Devon and Exeter contained more gentlemen per head of population than did the other two regions. The prominence of gentlemen in Exeter is explicable by the fact that the city was the centre of county society, a magnet for the rich and fashionable. In North and Mid-Devon the high number of gentry reflects a different social pattern. In these relatively poor areas impoverished gentlemen clung fiercely to their ancient status, because they could not be differentiated from their neighbours by wealth alone. That North and Mid-Devon contained more gentlemen than East and South Devon should not blind us to the fact that it was in the latter regions that the most important gentry families tended to dwell. The difference was one between quantity and quality, in both senses of the word.

Gentry Allegiances

Which side did the majority of the Devon gentry support during the Civil War? At the highest level of local society, Parliament held a distinct advantage. Around fifty knights and baronets lived in Devon in 1642. Of these, ten—Sir John Bamfield, Sir Shilston Calmady, Sir Francis Drake, Sir Nicholas Martin, Sir John Northcote, Sir John Pole, Sir Samuel Rolle, Sir Henry Rosewell, Sir John Speccot and Sir Richard Strode—supported Parliament throughout the war. In addition, Sir George Chudleigh, Sir John Davy, Sir Thomas Drewe and Sir Peter Prideaux rallied to Parliament during the opening stages of the conflict but later fell away when the tide began to turn towards the King.[10] The Parliamentarian group was remarkable not only for its strength, but also for its cohesion and effectiveness. There can be little doubt that these men played a vitally important role, both in securing Devon for Parliament and in maintaining the cause thereafter.

Numerically speaking the Royalist knights and baronets were roughly equivalent to the Parliamentarians. Of those individuals of knightly rank resident in Devon, at least eleven—Sir Ames

Amerideth, Sir Henry Carew, Sir Edward Carey, Sir John Chichester, Sir Francis Fulford, Sir Thomas Hele, Sir William Pole, Sir Hugh Pollard, Sir Edward Seymour, Sir Popham Southcott and Sir Ralph Sydenham—more or less enthusiastically supported the King, as did Henry Bourchier, 5th Earl of Bath. Yet in terms of local prestige these men were no match for their Parliamentarian rivals. Carey was a catholic, while Pollard had been damagingly implicated in the Army Plot of 1641. Several of the others were men of little local significance[11] and it seems probable that only Chichester, Fulford, Hele, Seymour and Southcott wielded real power in the county. This being the case, it was unfortunate for the King that Southcott died in 1643 while Seymour laid down his commission during the following year.[12]

Amongst the knights and baronets it was the Parliamentary faction which was the stronger. Yet at slightly less exalted levels of gentry society the situation was very different. Of more than 300 esquires who lived in Devon on the eve of the Civil War, forty-six went on to support the King, while only twenty-eight are known to have supported Parliament (three more were turncoats, while the allegiance of the rest is unknown).[13] One must remember that, owing to the nature of the surviving sources, it is easier to identify Royalist than Parliamentarian gentlemen. Even so, it is clear that the King had a strong group of supporters amongst the local squirearchy, and some of these individuals were as rich and influential as their titled fellow countrymen.[14] Amongst the lesser Devon gentry Royalism was even more widespread and of those gentlemen below the level of the knights and esquires, no fewer than 118 are known to have supported the King. The equivalent figure for the Parliamentarians is just eleven.[15] Again one must not forget the proviso that it is easier to identify Royalists than Parliamentarians, yet having made all due allowance for the shortcomings of the sources, it is still tempting to conclude that the Royalist group was the stronger.

Contemporary comments show that the King received a great deal of support from Devon gentry. From the very beginning of the war, Royalist sentiment was clearly visible amongst this group. In August 1642 a number of local gentlemen came out in support of the King's Commission of Array, which was then arousing such bitter (and apparently unanimous) hostility amongst the common people of Devon. Even as early as this then there is evidence to suggest that Royalism was more prevalent amongst the gentry than the commoners. One cannot claim that the majority of local gentlemen favoured the Array, of course. Many clearly opposed it, while several of the individuals who had been chosen as commissioners themselves refused to serve, one going so far as to declare his reservations before a popular assembly gathered on a hillside.[16] Nevertheless, at least a score of local gentlemen are definitely known to have supported the Array.[17]

Their behaviour was a sign of things to come. If some members of the elite had been prepared to come out in support of the King during August and September 1642, many more were ready to do so by the end of the year. It is significant that the initial foray of the Cornish Royalists into Devon was made at the invitation of 'Mr Culme then High Sheriff ... and divers other well affected [Royalist] gentlemen of that County'.[18] Many Devon gentlemen helped the Cornish in their subsequent attempts to reduce the county to the King's obedience. Some 200 loyalist gentry, a huge number, were reported to be gathering in North Devon during December.[19] Twenty more gentlemen were captured by the Parliamentarians at Modbury later that month, and others were imprisoned after Hopton's retreat from Exeter.[20] By February 1643 at least thirty of the King's most enthusiastic gentry supporters were behind bars. Even so, many other loyal gentlemen remained at liberty. Several left their homes and went into Cornwall to join the King's forces and when Hopton advanced into Devon for a third time during April, he was again accompanied by 'divers volunteers of the gentry of that county'.[21]

After Stratton the Devon gentry again flocked in to assist the King. Royalist forces near Exeter received a great deal of gentry support in summer 1643, and later that year country gentlemen helped Maurice to raise men and supplies for the assault on Plymouth.[22] Further signs of gentry attachment to the King's cause appeared throughout the war. When Essex tried to win the Devon gentry over in 1644 he failed dismally, 'not a person of any note deserting his Majestie's cause'.[23] When Fairfax captured Dartmouth in 1646 'many country gentlemen' were found sheltering there,[24] and whenever Royalist meetings took place in the county they were well attended by the local gentry.[25] Clarendon, who had himself spent some months in Devon, summed up the overall situation by observing that 'the gentlemen of that county [were] generally well devoted to the King's service'.[26]

Statistical analysis and contemporary comments both suggest

that the majority of the Devon gentry favoured the King. This casts doubt upon the theory that the attitude of the gentry was the crucial factor in determining popular allegiance, for most Devon commoners supported the Parliament. It might be retorted that the vital factor in deciding Devon's allegiance was not the attitude of the local gentry as a whole, but the attitude of the most vigorous members of the county elite. This argument is impossible to refute completely. The existence of a determined group of Parliamentarian sympathizers at the very top of county society undoubtedly helped to smooth Devon's passage into the Roundhead camp in 1642, but can the allegiance of the county as whole be explained by the behaviour of this one small group?

The effect of gentry allegiance upon popular behaviour

One problem with accepting such a theory is the fact that, at the regional level, the gentry influence model patently fails to work. In the first part of this book it was shown that popular Royalism was most prevalent in Mid-Devon and parts of East Devon, while in North Devon and the South Hams, opinion was strongly in favour of Parliament. If it were true that popular allegiances were chiefly determined by the attitudes and behaviour of the local gentry, one would expect to find that more Royalist gentlemen resided in the former regions of the county than in the latter. Yet this was not the case and contemporary comments make it clear that loyalist gentlemen were most numerous and powerful in the south of the county. The well-affected gentlemen of Devon told Hopton in November 1642 that 'their chief strength' lay in the South Hams.[27] Next month a Parliamentary writer in Dartmouth confirmed this, lamenting that 'almost all the gentry in these parts are for the Commission of Array'.[28]

Few contemporary statements as explicit as this have survived, but there are other ways of gauging the strength of the loyalist gentry in each region.[29] Peter Newman has identified thirty-four Royalist field officers who came from Devon.[30] During the course of research for this book, another twenty-nine names have come to light, making a total of sixty-three in all.[31] Military rank was generally concomitant with civilian status in the King's army, so one can be confident that these individuals—colonels, lieutenant-colonels and majors—were amongst the most socially prestigious of the local loyalists.[32] As high-ranking field officers, moreover, these are the very men who would presumably have been most assiduous in urging their tenants and neighbours to fight for the King. If gentry behaviour really was decisive in determining popular allegiance, one would expect to find that the regions in which these important officers were most heavily concentrated would also be the regions in which popular support for the King was greatest. Yet, once again, this was not the case. Of the sixty-three Royalist field officers whose places of residence can be established, well over half lived in the regions of the county in which popular affection for the King was weakest.[33] Thus South Devon produced twenty field officers, almost a third of the total, while the Parliamentarian stronghold of North Devon was not far behind with seventeen. Mid-Devon and East Devon, the regions of the county in which popular Royalism has most frequently been identified, produced only twelve and eight field officers respectively (19 per cent and 13 per cent of the total). Exeter produced another six field officers (10 per cent of the total).

A similar picture emerges if one looks at the regional origins of all Royalist officers of the rank of lieutenant or above. Of 293 such officers identifiable from Devon, the largest number, fifty-nine (20 per cent of the total), again came from the South Hams. The next largest number, forty-nine (16 per cent), came from North Devon, while forty-eight (15 per cent) came from Mid-Devon, forty-one (13 per cent) from East Devon and twenty-seven (9 per cent) from Exeter.[34] Again, one sees the confusing spectacle of the regions in which popular Parliamentarianism was strongest producing the largest number of Royalist officers. This surely supports Ann Hughes's claim that 'in areas where middling and lesser men supported Parliament, elites ... [became] alarmed about social order and hierarchy and more inclined to an authoritarian politics'.[35]

Because of the scarcity of the evidence it is hard to arrive at comparable figures for the Parliamentarians, yet something may still be learnt. Of a group of eighty-two Parliamentary leaders, identifiable from the county as a whole (Exeter excluded), twenty came from the south of the county, nineteen from the east, and twelve each from Central and North Devon, while the residences of the remaining eighteen are unknown.[36] The prominence of South Devonians in this list is a reflection of the unique experience of Plymouth which was the only Devon town to remain in

Parliamentary hands throughout the war. Therefore, a dispropor-
tionate number of the Parliamentary leaders were drawn from this
area. Taking the 'Plymouth factor' into account, South and East
Devon emerge as roughly first equal in terms of the number of
Parliamentary gentry they contained. It is hard to make very
much of this. Certainly, the South Hams was an area of strong
popular Parliamentarianism, but this was less true of East Devon
and, in terms of number of gentlemen activists per head of population, the Parliamentary gentry appear to have been weakest of all
in North Devon—the very region of the county which provided
them with the most fervent popular support!

The marked contrast between the geographical patterns of
allegiance found amongst the Devon gentry and the Devon commoners again points to the conclusion that gentry influence was
not the crucial factor in determining popular behaviour. Much
anecdotal evidence points the same way. We have already seen
how the Earl of Bath and his gentry supporters were repulsed by
angry crowds when they tried to publish the Commission of
Array at South Molton. It should be noted, too, that after the
Royalist gentry of North Devon had supported the Array, in
direct opposition to the wishes of the local countryfolk, it was
observed that 'those men will never get renown and credit again
of their Country'.[37] This comment shows that a gentleman's social
standing, far from allowing him to dictate how his poorer neighbours should act, could sometimes depend upon his espousing the
cause which was favoured by the local community. Not everyone
concluded that a course of action was right just because it was advocated by the local gentleman, and many commoners possessed
a healthy disrespect for the political opinions of their 'betters'.

Across England as a whole, tenants refused to obey their masters on many occasions during the Civil War,[38] nor was it only
Royalist gentlemen who had to face such insubordination. In
Devon, at least, the process worked the other way as well. When
a yeoman of Brushford learnt that Sir John Northcote, one of the
most powerful Devon gentlemen, was leading a force of Parliamentary volunteers to Sherborne, he retorted that 'Jack Northcott
was a fool ... & that he should be hanged when he came home,
& all his soldiers with him'.[39] Similar disrespect for the Parliamentary leaders surfaced on many other occasions. In November
1642 a cordwainer's wife spat in the face of Mr Adam Bennett, the
son of an Exeter Alderman, 'and called him Traitor, and said he

was against the King, and that she did not doubt but one time or other to meet with [him] ... and fit him a pennyworth'.[40] When a city chandler heard that the Parliamentarian merchant, Mr Richard Evans, had been chosen captain of the Exeter trained bands, he called Evans a 'Coxcomb' and swore 'that before he would go into the field after him, he would lie in Southgate [the city prison]'.[41]

Such anecdotes demonstrate that humble men and women had their own views and opinions and were prepared to follow a line independent of that taken by their social superiors. Gentlemen could not simply snap their fingers and depend upon the commoners to do their bidding. It is well known that officers who changed sides were sometimes able to persuade their men to do so too.[42] But the mere fact that a gentleman had turned his coat was no guarantee that the soldiers serving under him would do the same. When Captain William Putt of Gittisham deserted the Parliament's cause in 1643 and took service with the King, he tried to persuade his servant to follow him, but the man flatly refused.[43] Similarly, when Sir Alexander Carew attempted to betray his post at Plymouth to the Royalists, a group of the soldiers under his command refused to join their turn-coat officer and put him under arrest. Apparently '[Carew's] own man tooke his master by the choller of his dublet, and strucke up his heeles, and ... bound him hand and foot'.[44] Little sign of slavish deference here.

Contemporary gentlemen themselves were, of course, reluctant to admit that their influence over the commoners was limited in any way. Many gentlemen, particularly Royalist ones, were supremely confident of their own ability to sway their tenants and neighbours. In October 1644 the young Sir John Grenville airily assured Prince Charles that he would be able to raise a whole regiment of men from his family's estates in North Devon.[45] Yet—as Grenville's subsequent failure was to show—gentlemen notoriously exaggerated the influence which they possessed over their poorer neighbours. Clarendon observed that 'it was a general ... miscomputation of the time that the party ... which wished well to the King (which consisted of most of the gentry in most counties) ... had so good an opinion of their own reputation and interest' that they believed themselves able to order events in their own localities with little or no outside assistance.[46] As Clarendon himself knew only too well, this rarely turned out to be the case and West Country commoners disappointed gentry expectations on numerous occasions during the Civil War. In 1642 loyalist gentlemen near Exeter made 'frank promises of supplies of men' if the Cornish army 'would but advance into those parts', but when the Cornishmen accordingly advanced the promised recruits were not forthcoming.[47] Similar assurances of popular support were given to Essex by a group of Cornish gentry in 1644.[48] Yet when he acted upon these assurances and marched into Cornwall, the people rose against him. Such incidents warn us against accepting gentry assessments of their own influence at face value.

It was only when gentlemen were backed by overwhelming military force that they could be confident of dictating popular behaviour. Bullying and coercion could often bring in large numbers of recruits and this was especially true where patterns of settlement worked to the gentry's advantage. In the South Hams, where there were numerous loyalist gentlemen and the terrain made it difficult for men to hide themselves from the press, the Royalists were able to obtain large numbers of soldiers, despite local hostility to the King's cause. But coercion was a deeply unsatisfactory way of raising troops. The South Devon levies were unreliable, as troops raised in this way almost always were. Men who had had to be coerced into fighting were prone to run away at the first opportunity, and sometimes deserted to the enemy *en masse*.[49] Occasionally they even killed their officers. For example, the Royalist Colonel Bluett was apparently murdered by his own men during the siege of Lyme.[50] Bluett's troops had been raised in the strongly-Parliamentarian communities of north-east Devon. His fate vividly illustrates both the ineffectiveness of troops raised by coercion and the gentry's basic inability to override popular allegiances.

The Devon gentry did not have the power absolutely to determine popular allegiances then. Yet one should not take this line of argument too far and conclude that gentry influence over the political behaviour of the lower classes was negligible. Although commoners were prepared to resist the gentry over matters of strongly-held belief, county society as a whole remained intensely deferential. Political radicalism was rare in Devon, even during the 1640s, and while criticisms of individual gentlemen were common, resentments against the gentry as a group were seldom articulated. In Devon, as elsewhere, the Civil War possessed few of the characteristics of a class conflict.[51]

There were some ominous mutterings. In August 1642 two East

Devon husbandmen were overheard 'conferringe together in theire worke ... concerninge the raiseinge of forces in Cullyford, Beere and Seaton ... for riflinge howses in these tymes of trouble', and a month later there was concern that decay of trade might lead to popular unrest.[52] A garbled report spoke of 'great combustions' amongst the Devon commonalty at this time and claimed that 'the poor for want of trading have gotten head, and have done great spoils, forcing those of ability to relieve their distress, [so that] in many repulses, divers ... have been slain'.[53] This report seems to have been inspired by the South Molton riot, however, and it is significant that—on the one or two occasions when gentlemen were attacked or abused at this time—it was because they were Royalists, rather than because they were gentlemen. If wealthy Devonians really did fear an imminent *jacquerie* in 1642 it failed to materialize.

On the eve of the Civil War, as for centuries before, the gentry were universally regarded as the leaders of local society. If given the choice between serving under a yeoman or a gentlemen, most Devonians would unhesitatingly have adopted the latter course. It was only when gentlemen attempted to dragoon people into fighting for a cause of which they disapproved that trouble arose. There can be no doubt that West Country men preferred to serve under local gentry commanders whenever possible. The attachment of the Cornish to the gentlemen officers of their own county was legendary, and it was later recalled that the Cornish soldiers had only been successful 'as long their own officers lived to command them'.[54] Comments like this have been used to suggest that Cornish Royalism owed more to 'a passionate and personal attachment to ... local leader[s]' than to any real affection for the Crown.[55] Such attempts to resurrect the model of feudal allegiance for Cornwall alone are unconvincing, and surely underestimate the sophistication of the Cornish people. The Cornishmen's attachment to their own gentry may well have been exceptionally strong, but it was by no means a blind devotion. Nor was it unique, and claims that 'the loyalty of the Cornish to their local squires ... was not to be found in the more independently minded ... county of Devon' are incorrect.[56]

A similar attachment to local gentry officers was revealed in Devon on several occasions. When the militiamen of the Cullompton area were ordered to march to Sherborne in 1642, they refused to go until John Weare, a local gentleman, managed to persuade

them 'by reason of my respects and vicinity with them'.[57] Similarly, those who gathered at Crediton in 1645 requested that they
should be put under Sir Richard Grenville's command.[58] The
evidence of the maimed soldiers' petitions shows that humble
Devon Royalists shared in the admiration for the Cornish officers.
Long after the war was over, a Mid-Devon husbandman referred
to the Cornish colonels Slanning, Godolphin and Trevanion as
'valiant' and to Bevill Grenville as 'heroiycke'.[59] Trusted local
gentlemen like these could win the respect and admiration of their
soldiers, and could sometimes spur them on to deeds which they
would never have performed under less inspiring leadership. But
even the most exceptional local officers were unable to persuade
men to fight in a cause of which they disapproved.

This survey supports the contention of Morrill and others that
it was not 'the gentry alone who determined the political align-
ment of a county in the Civil War'.[60] While Devon was a broadly
Parliamentarian county, the majority of the local gentry favoured
the King. At the regional level, too, no clear link has been found
between gentry allegiances and those of the commonalty. These
findings reflect the limitations of the gentry's influence over the
common people. The gentry could persuade, cajole and threaten,
but they could not simply command. As Wrightson has observed
'the acceptance of authority [by the commons] ... depended not
upon coercion, but upon assent'.[61] The picture altered from parish
to parish, of course, and it is probable that in one or two communities where gentlemen were exceptionally numerous, the local
population could indeed be swayed. The Royalism of Modbury
and Ottery may well have owed something to the large number
of Royalist gentry who dwelt in those towns, for instance.[62]
Yet even in communities like these, deference to social superiors
was by no means universal. Despite being castigated by a local
gentleman, who 'abused him and called him a rogue', Edward
Wyatt, a commoner of Ottery, still joined the Parliamentary
army.[63]

The gentry's ability to determine popular allegiances during the
course of the war itself has been overrated. But the true extent of
gentry influence upon the behaviour of the commonalty does not
emerge from a study of the war years alone. While the short-term
techniques of persuasion and coercion adopted between 1642 and
1646 were essentially stop-gap measures, unlikely to have any
real affect on underlying popular sentiment, the long-term

programmes of cultural and religious indoctrination sponsored by many of the leading gentry families during the seventy years before the Civil War were of vital importance. The effect of these measures on lower class allegiance will be examined in Chapter Ten.

Chapter 8

An Ecology of Allegiance?
Ethnology, Land Use
and Occupation

Having discarded gentry influence as a major determinant of popular allegiance, other reasons must be sought to explain why local people took the sides they did between 1642 and 1646. This chapter will focus on three possible answers. First there is the neglected question of ethnology. Did racial divisions play any part in determining Civil War allegiance in the far South-West? Second, and much more important, there is the question of divergent agrarian practice. Was there, as David Underdown has claimed, a link between regional patterns of agriculture and wartime allegiances? Finally there is the question of occupation. Does Devon provide any support for the traditional view that Englishmen divided along occupational lines during the 1640s, with agriculturalists coming out for the King, townsmen and clothworkers for the Parliament? Each of these questions will be examined in turn below.

The role of ethnology

To begin a discussion of Civil War allegiance in Devon by examining local ethnology may well seem a little perverse, for the county possessed few large minority groups during the seventeenth century.[1] Nevertheless it is too often forgotten that Devon was a marcher (or border) county, the River Tamar forming a racial frontier between Anglo-Saxon England and Celtic Cornwall. Well into the early modern period Cornish commoners

retained 'a kind of concealed envy' against their eastern neighbours, a 'desire for revenge' against those who had conquered
their forefathers.[2] This racial hostility may well have been reciprocated. Certainly the steady stream of poor Cornish migrants
who flowed across the Tamar during the pre-war period aroused
resentment and suspicion.[3] Did such sentiments help to determine
Civil War allegiances and might not ancient antagonisms have
played a least a minor part in impelling the Anglo-Saxon inhabitants of Devon towards the side of Parliament, once it became clear
that Cornwall supported the King? To give too much weight to
such a theory would probably be unwise. There were numerous
links between Devon and Cornwall, particularly amongst the
higher social classes, and the two counties had a long history of
mutual co-operation. Nevertheless fascinating scraps of evidence
survive to suggest that the racial differences between Anglo-Saxon
and Celt did affect wartime allegiances in some areas.

The case of Stratton in north-east Cornwall is particularly
interesting. This small town and the villages which cluster around
it lie in the most anglicized part of Cornwall. It has been observed
that, while along most of Cornwall's eastern border English and
Celtic names are confusedly intermingled, near Stratton 'the
boundary between English and British names is much more
sharply defined'.[4] In this region the River Ottery, a tributary of
the Tamar, marks a clear division between villages with English
names, such as Poundstock, Jacobstow and Whitstone, and those
which are entirely Cornish in their derivation, such as Egloskerry,
Treneglos and Tremaine. There can be little doubt that the river
was at one time 'a racial frontier'.[5] Intriguingly, evidence survives
to suggest that this ancient division continued to shape events as
late as the 1640s. During the Civil War the area around Stratton
was described by Clarendon as 'the only part of Cornwall eminently disaffected to the King'.[6] That this ethnologically distinct
corner should have behaved so very differently from the rest of
the county leads one to suspect that its past had set it apart in
some way. And other evidence survives to make the distinction
between Stratton and the rest of Cornwall more explicit still.

In late 1645 the Cornish parishes of Stratton, Whitstone,
Bridgerule, Marham Church, Launcells and Poundstock rose up
against the Royalists.[7] This was one of the first Club risings to
occur in Cornwall and that it centred upon Stratton, of all places,
is significant. For one thing, the outbreak of Club activity in this

'eminently disaffected' town tends to confirm the suggestion that it was anti-Royalist communities which produced pro-Parliament-ary Clubmen and vice versa. Yet even more intriguing is the fact that the parishes which rose at this time all lay directly to the east of the River Ottery. It was the inhabitants of the English enclave in north-east Cornwall, in other words, who had risen up against the Royalists, while the inhabitants of the more purely Celtic communities further to the west remained quiescent. In 1646 in-habitants of Morwenstow and Kilkhampton, two more English parishes in north-east Cornwall, took part in further Club risings, this time centred on Hartland in Devon.[8] These episodes demon-strate that the inhabitants of Stratton and its hinterland preferred to co-operate with the people of north-west Devon rather than with their fellow Cornishmen, and also suggest that their sym-pathies lay with Parliament rather than with the King. It is hard to resist the conclusion that the ethnographic links between north-east Cornwall and north-west Devon played some part in this.

The divide between Saxon and Celt should not be overstressed. In 1549 the people of Mid-Devon were fully prepared to join forces with their Cornish neighbours in the Western Rebellion, and similar co-operation took place during the Civil War.[9] It may well be that this particular region of the county, with its rugged terrain and its tin mines, had more in common with Cornwall than with other parts of Devon. As several historians have observed, popular loyalties throughout the early modern period were often attached to a 'pays' or country which straddled county boundaries, rather than to the county itself.[10] This was certainly true in Devon. During the 1620s the sheep-farmers of north-east Devon combined with those of Somerset in order to oppose plans to deforest Exmoor, while twenty years later the local countrymen joined forces once again, this time to resist Lord Goring's troopers.[11]

The role of market towns and farming regions

What was it that defined a seventeenth-century Devonian's coun-try if it was not the county boundary? The parish acted as the primary focus of local loyalties, of course, but this was too small a unit to be regarded as a country in its own right. The same was true of the Devon hundreds, which tend to be peculiarly con-voluted and misshapen (Stanborough hundred is a good example) and can hardly be regarded as fully-integrated territorial blocs. More important may well have been the attachment which an individual felt to his or her market town. Historians are becoming increasingly aware that these medium-sized trading centres served as focal points for distinct rural communities.[12] The local market town was the furthest that the average commoner travelled in the course of the working week. Celia Fiennes noted in 1698 that the country people of Cornwall were 'very ill guides, and know but little from home, only to some market town they frequent'.[13] As a result, it was from the limited circle of villages served by the local market town that the majority of an individual's social and business contacts would be drawn. In seventeenth-century Devon, relatively few communities lay on the cusp between the spheres of influence of two market towns. Instead the hinterland of each centre was usually pretty well-defined; by ranges of hills, by river systems or by considerations of distance.[14]

The cohesion of these small territorial units was considerably increased by the fact that they often followed the lead of the central town in politico-religious matters.[15] Much more research needs to be done on this subject, but it might not be too much of an exaggeration to view early modern Devon as a loose federation of around forty rural territories, each one based on its own market town.[16] The events of 1642–46 support the idea that the inhabitants of a market town and its hinterland tended to act in concert. One is reminded of the Club rising around Stratton and the subsequent revolt based upon Hartland. Similarly, the fourteen North Devon villages which rose in 1645 may well have comprised the hinterland of South Molton.[17] Market towns could not be sure of dominating local communities, of course, and the townsmen of Moreton signally failed to convert the inhabitants of the surrounding villages to the Parliamentary cause. Yet generally speaking, the wartime allegiance of Devon market towns often does seem to have been matched by that of the parishes round about.

To concentrate on market towns alone would be too simplistic. Like the hundreds, market towns and their hinterlands were too small to be regarded as countries in their own right. Instead many such towns were usually comprised within a single country. What was it that served to bind these large rural territories together? Patterns of land use may well provide a clue. In recent years, historians have become increasingly concerned with the influence which different types of agricultural practice could exert upon the behaviour and social organization of rural communities. Joan Thirsk has suggested that during the late medieval and early modern periods there were 'two rural peasant Englands', one based on arable farming, the other centred on cattle grazing and the exploitation of pasture and woodlands.[17] Thirsk and her supporters contend that, in the arable areas, community life was more stable, conservative and strictly regulated than in the pastoral areas. The lives of arable farmers, it is claimed, were centred upon the nucleated village, the church and the manor house. As a result they were more susceptible to control by an elite group. In pastoral districts things were different. Here the pattern of settlement was scattered and local people were less tightly bound by traditional hierarchies. As a result the farmers of the woodland and pasture areas were more independent than those of the arable districts, and more open to radical ideas.

These ideas have been enthusiastically seized upon by Christopher Hill and, more recently, by David Underdown, who makes extensive use of them in his study of wartime allegiances in Wiltshire, Dorset and Somerset.[18] In these three counties, Underdown contends, Parliamentarianism was most common in the pastoral districts, while popular Royalism was associated with 'the survival of a more homogeneous, paternalist society in the arable regions'.[19] Underdown has also identified intermediate areas, in which neither patterns of land use nor patterns of allegiance were quite so clear-cut. The theory that political behaviour was preconditioned by agrarian environment is an intriguing one, but it has not met with universal acceptance. The field/pasture dichotomy adopted by Underdown has been denounced by some historians as too crude, while others have stressed that certain areas of the three counties do not conform to the 'pasture = Parliamentarians, arable = Royalists' model.[20] Buchanan Sharp is particularly sceptical, arguing that, as far as occupational structure and settlement patterns are concerned, there is 'no obvious distinction' between many of Underdown's pastoral and intermediate districts.[21] Similar doubts have been cast on the suggestion that agricultural practice affected cultural outlook.[22]

Can a study of the relationship between patterns of wartime allegiance and agricultural practice in Devon throw any light upon this debate? Was it the arable parts of the county which supported the King, while the pastoral areas favoured the Parliament? Before examining the situation in detail, two preliminary points should be made. The first is that Devonian agricultural techiques were very different from those which were practised further to the east. William Marshall, whose *Rural Economy of the West of England* remains the most useful introduction to Devon's agrarian history, describes the agricultural systems of Devon and Cornwall as completely distinct in character. This being the case, theories based on agricultural conditions in Dorset and Wiltshire can hardly be expected to be precisely applicable here. The second point to stress is that the regions into which Devon has been divided for the purposes of this book do not always correspond to true farming regions. Marshall identified six 'natural districts' in South-West England: North Devon, the South Hams, the Vale of Exeter, the dairy district of East Devon, the Tamar Valley and 'the mountains of Cornwall and Devonshire'.[23] Only the first two correspond very closely to the regions employed in this book. Of the other four, Exe Vale and the dairy district have been assigned to East Devon, while the Tamar Valley and the mountains (i.e. Dartmoor) have been assigned to Central Devon.

East Devon was the most deeply divided part of the county during 1642–46. Generally speaking the parishes in the north and east of the region supported Parliament, while those in the more westerly areas—especially in the countryside between Exeter and Ottery—favoured the King. Interestingly enough, these divisions coincide very neatly with the basic topography of East Devon. In the Vale of Exeter the land is flat and low-lying. As a result arable farming was widespread here, and the pattern of settlement reflects this fact.[24] Parishes like Broadclyst, Budleigh, Silverton and Thorverton are based around large, tightly nucleated villages. East of Ottery the landscape is very different. Here in the dairy district a band of rugged and very hilly terrain, five to ten miles broad, thrusts south from the Blackdown Hills to the sea, cutting off the fertile land of the Exe valley from the low-lying country near Axminster. Both this tongue of land and the Blackdown Hills proper (which stretch along the north-east of the region, from Burlescombe to Membury) have traditionally been used for pastoral farming. There is a good deal of woodland in these areas and the pattern of settlement is scattered.

It is remarkable that almost all the Parliamentarian petitioners identified from East Devon were inhabitants of the wild and hilly parishes of the Blackdown hills and its outliers. Royalist petitioners, by contrast, were concentrated in the arable villages of lower Exe Vale and in Axminster (also the centre of a small arable district). Similar divergences can be seen in the distribution of those towns and villages which are known to have demonstrated firm support for either side. Thus the Royalist communities of Axminster, Bradninch, Ottery and Thorverton lie in the low-lying arable areas, while the Parliamentarian parishes of Awliscombe, Halberton, Hemyock, Tiverton and Uffculme are all situated on the fringes of the pastoral dairy district. This suggests that patterns of settlement and land use did have a considerable effect upon popular allegiances in East Devon. Yet there is an important caveat to be made here. The hill-country in the north-east of the region was not only a dairy district, it was also the stronghold of the local cloth industry—and clothworkers tended to support the Parliament. It would be unrealistic to ascribe the political allegiance of this particular area to agrarian factors alone.

What was the position to the west of the Exe, in the highland zone which makes up the rest of Devon? North Devon was the most strongly Parliamentarian region of the county, and the dominant type of land use in this area is pastoral.[25] At first sight the field/pasture model seems to be vindicated once again. Yet on closer examination worrying inconsistencies appear. There is no sign whatsoever of support for the King in the important arable district of the Taw and Torridge valleys.[26] On the contrary, several local communities demonstrated determined resistance to the Royalist forces. In this area, at least, there is apparently no correlation between patterns of land use and political behaviour. Similar conclusions can be drawn from an examination of the situation in the South Hams. This was the richest part of Devon. It was also the region which contained the largest amount of arable land. Fraser noted in 1794 that 'scarcely any of the land [here] is kept wholly in grass'. The scarcity of permanent pasture was matched by a scarcity of woodland, South Devon was 'not so well accomodated with ... timber as other parts'.[27] The pattern of settlement reflected the dominance of arable farming as most South Devon villages are of the nucleated type.[28] According to the field/pasture model, the South Hams should have been politically conservative, yet it was not. Even in the parishes around Torbay, an area renowned for its rich corn land, popular risings against the King took place.[29]

In both North Devon and the South Hams, popular support for Parliament existed in predominantly arable districts, that is to say in precisely those areas which proponents of the field/pasture model would claim to have possessed an inbuilt bias towards the King. In Mid-Devon the position was exactly reversed. In this wild, rugged and very remote region, where the pattern of settlement was almost invariably dispersed, and where the hegemony of the gentry must have been extremely hard to enforce, the common people—far from being Parliamentarians—were supporters of the King. There is a clear parallel here with the situation in Wales and Northern England, other upland pastoral regions where Royalism was strong.[30]

Surveying the effects of agrarian practice on political behaviour has thus produced rather disparate results. It seems fair to say that the field/pasture model works best in East Devon, a region which possesses a landscape broadly comparable to that of the areas upon which Underdown's own research was based. Yet even here the apparent correspondence between pastoralism and Parliamentarianism may well owe more to the local distribution of the cloth industry than to anything else, suggesting that the 'wholly agrarian/partly industrial' divide was more important than the field/pasture one.[31] West of the Exe, the field/pasture dichotomy breaks down altogether. This is not too suprising and Underdown never suggested that his hypothesis would be applicable to all areas of the country. He has admitted (with scrupulous honesty) that, even in his own three counties, many regions do not fit the model, for example, Blackmore Vale was a pastoral region and it was also pro-Royalist.[32] In Devon there are many such inconsistencies and it is tempting to conclude that, in this particular county, patterns of land use and settlement were at best peripheral in determining wartime allegiance.

The role of occupation

If the suggestion that pastoral and arable farmers supported different sides is difficult to uphold, might not clearer divisions have existed between other occupational groups? Chapter Four suggested that local seamen and clothworkers had generally favoured the Parliament, while local tin-miners had supported the King. It was also suggested that the King had derived more support from rural dwellers than from townsmen. The geographical spread of allegiance in Devon is consistent with the pattern outlined above. All of the county's major seaports supported the Parliament, as did the fishing villages and coastal areas in general. The same could be said of most of the larger towns and, of Devon's ten most populous communities, at least eight were strongly Parliamentarian.[33] Most of the local cloth towns also favoured Parliament. One thinks of Moreton and Crediton in Mid-Devon, of Chulmleigh and South Molton in the north and of Tiverton and Cullompton in the east. It can hardly be coincidence that the area in which popular support for Parliament was strongest, the countryside along the county's north-east border, was also the area in which cloth manufacture was most firmly established.[34] The links between the tin-mining areas and popular Royalism are also clearly apparent. Of the thirty-five Devon parishes which the evidence of the maimed soldiers' petitions indicated to be most strongly Royalist, seventeen lay within the Stannary jurisdiction.

Why was it that some occupational groups supported one side, while others supported another? In the case of the tin-miners, the explanation is pretty clear. As we have seen, tinners received many benefits from the Stannary system as working miners possessed rights and privileges which placed them above the common law.[35] Obviously tensions arose from this. The miners' privileges were actively resented by the surrounding countrymen and remonstrances against the tinners were presented in several national Parliaments.[36] There were also jurisdictional disputes between the Warden and the county JPs, who saw the Stannaries' exemption from their authority as a personal affront.[37] Yet the Crown upheld the tinners against every attack and their opponents were continually thwarted. The tinners did not scruple to challenge the authority of Parliament itself, and once imprisoned an MP for an alleged breach of Stannary Law.[38] By the 1630s, however, the Stannaries were in crisis. Tin prices had long been in decline and the Dartmoor seams were becoming exhausted. The tinners petitioned the King for assistance in 1636, pleading that the price of tin should be artificially raised in order to protect their livelihoods.[39] Once again, Royal help was forthcoming and prices were accordingly increased. Yet the episode had served to demonstrate just how reliant the tinners really were upon the monarchy, so it is hardly suprising that the tinners rallied to Charles I in 1642–46.

Their economic well-being was completely dependent upon the monarchy, for Royal support was all that prevented the collapse of the tin industry. The privileges and tax-exemptions which cushioned the miners from the full effects of the slump were also derived solely from Royal favour. Economic reasons aside, the tinners' long-standing feud with the county authorities doubtless helped to ensure that, when the latter chose to support Parliament, the former would swing the other way. In any case the Stannary had its own differences with Parliament, and the tinners were well aware that their juridical privileges were looked upon with hostility by the national assembly.

Can similarly plausible explanations be found for the political predilections of the county's seamen? It should be pointed out at once that the Devon mariners were by no means unique in their affection for Parliament. Historians have long recognized that, across the country as a whole, seafaring men were amongst the most determined opponents of the King.[40] This may well reflect the fact that seamen were unusually exposed to new ideas and influences. Through trade links with other regions and countries, mariners came into contact with radical systems of thought, and this must have encouraged them to ponder on radical ideas themselves. Seamen were also unusually literate (probably because of the long periods of enforced idleness which their trade entailed), again exposing them to all sorts of influences. Studies of Restoration Bristol have shown that seamen possessed the highest literacy rate of all occupational groups below the gentry. Some 86 per cent of Bristol seamen were able to sign their names in 1660, and no doubt even more were able to read.[41] This high rate of literacy may well have prevailed in the period 1600–40 as well.

Other explanations for the seamen's Parliamentarianism could also be advanced. This particular group had been at the forefront of the Elizabethan wars against Spain. Many seamen had suffered at the hands of the Inquisition, and it may well be that they retained a particular hatred of catholicism as a result. Mariners may also have been more conscious than landsmen of a general 'popish threat', because they had a better idea of the situation in the rest of Europe. It is also worth pointing out that seafaring communities were less tightly controlled by local elites than were inland, agricultural parishes. Many of the men engaged in the Newfoundland fisheries spent a good part of the year away from home, effectively removed from clerical and gentry supervision.

This may well have been significant, contributing to a distancing from the hierarchical landed society of which the King himself was the capstone.

These are general points which would be applicable to seamen across the country as a whole. How might the experiences of Devon mariners in particular have predisposed them to favour Parliament? The events of the 1620s may well be crucial here as Devon mariners had suffered greatly as a result of the expeditions which Charles I sent to Cadiz and the Isle of Rhe. Thousands of local seamen were impressed at this time, many only to die of disease and neglect in the Royal fleet. Conditions were so bad that, in March 1628, a mutiny broke out amongst the sailors. One hundred newly-pressed men seized control of Plymouth Guildhall and openly defied their officers. The disturbance was quickly suppressed, yet when the authorities tried to hang one of the ringleaders 'the mariners resorted to [Plymouth] Hoe, tore down the gallows and cast it into the sea'. The seamen then surged into Plymouth itself in order 'to force the prison'.[42] The violence of these disorders provides powerful testimony of the mariners' discontent.

Angry murmurs persisted amongst the sailors for months afterwards, and their resentment can only have been fuelled by the havoc which the war was wreaking on local maritime industries.[43] There was 'an almost total cessation of fishing activity' in Devon between 1625 and 1630.[44] Economic hardship, combined with the effects of plague and billeting, devastated the South Devon ports during the late 1620s. Nor did the lot of local seamen improve much after the wars came to an end. Piracy was endemic in the South-West during this period and hundreds, even thousands, of local mariners were carried off as prisoners by the Muslim corsairs.[45] Anguished protests went up from the seafaring communities, but, for what must have seemed an agonisingly long time, little effective action was taken. As a result trade suffered badly, seamen dared not put to sea, and more and more mariners were carried off into captivity. During the early 1630s resentment against the government was running high. One naval officer complained of the 'disrespect' shown to the Royal fleet by South-Western merchants, while it was reported from Plymouth in 1633 that 'no ships [are] more stubborn and unwilling to give his Majesty's ships respect than our own merchants. They hate all gentlemen, especially such as serve his Majesty at sea'.[46] The

Royal fleets paid for by Ship Money may have done something to ease local resentment. Even so, it seems probable that the enthusiasm with which the Devon seamen embraced the Parliamentary cause in 1642 owed much to the harassment and neglect which they had endured at the hands of Charles I's government during the previous seventeen years.

It is more difficult to find specific explanations for the Parliamentarianism of the clothworkers and the townsmen. No doubt many of the points made above in relation to seafaring communities applied to clothing districts and urban areas as well. In these communities too, literacy rates were higher than in the country (possibly because clothworkers, like seamen, but unlike agricultural labourers, had the opportunity to study books while they were working).[47] In these communities too, there was a greater receptiveness to new ideas, partly as a result of business contacts,[48] and elite control tended to be less absolute than in agrarian parishes. In addition it is probably true to say that the economic vulnerability of the clothworkers made them more susceptible to radical ideas and even, perhaps, more prone to insurrection. Robert Cecil believed that 'the people that depend upon making of cloth are of worse condition to be quietly governed than the husbandmen', while John Aubrey claimed that the meagre wages of the Wiltshire spinners kept them 'but just alive', so 'they steal hedges, spoil coppices and are trained up as nurseries of sedition and rebellion'.[49] Aubrey's comments support the view of the Civil War as a class struggle, implying that it was the grinding poverty of the clothworkers which had eroded their respect for traditional values and thus, by extension, for the system of government itself.[50] Whether or not this view is correct, what little evidence there is for political radicalism amongst the common people of pre-war Devon is certainly associated with the cloth industry.[51]

The final subject which needs to be addressed is that of personal mobility. The influence of new ideas has already been examined, but the influence of incomers may well have been just as important in determining the political allegiance of a parish.[52] Significantly, the types of community which provided most support for Parliament in Devon were also those in which turnover of population was high. Cloth districts possessed fluctuating, unstable, populations, as did the larger towns, while there was a very high rate of internal migration amongst local sailors.[53] In the remote moorland parishes of Central Devon, by contrast, population turnover seems to have been low. Of the forty-eight family names recorded at Lustleigh between 1600 and 1634, twenty-one (44 per cent) could still be found there in 1700–34.[54] Similarly, of the 107 family names recorded at Widecombe between 1600 and 1634, fifty-four (51 per cent) were still there in 1700–34.[55] These figures compare strikingly with those for parishes elsewhere in England. At Honiger, Suffolk, only 3 per cent of the family names recorded in 1600–34 were still there in 1700–24.[56] It may well be that stable populations helped to preserve more traditional social, cultural and religious attitudes, and that these attitudes in turn contributed to popular Royalism.

Many aspects of traditional theories about the effect of economic occupation on Civil War allegiance have received at least qualified support from this survey. In Devon, Parliamentarianism does indeed seem to have been centred upon the ports, the larger urban communities and the clothing districts, while Royalism was concentrated in the rural areas and smaller towns. Some general trends can be identified, therefore, and these trends accord with those which have been identified by previous historians. It is also possible to find plausible reasons to explain why some occupational groups should have favoured the King, others the Parliament. Yet time and again, exceptions have been found to the general rules posited above. Most of the tinners supported the King, but those from the countryside around Plymouth did not.[57] Most of the larger urban communities supported the Parliament, but Tavistock, and perhaps Exeter, did not. The majority of the Devon cloth towns supported the Parliament, but Axminster, Bradninch and Ottery did not. Even in the case of the seamen, where the fit between occupation and allegiance seems most nearly exact, there are inconsistencies. The Exe estuary port of Topsham clearly favoured the King, for example. One can only concur with Underdown when he suggests that the effect of economic occupation upon popular allegiances could always be overridden by 'other factors'.[58] Yet what were these other factors? Inexorably, our attention is drawn back to religion and politics.

Chapter 9

'True Blades for Liberties': Pre-war Opposition to the Caroline Regime

Writing in 1972 Eugene Andriette described the years 1625–40 as a time of growing discontent in Devon, a period in which Royal policy 'irritated and antagonised the populace and created opposition, ... opposition which could be built upon and enlarged by a daring leadership'.[1] Since Andriette wrote these words the tidal wave of revisionism has swept away many of the old historical certainties. Few scholars today would be prepared to make such bold statements about the existence of a pre-war opposition, let alone its smooth transformation into wartime Parliamentarianism, without a great deal of supporting evidence. Nevertheless an attempt to relate pre-war political attitudes to wartime behaviour and allegiance must be made. Did the fact that Devon was a broadly Parliamentarian county reflect particularly strong pre-war antagonism among local people towards the policies of the Crown?

The attitude of the local governors

During the first four years of Charles I's reign, Devon's Deputy Lieutenants and JPs made many trenchant criticisms of Royal policy. This is hardly surprising, for the military expeditions which the King launched from Plymouth during these years brought misery upon the entire county. Decay of trade and the billeting of thousands of unruly soldiers reduced many people to miserable poverty.[2] Desperate to relieve their countrymen, local governors made numerous complaints to the Privy Council during 1625 and 1626.[3] Yet these petitions met with no effective response, nor even 'so much as a cordial answer'.[4] By mid-1626 tempers were rising. In July three local gentlemen wrote to the Council, setting out the county's burdens and noting that, to these self-evident ills in Devon's body politic, 'your own ... judgements will add (as the worst of evil signs) an apparent distraction in the head by our rude and passionate letters'.[5] This was a clear warning that Crown policies were alienating local governors, leading them to abandon their customary habits of deference. Even so billeting was resumed in 1627. Not until the Lord Lieutenant himself joined the chorus of protest did the Council finally free the county from soldiers.[6]

Billeting was not the only grievance to exercise local governors, during the late 1620s, for these years also saw the imposition of a series of unpopular taxes. Resistance to the levy known as the Forced Loan was not particularly strong in Devon. This was chiefly because the Crown agreed that monies raised locally should be handed back to the billeters.[7] Even so, the loan was clearly seen as a grievance, and when demands for more money went out in 1628 the Devon JPs flatly refused to co-operate. In a letter to the Council they stated that 'the summe enjoined to be leavied ... is not to be raised ... out of this county by any means'. Only 'extremities' could force local people to contribute, they said, adding pointedly that such extremities 'had need be backt by Law'.[8] Richard Cust has suggested that the letter was part of a wider campaign, aimed at preventing Charles from raising money through extraordinary means and thus at forcing him to summon a Parliament.[9] It was rumoured in 1629 that the Devon Deputies were so unhappy with Crown policy that they were planning to petition Charles I to halt 'innovations in the Commonwealth'.[10]

Open protest subsided following the dissolution of the 1629 Parliament. Yet throughout the Personal Rule of 1629–40 (the period during which Charles I ruled England alone, without Parliaments) intermittent criticisms of Crown policy continued to be voiced. In 1634, for example, five Devon JPs were summoned before the Council for expressing doubts about the financial levy known as Ship Money.[11] Following Scotland's rebellion against the King in 1637, criticism became more explicit. In 1639 Justice Finch had to manoeuvre to prevent a grand jury presentment against Ship Money at Exeter, while in the elections to the Short

Parliament of April 1640 Devon returned several 'oppositionist' MPs.[12] After the Short Parliament's dissolution, the Devonshire Deputies were ordered to raise 2,000 men to serve against the Scots. Somehow they managed to do so, but when the conscripts were ordered to march, a serious mutiny ensued. An officer was murdered, and the Deputies themselves were insulted and harangued. This was the last straw for the local governors. Hitherto they had carried out the King's orders as best they could, but now it seemed that Crown policy was threatening the peace of the entire county, and their own local reputations besides. Fearful of popular disturbances, Devon's ruling class effectively suspended its support for the regime.[13]

In September 1640 a petition against Royal ecclesiastical policies was presented to the Privy Council by a delegation of Devon gentry.[14] An official at first offered to read the document out, 'but looking upon the names of the petitioners and observing the tenour of the same [he then] refused ... to tender it' for fear of incurring the Council's wrath. When the petition eventually was read, the councillors were sharply disapproving and the names of the petition's gentry sponsors were taken down. One councillor claimed that the petition bore witness to an unlawful 'League', while another 'said with a soft voice, it seems the gentlemen of Devon have more witt than this board'.[15] Devon's local governors were not intimidated by this hostile reception. Some weeks later the Deputies and JPs wrote a letter to the Council in which they politely but firmly refused to send any more troops to the North. The twenty-one gentry subscribers cited the county's vulnerability to attack and the lack of money to pay the men. In addition they openly questioned the legality of the Commission of Array, which had been sent down to Devon in September. The letter concluded by expressing the hope that the forthcoming Parliament would 'quiet all disputes about these necessary services'.[16] The missive demonstrates a quite striking willingness to disobey Royal orders and slight Royal authority.

Does the frequency with which Devon's local governors criticized Royal policy between 1625 and 1640 explain the county's later Parliamentarianism? Not necessarily, for Cornwall was also forward in complaining against Crown policy during these years, but later behaved very differently. Like Devon, Cornwall protested against billeting, muttered against the Forced Loan, fulminated against the expense of Ship Money and complained about having to send troops to the North.[17] Between 1625 and 1640 the two counties reacted to Royal policy in very similar ways. Yet, when war broke out in 1642, Cornwall sided with the King, Devon with the Parliament. This suggests that pre-war political attitudes were not the decisive factor in determining wartime allegiance. Analysis of those Devon gentlemen who put their names to criticisms of Crown policy in 1639–40 points the same way. Andriette claimed that the thirty-eight men who signed the petition of September 1640 were 'supporters of the Parliament'.[18] Yet the true picture is more complicated. Eighteen of the signatories were indeed future Parliamentarians, but of the others fourteen went on to support the King.[19] Similar divisions can be seen amongst those who signed the letter questioning the legality of the Commission of Array. Of the twenty-one individuals who subscribed this document, eleven were future Parliamentarians yet eight went on to support the King.[20] Amongst the latter was John Peter, described in 1642 as 'a great Array man'.[21] Peter's opinions had clearly undergone a sea change between 1640 and 1642.

The apparent disparity between pre-war and wartime attitudes has often been remarked on. R.N. Worth noted with some surprise in 1895 that William Coryton, the MP who had been such a thorn in the government's side during the 1620s, eventually became a Royalist.[22] More recently, John Morrill has shown that, although the Cheshire gentleman William Davenport filled his commonplace book with criticisms of Royal policy during the 1620s and 1630s, he eventually took up arms for the King.[23] Such studies appear to confirm that an individual's pre-war political opinions had little or no bearing on the side which he eventually chose to take during the Civil War. But is such an argument really credible? Do we really enter a new world in 1642, one which had been turned so thoroughly upside down that previous political convictions were no longer of any importance? Or did certain traditions of political behaviour, both individual and communal, survive the turmoil of the Long Parliament's opening months and emerge as support for one or other of the two warring sides? Amongst the Royalists such continuity is hard to discern. There were few indeed who ardently supported the policies of the Personal Rule, especially during its latter years, and many historians have commented on the King's dismally narrow base of support in 1640.[24] To suggest the existence of a large group of pre-war monarchist ultras, delighting in the abrogation of parliaments and eagerly queuing up to pay their Ship Money, would be absurd. Yet it is harder to deny the existence of a proto-Parliamentarian group. Scraps of evidence suggest that, in Devon as elsewhere, certain individuals kept up a principled opposition to the pre-war policies of the Crown.

Evidence of individual opposition

Conducting a survey of political dissent in Caroline Devon is difficult, for outright opposition to Crown policy was scarcely ever voiced. Nevertheless, it would be unwise to presume that such sentiments did not exist. One need not posit a reign of terror or Stuart despotism to appreciate why critics of Royal policy might have been reluctant to commit their opinions to paper. While it is impossible to prove the existence of a coherent ideology of opposition in Devon, the frequency with which certain individuals came up against the Crown is suggestive. Ignatius Jurdain, the Exeter alderman, provides a good example. As early as 1618 a local man claimed that 'there were some in the Citty that didd not love the Kinge and didd not care yf he were dead or hanged'. It is clear that he had Jurdain in mind.[25] Over the succeeding years Jurdain frequently opposed Royal policy, refusing to contribute to the Forced Loan, speaking and writing against the Book of Sports (which ordered that people should be permitted to enjoy sports and recreations on Sundays) and showing a very public disapproval of the Scots War. Jurdain seldom pulled his punches. So vehement was his hostility to the 'Dancing Book', indeed, that the King complained that a letter Jurdain had sent him on the subject 'seemed to call his prerogative into question'. Charles angrily threatened to hang Jurdain.[26] Yet despite the King's hostility, Ignatius retained his local position throughout the period 1629–40.[27]

Few possessed Jurdain's ability to combine principle and outspokeness with political survival. But others clearly shared in his opposition to Crown policy. Walter Yonge of Colyton kept a diary which can only be described as an opposition document.[28] Similar, though much more muted, criticisms can be seen in the chronicle of the Exeter merchant James White.[29] In the section of this manuscript which deals with the period 1625–40, White makes few personal judgements on national events. Yet the evidence of his chronicle should not be dismissed on this account, for the political stance of Caroline diarists is often revealed by the events which they chose to record.[30] It may well be significant that in White's chronicle Charles I's accession is juxtaposed with the fact that there was 'a great sickness in London'. That White was no admirer of Charles I's favourite, the Duke of Buckingham can be gleaned from his reference to the Duke's physician, Dr Lambe, as 'a man of dissolute conversation'.[31]

From 1639 onwards the chronicle becomes less impersonal. In 1639 White recorded his impression that religious radicals were becoming more numerous, and noted that they had been punished severely (is there a note of criticism here?) by the court of High Commission.[32] In 1640 he commented that 'the Parliament affaires goe on ... with good successe', and in 1641 he referred to the London mob's desire for justice on 'delinquents', gave thanks for the discovery of the Army Plot and noted the King's declaration 'that his subjects of Scotland were good subjects'. By early 1642 White was plainly in the Parliamentarian camp, but even now he remained nervous about committing his opinions to paper. A comment that 'Lord George Digbie much infested the Kingdom' was later thought better of and crossed out.[33] Sadly, White's chronicle ends in October 1642. Almost certainly this was because he himself had now become swept up in national events. In November 1642 White enlisted as a Parliamentary Captain.[34]

It is significant that both White and Yonge eventually became Parliamentarians. For these men, at least, it is possible to demonstrate continuity in opposition throughout the pre-war and wartime periods. Did similar continuities exist at less exalted social levels? In Devon, as elsewhere, evidence about the political attitude of individual commoners is almost non-existent, however, much can be learnt by examining broader patterns of behaviour. This has been admirably demonstrated by Richard Cust, who has shown that most of the subsidymen who refused to pay the Forced Loan in Essex came from areas in which puritan influence was strong.[35] Cust's discoveries not only suggest that principled popular resistance to Royal policies existed, they also tend to confirm that patterns of popular behaviour could differ widely across a single county. How much evidence is there for popular resistance to Crown policies in pre-war Devon?

Popular opposition to Crown policy: Mutiny

Crown policy sparked off two major disturbances in Devon between 1625 and 1640. The first of these was the sailors' mutiny of 1628 described in Chapter Eight, p. 159. Little more needs to be said about this incident, except to stress that the participants were all mariners—members of an occupational group which later proved overwhelmingly hostile to the King—and that the mutiny took place at Plymouth, later a bulwark of the Parliamentary cause. The second major disturbance was the soldiers' mutiny of July 1640. This incident centred upon a group of 600 North Devon conscripts who had been impressed to fight the Scots. On 11 July these men arrived at Tiverton where they were met by Lieutenant-Colonel Gibson, the officer who was to conduct them on their march. Gibson led the first company of soldiers away soon afterwards, assisted by a young lieutenant named Compton Evers. That night the unit quartered at Wellington in Somerset and the troops remained there all the next day. This period of enforced idleness was to have disastrous results.[36]

During the course of 12 July, a Sunday, the soldiers noticed that Lieutenant Evers had not attended church and suspicions were immediately aroused that the young officer was a catholic. Towards dusk, the soldiers made their way to the house where Evers was quartered. Scores of angry men were soon milling around in the street outside. Some broke into the building, while others climbed upon the roof and began to rip off the tiles above the lieutenant's chamber. Eventually three of the boldest forced their way into Evers's room, and the terrified lieutenant was dragged from his lodgings by main force. An eye-witness recalled that the soldiers pulled Evers 'out of his chamber, dragging him by the armes and legges downe the staires & soe into the street'. Once he had been brought out, the soldiers 'fell upon him and beate him violently ... with theire cudgells', continuing to belabour him 'both with swordes and staves untill they had killed him'.[37]

As Evers lay dying the mutineers stripped his body. One of the soldiers took the lieutenant's money, while another tore off his pockets. A third man took 'from about [Evers'] necke a crucifixe tyed in a riband', proof of the murdered officer's catholicism. Afterwards Evers's body was left lying in the street and not until the next morning was the corpse carried to a nearby inn. With Evers dead the soldiers 'took occasion to retire', deserting their officers and hurrying back to Devon. As they went they boasted of what they had done, crowing exultantly 'that they had dispatched theire Lieutenante'.[38] News of the mutiny soon reached another company of soldiers, who promptly 'forsook all command and returned home'. According to one account these men 'called upon the drummer to beat a march back, crying out that they would not march forward unless they were led by their own county conductors'.[39] With one company in open rebellion and another dispersed to the four winds, the panic-stricken deputies ordered the entire force of North Devon soldiers to disband. But this was not enough to quell the disturbances and the mutineers refused to disperse. Instead they remained in arms, 100 strong, openly defying the deputies' orders.[40] It was not until 12 August, a month after Evers's death, that the principal suspects were interrogated. What happened in the interval is unclear but the mutineers may well have remained at large for some time.[41]

The mutiny of July 1640 was probably the most serious popular disturbance to occur in Devon between the Western Rising of 1549 and the Civil War itself. That it broke out in Wellington, of all places, is significant, for the town was later a hotbed of Parliamentarianism (the term 'Wellington Roundhead' became proverbial in Somerset, just as 'Moreton Roundhead' did in Devon). It is hard to resist the suspicion that the townsfolk had a hand in the mutiny, certainly they did nothing to stop it.[42] The places of residence of the soldiers who actually killed Evers are also significant. Of those who were examined or sought in connection with Evers's death, nine came from Bishop's Nympton and South Molton, and the remaining twelve from the nearby parishes of Landkey, Chawleigh, West Anstey, Chittlehampton, Bishops Tawton, Oakford, Rackenford, Swimbridge, and Witheridge.[43] This was a zealously Parliamentarian area during the Civil War, and South Molton was the centre of a huge popular demonstration against the Royalist Commissioners of Array in 1642 (see Chapter Two, pp. 39–40). It is surely no coincidence that the men who took part in Evers's murder were drawn from these particular communities.

Popular opposition to Crown policy: The Exmoor tithes

The mutiny of July 1640 provides an impressive example of active popular resistance to pre-war Caroline policies. Yet displays of passive resistance (which were much more frequent) are equally worthy of attention. During the 1630s, attempts to augment the Royal revenues through improvement and enclosure met with resistance right across England.[44] Devon also suffered at the hands of court-backed 'improvers' during this period and in one corner of the county a major dispute blew up. Although this affair has been ignored by most historians, its impact on local affairs was considerable. The controversy centred upon the Royal Forest of Exmoor, a moorland district lying on the Devon/Somerset border.

Exmoor was used for the pasture of 'great numbers of sheep, cattle and horse beasts' during the early Stuart period.[45] Some 30–40,000 sheep were pastured here annually, and animals were brought in from all over North Devon. Those who wished to graze their animals in the forest had to pay the King's under-forester for the privilege but, as the fees had remained unchanged since 1570, local people were getting something of a bargain. In 1629 prices were suddenly raised. The countryfolk were outraged, and were well enough organized to send to Taunton for legal advice. Nevertheless, the new rates remained in force, and in 1630 local people became aware of a Royal plan to deforest Exmoor altogether and abolish the privileges which the inhabitants of nearby parishes enjoyed. Such a scheme had been suggested once before and had only been scrapped after strenuous local resistance. Much to the relief of 'the country', the second proposal eventually went the way of the first.[46] But the scare of 1630 heralded a sustained Royal attack upon local privileges.

The Crown's attention had first been drawn to Exmoor by a case in the Court of Exchequer. Traditionally, sheep kept in the Royal forest had been exempt from tithes. Local clergymen attempted to challenge this exemption in 1628, but the Exchequer upheld the status quo, ruling that the parsons possessed no right to tithe. Yet the Court also stated that if the money due for pasturing animals on Exmoor belonged to anyone, it belonged to the King. Crown officials, ever alert for profit, siezed on this. In 1633 the Exmoor tithes were awarded to George Cottington, probably a relative of Francis Cottington, the Chancellor. It was not long before George arrived in North Devon demanding that local farmers should pay him his tithes. Naturally enough these activities greatly 'vex[ed] the country'. Many tried to ignore Cottington's claims, but in 1634 he commenced a series of suits against his opponents. Prominent amongst those assailed was Humphrey Venner, the under-forester, but Cottington troubled all sorts of smaller fry too, issuing process against 100 of the 2,000 local people who kept sheep on the moor.[47]

The farmers tried to resist Cottington, but the courts consistently found in his favour. As a result local people stopped sending their animals to the moor altogether, and the number of sheep annually depastured on Exmoor fell from 43,000 to 16,000. This was ruinous for Venner, the under-forester, whose livelihood depended on the pasturage fee. In 1637 he was forced to raise the fee once again, this time to 3s. 4d. per beast. No doubt this caused even more farmers to keep their sheep away, contributing still further to the spiral of decay into which Exmoor's economy had fallen. The shepherds feared they would be ruined and complaints about Cottington's activities continued to be voiced until 1641.[48] Clearly the grant of the Exmoor tithes to Cottington, a man whose very name revealed his intimate links with Royal officials, had stirred up an immense amount of resentment against the Crown. Such sentiments surely contributed to the wartime Parliamentarianism of the district around Exmoor.[49]

Patterns of resistance:
Billeting and the Forced Loan

How much resistance did other Crown policies stir up in Devon? Elsewhere in England there are interesting continuities between pre-war opposition to billeting and Parliamentarianism.[50] The universal opposition which billeting encountered in Devon makes it difficult to identify particular centres of resistance here. The sheer number of men imposed on the county, and the incompetent way in which they were supplied (or, in most cases, were not) meant that even the most conformable local communities were bound to complain. Yet with this said, the countryside around Plymouth clearly suffered more than anywhere else.[51] Once the soldiers had gone, bitterness may well have remained particularly strong in this district and also in those places which had to wait longest to be repaid. In 1631 ten North Devon hundreds were still trying to recover money laid out on billet in 1627–28, while Tiverton was still owed £160 in 1634.[52]

Patterns of resistance to the Forced Loan are slightly easier to discern. Thirteen East Devon men were reported to the Council in February 1627 for their 'refractory contempt' in refusing to lend. Five months later a second list of fifteen 'able ... [but] refractory persons whose examples have been very prejudiciall to this service' was compiled, while in September the names of twenty-four defaulters were sent up from Exeter.[53] From these lists it is possible to identify two main centres of resistance to the loan. The first is Exeter and the second is the cloth district of north-east Devon. Of the twenty-four 'refractory persons' recorded from the county as a whole (Exeter excluded), thirteen came from here. Moreover, these were only the most prominent among 'diverse others within the hundreds of Haydridge, Hemyock, Bampton, Halberton and Tiverton ... who have refused to pay'.[54] It is tempting to conclude that north-east Devon was the area in which popular opposition to the loan was strongest.[55] Resistance apparently centred upon the cloth town of Collumpton as four of those informed against came from here. Cullompton was later a Parliamentarian town, so it may be significant that such a large proportion of the defaulters came from this area.

Patterns of resistance: Ship Money

Another way of gauging patterns of resistance to Crown policy is to examine Devon's reaction to the Ship Money levies of 1634–40. This tax (technically a service, or payment in lieu) was levied by the Crown in order to provide money for the strengthening of the Royal fleet. Towards the end of the 1630s there were complaints that the tax was unconstitutional and, across the country as a whole, many people refused to pay on grounds of principle.[56] As one of England's wealthiest shires, Devon was expected to provide large sums of money towards the shipping rate—as much as £9,000 in 1639–40. This was a considerable sum and the Sheriffs met with bitter complaints of inability to pay.[57] Such grumbling was to be expected, however, and it did little to impede the service. Generally speaking, the Sheriffs were very successful in raising the sums assessed upon the county. Thus the Ship Money demanded in 1635–36 was 'wholly paid', as was all but £19 of the sum requested in 1636–37.[58] Collection became appreciably harder during 1637–38 and 1638–39, but despite this, Sir John Pole, Sheriff in the latter year, received a congratulatory note from the Privy Council for his achievements.[59] Only in 1639–40, when resistance to Ship Money hardened across the entire kingdom, did local payments cease. And even in 1640 the prospects for compliance at first seemed relatively good. As late as February 1640 a local man could claim that, in spite of Devon's large assessment, 'there [is] no grudging, so as I think we are the King's best subjects'.[60]

Most Devonians acquiesced in the tax, therefore, almost certainly because—as residents of a county which depended on the sea and had suffered particularly badly from piracy—they appreciated the need for a strong navy.[61] Yet not everyone felt the same way. Sheriff Rolle noted in 1637 that some were so refractory over Ship Money that they deserved physical punishment.[62] There is good reason to think that these malcontents were concentrated in particular areas of the county. Thomas Drewe reported in 1635 that he had sent his undersheriff to distrain and imprison in 'those parts … that are … slow', while in 1640 Sheriff Martin observed that 'some hundreds and parishes do yet stand out and refuse to pay'.[63] Both comments imply that opposition to the tax was stronger in some areas than others. It was the corporate towns which were most obdurate. Drewe reported in 1635 that 'the towns are slow', while his successor observed that 'from the towns corporate he has only received £30, [though] £1250 is due from them'.[64] Sheriff Thomas Wise noted in January 1639 that 'there is about £600 due from the corporations', and in April they still owed him £100.[65]

Between 1634 and 1640 petitions about Ship Money poured into Whitehall from the Devon towns. Which communities complained the most? Unsurprisingly, it was those which had been assessed at the highest amount and of the five towns ordered to contribute £100 or more, at least four made representations to the Council. Exeter was the most restrained in its protests. The town governors limited themselves to an observation that the Ship Money for 1638 would be levied with 'much more difficulty than the former rates' and a request for more time to collect arrears.[66] Totnes made more of a fuss. In 1636 and again in 1639, local officials sent woeful letters to the Council, complaining about the town's decay and the difficulty of extracting the requisite sums from the townsfolk. It was asked that the town's assessment should be reduced.[67] Tiverton tried to get out of paying altogether. In 1634 the inhabitants petitioned that they were still owed £160 for billeting and were therefore unable to raise 'the sum now imposed on them for shipping', a complaint which, as Kevin Sharpe observes, had 'broader implications' than usual.[68]

Yet of all the Devon towns it was Barnstaple which complained most bitterly. Ostensibly at least, the townsmen's grievance stemmed from the fact that they considered themselves to have been unfairly assessed. At the initial meeting to fix the county assessments, Barnstaple had been rated at £100. The Barumites felt this sum to be excessive, and claimed that their town was decayed and that the assessment should be reduced. Far from reducing the original sum, however, the Sheriff and representatives of other local towns decided to increase it, to £150. The Barumites were outraged. In 1635 the Mayor petitioned the Council, begging that Barnstaple's contribution should be reduced to £85 and stating that the inhabitants were utterly unable to pay the higher sum.[69] This petition was met with indifference by the Councillors, who noted that 'since they could not prevail with their neighbours, who best know the ability of that town, the Council think it not fit to alter what has been assessed'.[70] Barnstaple remained obstinate and in March 1635 the Council was forced to administer a harsh rebuke to the town, berating the townsmen for their 'undutiful and refractory carriage ... towards his Majesty's service', and complaining of Barnstaple's 'great neglect and backwardness in the execution of his Majesty's writ (the like whereof hath not been found from any part of the Kingdom)'.[71] The Crown's displeasure could hardly have been made more plain. Even so, the inhabitants of Barnstaple continued to make bitter representations against their assessment but none met with any success.[72]

There are echoes here of previous disputes. Between 1600 and 1630, Barnstaple had frequently refused to pay its share of local rates and, always, the townsmen had put forward the 'decay' of their town as an excuse, though never to any avail. By the late 1630s the Barumites clearly felt themselves to be very hard done by. A remarkable memorandum of November 1637 survives among the town records, in which the Corporation bitterly complains that 'we ... of Barnstaple do find by daily experience, that through the envy of others maligning the prosperities of this town, we have many heavy burdens laid upon us, and are ... like to be without remedies, unless we may procure the assistance of some great man, who is powerful at the Court and Counsel board'.[73] This memorandum neatly encapsulates two of the Barumites' chief grievances; the excessively heavy burden of Ship

Money and other rates, and the failure of the Earl of Bath (who lived nearby and might have been expected to act as 'Good Lord' to the town) to defend their interests at Court. The reference to 'the envy of others, maligning the prosperities of this town' suggests a hint of paranoia. One gets the picture of a community which felt itself to be isolated and under attack: by the local magnate, by its own neighbours, and even, perhaps, by the central authorities.[74]

The fuss made over Ship Money by Barnstaple, Tiverton and Totnes was untypical. Of Devon's smaller towns, those rated at £80 or less, only one—Plympton—is known to have complained about Ship Money.[75] The smaller towns generally paid up without too much trouble, and this was also true of Plymouth. The Mayor informed the Council in 1635 that he had collected the Ship Money imposed upon the town. His appended comment, that 'it is heavy upon them, but they are willinger than able to undergo the service', implies that while the Plymothians were poor, they saw the need for the tax to be raised.[76]

That resistance really was stronger in Exeter, Totnes, Tiverton and Barnstaple than elsewhere is confirmed by a document which was drawn up by Sheriff Thomas Wise listing all those who were in arrears for the Ship Money payment of 1637. Wise's memorandum deals chiefly with the rural areas, but a brief schedule notes the sums still due from the corporate towns. Only five communities are named. One is Bideford, which owed £8. The other four towns referred to are those which were noted above as particularly recalcitrant; Exeter (which owed £35), Totnes (which owed £4 18s), Barnstaple (which owed £11 12s.) and Tiverton (which owed no less than £130).[77] As well as noting the sums due from the towns, Wise's list sets out the names and residences of 881 individuals (often quite humble ones) who had failed to pay their Ship Money. The document thus provides a valuable snapshot of patterns of local resistance to the tax.

Of those who had failed to pay, the smallest number lived in the South Hams. Only seventy-nine of the defaulters, just 9 per cent of the total, dwelt here. We have already seen that the South Devon ports made few complaints about Ship Money. It may well be that, because South Devon possessed more fishermen and merchants than other parts of the county, and because it had suffered more severely from pirates, it was more willing to contribute to the levy. Mid-Devon produced a few more defaulters, but here too, numbers were relatively small (121 non-payers, 14 per cent of the county total). Between them, Mid-Devon and the South Hams supplied only 22 per cent of the county's defaulters. Over 75 per cent of those who refused to pay came from the North and the East. The precise figures are 236 defaulters (27 per cent of the total) from North Devon, and 445 defaulters (a massive 51 per cent of the total) from East Devon.[78]

Cullompton was the community which produced the largest number of defaulters, 128 in all. Next came Colyton, Newton Abbot and Crediton with sixty-nine, thirty-eight and twenty-six defaulters respectively. Then came Beer, Bishops Nymet, Braunton, Churston Ferrers, Chulmleigh, East Down and Rockbeare —all with more than twelve persons refusing to pay.[79] The distribution of the defaulters provides further evidence of continuity between pre-war opposition and Parliamentarianism. This can be seen from Map 2 (p. 53) and Map 8. Map 2 shows the pattern of wartime support for Parliament and Map 8 the areas which refused to pay Ship Money or demonstrated other kinds of resistance to the Crown during 1625–40. Comparison of the two maps shows that pre-war and wartime dissent were rooted in broadly the same locations. During 1642–46 support for Parliament was strongest in North and north-east Devon, and in the towns, ports and clothing centres. During 1625–40 opposition to Crown policies was strongest in precisely the same areas. During 1642–46 individual communities like Tiverton, Barnstaple and Cullompton exhibited strong support for Parliament. During 1625–40 the same towns demonstrated a striking willingness to resist the Crown's financial exactions. The reverse is also true and in Mid-Devon, the region which demonstrated least wartime support for Parliament, there is very little sign of pre-war dissent.

The causes of opposition

What can account for these striking continuities? It could be argued that communities which had already opposed royal authority once would find it easier to do so again, having broken the habit of obedience. More broadly, one could cite the connection between poverty and resistance to taxation, suggesting that it was the poorest communities—those which had suffered most from pre-war exactions—which had felt most resentful towards the

Plate 1.   Royal Coat of Arms, St Martin's Church, Exeter, 1635. Concealed by the Royalist parishioners of St Martin's during the 1640s in order to protect it from Roundhead despoliation, this beautiful wooden panel remained hidden for almost 300 years. (Photograph by S. Goddard)

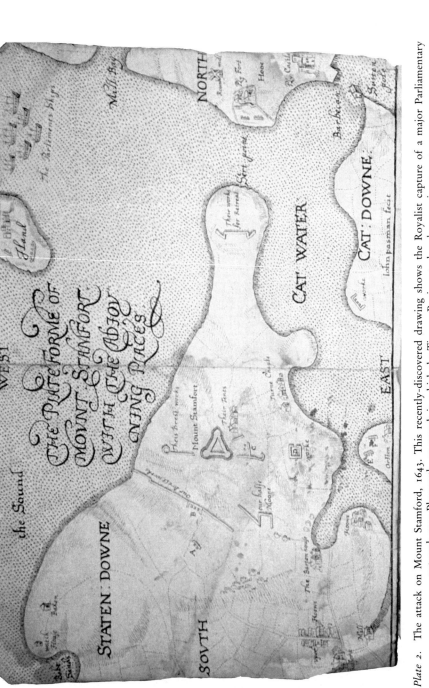

The Sound

WEST

The PLATEFORME OF MOUNT STANFORT WITH THE ADJOYNING PLACES

Milbay

NORTH

A Defensive Ships

Oyster Iland

Mount Stanfort

Plus bread worke

STATEN · DOWNE

SOVTH

Boat

The Burgen house

EAST

CAT · WATER

CAT · DOWNE.

Iohn pasman fecit

Plate 2. The attack on Mount Stamford, 1643. This recently-discovered drawing shows the Royalist capture of a major Parliamentary outwork near Plymouth, an assault in which the Tinners Regiment played a prominent part.

Plate 3. The Gidley Medal: struck after the Restoration to commemorate the loyal service of Bartholomew Gidley, Captain of the Tinners. (By permission of the British Museum).

Plate 4. Roof decoration, Throwleigh Church: showing the 'Tinners Rabbits', reputed to be the badge of the Devon tin-miners. (Photograph by C. Chapman)

(a)

Plate 5. Defaced images, Exeter Cathedral. These representations of Aaron (a) and Moses (b) formed part of the 'Helliar Reredos', a screen erected by a Laudian clergyman shortly before the Civil War. The faces were gouged and mutilated by puritan iconoclasts in 1643. (Photographs by D. Garner)

(b)

We are highly senſible of the extraordinary merit of our
County of Cornwall of their Zeal for the defence of our Perſ=
=on and the juſt rights of our Crown, in a time, when we cou-
-ld contribute so little to our own defence, or to their aſiſtance
in a time when not only no reward appeared, but great and
probable Dangers were threatned to obedience and **Loyalty**:
of their great and, eminent courage and patience in the ind-
-efatigable Proſecution of their great work againſt so potent
an enemy, backed with so ſtrong, rich, and populous Cities, and
plentifully furniſhed, and ſupplied with Men, Arms Money
Ammunition and, Proviſion of all kinds, and, of the wonderfull
Succeſs with which it hath pleaſed Almighty God, although
with the loſt of ſome moſt eminent Perſons, who ſhall never be
forgotten by us to reward their Loyalty and Patience by many
ſtrange Victories over their, and our Enemies, in diſpight of all
human Probability, and all imaginable Diſadvantages; that as
we can not be forgetfull of so great Deſerts, so we cannot but
deſire to publiſh to all the World, and perpetuate to all time, the
Memory of theſe their Merit, and of our acceptance of them;
and to that end, we do hereby render our Royal Thanks to
that our County, in the moſt publick, and laſting Manner
we can deviſe, Commanding, Copies hereof to be Printed
publiſhed, and one of them to be read in every Church, and
Chappel therein, and to be kept for ever as a Record in the
ſame, that as long as the Hiſtory of theſe Times, and of this Na-
-tion ſhall continue, the Memory of how much that County hath
merited from us, and our Crown, may be derived with it to Poſterity.
Given at our Camp at Sudely Caſtle, the tenth of Sep:
1643 His Majeſties Gratious letter to the County of Corn
wall, after the death of S:ʳ Bevill Grenville

Plate 6. Wall tablet, Landulph Church: reproducing Charles I's commendation of the
Cornish people for their loyalty. (Photograph by D. Garner)

The VVelſh-Mans Poſtures,

OR,

The true manner how her doe exercise her
company of Souldiers in her own Countrey in a
warlike manners with ſome other new-found
experiments, and pretty extravagants fitting
for all Chriſtian podies to caknow.

Vp Morgan. up Shinkin. Maurice.

Taſſie

f:6: 10

Printed in the yeare. When her did her enemy jeere, 1642.

Plate 7. 'The Welshman's Postures': Roundhead propaganda pamphlet, satirizing the
military prowess of the King's Welsh soldiers. (By permission of the British Library)

Plate 9. The Three Crowns Inn, Chagford: showing the porch in which Sidney Godolphin is reputed to have died. (Photograph by M. Stoyle)

Plate 8. The village of Dunsford with, in the background, the church which was the site of Captain Nicholas Vaughan's murder in December 1642. (Photograph by M. Stoyle)

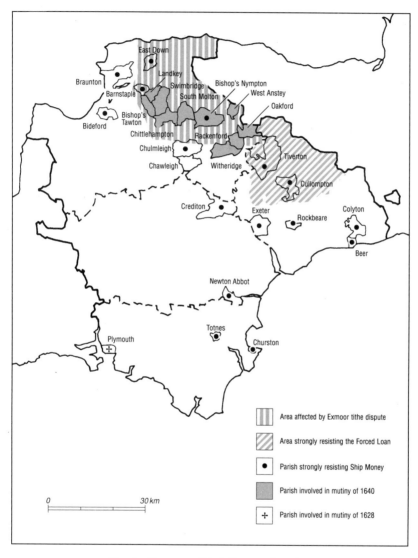

East Down

Landkey

Braunton

Swimbridge

Bishop's Nympton

West Anstey

Barnstaple

South Molton

Oakford

Bishop's
Tawton

Bideford

Chittlehampton

Rackenford

Chulmleigh

Chawleigh

Witheridge

Tiverton

Cullompton

Crediton

Exeter

Rockbeare

Colyton

Beer

Newton Abbot

Totnes

Plymouth

Churston

	Area affected by Exmoor tithe dispute
	Area strongly resisting the Forced Loan
●	Parish strongly resisting Ship Money
	Parish involved in mutiny of 1640
+	Parish involved in mutiny of 1628

0   30 km

Map 8. Pre-war political dissent, 1625–1640.

177

Caroline regime, and had therefore gone on to support the Parliament. The problem with this line of argument is that not all of Devon's poorest communities were Parliamentary strongholds. Newton Abbot, a town which suffered hard times during the 1630s and produced many Ship Money defaulters, later went on to support the King.

The alternative explanation is that towns like Cullompton and Barnstaple were intrinsically 'froward', or recalcitrant, places, communities in which there was a degree of principled opposition to the Crown. How much evidence is there to support such a claim? Did politico/religious principles underlie the incidents of popular hostility to Royal policy noted above? There is nothing to suggest that such sentiments played a part in the Plymouth mutiny or the Exmoor tithe dispute, but in the mutiny of 1640 they clearly did. It was Evers's catholicism which led the North Devon soldiers to attack him. Yonge noted unambiguously in his diary that the 'souldiers killed Leiftenant Evers ... for that he was a papist' and the Deputy Lieutenants concurred with this judgement, observing that the soldiers had killed Evers '[because they] suspected him to be a papist; and for no other cause that we can learn'.[80] In this case, at least, popular protest was clearly fuelled by the virulent hatred of catholicism so often associated with zealous protestant belief. One is reminded of Cust's findings in Essex. Here, too, popular opposition to Crown policies was linked to fervent protestantism, or puritanism.

Was there a similar association in Devon? One way of finding out is to scrutinize the defaulters reported in 1627. These individuals make up a curiously mixed bag. At least four were catholics,[81] but a number of puritans also appear, amongst them Ignatius Jurdain of Exeter and John Delbridge of Barnstaple. Jurdain's reputation has already been touched upon, while Delbridge was once described as 'the factious, schismaticall head' of all the North Devon puritans.[82] That two of the most notorious Devon puritans should have been amongst those who were most prominent in resisting the Forced Loan strongly suggests that ideological principles underlay at least some of the opposition.

Can one see similar associations in the case of Ship Money? Were the individuals named on Wise's list making a principled stand on a matter of firmly-held political opinion? In many cases the answer is clearly no. To view the list of those who refused to pay Ship Money as a roll-call of incipient revolutionaries would be a mistake. In Devon, as elsewhere, future Royalists as well as future Parliamentarians were unwilling to pay.[83] John Northcote and other future luminaries of the Parliamentary cause can be found rubbing shoulders on Wise's list with the likes of Francis Bluett and Thomas Wood, later ardent loyalists.[84] The comment made by a Royalist yeoman in 1642 that 'the Shipp Money was bad' proves that, amongst commoners too, a distaste for Ship Money was not necessarily a sign of political opposition.[85]

But this line of argument must not be taken too far. Many contemporaries saw a definite link between puritanism and the staunchest opposition to Ship Money, and the Devon defaulters include a number of extremely zealous puritans.[86] Moreover, many of the communities which exhibited the strongest resistance to the levy, Barnstaple, Bideford and Colyton for example, were puritan strongholds. Evidence that local people saw a clear link between opposition to Ship Money and opposition to the Crown was provided by the vicar of Ilsington, who claimed that Thomas Wise, Sheriff in 1637, was 'a factious mann, and ought not to be elected for a knight for this countye ... because [he] did not levy the Ship Monye, as wilbe proved'.[87] The description of Wise as factious suggests that he was seen as an opponent of the regime. That such suspicions were well-founded is implied by the fact that so many Devonians refused to pay their Ship Money during Wise's shrievalty. Determined Sheriffs usually managed to raise the sums assessed, even in the most unwilling areas.[88]

Elsewhere in England protests about the rate of assessment often served as a cover for more principled opposition.[89] This was probably the case in Devon too. Plympton, the only small Devon town to petition the Council about its Ship Money rate, was the home of Sir Richard Strode, a fierce opponent of the levy on expressly constitutional grounds.[90] That Barnstaple was the town which complained most of all, and was the town, indeed, which the Council picked out as the most recalcitrant in all England, is particularly significant, for within a few years the town was to emerge as a hotbed of Parliamentarianism. This conjunction alone suggests that there was a tradition of principled opposition in the town. But in Barnstaple's case there is further evidence of a willingness to question and oppose Crown policy. The town had a marked propensity to elect critics of government policy as MPs. More revealing still is the fact that, as early as 1629, the inhabitants were pressing their lecturer for his opinion about the lawfulness of certain royal policies, causing him to comment: 'I wonder that you could so much forget yourselves as to enquire so many things in a Parliamentary manner concerning the rights and prerogatives of Kings'.[91] Here, surely, is evidence of pre-war opposition of the most nakedly political kind. And it is clear that this specifically political opposition contributed to Barnstaple's wartime allegiance. A pamphleteer commented in 1643 that Parliament would sorely rue Barnstaple's loss, for that town contained 'more true blades for Religion <u>and Liberties</u> than ... any town in England'.[92]

Was Barnstaple typical of the rest of Devon? Was it a concern for religion and liberties which chiefly underlay the continuity between pre-war opposition and wartime Parliamentarianism? Almost certainly it was, for such principles are known to have animated at least two local men to support the Parliament. John Weare of Halberton came out for Parliament because he felt the King's cause 'tended both to the dishonour of God, and the overthrow of the common liberty'.[93] In the will which he made shortly before setting off to war in 1643, Thomas Prowse of Cullompton stated that he was determined to fight the Royalists because they 'doe endeavour ... to alter the fundamental lawes of this Kingdom ... [and] the Protestant Religion'.[94] Again, the only individuals about whom detailed evidence survives are members of the county elite. Yet the pamphleteer's comment about Barnstaple leads one to suspect that a desire to defend religion and liberties motivated more humble Devonians, too.

'Religion and Liberties'; the conjunction is a familiar one. Most historians now agree that religious and secular opposition were inextricably intertwined during the period 1625–40, that innovations in religion were regarded as part and parcel of an assault upon the subjects' rights.[95] This association was made particularly readily by puritans, it is argued, and as a result, it was puritans who stood at the forefront of pre-war opposition to the regime. These claims receive ample confirmation from Devon. The local men who were most forward in opposing the government's temporal policies were invariably protestants of the hotter sort. One thinks of Walter Yonge and Richard Strode, of Ignatius Jurdain and John Delbridge, and of Thomas Sherwill of Plymouth, a 'godly magistrate', who opposed Buckingham's attempts to impose an MP on the town and possessed a local reputation as a patriot.[96] These individuals were all gentlemen or merchants.

But there are hints of a connection between opposition to the regime and the more zealous strain of protestantism at the bottom of society too. And the fact that Jurdain, Delbridge and Sherwill were all elected as MPs and Mayors of their respective communities surely suggests that their political ideas struck a chord with many of their fellow townsmen.[97]

Most contemporaries cared about the liberties of the subject, of course, but the puritans cared most of all. And while the collapse of the Caroline regime in 1640 was undoubtedly caused first and foremost by a nationwide revulsion against the temporal policies of the Crown, it seems unlikely that the same concerns determined wartime allegiance. Many Devonians who had opposed the government's temporal policies eventually became Royalists, while several communities which had produced many Ship Money defaulters came out on the same side. This hardly suggests that constitutional issues were the prime determinant of allegiance. It is tempting to suggest that it was only in those communities where concern for liberties was directly inspired by puritanism that a direct continuity can be found between pre-war opposition and wartime Parliamentarianism.

Chapter 10

'True Blades for Religion':
The Role of Puritanism

'Very zealous in all causes that concern the hindrance of his Majesty's service': this exasperated judgement on the puritans of Essex could equally well have been applied to their counterparts in Devon.[1] As the previous chapter has shown, advanced protestants formed the hard core of Devonian resistance to the pre-war regime. It was they who were most prominent in resisting the Book of Sports, they who stood out most boldly against Ship Money, they who were most bitterly opposed to the Scots war. That this should have been so, both in Devon and elsewhere, is hardly suprising. The 'hotter sort of protestants' had little reason to feel affection for the Caroline regime. Over the past century, Charles I has been variously portrayed as a quasi-catholic, as a pawn in the hands of the high-church Archbishop Laud and as a doctrinal revolutionary intent on foisting a novel anti-puritan creed (Arminianism or Carolinism, according to taste) on a reluctant Church of England.[2] In none of these guises was the King likely to appeal to puritans. Even if one takes a more positive view of Charles I's religious policies and accepts that he was a conscientious ruler, striving to maintain the monarchical church of his predecessors, it is still hard to deny that the King was widely regarded as a religious innovator.[3] When Mr Thomas Prowse of Cullompton set off to join the Parliamentary army in 1642 he stated explicitly, in his will, that he was taking up arms in order to 'extirpate those locusts and caterpillars who ... doe [now] endeavour ... to alter that which is most dear to a christian, the protestant religion ... established within [this] kingdom'.[4] Were

Prowse's views shared by his neighbours and was it an unusually deep concern for protestantism which inspired other local people to assist the Parliament's forces?

The links between Puritanism and Parliamentarianism

Some evidence to support this view has already emerged. Chapter Five, pp. 96–97, demonstrated that, at Exeter, it was the activities of a determined puritan clique which led to the city being secured for Parliament. Chapter Eight, pp. 157–60, showed that, across the county as a whole, it was seamen and clothworkers, members of the trades most commonly associated with advanced protestant belief, who offered the most fervent support to Parliament. Nor is this the only evidence to suggest that intimate links existed between puritanism and Parliamentarianism. Royalist propaganda constantly stressed that the Parliamentary armies were made up of 'schismatics', and such claims should not be regarded as mere rhetoric.[5] Devon Royalists sincerely believed their enemies to be religious radicals. Instructions sent out to the constables of Peyhembury in 1643 make this point crystal clear. The constables were told to report not only those who had served in the Parliamentary armies, but also all 'seditious preachers, sectaries [and] separatists ... [who] have accompanied, abetted, assisted or incited the ... present rebellion ... or defaced any churches, church windows, monuments or any other ornaments of any church or have resorted to ... conventicles or have depraved the booke of Common Prayer or neglected to use the same'.[6] No distinction is drawn here between disaffection to the Church and rebellion against the Crown: the Royalists who drafted these instructions clearly saw the Civil War as *Rebellio Puritanica*, pure and simple.[7]

Humbler loyalists shared this view. Having berated Richard Syms, the puritan minister of Sheepstor, for not wearing his surplice in 1643, two Royalist soldiers went on to complain that Syms and others like him 'were the cause of all the affrayes and bloodshed in the Kingdom'.[8] Many other humble people linked Parliamentarianism with religious dissent. One female loyalist from Exeter termed a Parliamentary captain 'an excommunicated roague'.[9] More significant still are the words of John Austen of Sidmouth, yeoman, who asserted in June 1642 that 'the Parliament ... were all puritans, for the protestants were all gone away from them to the King'.[10] Another Exeter Royalist was apprehended for speaking 'seditious words against puritans and rownd-headds'.[11] It is clear that in Devon, as in Herefordshire, the two terms were considered synonymous.[12] Even Parliamentary writers admitted this, Thomas Larkham observing that, before the Civil War, 'the people of God' had been referred to by 'that name of reproach which was then in use ... Puritanes ... for the term of Roundhead was not then in being'.[13]

That the perceived links between puritanism and Parliament-arianism were real is further suggested by the wartime behaviour of the Devon gentry. Almost all the great local families with a pre-war reputation for puritanism went on to support the Parlia-ment.[14] So did the county's puritan ministers. One thinks of George Hughes, Thomas Larkham and Henry Painter, all of whom had been thorns in the side of the Laudian establishment and all of whom went on to give sterling support to Parliament.[15] Was what was true of the gentlemen and the clergy true of the common people as well? Puritan preachers were certainly credited with a great deal of influence. The pro-Parliamentary rebellion at Hem-yock in 1644 was attributed to the exhortations of a single godly minister.[16] And most of the Parliamentary units in Devon were provided with puritan chaplains, suggesting that Roundhead com-manders recognized the preachers' efficacy.[17] The Royalists, for their part, regarded puritan ministers as a kind of deadly bacillus, spreading the disease of rebellion wherever they went and, accord-ingly, they did their best to prevent the people from coming into contact with them.[18] Even puritan sermon notes were regarded as dangerous by the King's Devonian soldiers, who hunted such documents down and destroyed them whenever they could.[19]

Were the Royalists' anxieties justified? Was it puritan doctrine which underlay popular Parliamentarianism? Chance references make it clear that the message of the puritan preachers had been internalized by at least some of the common soldiers on the Par-liamentary side. One Roundhead soldier, taken at Warminster in Wiltshire in 1644, told a local clergyman that he would 'stick in his skirts' for reading the Book of Common Prayer.[20] During the same year, another clutch of Roundhead prisoners, when asked why they fought against the King, replied 'Tis prophesied in the Revelation that the Whore of Babylon shall be destroyed with fire and sword, and what do you know but this is the time of her ruin, and that we are the men that must help to pull her down?'.[21]

Were such men typical? It is impossible to be sure, for the religious beliefs of the bulk of the common people will always remain elusive. Even amongst the gentry and the clergy, the line between protestants and puritans remains difficult to draw and amongst the common people—for whom so much less information survives—the task is usually impossible. Yet even if one cannot define the beliefs of individual commoners, one can discern general patterns. It is the argument of this book that popular Parliamentarianism flourished most strongly in those areas which had been most exposed to radical protestant ideas during the century which preceded the Civil War. The following discussion attempts to prove the point by mapping out the geographical and chronological spread of puritanism in Devon. Yet first something should be said about the vexed question of definition.

Patrick Collinson once spoke of 'the secondary academic industry' devoted to the definition of puritanism, and this is one contemporary industry which shows little sign of recession.[22] Most scholars would agree that puritanism was a broad spectrum of belief, one which embraced godly conformists on the one hand and those with more radical views on the other.[23] Yet the precise width of the gap between puritanism and out-and-out separatism remains a matter for fierce debate. Some historians have claimed that the vast majority of the godly were loyal and respectable subjects, clearly set apart from the radical sectarians.[24] But others have argued that godliness 'was never far from, indeed in a way constituted a form of, separatism', and it is the latter view which will be taken here.[25] In Devon, as in Cambridgeshire, 'dissent bred dissent' and wherever moderate puritanism took root, more radical nonconformity usually followed on behind.[26] The limitations of the sources make it impossible to distinguish the vast majority of conformist puritans from their non-puritan neighbours. Nonconformists are much easier to track down, however, and it is they who form the visible tip of the hidden puritan iceberg. In which areas of pre-Civil War Devon were such protestant nonconformists most heavily concentrated?

Devon and the Reformation

Heresy was virtually unknown in the South-West during the century which preceded the break with Rome.[27] As a result those few protestants who arrived in Devon during the 1530s found themselves working virgin soil.[28] This, together with the county's remoteness from London and other centres of early protestantism, helps to explain why Devonians were relatively slow to embrace the Reformation. As late as 1549 many of the county's inhabitants were prepared to rise up in arms against the religious innovations of the Edwardian regime.[29] Although this rebellion was crushed there was no great upsurge in enthusiasm for protestantism during the years which followed.[30] It took some time for even the most rudimentary system of protestant worship to become established, let alone any more radical beliefs. As a result 'the greater part ... of Devon' remained 'some of the dark corners of England', until well into the last quarter of the sixteenth century.[31]

It was not until the 1570s that radical protestantism began to make real advances in Devon, but thereafter its progess was swift.[32] By 1576 Bishop Alley was complaining that 'the puritance and sectaries daylye doe increase' and during the 1580s and 1590s puritan ministers flooded into Devon.[33] William Cotton, Bishop from 1598 to 1621, at first made determined efforts to halt the radical tide. During the early 1600s many puritan ministers were deprived. Yet as Cotton's episcopate wore on, he grew less combative, gradually subsiding into old age and inactivity.[34] Cotton had at least tried to contain the puritans. But Joseph Hall, diocesan from 1627 to 1642, was extremely tolerant of the 'hotter sort of protestant'. Indeed one writer claimed that Hall himself was 'a doctrinal puritan'.[35] Only the most blatant separatists had anything to fear from Hall and during the 1620s and 1630s Devon puritanism was able to flourish and expand. As late as 1637 Priscilla Painter—the wife of a minister teetering on the edge of outright nonconformity—was able to state that, in Exeter, 'we yet enjoy the ordnance of God ... in a most powerfull and plentyfull manner'. She was well aware that it was far 'otherwise in some parts of our land ... [where] the flame [of persecution] is so violent'.[36] Hall's tolerance, some might have termed it his criminal inactivity, enabled Devon puritanism to emerge from the Personal Rule largely intact.

Puritanism in Exeter

Exeter was the community which had first been exposed to protestant ideas. A heretic was martyred here as early as 1531 and by 1549 a substantial minority of Exeter's inhabitants had become adherents of the reformed faith.[37] During the 1580s signs of really zealous and widespread protestantism began to emerge, with calls for the establishment of a city lecture. In 1599 Exeter's governing body agreed to fund a preacher. The man chosen was Edmund Snape, a nonconformist. Not surprisingly, Bishop Cotton was opposed to this choice and Snape was soon dismissed. The city's second hired lecturer, William Hazard, fared little better. Although less radical than Snape, he was still too extreme for Cotton, who refused to allow him to preach.[38] The swiftness with which the preachers were dismissed hardly suggests that Exeter was a radical hotbed, and Wallace MacCaffrey has concluded that there was 'very little evidence of overt discontent with the religion established by law' in the city.[39] Yet one should not forget that Exeter was a cathedral city. Religious radicals could not be as open here as in more remote parts of the diocese, and while MacCaffrey is right to state that overt dissent was rare, much evidence suggests that a strong, but hidden, radical network existed beneath the very nose of the Bishop of Exeter.

Predictably enough the forbidding figure of Ignatius Jurdain stood at the centre of this radical web. Historians have long been aware that Jurdain was a leading Exeter puritan,[40] but what has not been fully appreciated hitherto is just how central Jurdain's role was, both in sustaining puritanism in Exeter and in maintaining religious dissent throughout the entire South-West of England. Jurdain's contemporary biographer, Ferdinando Nicolls (another radical), admitted that his subject was termed 'Archpuritan' and 'Hospes Schismaticorum' by his enemies. However Nicolls claimed that these charges were false, alleging that Jurdain was a moderate who never 'cast off ordinances'.[41] The latter part of Nicolls's statement may well be true. In public, at least, Jurdain usually conformed to the law. Yet charges levelled against him in Star Chamber in 1624 suggest that his public conformity was a mask.

Jurdain, the charges alleged, was 'held and esteemed the principall patron of factious and seditious persons in all the westerne parts, and especiallie in ... Exeter and ... Devon'. Not only this, he was 'a common and vehement abettor of such as doe oppose the present discipline and government of the State and [the] Church of England'.[42] The perceived link between faction and sedition, between opposition to the Church and opposition to the State is again made explicit in these charges. The allegations support the contention made in Chapter Nine, pp. 178 and 180–81, that Jurdain's resistance to many aspects of Crown policy sprang from a principled sense of opposition, grounded in his own religious beliefs. Many further charges were made against Jurdain: he was a 'cherisher of ... such as [have been] deprived of their ministeriall functions' (including Melanchthon Jewell, one of the most important of the early Devon puritans). He was said to be cruel and unjust. And several of his closest associates, including Reverend John Mico, were regarded as confirmed schismatics.[43] Jurdain somehow managed to clear himself of these charges. But there can be little doubt that they were substantially true. Preliminary research has uncovered numerous links between Jurdain and religious radicalism, and he was clearly the leader of the puritan group in Exeter.[44] Jurdain was not the only prominent city radical. Robert Tyrling, minister of St Kerrian, was a noted puritan minister, and in 1639 a Laudian cleric noted anxiously of Henry Painter, minister of St Petrock, that '[he] is a man, like the patriarchs of our time, too dangerously bad to be easily discovered'.[45]

Whereabouts in Exeter were puritan ideas most firmly established? A survey of the leading radicals' home parishes reveals a significant pattern. Tyrling lived in St Kerrians, Painter and Mico in St Petrocks, and Nicholls and Jurdain in St Mary Arches.[46] These three parishes are precisely those in which wartime Parliamentarianism was strongest (see Chapter Five, p. 107). The correlation can hardly be coincidental. That St Mary Arches was the power-house of the Parliamentarian cause in Exeter during the Civil War almost certainly reflects the fact that, for at least forty years before this, it had also been the powerhouse of local puritanism and dissent.

Puritanism in East Devon

During the early Stuart period nonconformity in East Devon was concentrated in two main areas, the extreme south-east and the clothing district around Tiverton. The former district possessed a long radical tradition. Advanced heretical ideas had been circulating at Axminster as early as 1535 and a century later the town was still a centre of religious dissent.[47] It was reported in 1630 that the curate at Axminster refused to wear the surplice or read the litany, that several of his parishioners did not kneel during communion and that conventicles were being held in a private house.[48] The nearby village of Axmouth was another puritan stronghold and radical clergymen were continually active here between 1590 and 1640. Richard Harvey, minister from 1590 onwards, was a contact of Melanchthon Jewell.[49] Following Harvey's death in 1632 William Hooke, another 'puritanical preacher', was presented to the benefice.[50] Significantly, the patron of the living at this time was Sir Walter Erle whom Archbishop Laud clearly (and rightly) regarded with great suspicion.[51] Hooke remained at Axmouth for the next seven years until eventually even Bishop Hall decided he was too extreme, and deprived him.

Harvey and Hooke aside, several radical preachers were active in Axmouth. Walter Layman, 'a perfect separatist in heart and a dangerous anabaptisticall fellowe', was licensed to preach there in 1619. During the mid-1630s John Salway, another who refused the surplice, was preaching in the town.[52] Many inhabitants of Axmouth supported the radical clerics and when Leyman was driven away for nonconformity, several of his old auditors began to 'gad' to Lyme Regis in order to hear sermons there. One of these individuals flatly refused to kneel at communion. Further evidence of lay nonconformity surfaced in 1625, when four Axmothians were accused of gadding to sermons, speaking against the liturgy and belonging to 'that [puritan] faction'.[53]

The third main centre of religious radicalism in south-east Devon was Colyton and by 1632 residents of the town were refusing to kneel at communion.[54] During the same decade the feoffees of Colyton displayed a quite remarkable willingness to flout ecclesiastical authority, noting in their account book that 'if any of their body, being elected churchwarden, [should be] ... prosecuted by the Ecclesiastical Court for refusing to take the oath of churchwarden, that the person so prosecuted should have his charges allowed him out of the publick stock'.[55] A reluctance to take oaths was a sure sign of advanced protestantism, and such scruples were clearly widespread in Colyton by this time. In 1641 twenty-six of the townsmen declined to take the Protestation, one man hastening to assure the Parliamentary authorities that he was 'not obstinately refusing but scrupulously forbearing'.[56]

Axminster, Axmouth and Colyton lay at the centre of a wide penumbra of religious dissent. Puritan activity was frequently discernible in the parishes round about. In 1613 lectures were being held at Axminster and Honiton.[57] Six years later inhabitants of the Blackdown village of Yarcombe were apparently gadding to other churches.[58] In 1630 the parsonage of Beer and Seaton, just west of Colyton, was purchased by the notoriously puritan town of Dorchester.[59] No doubt the people of Dorchester later appointed clerics whose religious beliefs agreed with their own and it is noteworthy that Henry Painter, already encountered at Exeter, was active at Seaton by 1614.[60] A minister refused to wear the surplice in nearby Shute in 1636–37, and his stand was supported by the vicars of Lyme, Sidbury and Seaton and the curates of Membury, Colyton and Combe Pine.[61] In 1640 Sir Henry Rosewell was fined for holding conventicles in Thorncombe and soon afterwards popular iconoclasm broke out in the region.[62] The vicar of Awliscombe later recalled that 'a little before the Rebellion, some of the puritan party in my parish ... did in one night break in pieces, all the painted glass, pictures of Saints &c in the church-windows'.[63]

Away from the extreme south-east, Tiverton was the main centre of dissent. A staymaker and a fuller of the town were committed by the Mayor in May 1622 'for contempt of the booke of Common Prayer'.[64] Two months later William Chilcott and Henry Hobbs, shoemaker and tucker of Tiverton respectively, were informed against as 'men ... reputed and held to bee Brownistes and schismaticall persons, holding and maintayning divers things against the orders and good government of the Church of England'. Both Chilcott and Hobbs were accused of attending 'secret conventicles and meetings abroad, in woods and other places'. In addition, they were said to have affirmed that 'all preachers were and are false prophetus [sic], and that they goe upp into the pulpitt to tell a tale, and that the church was but a howse built upp, and noe more to be regarded than any other howse for any service or prayers to be used therein'.[65] Religious disturbances continued in Tiverton long after 1622. In 1624 Richard Berry, a local clothier, was jailed for holding conventicles, and four years later he was imprisoned once again, this time on a charge of 'Brownisme'.[66] A strong anabaptist group had been established in Tiverton by this time, and in 1630 one of its leading members, James Tapp, was in contact with Dutch baptists.[67] Both Tapp and John Fort, another Tiverton clothier, were later charged with anabaptism by the Court of High Commission.[68] Shortly before the outbreak of the Civil War popular iconcoclasm surfaced in

Tiverton, when a crowd of local people demolished the Earl of Devon's chapel.[69] Radical ideas also circulated in the nearby cloth town of Cullompton.[70]

Pre-war radicalism was most prevalent in the south-east of East Devon and in the clothing district around Tiverton, that is in precisely those areas which later proved most recalcitrant over Ship Money. It can hardly be coincidence that the radical strongholds of Tiverton, Cullompton and Colyton were the three local communities which produced the largest number of Ship Money defaulters. The links between puritanism and Parliamentarianism have also been made very clear. Tiverton, Awliscombe and Thorncombe—all of which contained strong radical groups—were all pro-Parliamentarian parishes, while the majority of the Roundhead maimed soldiers came from the villages of the Blackdown hills, in which radical traditions were also strong. In the western half of the region, the area which provided least support for Parliament, puritan activity was confined to a narrow coastal strip. Lectures were held at Budleigh and Withecombe Raleigh in 1628, while puritan ministers were active at Newton Poppleford and Sidbury.[71] Further inland, however, in the rich arable parishes between Ottery and Exeter, lay-radicalism was conspicuous by its absence. This district provided little support for Parliament during the war and it was probably the absence of a strong dissenting tradition which had set the area apart.

Puritanism in North Devon

Advanced protestantism was deeply entrenched in East Devon, but it was in the north of the county that radical ideas were most widespread. By the late sixteenth century the region was fairly awash with radical clerics. Melanchthon Jewell was established at Thornbury by 1572. Conan Bryant—who advocated disobedience to Queen Elizabeth I herself—was presented to Parracombe in 1574, and to Challacombe a few years later. The notorious Eusebius Paget was at Kilkhampton by 1580. John Holmes, subsequently deprived for nonconformity, was at Tettcott by 1585, while George Close, the virulently puritan author of *The Papist's Parricide*, was presented to Black Torrington in 1585, and to Bradford in 1591.[72] All five of these men, radicals by any standard, were able to retain their benefices for many years, suggesting that they had considerable local support. By 1600 there was a galaxy of godly ministers in North Devon, including Richard Burton of Shirwell, Richard James of Thornbury and Roger Squire of Tettcott.[73] Radical clerics continued to pour into the region over the next forty years. John Cann, the Brownist, was at Pilton by 1628, while Thomas Larkham—whose religious convictions defy neat categorization but were clearly of a very radical nature—was at Northam by 1626.[74]

These were only the most notorious of the many extreme puritans who were active in North Devon between 1600 and 1640. Benedict Browninge, vicar of Pancrasweek, was presented at the sessions in 1605 for having 'openlie ... [said] that the ceremonies in the church which are now observed ... are not the lawes of God nor warranted by his worde ... but are new lawes made by the Kinge, which he will observe as farr as God's worde will allowe'.[75] John Leigh of Eggesford was similarly presented in 1621 for having 'neglected to reade divine service in such manner as the lawe requireth'.[76] In October 1639 Benjamin Coxe of Sandford 'vented doctrine foully prejudicial to the divine institution of episcopal government'.[77] Two months later Richard Down was told to make public submission at Marwood for 'his nonconformity practised and his erroneous doctrine delivered in the ... Church' there.[78]

Whereabouts in North Devon were radical ideas most firmly established? South Molton is the first community known to have produced zealous adherents of the reformed faith. A group of 'professors', as the godly liked to term themselves, was active in the town during the Marian period and in 1562 the Moltonians were described by their ex-minister as 'the ensample of Godlynes, out through all the costes [regions] rounde about you'.[79] South Molton remained a zealously protestant town throughout the seventeenth century. Yet any discussion of puritanism in North Devon must, of necessity, focus upon Barnstaple, the regional capital. As early as 1584 Barnstaple was riven by bitter religious rivalries. These rivalries had been exacerbated by the appointment of Eusebius Paget as town preacher. Paget was an extreme antiepiscopalian who had already been ejected from Northampton for nonconformity.[80] Once established in Barnstaple he launched bitter tirades against organs, singing in church and non-preaching ministers, while his allies spoke out against the communion service. Paget had many local supporters, who countenanced and encouraged his activities. One of them 'brake and spoiled' the church organs, presumably in obedience to Paget's exhortations. Those who dared to disagree with the preacher were simply 'counted papists'.[81] Already one can see the potential which puritanism had to split the Church of England, and ultimately the Kingdom itself, in two. Under the baleful influence of Paget and his allies, the middle ground of local religious opinion had simply disappeared and Barnstaple's more zealous protestants had come to regard their conservative/conformist neighbours as crypto-catholics.

Paget was deprived in 1585 but he left a maelstrom of religious dissent behind him. By 1586 many Barumites were gadding to Pilton and Shirwell in order to hear sermons there, and from 1590 onwards Barnstaple's ruling body funded a series of 'Friday preachings'.[82] Evidence that separatism was entrenched at the very highest levels of local society emerged in 1596 when the vicar scolded the aldermen for not coming to church 'whom, he said, were like two fat oxen, that they would not hear when [Christ] call'd unto them, but drew backwards and drew others from [Christ]'.[83] Three years later the town schoolmaster, 'one of the anabaptistical and precise brethren', requested the vicar to christen his child 'Do Well'.[84] As Nicholas Tyacke has shown, the short-lived craze for such godly baptismal names was chiefly confined to the Kentish Weald and to Northampton, both puritan strong-holds. That the practice was exported to Barnstaple is further evidence of the town's links with dissenting groups elsewhere.[85] It is remarkable, too, that one described as an anabaptist should have held the responsible post of schoolmaster.

In 1600 the preacher of Barnstaple and the lecturer of Pilton were inhibited from public speaking as they refused to wear the surplice.[86] The hired preachers' attitudes clearly reflected those of their paymasters for in 1601 John Delbridge, the mayor of Barnstaple, was described as 'the factious schismaticall head' of all the North Devon puritans.[87] Between 1600 and 1625, Barn-staple employed no fewer than eleven temporary lecturers.[88] The most influential of these was probably Benjamin Coxe, an anti-episcopalian.[89] Coxe was succeeded as lecturer in 1628 by another radical, William Crumpton.[90] Soon afterwards, Delbridge—who had somehow managed to secure the right of presentation to Barnstaple Church—appointed his son-in-law, Martin Blake, as vicar. Needless to say, Blake was puritanically inclined but, even so, he quickly fell out with Barnstaple's radical extremists.[91]

The lecturer of Pilton at this time was John Cann, 'a rigid Brownist' who had previously led an independent congregation in London.[92] Cann 'drew many after him, not in Pilton only but in Barnstaple also'. As a result many local people became Brownists and 'semi-separatists ... exceedingly disaffected ... to ... [the established] Church'.[93] Cann eventually emigrated to Amsterdam, but before he left he 'prevailed so far' with some of the townsfolk that they agreed to go to Holland with him.[94] Cann's departure did little to halt the spead of semi-separatism in Barnstaple. In 1634 a factious man was appointed to the post of town bookseller and unlicensed and seditious books were soon flooding into Barnstaple. As a result, Vicar Blake later complained, 'my ministry was much weakened in the minds of the people; so much that in a short time they had my preaching in contempt, which ... [they] abundantly testified by their often gadding abroad in great troops to other churches upon the Lord's day'.[95] Many of Barnstaple's elite were hostile to Blake, partly because they disagreed with his theology, partly because he had attempted to halt their 'encroachment upon ecclesiastical and episcopal jurisdiction' within the town.[96]

In 1634 Bishop Hall informed Archbishop Laud that a 'strange puritanical monster' had been discovered in Barnstaple. The individual referred to, one John Cole, had been holding forth upon spiritual matters for some time. Although unlearned, he had gained many followers 'among the simpler sort, especially women'. Cole had then begun to seduce his female disciples, persuading them that '[sexual] acts might stand with Grace'. Hearing of Cole's activities, Hall ordered the town authorities to put him under arrest.[97] This incident shows just how unorthodox some of the ideas circulating in Barnstaple at this time really were. In addition they show that radical ideas were filtering far down the social scale—and that local commoners were not only receiving such opinions, but beginning to expound them for themselves.

Barnstaple's religious history cannot be explored in further detail here.[98] What has already been said is quite enough to demonstrate the unique strength and influence of nonconformity in Barnstaple. The effects of sixty years of continuous radical dissent upon the religious attitudes of the townsfolk can only be imagined. Nor was the impact of the preachers confined to Barnstaple alone. When the puritan minister of Dedham, in Essex, died after thirty years of preaching it was observed by a conservative cleric that he had 'poyson[ed] all those partes for 10 myles round about'.[99] A similar situation obtained in North Devon, where it was reported that the activities of radical ministers in Barnstaple had bred 'tumults and frivolous opinions in the peoples' hearts', so that 'not only the people of the said town but also of the country near adjacent are divided and distracted to sundry opinions and strange conceits, unreverently using the ministers and ministry also'.[100]

Barnstaple and its immediate hinterland aside, the market town of Holsworthy was probably the most important centre of local dissent. Melanchthon Jewell was established in the adjoining parish of Thornbury by 1572, and during the 1580s David Black, the radical schoolmaster of Kilkhampton, was active in the town. Puritan lectures were being held in Black Torrington in 1605 and, from 1632 onwards Holsworthy's vicar was the puritan Humphrey Saunders.[101] During James I's reign heretical blasphemy surfaced in the area. A yeoman and a husbandman of Cookbury were presented at the sessions in 1617 for 'namyinge a dogge John and puttinge water uppon [it] & saying [they] did yt in the name of the father, sonne & holy ghost & signyinge yt with the signe of the Crosse'.[102] These mock ceremonies were part of radical tradition—similar cases occurred in Essex—and the practice was kept up by Parliamentary soldiers during the Civil War.[103] Chulmleigh was another radical centre. In 1630 conventicles were being held in the town, and in 1634 a hired preacher arrived here from London, though Laud drove him out soon afterwards.[104] Bideford was another North Devon town where radicals were active and lectures held during the pre-war period.[105] Finally the persistence of nonconformist ideas at Sandford should be noted. Thomas Larkham and Benjamin Coxe, both extremist firebrands, were successively presented to the benefice here, and there are hints of conventicles during the later 1630s.[106]

In North Devon, as elsewhere, the parallels between the geographic spread of pre-war puritanism and wartime Parliamentarianism are striking. North Devon was the region in which pre-war dissent was most widespread and firmly established: it was also the region which provided the greatest amount of support for Parliament. Of all the North Devon towns, Barnstaple was the one in which religious radicalism was strongest: it was also the town which did most to assist the Parliamentary forces.

South Molton, Holsworthy, Bideford, Northam, Chulmleigh and Sandford were all communities in which pre-war dissent was strong and all six parishes exhibited wartime support for Parliament. The link between religious radicalism and Parliamentarianism was made especially clear by Martin Blake, who remarked that, when the governors of Barnstaple reluctantly decided to surrender the town to the King's forces in August 1643, 'a company of factious schismatickes' riotously opposed the decision, even though Parliament's cause seemed lost.[107] The connection between extreme radical beliefs and intransigent Parliamentarianism is once again made very clear.

Puritanism in South Devon

In South Devon Plymouth was the chief puritan stronghold and, like Exeter, had long been exposed to protestant ideas. An embryonic protestant cell was in existence here by the 1530s and radical ideas quickly took root thereafter.[108] By the end of the sixteenth century local puritanism was well established. Plymothians flocked to Modbury during the 1580s in order to hear the sermons of the far-famed nonconformist preacher Samuel Hieron, the 'Star of the West'.[109] Financial contributions from Plymouth helped to sustain Hieron's ministry and this was not the only assistance the townsmen gave him. When Hieron was unable to get his pamphlet defending 'Refusall of subscription to the Book of Common Prayer' published, the text was sent into Holland. Once it had been printed copies were sent back to England 'packt up in the goods of an eminent merchant of Plymouth, Mr Thomas Sherwill'. No bookseller dared to sell the book, so copies were distributed for nothing, being 'dropped in the streets [and] hung on hedges'.[110]

It is striking that Sherwill, one of Plymouth's governing elite, was already prepared to break the law of the land in order to further his religious beliefs. Nor was he alone for during the early Stuart period, Plymouth was ruled by a formidable group of 'godly magistrates'.[111] The religious sympathies of these men are best revealed by their attitude towards the clergymen employed in the town. From 1603 to 1635 Plymouth's vicar was Henry Wallis. He was probably a puritan.[112] Even so the corporation felt it necessary to maintain a string of radical lecturers between 1618 and 1642 and the first of these was John Barlow. 'Much beloved and honoured' in Plymouth, he was quickly driven out by the ecclesiastical hierarchy for his nonconformity.[113] Barlow was replaced in 1620 by Mr Nicols, another radical. Nicols received a stipend of £100 per annum and was clearly being groomed for the post of vicar.[114] However in 1631 he died and the town governors asked Thomas Ford to be their minister instead.[115] This invitation can only be seen as a calculated provocation to the church hierarchy as Ford, who was openly hostile to Laud, had recently been expelled from Oxford for his beliefs. Not surprisingly, Laud and the King refused to allow him to be entertained in Plymouth.[116] The corporation at once appointed another puritan, Alexander Grosse, as lecturer and in 1632 they agreed that Grosse would eventually become vicar. Yet Laud was opposed to Grosse too, and 'would not suffer him to be quiet ... in Plymouth'.[117] He was packed off to the remote Mid-Devon parish of Bridford, and when Wallis finally died in 1635, Laud ensured that the vicarage went to Aaron Wilson, a moderate.[118]

Wilson encountered stiff opposition at Plymouth. He was soon complaining that 'the vicarage is much wronged, partly by some ill-minded persons who combined together ... before the death of the last incumbent to set up certain customs to the great damage of the church, and partly by the usurpation of the ... town upon the rights of the vicar'.[119] Squabbling between the vicar and the corporation continued, but the townsmen were unable to get Wilson removed. In 1637 the town asked the King for permission to erect a second church in Plymouth. Somehow they managed to secure his assent, and in 1642 Charles granted the advowson of the new church to the corporation.[120] If this was an attempt to win the Plymothians over to the Royalist cause, it failed. As soon as the Civil War began 'the liturgy of the Church of England was layd aside' in Plymouth, and 'he that first did it was the first incumbent of the new church, Mr Porter'.[121]

Outside Plymouth the main puritan centres were Dartmouth, Kingsbridge and Totnes. Dartmouth does not seem to have been an early radical centre, but during the 1610s and 1620s the religious atmosphere of the town began to change.[122] Between 1632 and 1640 the puritan minister Anthony Harford preached constantly in Dartmouth and by 1642 local puritanism was very strong.[123] In 1643 one loyalist clergyman complained that many in the town were 'too much' disaffected to the established church. Prince Maurice also suspected the inhabitants of nonconformity, demanding 'that the Booke of Common Prayer ... shall be freely exercised within this towne ... without any depravation or irreverence by any form of sectaries'.[124] The vicar of Kingsbridge during the mid-1630s was the puritan George Gefferyes. It was later recalled that 'all the people of the South Hams [had] loved him dearly' and that 'multitudes came in flocks' from West Alvington, Thurlestone, Milton, South Huish, Malborough and Charlton to hear him preach.[125] Lectures were also held at Kingsbridge from 1630 onwards and radical clerics were active in the surrounding countryside.[126] The most important of these was William Dodding, of South Pool, who in 1621 was refusing to read the litany or wear the surplice.[127] At Totnes there were lectures from 1621 onwards and the preacher was favourably regarded by local puritans.[128]

In South Devon, as elsewhere, the preachers drew their audiences from miles around. This was most clearly demonstrated in the case of Samuel Hieron, who had remarkable pulling power, 'all the country far and near, from all ... the neighbour parishes and villages of the South Hams flocked in like doves into ... [his] lectures' at Modbury. Hieron made puritan converts in as many as seventeen South Hams parishes; West Alvington, Bigbury, Brixton, Charlton, Ermington, South Huish, Kingsbridge, Malborough, Newton Ferrers, Plymouth, Plympton, Plymstock, Revelstoke, Shaugh Prior, Thurlestone, Ugborough and Wembury. (Surprisingly, Modbury itself remained largely immune to Hieron's teachings.[129]) This brief summary cannot do justice to the vitality and strength of the South Devon puritan movement. Even so, the connections between the geographical spread of pre-war puritanism and Parliamentarianism have once again been made clear. Plymouth and Dartmouth—the bastions of the Parliamentary cause in the South Hams—were radical strongholds, whilst Kingsbridge and its neighbourhood—the district upon which the anti-Royalist uprising of 1644 was centred—was similarly suffused with puritan belief.

Puritanism in Central Devon

Central Devon has been left until last in this discussion, chiefly because radical ideas made relatively little impact here. Only two Mid-Devon towns displayed any considerable degree of puritan activity. The first of these was Crediton, where moderate puritanism was encouraged by the town elite. William Cooke, a contact of Jewell's, was appointed vicar here in 1596, Snape preached in the town during the early 1600s, and Richard Coles, vicar from 1616 to 1650, was a puritan activist. Yet despite the presence of these radical clerics, there is no evidence of extreme lay nonconformity of the type seen elsewhere in Devon.[130] The other stronghold of Mid-Devon puritanism was Moretonhampstead, a town which has a particularly intriguing religious history. Situated on the edge of Dartmoor, Moreton was far removed from the sea and from major population centres. It seems an unlikely focus of radicalism. Yet the town was deeply involved in the cloth trade and during the 1560s advanced protestant ideas were brought here by exiled Flemish weavers.[131] The new ideas gradually took root in Moreton and, from the 1590s onwards, they received vital encouragement from a local gentleman, John Southmead of Wrey. How Southmead came by his puritan beliefs is unknown, yet he clearly held them with passionate conviction. Indeed Southmead emerges as the Dartmoor equivalent of better-known puritan patriarchs like Delbridge and Jurdain. For half a century, he battled tirelessly to transform Moreton into a godly 'town upon a hill'. Drunks were punished, revels discouraged and alehouses suppressed.[132]

Like Delbridge at Barnstaple, Southmead eventually managed to secure the right of presentation to Moreton church and in 1626 he presented his puritan son-in-law, Francis Whiddon, to the benefice.[133] The two men subsequently worked together to erect a godly commonwealth in the town. It is significant that, in August 1642, Southmead came out in open opposition to church and state, being presented at the assizes for speaking 'scandalous words' of the King and the Book of Common Prayer.[134] Predictably enough both Southmead and Whiddon opposed Charles I during the war. They also survived long enough to see, and presumably exult in, the eventual Parliamentary victory. Southmead died in 1650. In a subsequent sermon Whiddon spoke of his patron's curbing of 'prophaneness', his 'paines in getting a faithfull teacher to instruct the people' and his behaviour 'at home in his family, in repeating sermons ... [and] reading, opening and applying scriptures'. Whiddon also reminded the townsfolk that they had had 'a great advantage over other places adjacent' because of Southmead's 'zealous ... striving for the inlargement of the Kingdom of Christ'.[135]

These last words make the point that Moreton's conspicuous godliness was all the more surprising because of its position at the heart of Central Devon. In other Mid-Devon communities, lay puritanism was hard to find. There were stirrings of puritan activity at Tavistock during George Hughes's ministry of 1638–42, while in 1630 a lecture was begun at Okehampton, though not with any great success.[136] It is also true that several radical ministers had been active in Mid-Devon: Randall at Lydford in 1581, Stevens at Spreyton in 1588 and Grosse at Bridford from 1635. But there is no evidence that these men established strong groups of lay supporters.[137] It is tempting to conclude that puritan doctrines were still regarded with hostility by the people of Central Devon. This in turn probably explains why so few local communities joined Moreton in embracing the Parliamentary cause.

It is hard to doubt the intimate link which existed between puritanism and Parliamentarianism in Devon. In every region of the county the communities which supported Parliament during the war were those which had boasted the strongest puritan groups before it. This was true of Barnstaple, Chulmleigh, Dartmouth, Exeter, Holsworthy, Kingsbridge, Moreton, Plymouth, Tiverton and many other places besides. At the regional level the picture is the same. In North and South Devon, regions which supported Parliament, puritanism was strong. In Mid-Devon, on the other hand, where little support for Parliament was forthcoming, it was weak (see Map 9). The same link is clearly discernible at the county level. A Parliamentary stronghold, Devon was also 'one of the most puritan counties in England'.[138]

Why did puritanism take root in the areas where it did? There can be no doubt that in Devon, as elsewhere, radical ideas were transmitted through trade. It is this which explains the concentration of puritanism in the county's towns, ports and cloth districts. Certain trades were more prone to radicalism than others, and it is probably no coincidence that the radical stronghold of Barnstaple was also an important centre of the shoemaking industry.[139] The influence of the exiled Flemish cloth workers (about whom too little is known) was also important. The example of Moreton has already been noted, and foreign clothworkers probably contributed to the spread of religious dissent in East Devon too. Lysons was told in 1820 that it was 'Lollards', fleeing from Antwerp, who had established the lace industry along the East Devon coast. The description of these refugees as Lollards

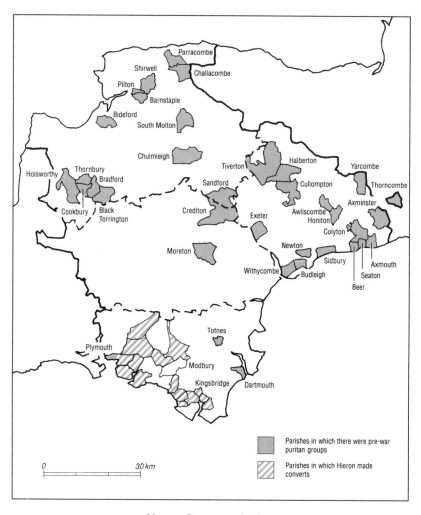

Map 9. Pre-war puritanism.

suggests that their religious beliefs were regarded as heretical by the indigenous population, so it may be that the Flemings were the first to bring radical beliefs to the area. Lysons also noted that the lacemakers of Devon 'are only to found between the Rivers Ax and Exe and in ... the villages and hamlets throughout that line of coast home to the first market towns inland'.[140] This is an intriguing comment. It suggests that the restriction of puritanism in the western half of East Devon to a narrow coastal strip was a direct reflection of the local distribution of the clothing industry.

Trade links apart, the spread of puritanism was crucially influenced by the attitude of the local gentry. Ian Gowers has shown that gentry support was vital in nurturing and sustaining Devon puritanism and similar conclusions have been drawn from studies elsewhere.[141] The example of John Southmead at Moreton provides further support for this view, while the examples of Delbridge, Jurdain and Sherwill again stress the importance of the urban oligarchs. Where elite support was forthcoming, puritanism could flourish. It only required one gentry household to patronize puritan preachers for the surrounding area to become infiltrated by radical ideas. And when the habit of puritanism was sustained in a gentry family over two or even three generations, as often happened in Devon, zealousness became entrenched in the fabric of local society. It was in this sense that gentry influence was most vital in determining popular allegiances. By presenting and supporting puritan clerics, Elizabethan and early Stuart gentlemen ensured that the local populace would become imbued with puritan beliefs, the very beliefs which later led to Parliamentarianism. In this sense, patterns of allegiance were determined almost by accident, many years before the war itself broke out.

Yet is it really credible to suggest that the fierce puritanism which sustained the Parliamentarian clergy and gentry could also have motivated the common people? As Kevin Sharpe has observed 'the puritanism of the ... plain folk, remains a dark corner of religious history'.[142] Even so, it is sometimes possible to discern a little through the gloom. The writings of the London artisan Nehemiah Wallington are justly famous. They show that, in the capital at least, many humble people were fiercely committed to puritanism and that this commitment later emerged as wartime Parliamentarianism.[143] Was Wallington exceptional? Could such committed individuals have existed only in London and the largest cities, or did humble 'village Wallingtons' flourish in the towns and villages of provincial England too?

The evidence from Devon suggests that they did. In his little-known work *Icones Sacrae Anglicanae*, the Devon minister John Quick provides many insights into the mentality and outlook of puritan commoners in early Stuart Devon. A post-war non-conformist, Quick was keenly interested in the antecedents of local dissent and during the 1650s he talked to many of those whom he termed 'old puritans' about their experiences under the prelacy. Forty years later Quick used the testimony which he had accumulated to compile a set of portraits of radical ministers. These 'lives' are immensely valuable in their own right, yet perhaps most important of all is the light which Quick's biographies throw upon the footsoldiers of the Devon puritan movement. Quick was told that the common people, 'the meaner or midling sort', had flocked to hear puritan ministers like Crumpton and Hieron. He was told that yeomen and their families had travelled ten or twelve miles to hear the godly preachers. And 'in those many long miles that they went to be instructed', the old puritans later recalled, 'all their discourse on ye highways and open fields ... was onely of those divine and heavenly matters which had been delivered to them'.[144] Quick also depicts the character of a pre-war artisan from South Devon, 'a parchment maker ... who besides reading the scriptures morning and evening in his family, with singing of psalmes & fervent prayers with his children and servants, would shut himself up frequently every day in secret for private communion with God, and spend his time in sighes, groanes and tears, thus wrestling with God for his blessing'.[145] Nehemiah Wallington would clearly have felt at home here.

It is simply impossible to believe that the individuals whom Quick describes would ever have acted as unthinking pawns, that they would ever have deferred to the commands of gentry, clergy, or even the King himself, if they had felt their religious beliefs were at stake. Indeed Quicke specifically states that the 'old professors ... retained their integrity in those hours of temptation and power of darkness, those fiery trials that passed upon them in the Civill Wars'.[146] It was men such as these who stood at the forefront of the Parliamentary armies. It was men such as these who were the shock troops of the puritan revolution.

Chapter 11

'Mere Conventicles of Bad Fellows': The Cultural and Religious Determinants of Popular Royalism

If the Parliamentarian areas of Devon were those in which puritanism was strongest, what was it that defined the Royalist areas? It is tempting to suggest that they were simply the districts in which puritanism was weakest, in which hostility to 'godly reformation' was most keenly felt. Study after study has shown that, across the country as a whole, the King's party formed later than Parliament's and that the Royalist party was defined as much by what it was against as what it was for. Such claims receive a great deal of support from Devon. All the evidence suggests that the chief thing which united the King's supporters here was their hatred of the 'professors', and their desire to protect the established church, and all its appendages, from puritan defilement.

The link between Royalism and anti-puritanism

The process by which even pre-war critics of Crown policy could be transformed into Royalists through their distaste for religious radicalism is well illustrated by the case of Sir William Courtenay of Saltash. In a series of letters sent to Sir Richard Buller in early 1641 Courtenay praised the proceedings of the Parliament, expressed the hope that it would 'locke into all things for the advansing of honour and profitte of these 3 kingdomes' and made many criticisms of the way in which national finances had hitherto been managed. There is nothing in any of these letters to suggest that Courtenay was a proto-Royalist. Yet in August 1641 he heard rumours that the soldiers in the north 'committe deeds of hostellitie ... breack[ing] doune organes and crissininge vonntes with many other disorders'. This news greatly alarmed Sir William and soon afterwards he wrote to Buller that 'if this that I have harde be true, the honour of the state is ingaged to see these [f]oull disorders punishadd or ellste greatter oppression will sertenlly folloe on men of the best ranckes'. Courtenay's association of religious radicalism with social disorder is made abundantly clear. What he thought of the religious developments of the next few months can only be surmised, but it is significant that, when he next wrote to Buller, it was as an officer in the Royalist army.[1]

In Devon, as elsewhere, distaste for religious radicalism clearly propelled many gentlemen into the King's camp.[2] Those Devon gentlemen who were most prominent in the King's service lay at the opposite end of the religious spectrum from the puritans. Of the sixty-three Royalist field officers identifiable from Devon, no fewer than eight (13 per cent of the total) were either catholics themselves or the sons of catholics. At least five more Devon recusants served as junior officers.[3] The representation of local catholics in the King's armies was out of all proportion to their numerical strength, and it is clear that in Devon, as across the kingdom, 'most ... [catholics] were active Royalists'.[4] Significantly, the one Devon town in which Catholic influence was strong—Ottery St Mary—was a notorious Royalist stronghold.[5] The religious sympathies of the non-catholic field officers are harder to ascertain. Yet only one of them came from a family with a reputation for godliness, and this was James Chudleigh the turncoat. Many of the others came from distinctly ungodly backgrounds. This was true of Philip and Henry Champernowne, for example; one puritan writer describing their 'whole family [as] very wicked'.[6]

Amongst the Devon clergy, too, the King's most enthusiastic supporters were the anti-puritans, those who stood on the 'superceremonious' wing of the church. Chapter Five, p. 107, demonstrated that in Exeter the Cathedral Close was the focus of Royalist sentiment and that most of the Cathedral Clergy were Royalists. It is significant that the Close had also been the centre of local opposition to puritanism before the war and that the clergymen had a reputation for Arminianism. A city cordwainer claimed in 1641 that most of the cathedral clergy 'were Arminians' and that the Cathedral service 'was poperye'.[7] Here, pre-war anti-puritanism fused seamlessly into wartime Royalism, and similar connections can be seen in the case of Anthony Short, rector of Drewsteignton. A prominent Royalist, Short later boasted 'that noe man in Devonshire ha[d] done more for the Kings partie than he'.[8] It comes as little surprise to find that Short was a personal enemy of pre-war puritans like John Southmead.[9]

Like the puritan ministers, conservative clergymen attempted to influence the political behaviour of their parishioners. A fascinating description has survived of the way in which Anthony Short read out a Parliamentary declaration in 1642. According to the man who reported him Short recited this document in 'a disdayneful manner', 'descant[ing] upon it' at length. Thus when he came to the part of the text which mentioned the Lords and Commons assembled in Parliament, Short commented, 'How many be then there, 14? I am sure there are not 40, and of all the Cornish burgesses which hath most of any county in the Kingdom, ther is but one'. When he came to Parliament's claims that 'religion & liberty are already supprest', Short, 'lifting up his hands and eies to the heaven, said "O what damnable lies doe they divulge"'. When he came to claims that royal agents had tried to kill Sir John Hotham, Short averred that they would have been fully justified in doing so. And when he read out the MPs' solemn declaration 'that they propose to alter nothing in the church government ... [without] having first had consultation with reverend and learned divines', Short could not resist altering the last line to 'reverent and cockscomblike divines'! Throughout the war Short did his utmost to whip up support for the King, and indeed, it was later claimed that he had gone so far as to threaten 'damnation to the Parliaments partie'.[10] Clearly puritan ministers did not have a monopoly on hellfire.

How successful were the efforts of men like Short? The attempts of loyalist clergymen in Essex to influence public opinion have been described as 'pitifully ineffective'.[11] Yet in many parts of Devon the 'cavaliering priests' enjoyed considerable success. One Parliamentarian fumed that the Royalist cleric John Whynell 'did more mischife than a littell armey' in Exeter.[12] During 1642–43 clergymen in the hill-country to the west of Exeter helped to organize several pro-Royalist disturbances. Mr Garnett, vicar of Dunsford, and Anthony Turner, curate of Tedburn, were implicated in the meeting at Dunsford, and Turner himself was later accused of having shot a Roundhead captain. And when rumours reached nearby Ide that Parliamentary horsemen were about to arrest the rector, Mr Satterlie, his parishioners rose in arms to defend him. That local people fought alongside their Laudian vicars and helped to protect them surely suggests that they sympathized with their religious beliefs.

This is not to suggest that Royalist commoners were doctrinal Arminians of course. But like their social betters, they clearly disliked religious innovation in general and puritanism in particular. We have already seen that humble Royalists regarded Puritan and Roundhead as synonymous, that they castigated Parliamentarians specifically for their religious heterodoxy, and that a group of the King's soldiers accused radical ministers of being the begetters of the conflict. Nor was this the only occasion upon which Royalist soldiers vented their feelings against the godly. When the defeated Parliamentary garrison marched out of Exeter in 1643 they were jeeringly reviled by 'divers of the illiterate, ignorant and sottish common souldiers' of Prince Maurice's army, who 'belched out ... taunting blasphemies ... as "Where are now your long sanctified prayers by the spirit? What is become of your holy humiliations and supplications? ... Where is your God now, O ye hypocrites? Where is your holy Cause, your Cause and all your hopes?"'.[13] Here, as on so many other occasions, the bitter hatred which ordinary Royalists felt for the professors is made plain.

The frequency and vehemence with which this hatred was expressed suggest that, amongst Royalist commoners, just as amongst the gentry and clergy, hostility to puritanism and a desire to protect the established church were the chief determinants of allegiance. This view is supported by the words of John Austen of Sidmouth, yeoman. Arguing with a neighbour in June 1642 Austen made a speech which provides a fascinating, and extremely rare, glimpse into exactly what it was that motivated individual commoners to take up arms for the King. Austen began by expressing his fear that Parliament would subvert the old ecclesiastical order, that '[they] would have new tricks'. Next he criticized those local ministers who had already tried to implement religious innovations, revelling in the fact that a certain Mr Babbington had been questioned 'because he would not say the Epistle and Gosple', and cursing 'another such coxcombe foole' at Newton Poppleford, who 'would not say the Epistle or Gosple nor the Common Prayers'. Austen then went on to affirm that 'the Parliament were all puritans, for the protestants were all gone away from them to the kinge', adding that 'ther were none left [in Parliament] but a few puritans, and ... that yf yt came to [it], he would fight against that sort'. To make sure his neighbour was in no doubt as to his meaning, Austen later reiterated that 'the puritans should be the first he would fight against'.[14]

Austen's words indicate the primacy of religious conservatism in fostering popular Royalism. How much evidence is there to suggest that similar connections existed elsewhere? Was it from the most religiously conservative areas of Devon that Charles I drew most support? Chapter Ten, pp. 191 and 198–200, has already supplied some important clues, demonstrating that the regions in which the puritans were least active before 1642 were precisely those which later went on to support the King. The comments of contemporaries make the link between anti-puritan communities and Royalist ones explicit.

Popular resistance to puritanism: The mines and the moors

Most important of all is the testimony of the puritan minister John Bond. In a sermon of 1645 Bond sought to explain how the South-West had been lost to Parliament by identifying the weak points, or 'speciall sins', which had made each county vulnerable to the Royalists. Crucially, Bond ascribed the loss of Devon and Cornwall to 'the sins of the mines, and the sins of the moores'. Godly ministers, Bond argued, had neglected the inhabitants of the moorland districts and mining areas during the pre-war period. As a result those areas had been left in unreformed ignorance and had therefore become the seed-beds of popular Royalism. 'Alas, those poore creatures that laboured in the pits of tinne', lamented Bond, 'how were their souls made more black and rude with ignorance and prophanesse then their bodies with soot and oare! And yet who did pitie their condition? How few did looke after their salvation? And therefore now you see, those pits and places have been mines of men and storehouses of ... soldiers, for the black and prophane cause of the enemie'.[15] Bond's words are vital. They confirm the view that patterns of wartime allegiance were chiefly determined by pre-war religious history. They confirm the view that the western tin-miners were overwhelmingly Royalist. They confirm the view that popular

Royalism was particularly associated with certain geographical areas—in this case with the mining districts and moorlands of Mid-Devon and Cornwall. In addition, Bond's words suggest that the pro-Royalism of these areas was a direct result of the ignorance and religious conservatism of the local population.

Bond's suggestion that the inhabitants of the moorland districts were culturally backward is confirmed by many later authorities. It was claimed in 1713 that 'the inhabitants of ... [Dartmoor] are the most ignorant and rustick people in the west of England', while a century later it was noted that the inhabitants of 'the upper part' of Teignbridge hundred (on the eastern edge of Dartmoor) 'are considered by the rest of the county as uncouth'.[16] The 'peculiarity' of the local people was ascribed by a nineteenth-century writer to 'the situation, which is retired, there ... [being] not much intercourse with other parts'.[17] If this was true in the 1800s, it must have been even more true during the 1600s, and such physical isolation had important consequences. The role of trade routes in facilitating the advance of radical protestant ideas has already been touched on. The sequestered inhabitants of Mid-Devon were little exposed to such influences. It is this physical isolation which explains why local people were so slow to embrace the hotter sort of protestantism—and this, too, which explains the tradition of cultural backwardness which persisted in Central Devon right up to the twentieth century. As late as 1892 it could be observed that many 'superstitious observances' which had long since disappeared elsewhere in Devon might yet be found 'sheltering themselves under the Dartmoor Tors'.[18]

Bond's claim that the western tin-miners had imbibed little godly doctrine by 1642 is also hard to doubt. Parliamentary sources often commented on the irreligion of the miners. In 1644 the King's Cornish soldiers were described as 'ignorants and aetheists drained from the mines'.[19] The tinners' imperviousness to puritan teaching probably owed much to the demanding nature of their work, which afforded little time for religious contemplation. Aubrey's explanation as to why there were no anchor-smith 'fanaticks'—'for it is a mighty laborious trade; and they must drinke strong drinke to keep up their spirits; so they never trouble ... their heads with curious notions of religion'—was equally applicable to the tinners.[20] And, like the people of Mid-Devon as a whole, the tinners combined their hostility to godly teaching with a particularly strong attachment to superstitions and 'idle exercises'.²¹ It is easy to see why horrified Parliamentary writers should have branded the miners as 'subterraneous spirits of darknesse'.²² In puritan eyes the tinners were, figuratively as well as literally, denizens of some of the very darkest corners of the land.

Popular resistance to puritanism: 'Unprofitable places'

Bond's comments, combined with the negative evidence of Chapter Ten, amply confirm that Mid-Devon was the most religiously conservative region of the county. Yet can one be more specific? Is it possible to descend below the regional level and identify those individual parishes in which hostility to puritanism was strongest? It has been suggested that the pattern of clerical ejectment might be helpful in this respect, that parishes whose ministers were removed by the Parliamentary authorities after 1646 may well have been regarded as particularly in need of godly reformation.²³ The problem with this line of enquiry is that one cannot usually tell why the individual clergymen were ejected. Conservative clerics might have been removed because the Parliamentary authorities feared their local influence, yet they might equally well have been removed because their own parishioners had denounced them, or because of personal feuds. The pattern of ejection was an extremely haphazard one, in fact, with the shortage of replacement clergy permitting many Anglican ministers to remain in office, to the 'frustration ... [of the] zealous'.²⁴ As a result, analysis of the places of residence of the ejected clergy reveals little.²⁵

Puritan writers are more helpful, lambasting several Devon towns for their resistance to godly reformation. John Quick described Modbury as singularly resistant to the teachings of the great puritan preacher Samuel Hieron. 'It were well if the inhabitants of that most populous place had known the day of their visitation', commented Quick piously, adding that 'Mr Hieron did very little good among them'.²⁶ The 'rough-hewen people' of Ashburton were similarly criticized for their 'unprofitableness' under the ministry of the puritan Thomas Grosse.²⁷ Yet of all the Devon towns, it was Tavistock which the puritans regarded as the very heart of darkness. Even in the 1630s this populous place was still without a preacher. Horrified by 'the miserable estate of

Tavystock', Lady Maynard, a gentlewoman of 'exemplary prudence, zeale and piety', arranged for George Hughes of London to be appointed to the parish. Hughes was a radical and an extremely formidable man. This was just as well, for when he arrived at Tavistock in 1639 he found a herculean task awaiting him. According to Quick, Tavistock was no 'well-dressed garden' but a 'field overgrowne with bryars and brambles ... a mere waste desolate wilderness, breeding and feeding ... all kinds of abominations. There was a vast congregation, consisting of many thousands of soules, but miserably ignorant, prophane and debauched. And how could it be otherwise, when ... sermons were as rare among them as black swans, [when] impudent sinners and dareing despisers of true holiness swarmed in every corner?'. How indeed? One can only agree with Quick's assessment that 'here was work enough for Mr Hughes'.[28]

Hughes set about the work with a will, but was soon forced to flee by the outbreak of the Civil War.[29] When Thomas Larkham, another radical minister, was appointed to the benefice in 1647 he found the situation basically unchanged. Larkham once termed Tavistock a 'poor, profane, populous town, wherein many are very ignorant of God, and the generality enemies to religion'.[30] On another occasion he complained that 'we have many bad examples in this place, I have hardly known the like in any place where I have been'.[31] Larkham was a much-travelled man and his comments make it hard to doubt the strength of religious conservatism in Tavistock. Even so, the town's backwardness paled into insignificance when compared with that of the parishes round about. During the 1650s Larkham, observing that Tavistock had been 'the first in church resurrection in these parts', reminded his congregation that 'darkness hath been upon the face of the country (for the most part) round about you'. He later reinforced the point by lamenting that 'most parishes about us are strangers unto [the Gospel]' and speaking with stern disapproval of 'such as live in holes by the mooreside, and scarce heare of God'.[32]

The religious conservatism of Tavistock and its hinterland can hardly be doubted. Nor was this the only Dartmoor town in which godly ministers met with an unfriendly welcome. At Okehampton the populace was unimpressed by attempts to tamper with established church practice. In 1636 the vicar sent a letter to Bishop Hall complaining that 'the liturgie is much neglected in your chapple at Okehampton being not fully read at any time by the curate there, and not at all by the lecturer, and not well frequented by the people when it is imperfectly read'.[33] In the light of this final comment, it comes as no surprise to learn that a lecture established at Okehampton by 1630 was poorly attended, nor that the town authorities made careful arrangements to ensure that the lecturer should not speak for too long.[34]

Popular resistance to puritanism: In defence of images

Only a few Devon parishes can definitely be shown to have demonstrated opposition to godly ministers in the 1630s and 1640s. How else can the anti-puritan strongholds be identified? One way is to pick out communities which were unwilling to destroy ancient church fittings and furniture. Courtenay's disgust at the soldiers' attack on rails and fonts has already been cited and other local Royalists shared his point of view. In October 1641 Thomas Minshall, one of the Exeter Cathedral Chapter, responded to Parliament's order that 'superstitious' church furniture should be destroyed by warning his listeners that 'the images and railes in the churches cost blood in setting of them upp, and that hee did thinke that they would cost some what adoe before they would be pulled downe'. Only 'such fellowes as [the puritans] were', he added, 'would have the old order putt downe and putt in newe'.[35] Minshall's words reveal just how strongly some religious conservatives felt about the retention of the altar rails and decorated glass, and just how much they despised the puritan despoilers of such objects. Nor were such sentiments confined to the gentry and clergy alone. In many areas of England 'the rabble', too, 'defended the familiar images' from puritan attack.[36]

A concern to preserve ancient church furniture was a telling indicator of religious conservatism. Did any parts of Devon exhibit such concern? Sadly no major incidents like that which occurred at Norwich in 1641—when a motley group of conformists turned out to defend the Cathedral organs—are recorded.[37] But this is not to say that such incidents did not take place, or that there was no affection for what Minshall termed 'the old order' in Devon. The surviving evidence, fragmentary though it is, suggests that some local communities were much less willing than others to participate in acts of iconoclasm. In some parts of Devon church furniture was destroyed by local people during 1641–42. Yet in other areas it was only when Roundhead troops arrived upon the scene that such destruction occurred. It is tempting to conclude that the inhabitants of these latter areas retained a deep affection for their accustomed church fittings and had therefore refused to implement Parliament's orders.

Roundhead troops are known to have embarked on iconoclastic rampages in at least four places in Devon; at Exeter Cathedral in 1643, at Tavistock in 1644, and at Ottery St Mary and Bovey Tracey in 1645–46.[38] The first three places have already been identified as strongholds of religious conservatism and it seems fair to assume that Bovey was as well. That two of the four churches which were attacked lay in Central Devon is also significant, tending to confirm that it was in this region that religious conservatism was strongest. Other pieces of evidence point the same way. On several occasions Mid-Devon folk are known to have rescued church furniture from destruction. At Dunsford a carpenter and a churchwarden hid the communion rails and Royal arms when an intruded minister tried to destroy them, and at Bovey Tracey the lectern stand was buried in order to protect it.[39] Clear proof that Mid-Devonians were exceptionally active in preserving church furniture can still be seen today. Writing in 1912 the church historian B.F. Cresswell noted that 'the most remarkable feature of the Teign Valley is the remarkable preservation of its church treasures', and added that, 'judging from what may be found among these churches', Parliament's orders 'must have been judiciously disregarded throughout the deanery of Kenn'.[40]

Intriguingly, the area to which Cresswell refers is the same small Mid-Devon district which was identified above as particularly backward and uncouth. That the Teign Valley was unique both for its isolation and for the richness of its church furniture is suggestive. It is hard to doubt that the two facts are connected. The unique survival of church furniture in this area probably reflects the fact that, because of the district's extreme isolation, radical protestant ideas had made little headway here by 1642. As a result there were few godly activists in the Teign Valley to implement Parliament's iconoclastic orders. Instead local people rallied to defend the church decorations and, significantly, this is the only part of Devon which provides any evidence of armed resistance to Parliamentary iconoclasm. According to nineteenth-century tradition, Nicholas Vaughan, the Roundhead officer slain at Dunsford, was killed by the villagers because he had tried to damage the church there.[41] If true, this story provides still further evidence of the vital part which an attachment to church furniture played in motivating the enemies of Parliament.

Popular resistance to puritanism: 'Ancient pagan customs'

Hostility to iconoclasm and the comments of contemporaries have helped to identify several anti-puritan strongholds. Tavistock, Okehampton, Bovey, Dunsford, Ottery and the Teign Valley all seem to have been places in which religious conservatism was particularly strong. That so many of these places lie in Mid-Devon can only be said to confirm Bond's assertion that this was the most 'prophane' region of the county. A pattern is beginning to emerge, therefore, but the overall view remains impressionistic and patchy. How can a more accurate picture of the relative strength or weakness of anti-puritanism across the county as a whole be obtained?

One possible answer is to examine the role of popular culture. In recent years there has been an explosion of interest in this subject. It has been demonstrated that, during the century which followed the break with Rome, many religious conservatives retained a marked affection for the festive culture which had been associated with the old catholic faith. Thus they continued to hold church ales (dedication feasts, intended to raise money for the repair of the parish church), to enjoy music and dancing and to participate in other communal festivities. These diversions were viewed with intense disapproval by fervent protestants, who regarded them as tarred with the brush of popery. Throughout the period 1560–1640, therefore, religious and cultural conflict took place across the land, as the godly strove to sweep away all vestiges of catholicism, and the embattled traditionalists tried, just as doggedly, to cling to their ancient practices. Can these cultural rivalries throw any light on wartime allegiances? David Underdown contends that, in Dorset, Somerset and Wiltshire, there was a close correlation between cultural conservatism and Royalism, with the regions in which popular festivities survived for longest going on to support the King.[42]

Underdown attributes this geographical convergence to two things. First he puts forward the 'ecological explanation' examined in Chapter Eight, pp. 152–53, suggesting that both popular Royalism and cultural conservatism flourished best in the arable and downland districts, where traditional social structures were better preserved. Second he claims that affection for the festive culture was a manifestation of a specifically religious conservatism, the same religious conservatism which lay behind wartime Royalism. Where puritanism was weak on the ground, Underdown argues, the godly campaign for moral reformation had little local support. As a result church ales and revels were able to survive for longer in these districts than in areas where radical protestantism was strong.[43]

These claims are exciting. They suggest that the relative survival of popular festivities can be used as a touchstone to denote the strength or weakness of religious conservatism in different areas. But Underdown's ideas have not gone unchallenged. Martin Ingram has cast doubt upon the claim that a dichotomy existed between conservative chalkland communities where popular festivities survived, and more radical, pastoral communities, where they did not.[44] Scepticism has also been voiced about the very concept of a puritan campaign against the festive culture. John Morrill and Anthony Fletcher have requested more evidence on this point, and observed that Underdown does not tackle T. Barnes's contention that a concern for order, rather than a desire for godly reformation, lay behind the order against church ales by the Somerset JPs in 1633.[45] Ingram has voiced similar reservations, claiming that 'growing bureaucratisation', not puritan ideology, was the driving force behind the campaign to replace church ales with rates (i.e. regular parish assessments). Ingram suggests that it was the size of the individual community, not its cultural preferences, which mattered most. Ales survived longest, he claims, in small communities, 'where the smaller number of households made festive fund raising still practicable'.[46]

If there was no puritan campaign against the festive culture, then the suggestion that popular festivities survived best in districts where puritanism was weakest will lose much of its force. This in turn will mean that cultural survival can hardly be used as evidence of religious conservatism. Before attempting to link the two things together one must therefore examine the history of popular festivities in pre-war Devon. Did the incidence of such celebrations decline in the years before 1640, and if so, why?

I have chosen to approach this subject by concentrating upon church ales, for two reasons.[47] First, ales were the festivities against which godly opinion was most firmly set and, second, evidence for Devon church ales is particularly good. Although no references to ales have yet been found in the local consistory court records, such gatherings are regularly mentioned in the sessions records and sometimes in the papers of the central law courts too.[48] Most important of all is the information preserved in local churchwardens' accounts. Fifty-two sets of accounts survive, in whole or in part, for the period 1570–1640 and all have been examined for the purposes of this book.[49] Together the wardens' accounts and legal records provide a rough idea of the distribution of church ales in early modern Devon. These sources reveal that, during the early years of Elizabeth's reign, ales were widespread. Of the twenty-two parishes for which accounts of the 1570s survive, ales were held in at least twenty.[50] Yet ales gradually started to be replaced by rates as the sixteenth century wore on. Barnstaple had set up a rating system by 1563.[51] Other urban communities soon followed suit and during the 1580s and 1590s ales started to be phased out in rural communities as well. By 1600 rating systems had been established in the majority of Devon parishes.[52]

The ales did not disappear overnight. Old habits died hard and many communities contrived to raise funds through both rates and ales, at least for a while. Kilmington adopted a rating system in 1580 but, nevertheless, ales continued to be held in the village for the next fifteen years. The sums brought in gradually declined but as late as 1592, £2 6s. was raised by the church ale, just four shillings less than was raised by the rate and not until 1595 did the ales finally cease.[53] A similar sequence of events took place at Halberton. Here, too, a rate was introduced during the early 1580s and henceforth rates brought in the bulk of church funds. Yet ales continued to be held, albeit less frequently and less profitably, for the next forty years.[54] This was a common pattern right across the county. By 1600 the situation had become extremely complicated. In many parishes ales had ceased for good but in other places they were still intermittently held, despite the adoption of a rating system. In one or two particularly isolated places, moreover, rates had not been introduced at all, and ales continued to be held as usual.[55] The situation remained broadly similar over the next forty years, yet all the time the ales were fading. Between 1600 and 1609 only forty-one church ales are known to have been held in Devon. This is only a third of the number recorded in the 1570s. Even so the figures for 1600–09 are high compared with those for the following decades. During 1610-19 only twenty-six ales were recorded, in 1620–29 the figure slipped to fifteen and in 1630–39 to eight. By the time the Book of Sports was re-issued in 1633 it was already too late to save church ales in the vast majority of Devon parishes.[56]

What lay behind the shift from ales to rates? In part it was the efficiency of the rating system which made it more attractive. Rates certainly produced a steadier supply of cash than ales, the profits of which tended to fluctuate wildly from year to year. Ingram is surely right, moreover, to claim that ales were abandoned in the larger towns first, and that this owed more to administrative considerations than religious ones. It is significant that 'prophane' Tavistock switched from ales to rates at around the same time as puritan Barnstaple.[57] The two towns were roughly the same size and may well have experienced similar difficulties in gathering funds. Even so it is hard to believe that administrative considerations alone can explain the ales' demise. The chief reason must surely be the steady stream of sessions orders which were issued against them between 1584 and 1627. This was certainly the view of the clerk of the peace, who noted with some satisfaction in 1631 that, due to 'divers orders ... made at the assizes ... [and sessions] for the suppressing of ... disorderlie assemblies' the incidence of church ales and other such gatherings had been much reduced.[58] His claim seems a fair one; the sudden collapse of the ales between 1580 and 1620 surely reflects the fact that at least five sessions orders had been directed against them during the same period.[59]

Why were these orders issued? In part, the drive against the ales reflected a distaste for disorder amongst the local elite. This is made clear by several of the sessions orders, one of which claimed that the feasts were 'a speciall cause ... [of] many disorders [and] contemptes of lawe'.[60] The order of 1615 was similarly justified by the fact that there had recently been 'severall manslaughters committed at two church ales within the countie'.[61] That the JPs' directives were concentrated in the period 1580–1620 may also reflect the fact that, during these years of acute depression, fear of disorder was particularly strong. Yet a concern for order is not enough in itself to explain the sudden growth in hostility to the ales. During previous periods of heightened social control (in

1460–1500, for instance) ales had not come under special attack. Only after the Reformation did they face a sustained assault.[62] The inference must surely be that hostility to the ales possessed a specifically protestant dimension.

This was certainly the view of Richard Carew. His *Survey of Cornwall* (1601) contains a mock debate between a defender of the church ales—who describes them as 'a matter practised amongst us from our eldest ancestors, with profitable and well pleasing fruit'—and an opponent, who condemns them as the cause of drunkenness, idle living and disorder. Significantly, the latter is eventually 'twitted' by the former 'of being precise, as those who say Christ tide ... rather than Christmas ... etc'. The perceived link between puritanism and opposition to church ales is again made clear. Elsewhere in the book Carew specifically attributes the suppression of the ales in Cornwall to 'the earnest invective' of ministers, who had 'condemned these church feasts as superstitious'.[63] Thomas Westcote made a similar point in his *View of Devon* (1630), observing that the old holiday exercises had been 'by zeal discommended and discountenanced'.[64]

Legal records tend to confirm Westcote's opinion. The suppression of church ales was regularly justified by the Devon Bench on explicitly religious grounds. It was claimed in 1595, for example, that the feasts led to 'the prophaning of the Lords Saboth, [and] the dishonour of almighty God'.[65] In 1615 the Bench complained of the 'continuall profanacon of Gods saboathe att those and other such like unlawfull meetinges'.[66] And in 1622 it was noted that an ale held at Ashburton had resulted in 'greate disorder' being committed, 'to the great dishonour of Almightie God, prophanacion of the Sabboth and the withdrawinge of many well disposed persons from good and godlie exercises'.[67] The wording of this last order is particularly significant as no mention is made of any disorder having occurred. Instead the JPs' condemnation of the ale is justified on religious grounds alone. They abhorred the feast, first, because it had dishonoured the sabbath and, second, because it had discouraged people from attending lectures or other forms of 'godlie' instruction.

The phrasing of the sessions orders suggests that, in Devon at least, specifically puritan sentiment did contribute to the elite assault upon popular culture. This discovery may not negate Barnes's claim that, in Somerset, the sessions and assize orders against church ales arose from a simple concern for public order 'rather than any dislike for church ales as profanations of the Sabbath', but it certainly acts as an important counterweight.[68] Nor can it be claimed that the Devon sessions orders were mere paper tigers. Between 1604 and 1628 churchwardens were regularly dragged before the justices for holding church ales.[69] Morrill's request for evidence of puritan JPs applying 'pressure on parish officers' is surely answered.[70] Puritan oligarchs also assisted in the campaign. In Exeter Ignatius Jurdain 'did much to reform the open prophaning of the sabboth, for ... whereas it was usual to sell fruit and herbs ... on the Lord's Holy day, and bowling and cudgel-playing, and profane pastimes were then much used; [Jurdain] by his zeal and vigilancy, and the care of good officers under him ... wholly removed [them]'.[71] Another godly activist was John Southmead of Moreton. The Vicar of Moreton, Francis Whiddon, later recalled that Southmead had been 'a great curb ... to prophanesse', citing 'his great paines and travell in overthrowing those heathenish sports and pastimes, which were too common even upon the Lords day'. 'God made ... [Southmead] the instrument to abolish Wakes, Revells, Maypoles and Maygames', Whiddon observed, 'not only in his owne, but in many other parishes adjacent'.[72]

Men like Jurdain and Southmead obviously played a crucial role in quashing the popular festivities, and there can be little doubt that these two individuals were motivated by godly zeal. The case for a specifically puritan campaign against the ales again seems hard to deny. Significantly, Jurdain's success in halting 'profane pastimes' in Exeter was attributed partly to 'the care of the good officers under him'; to the city constables, in other words, who put his orders into force. Without the help of such committed middling-sort supporters, even godly champions like Jurdain would have found it impossible to achieve a true reformation of manners. It is surely plausible to suggest that, where few middling-sort puritans existed, ales were able to survive for longer.

The defenders of the festive culture

The assault on the ales aroused considerable hostility. Many people wished to preserve their ancient pastimes, and Jurdain's campaign in Exeter provoked 'much reluctancy and opposition, and danger at the first; for there were commotions and tumults and great resistance ... [until] they were suppressed and quel-led'.[73] Ales, maypoles and revels clearly possessed a powerful local constituency, but what were these cultural conservatives like? Were they a mere rabble of drunken reprobates as the godly liked to claim or did they include respectable, articulate individuals within their ranks? Information about culturally conservative commoners is very sparse, but the career of William Elliott, of Holy Trinity parish in Exeter, helps to cast some light into this dark corner. Elliot was a member of the city cordwainers' com-pany and a man of considerable means. In 1619 he claimed that 'he paid more to the King and the poore' than the master of the company himself.[74] The son of an apothecary, Elliot was respect-able enough to be made churchwarden of a city parish but, nevertheless, he seems to have made a habit of opposing himself to persons in authority. Elliott first surfaced in the Exeter sessions records in 1619, after an angry dispute with a business associate, whom he termed 'a puritante knave'. This, and Eliot's subsequent disparaging references to Exeter's 'puritant justices', suggests that he himself was no admirer of reformed church practice.[75]

A year later Elliot was thrown into prison for questioning the Mayor's impartiality.[76] Elliot blamed this misfortune on an old enemy, Edward Searell, and, once he was released, he set about planning his revenge. It is interesting to note the form which this revenge was intended to take. Elliott informed a confidant in 1622 that 'he would have ... Searell's picture to bee drawne by Hart the paynter and ... would have it carryed aboute the citty uppon a maye pole'. Clearly the cordwainer was intending to use the symbols of the festive culture to deride his opponent's good name. Yet Elliot's plan contained a flaw, for maypoles were disapproved of by Exeter's 'puritante justices'. Elliot's friend seized upon this and reminded him, rather primly, that 'you cannot doe it [parade with a maypole] without leave of Mr Maior'. The cordwainer was in no mood to be brought down to earth, however, and airily dis-missed his friend's objections, saying 'that he made noe question but that he would gett Mr Maior's leave'.[77] That year's Mayor was John Modiford, an enemy of Ignatius Jurdain's.[78] Modiford might well have proved more amenable to Elliott's scheme than some of his predecessors in office. Even so, Elliot had said quite enough to get himself into trouble and he was lucky to be let off with a caution on this occasion.

In 1624 Elliott appeared before the court again, this time

charged with organizing a church ale in Trinity parish. It is significant that Elliott not only admitted to his actions, but vigorously defended them. When questioned as to whether he had sold any ale, he replied that 'he doth sell it and will sell it, for it is an aunciente custome that the wardens of the parish ... have used to sell drinke for the space of 3 hundred yeres, and it is for the good of the parishe, and he is nowe warden'.[79] For this offence, and no doubt for his impudence as well, Elliott was bound over. The cumulative effect of all these court appearances may well have had a chastening effect as Elliot did not reappear in the sessions records for some years. Yet in 1633 he emerged once more, this time charged with illegal gaming on the Sabbath.[80]

William Elliott's trials and tribulations provide a fascinating portrait of a defender of the festive culture. Elliott was a respectable man, but he was prepared to speak his mind and challenge authority. He was hostile to puritans and antagonistic towards the city authorities (probably because of their puritanical leanings). He was in favour of church ales, maypoles, and gaming on Sundays, and he actively tried to promote these pastimes. What is more he was fully aware of the centuries of tradition which underlay and, to him at least, legitimized these popular practices. Finally he was prepared to suffer imprisonment and harassment in defence of his beliefs. Elliot's stormy career suggests that the defenders of the festive culture were every bit as determined as those who wished to bring it down.

Elliott's opinions exude the true flavour of the religious and cultural conservatism which later underlay popular Royalism. Hatred of puritans, reverence for tradition, attachment to the festive culture; these three things were repeatedly cited by Parliamentary diurnalists as symptomatic of support for the King. In 1644 a Roundhead pamphleteer printed a satirical letter purporting to emanate from the 'loyallists inhabitinge in the wilde of Kent'. The supposed authors of this document begged for a resumption of church ales, and ended with a plea to 'let us serve God, after the old Protestant religion, and be merry together without preciseness'.[81] The belief that popular Royalism was intimately bound up both with an affection for the festive culture and a hatred of puritan 'preciseness' is made crystal clear.

Even more telling is the evidence of the Parliamentary diurnal *The Spie*. This noted in June 1644 that the last issue of *Mercurius Aulicus* had made 'a plea in the behalf of the vulgar rabble, for whitson-ales and morris-dancing and may poles'.[82] *The Spie* went on to claim that this plea had been inserted at the behest of the Royalist bishops, in order 'to ingratiate themselves and their cause into the acceptation of the more ignorant sort'. It was particularly vital for *Aulicus* to stress the Royalists' attachment to the festive culture 'now [that] his Majestie is recruiting', the diurnalist added, for when the commons 'understand that he fights for such glorious parcels of the protestant religion, they cannot choose but to come in unto him, to helpe defend these, and such like ancient pagan customes'.[83] The connection between religious conservatism, affection for the festive culture and popular Royalism could hardly be better expressed. Royalist commoners were not only prepared to fight in defence of the ales, they also regarded them as 'parcels of the Protestant Religion'.

One more contemporary comment begs to be included here. John Bond's description of what he termed 'our ejecting sins'; of the local weaknesses, in other words, which had led to the Parliamentary forces being driven from the western counties, has already been noted. In Devon it was 'the mines and the moores' which had acted as reservoirs of malignant backstabbers. Yet in the case of Somerset it was upon 'those wakes, revells, may poles &c that so much abounded in those parts' that Bond laid the blame for Parliament's defeat.[84] The intimate link between popular festivities and Royalism is once again confirmed.

The pattern of festive survival

Can this link be discerned on the ground in Devon, as Underdown has claimed that it can be elsewhere? Was the decline of church ales and popular festivities less marked in some regions of Devon than others? And if so, were the areas in which the festivities survived longest the same regions in which pre-war puritanism was weakest and wartime Royalism strongest? The answer, in every case, is yes. It has already been seen that different communities reacted in very different ways when ordered to abandon the old festive culture, some obeying the JPs' commands very quickly, other clinging to their traditional practices for as long as possible. This contrasting behaviour at once suggests that certain areas of the county were more culturally conservative than others—and Map 10 demonstrates that, by 1600, the distribution of church ales and other popular festivities in Devon had begun to

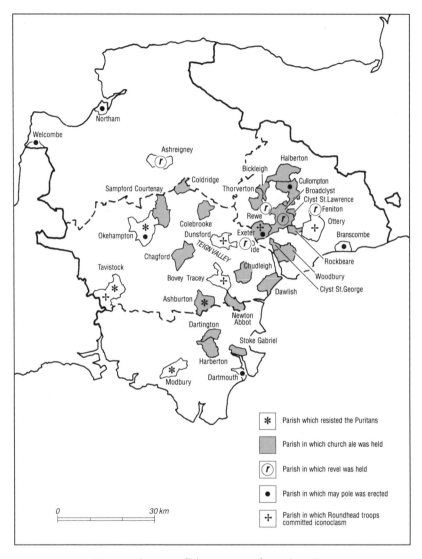

Map 10. Pre-war religious conservatism, 1600–1642.

exhibit striking regional variations. Of the thirty-two parishes in which ales, revels and other forms of festive disorder are known to have occurred between 1599–1600 and 1641–42, eleven lay in Mid-Devon and fourteen more in East Devon and Exeter. In striking contrast, only four such festivities are recorded from the south of the county, while just three are recorded from the north (see Map 10). The regional contrasts are clear, and they accord with those which the county displayed during 1642–46.

In North Devon the decline of the festivities was dramatic. Church ales had flourished here during the 1570s, but none survived into the seventeenth century. Not a single church ale is known to have been held in North Devon between 1600 and 1642 and other types of festive disorder were also rare. In 1627 a reprobate clergyman set up a maypole at Northam, and in 1628 and 1637 there were revels at Ashreigney and Welcombe.[85] Otherwise North Devon was bare of such festivities and the explanation for this is surely a religious one. North Devon was the region in which radical protestantism had made the greatest gains during the 1580s and 1590s. The sudden disappearance of local church ales during the same period reflected the puritan advance, and the failure of festivities to resurface here shows that godly activists retained their grip right up until 1642. Sixty years of puritan hegemony made North Devon a uniquely sterile environment from the Royalist point of view. It is hardly surprising that the region went on to be the most fervently Parliamentarian part of Devon.

In South Devon the situation was broadly the same. Here too popular festivities had largely disappeared by 1600, and here too puritanism was strong. The South Hams were not as puritan as North Devon, however, and this is reflected in the survival of a handful of local festivities after 1600. Ales continued to be held at Harberton and Dartington, and at Stoke Gabriel until 1620.[86] The latter parish was one of the few Royalist strongholds in the South Hams, again demonstrating the link between cultural survival and popular Royalism. Harberton, Dartington and Stoke Gabriel aside, only one other South Devon community is know to have experienced festive disorder during the early Stuart period. This was Dartmouth where a maypole was erected by 'a company of younkers' in 1634. This particular incident can hardly be seen as proof that popular festivities were approved of in Dartmouth, however, for the offenders were swiftly bound over by the puritan town authorities, subsequently leading to a tussle with

Laud's Vicar General.[87] In Mid-Devon, the most Royalist region of the county, popular festivities survived much longer. Between 1599–1600 and 1641–42 ales and revels were held in at least ten Mid-Devon parishes; Ashburton, Chagford, Chudleigh, Colebrooke, Coldridge, Dawlish, Ide, Sampford Courtenay, Widecombe and Wolborough.[88] In addition a maypole was erected at Okehampton in 1641.[89] The late survival of popular festivities in such a comparatively large number of Mid-Devon communities surely clinches the argument that this was the most religiously conservative region of Devon.

East Devon was the most divided region of the county during the Civil War, with the northern and north-eastern districts favouring Parliament and Exe Vale supporting the King. Once again, this division was reflected in the relative survival of popular festivities. In lower Exe Vale the festive culture proved very resilient, with many ales and revels surviving long after 1600. Broadclyst, in particular, was a festive stronghold. In 1612 an ale was held here and next year a near-riot broke out when the parish governors switched to a rating system.[90] In 1615 and 1622 revels took place in the village, and as late as 1635 a parish ale raised the impressive sum of £14.[91] Most of the other parishes in which festive disorder is known to have occurred lay in a wide circle around Broadclyst. Ales were held at Clyst St Lawrence in 1604, Clyst St George in 1605, Bickleigh in 1607, Thorverton in 1610, Rockbeare in 1613 and Woodbury in 1620.[92] In addition revels were held at Feniton in 1601 and at Rewe in 1620.[93] All these parishes lay in the region which has already been identified as Royalist. In the Blackdown hills and on the coast, by contrast—the puritan/Parliamentarian part of East Devon—popular festivities were rare. Apart from the erection of a maypole at Branscombe in 1634, no organized festivities are known to have occurred in these districts.[94] Once again Underdown's thesis is confirmed.

One part of East Devon presents conflicting evidence. The district around Cullompton was strongly Parliamentarian, but Cullompton was also a centre of festive disorder. Ales continued to be held in the town until 1612 and in 1616 the wardens were examined by local JPs 'touching a stocke by them collected for the sellinge of churche ale'.[95] Fifteen years later 'great misdemeanours' were committed at Cullompton during 'the setting up of a maypole' there.[96] The erection of the maypole might perhaps be dismissed as the action of a few individuals, and thus as unrepresentative of the attitude of the community as a whole. The late retention of the church ales is harder to explain away, however, as is the fact that the neighbouring town of Halberton, another Parliamentary stronghold, saw ales clinging on until 1621.[97] In this district the link between cultural conservatism and wartime Royalism remains hard to prove. Yet in every other part of Devon, the survival of church ales serves as an accurate predictor of both wartime allegiance and the pre-war strength of puritanism.

In August 1642 Thomas Trescott, the puritan vicar of Inwardleigh in Mid-Devon, delivered a powerful sermon at the Exeter assizes, in which he begged the judge to stamp out those 'heathenish may-games', those 'church-ales and revells', those 'unlawfull assemblies (meere conventicles of bad fellowes) ... [which] yet in some places are more zealously observed, and stood for, than ... the Lawes of God'.[98] Trescott's words show that, as late as 1642, ales were still flourishing in certain parts of Devon (and particularly perhaps, in the region where the preacher himself dwelt). Yet the most fascinating aspect of Trescott's speech is its depiction of ales and revels not just as sinful pastimes, but as what amounted to almost a rival system of belief to that espoused by the godly. Trescott's words—and William Elliot's actions—confirm that ales and revels were 'zealously stood for' by many Devonians, just as puritan ideals were strenuously upheld by others. There can be little doubt that these rivalries later helped decide wartime allegiance. Just as puritan meetings were the chief breeding ground of popular resistance to the King, so church ales and revels—'mere conventicles of bad fellowes'—were the focal points of popular resistance to Parliament.

PART IV

The National Picture

Introduction

During the 1650s, Jane Jessup, the servant of Thomas Rich of Plympton, was asked which side her master had supported during the Civil War. Her answer—'that when the King's partye were quartered at the said Mr Rich his house they condemned him to bee of the Parliament's partye, and when the Parliament's partye quartered there they said hee was for the Kinge's partye, and more shee cannot depose'—would still be taken by many scholars to encapsulate the attitude of the vast majority of the common people to the events of the English Civil War.[1] Yet the evidence presented in Parts II–III of this book suggests that such a view can no longer be upheld. In Devon, at least, people from all ranks of society possessed very definite political views, and firm political commitment did exist amongst the common people. Moreover, wartime allegiances in this county displayed a clear geographical pattern. The inhabitants of Mid-Devon possessed a political and religious outlook which was markedly more conservative than that of their fellow Devonians. The fact that these divergent attitudes can be traced back to 1600 and beyond suggests the existence of long-standing traditions of conservatism and dissent, contrasting patterns of political behaviour stretching back over very many years.

During the Spanish Civil War George Orwell observed that 'the people of Barcelona are so used to street fighting and so familiar with the local geography that they know by a kind of instinct which political party will hold which streets and which buildings'.[2] The people of early modern Devon were not accustomed to street fighting of course (or at least not in the modern sense of the word). Nor did they possess organized political parties. Nevertheless it is tempting to suggest that they, too, had a clear understanding of political geography, knowing full well which local parishes would be more or less sympathetic to which particular causes. Just how deeply such ideas were ingrained in the local subconscious is demonstrated by the fact that, when Edward Wood of Culmstock was accused of being a Royalist after the Civil War, he tried to disprove the charges simply by stating that he had previously lived in Hemyock and Uffculme, well known to be 'parishes well-affected to the Parlyament'.[3] Wood's words bear witness to a complicated pattern of political geography, one which this study has mapped out in Devon for the first time. Did similar patterns exist across the whole of England? The fourth and final part of this book suggests that they did.

Chapter 12

'Out of the Dust of the Earth'?

Writing in 1993, Ronald Hutton dismissed belief in the 'mono-lithic loyalties of counties and towns to one party or another' as 'antiquated'.[1] He is in good company. Conrad Russell has noted that 'no area was unanimous', Gerald Aylmer that 'very few regions were solidly for King or Parliament' and R.C. Richardson that 'it was rare indeed to find unanimous allegiance to one side in the same place'.[2] Such statements are undoubtedly correct: unanimity was hard to find. Yet beyond this point scholarly consensus breaks down. While Aylmer believes that 'some counties and towns, and some districts within counties, were more or less Royalist or Parliamentarian than others',[3] Hutton finds such contrasts difficult to discern. Herefordshire was the only county which demonstrated genuine popular enthusiasm for the King, he claims, while popular Parliamentarianism was equally insignificant.[4] According to Hutton 'the only place in the future Royalist area which manifested ... unequivocal support for Parliament was the small town of Birmingham'.[5] This seems to ignore the example of Barnstaple, Dartmouth, Plymouth and a good many other places besides, but for the moment it can be allowed to pass.

Hutton's opinions owe much to the work of Clive Holmes, Roger Howell Brian Manning and John Morrill, all of whom have, at different times, stressed the importance of popular neut-ralism and indifference during the period 1642–46.[6] Hutton is probably the historian who has taken such ideas to their farthest extremes, but a similar tendency is visible in much recent writing on the Civil War. In a 1992 article R.C. Richardson observed that 'to describe a locality or town as either Royalist or Parliament-arian is misleading in a number of respects', adding that 'terms like "Royalist Newcastle" or "Parliamentarian Bradford" refer chiefly to the dominant elite of the place in question'.[7] Many scholars would agree with this point of view, indeed Richardson's words represent the dominant strand in contemporary historical thinking. Yet over the last decade a number of others, most notably David Underdown and Ann Hughes, have challenged the neutralist/indifference model.[8] While not seeking to resurrect the old idea of a country divided into a solidly Parliamentarian South and East and a solidly Royalist North and West, they agree, with Aylmer, that certain towns, regions and counties were more, or less, Royalist or Parliamentarian than others. The evidence from Devon strongly supports such a view. But what was the position across the country as a whole?

'In a perfect world', Underdown once noted, 'in which historians had unlimited time, unlimited funds and armies of research assistants at their disposal, it might be possible to investigate the patterns of Civil War allegiance throughout the whole of England'.[9] The world remaining manifestly imperfect, it may well be thought reckless to attempt such a survey here. Yet the regional patterns of behaviour which have already emerged from this book, from Underdown's own research and from that of other scholars working elsewhere seem clear and compelling enough for a preliminary attempt at a national plan of allegiances to be made. The following pages seek to construct such a model. Attention will focus most closely on Cornwall, Wales and the West, but an examination of affairs in the rest of the country will also be made.

Cornwall

Throughout the eighteenth and nineteenth centuries, Cornwall was regarded by historians as the Royalist county par excellence.[10] It is easy to see why. Cornwall was the one county in Southern England which remained in the King's hands throughout the war, and it produced many of the King's bravest commanders and soldiers. Yet ever since the publication of Mary Coate's great study of the county in 1933, Cornwall's Royalism has tended to be played down. Coate observed that Parliamentarianism had been strong amongst the Cornish gentry and claimed that many of the smaller towns had been indifferent to the Royalist cause.[11] She also noted that, according to the Royalist Joseph Jane, political opinion had been finely balanced in Cornwall in 1642, and, had it not been for the fortuitous arrival of Ralph Hopton with a body of Royalist horse, the county might well have declared for Parliament.[12] Later historians have seized upon this, claiming that Cornwall became Royalist chiefly thanks to the good luck, tact and timing of the King's local gentry supporters.[13]

This is surely to go too far. While currents of Parliamentarian opinion undoubtedly existed in Cornwall, they were largely restricted to the gentry and the clergy. The vast majority of the common people supported the King, a fact which was to be demonstrated again and again as the war progressed. In 1642 huge numbers of men rose up to eject Sir Richard Buller and his 700 or so Parliamentarian supporters from their headquarters at Launceston. One excited Royalist informed Lady Dorothy Mohun at this time (obviously with considerable exaggeration) that 'there were at Lanseston att least twenty thousand of armed men, besids ten thousand supplies, to [fight] ... with Sir Richard Buller's armye'.[14] Once Parliament's few local supporters had been chased out of the county, thousands of Cornishmen enlisted in the Royalist army. This rush to the colours cannot be attributed simply to fear or compulsion. Such an explanation ignores the fervour with which Cornish soldiers fought for the Royal cause. It also ignores the fact that, whenever Parliamentary armies subsequently ventured into Cornwall, they were stoutly resisted by the inhabitants. In summer 1643 Parliamentary troops from North Devon sallied across the Tamar whilst Hopton's Cornish army was away in Somerset. Had Cornwall's Royalism been feigned or reluctant, the inhabitants would surely have aquiesced in this invasion. Instead, as the Roundheads themselves admitted, 'the whole power of the county of Cornwall rose against them'.[15] Cornish hostility to Parliament was demonstrated even more clearly during summer 1644, when the Earl of Essex marched into the county with a Roundhead army. The entire adult male population took to their heels, causing Essex to note with bewilderment and growing alarm that 'through many townes and villages where my army passes, there is none but women and children left'.[16]

The King's army met with a very different reception. Before crossing the Tamar in pursuit of Essex, the Royalist soldiers had been told that 'they were now entering a country exceedingly affectionate to his Majesty'.[17] They were not to be disappointed and as soon as the King marched into Cornwall the able-bodied men who had hidden themselves from Essex came flocking to join him.[18] Clarendon speaks of 'the general conflux and concurrence of the whole people of Cornwall' to the King,[19] and Edward Walker was equally impressed. Indeed he saw the strength of popular support for the King in Cornwall as unique, commenting that 'not till now were we sensible of the great and extraordinary advantage the rebels have over his Majestie's armies throughout the kingdom by intelligence ... which by the loyalty of the [Cornish] people, the rebels here were utterly deprived of, no country in his Majestie's dominions being so universally affected to his Majesty and his cause'.[20] Richard Symonds, an officer in the King's lifeguard, confirmed Walker's statement, noting in his journal that 'divers of the country people came to the King with much joy to tell him of his enemyes, where they lay, and please his worship'.[21]

The King's subsequent defeat of Essex owed much to the support of the Cornish people, who hung like wolves on the flanks of the Roundhead army. According to Walker the Roundhead soldiers 'could not straggle out of their quarters but they were presently either slain or taken'.[22] Parliamentary sources confirmed this, Essex writing despairingly that 'intelligence we have none, the country people being violent against us, if any of our scouts or soldiers fall into their hands they are more bloody than the enemy'.[23] Following Essex's surrender 'the Cornish, both men and women, had no compassion' on their defeated foes.[24] After the Parliamentarian foot soldiers had been disarmed the King permitted them to march back towards the east, yet when the Roundheads reached Lostwithiel they were set upon and mobbed by 'the inhabitants and the country people'.[25] A crowd of 'Cornish dames' attacked the Parliamentarian camp followers, stripping them of their clothes and even hurling some poor unfortunates into the river beneath Lostwithiel Bridge.[26] Similar scenes were enacted in other towns on the Roundhead line of retreat, the Cornish women again proving especially violent.[27] Terrified, the Parliamentary soldiers fled for the Tamar, 'never thinking themselves secure till they were got out of this county of Cornwall'.[28]

During the Western campaign of 1645/46 the commanders of the New Model Army took quite exceptional pains to win over the Cornish, who were still regarded as 'generally disaffected to the Parliament'.[29] Fairfax spoke of 'good carriage ... [being] the best way to gain them' and made sure that all Cornish soldiers whom his army took prisoner during early 1646 were released on parole, with a small sum of money to cover their expenses on the journey home.[30] When the New Model Army finally entered Cornwall the Roundhead soldiers were told to treat the inhabitants with special respect. In addition a propaganda offensive was launched by the puritan preacher Hugh Peters, who, in a series of open air meetings, assured the country people that Parliament meant them no harm.[31] These exceptional measures—combined with the total collapse of the Royalist cause elsewhere—eventually persuaded the Cornishmen to lay down their arms, but they had already done as much as could humanly be expected of them.

Within the overall picture of Cornish Royalism there were distinct regional variations. Clarendon observed that it was 'the west of that county ... [which was] best affected', and his statement receives ample support from other sources.[32] West Cornwall is one of the few areas of England which really does seem to have been almost unanimous in its allegiance. Outside the fiercely independent port of St Ives, popular Parliamentarianism simply did not exist in this region, or if it did, not a scrap of evidence for it has survived. When Hopton first arrived in Cornwall a thousand men came in to his assistance from the two western hundreds of Powder and Pyder alone. Following the Royalists' decision to summon the county posse 'there appeared of the west part of Cornwall ... about three thousand foote well arm'd ... and divers others with clubbs'.[33] The remarkable enthusiasm of this response prompted the Royalist gentlemen of West Cornwall to send the local constables a special letter of thanks. This (previously unnoted) 'gratulacon to Cornish men' praised the 'great cheerefullnes that wee observed in the Countie's readye repayre uppon ... the Posse Comitatus' and promised that 'as [the local people] testified theire loyaltie and love to theire kinge and countrye in that action, soe we shal retaine a faithfull memory of [that] acte ... and ... represent theire forwardnes ... to his Majestie'.[34] The Parliamentarians drew what support they possessed at this time from 'the east division' of the county.[35] The same east–west division persisted throughout the war. Pamphleteers reported in late 1645 that many men were coming in to the Royalists from West Cornwall, but that 'Grenvill complaines of the eastern confines to be very untoward, like their Devonshire borders, loath to come in'.[36]

Where should one draw the line between the staunchly Royalist west and the more lukewarm east? The inhabitants of the countryside around Bodmin, halfway along the Cornish peninsula, were clearly loyal. In 1643 they fought at the barricades to resist a Roundhead cavalry force which was trying to enter the town (the fact that many of these troopers later became 'a prey to the country people', suggests that, even as early as this, the Cornish felt an unusually deep antipathy towards the Parliamentarians).[37] Liskeard, fifteen miles further east, was also strongly Royalist. In 1643 'the burgesses, leaving their homes, fought bravely in the memorable battle and victory of Braddock Down ... although their wives and families remained at the same time under the power of the rebels'.[38] When the King made his headquarters at Liskeard a year later 'the townsmen and contiguous countrymen shewed themselves very zealous and loyal towards his service'.[39] Walker noted that, from the moment the Royalist army arrived in the town, 'we had hourly notice of the rebels' actions'.[40] Even in the countryside around Saltash, the most south-easterly part of Cornwall, popular opinion was clearly on the King's side, the country people 'cheerfully coming in' to assist him.[41] Popular support for Parliament seems to have been restricted to Saltash itself and to the north-eastern corner of the county: to Launceston, the upper Tamar Valley and the district around Stratton—which Clarendon described as 'the only part of Cornwall eminently disaffected to the King's service'.[42]

Why was most of Cornwall so strongly Royalist, and why did the north-eastern corner behave so differently? Edward Walker gave the most detailed contemporary explanation of the Royalism of the Cornish commoners, ascribing it to 'that obedience to their superiors which the rest have cast off. For the gentry of this county retain ... their old tenants and expect from them their ancient reverence and obedience'.[43] Walker's explanation has been swallowed uncritically by historians, who have used it to argue that Cornish Royalism owed more to deference to social superiors than to any real affection for the Crown.[44] Such explanations fail to explain why the many Cornish gentlemen who supported Parliament, most notably Lord Robartes, were unable to rally their tenants to the Roundhead cause. Nor should it be forgotten that Walker himself was a deeply conservative man, one who instinctively linked Parliamentarianism with a lack of respect for the social hierarchy.[45] When Walker came across the Cornish—a group of commoners who were conspicuously loyal to the Crown—his own prejudices naturally led him to assume that their loyalty must have stemmed from deference to their social superiors. Walker's explanation of Cornish Royalism reflected the world as he would have liked it to be, rather than the world as it really was.

An alternative explanation for Cornish Royalism is that local people felt a particular affection for the Duchy of Cornwall. This theory was dismissed by Mary Coate, who concluded that 'the fact that a man was a Duchy tenant did not determine his choice [of sides]'.[46] While this may have been true of the handful of gentry activists whom Coate examined it was not true of more humble folk. Hals attributed the loyalty of Liskeard specifically to the fact that 'the town ... and manor of Leskeard was ... the Duke of Cornwall's lands'.[47] If the Duchy's influence has been played down, that of the Cornish Stannaries has been virtually ignored. Yet it is arguable that the Stannaries played a vital role, not only in securing Cornwall for the King, but also in establishing Royalist control over the entire South-west of England. The Cornish tin-miners were very numerous and, like their Devonshire colleagues, they had every reason to support King Charles. It was surely the presence of these 8–10,000 tin-miners which enabled Hopton to raise an army in Cornwall with such remarkable speed. And it was surely their toughness and endurance—combined with the fact that they were already inured to the semi-military discipline imposed in the mines—which enabled the small Cornish army to defeat much larger Roundhead forces again and again during 1642–43.

Important though the miners were, their presence alone is insufficient to explain the peculiar intensity of Cornish Royalism. In Cornwall, as in Devon, religion was probably the crucial motivating force.[48] Joseph Jane claimed that it was 'zele for the establisht liturgie' which had brought the majority of Cornishmen into the King's camp.[49] This opinion was shared by Hugh Peters, who identified popular affection for the 'service book' as a major determinant of local allegiance.[50] Roundhead pamphleteers agreed, stressing again and again the religious backwardness of Cornwall, which they variously described as 'a corner of ignorants', 'a place full of superstitious and popishly affected persons' and 'a pagan principality ... inhabited by a blind generation'.[51] Cornwall had a long tradition of religious conservatism. In 1549 the county had rebelled against Edward VI's religious innovations and as late as 1577 Bishop Alley was frightened of how 'the sympell Cornishe men' might react to 'straunge doctrine'.[52] On the eve of the

Civil War radical protestant ideas had still made relatively little headway amongst the common people of Cornwall and popular puritanism was largely confined to the eastern hundreds.[53] Significantly this is the very area which later came out for Parliament.

Why was Cornwall so resistant to puritanism? The county's remoteness and its lack of major urban centres was obviously important, as was the presence of thousands of ungodly tin-miners. The late survival of the Cornish language must also have had a part to play. In the far west of Cornwall there was still a substantial monoglot population in 1642. Those who could not speak English would have been largely immune not only to puritan religious teachings, but also to the flood of scurrilous ballads, libels and newsheets which increasingly came to tarnish the monarchy's reputation during the early Stuart period.[54] This surely helps to explain why the far west of Cornwall eventually became the most solidly Royalist area in southern England.

Wales

The situation in Wales provides some intriguing parallels. Like Cornwall, Wales was quickly secured for the King in 1642 and like Cornwall it went on to supply large numbers of foot soldiers to the Royalist army. Hutton regards the behaviour of Wales as mysterious but he and other historians agree that Welsh Royalism was primarily attributable to the influence of local gentry activists.[55] Is the deference model any more convincing for Wales than it is for Cornwall or Devon? A great deal of evidence survives to suggest that Welsh commoners felt a genuine commitment (or 'addiction' as one Roundhead commentator termed it) to the Royalist cause.[56] Clarendon noted that the whole of Wales was generally well-affected to the King and Royalist polemicists agreed, lavishing extravagant praise on 'the loyall Welsh'.[57] Roundhead pamphleteers responded with a torrent of anti-Welsh propaganda —including some of the most scurrilous publications of the entire decade.[58] Their efforts did nothing to reduce Welsh hostility to Parliament. By late 1644 Roundhead leaders in the Marches, like Fairfax in the west during the following year, were coming to realize that more positive measures would have to be taken if the hostility of the King's Celtic supporters was to be overcome. Having captured some Welsh prisoners in September 1644 the Parliamentarian General Massey 'used [them] very kindly, and soon after sent them to their homes, every one with a little note, directed to his master or the parish where he lived, to signify to them that the intention of Parliament ... [was] to preserve their lives and fortunes ... [and] to open the cause of justice'.[59]

These measures were not without effect,[60] but even so, most Welsh people remained hostile to Parliament throughout 1645–46. In March 1645 one local Royalist assured another that, although the strategic position in South Wales was deteriorating, the common people 'are yet for the most part loyal'.[61] In August 1646, with the war almost over, General Fairfax, conducting operations at Raglan, could still note 'how disaffected these parts are'.[62] Two years later a Roundhead correspondent wearily admitted that 'I am much afflicted that I can give no better account of South Wales, but in one word I must say again, that it is generally against the Parliament'.[63] In North Wales the populace was even more solidly Royalist. Norman Dore has noted the inhabitants' 'stubborn resistance to all the blandishments of the Parliament' and observed that 'Parliamentary troops did not dare to take up quarters over the Welsh border' until the very end of the war.[64] The Parliamentarian William Brereton complained in November 1645 that the people of North Wales 'remain so disaffected as that they rather prefer to bury [or] destroy ... their victuals' than that the Parliament's troops should get them.[65]

The Royalism of the North Welsh was similar to that of the Cornish in its intensity, and it probably sprang from the same basic root, namely, a deep religious conservatism, fostered by isolation and racial difference. Mid seventeenth-century Wales was 'a barren land for puritans', and Roundhead pamphleteers continually ascribed the malignity of the Welsh to their religious traditionalism.[66] 'Alas' cried one diurnalist, 'it is no wonder to see Wales for the King's service, for they have scarce had any more reformation than the Common Prayer Book, or Masse Book Junior'.[67] 'The word of God hath scarce appeared to the Welsh mountainers', agreed another, while a third observed that the Cornish and 'the ignorant Welch ... are very heathens ... that know no religion, or God'.[68] This was a common charge. One pamphleteer accused the Welsh and the Cornish of 'paganisme', going on to predict that 'when posterity shall see the Gospell shine cleere there, they will know what Turkes their ancestors were, and what advantage this rebellion against the Parliament had from thence by their forefathers' ignorance'.[69] That Welsh

Royalism had a cultural dimension as well as a purely religious one is suggested by the comment that the Welsh 'find no fault with any religion but Roundheadisme, nor hate any man but him that will preach against . . . good fellowship on Sunday about the Maypoll'.[70]

The pamphleteers' opinion that Wales was a stronghold of religious conservatism was confirmed by the reports of observers on the ground. A correspondent attached to the Parliamentary force which occupied Caernarvonshire in 1646 noted with distaste that 'they are here, for the matter of religion, most ignorant and brutish people who know very little of God, and it is heartily to be wished that some honest and godly painful ministers would come to preach to them', adding that, 'the country towns hereabouts have been quite without all manner of preaching almost'.[71] Symptomatic of the principality's religious conservatism was the affection which the inhabitants retained for the traditional church furniture and decoration. Roundhead soldiers smashed up what they could, but in Wales, as in Mid-Devon, local people removed and hid certain treasured items in order to protect them from destruction. Peter Gaunt observes that 'the finest [stained glass window] surviving in Wales—the Jesse of 1533 in St Dyfnog's, Llanrhaeadr—reputedly does so only because it was removed and buried in a chest during the war'.[72] Royalist soldiers were affronted by the violence offered to their churches and sometimes tried to repair the damage which the Roundheads had done. The Royalist Captain Harry Byrch noted in December 1643 that, after a group of Parliamentarian soldiers had dragged the altar at Hawarden in North Wales into the middle of the church, 'some of our soldiers came and swore it was not right . . . and set it close to the wall again'.[73]

The religious traditionalism of the Welsh must have owed a good deal to the principality's remoteness and its lack of major urban centres. Yet the biggest single barrier to the spread of puritan ideas was surely linguistic. In Wales, far more than in Cornwall, the population was shielded from advanced protestant views by incomprehension of the language in which those views were usually advanced. Welsh-speaking puritan ministers remained very rare until well after the Civil War, and even during the Interregnum the godly were slow to realize 'the need for a dialogue with the Welsh in their own tongue'.[74] It is crucially significant that the one part of Wales which demonstrated unequivocal support for Parliament during the Civil War was Pembroke-shire—the most anglicized part of the principality.[75] Sir John Birkenhead, the editor of *Mercurius Aulicus*, made a special point of this, observing that Pembrokeshire was 'the most seditious county of all Wales, or rather of England, for the inhabitants live like English Corporations, very unlike the loyall Welchmen'.[76] His comment suggests that social conditions, as well as language, had combined to set Pembrokeshire apart from the rest of Wales.

Birkenhead was obviously struck by the unusual loyalty of the King's Celtic subjects, for he returned to this theme elsewhere, commenting that 'Pembroke is the only remnant of Wales (if it be true Welch) which rebels against his Majestie, for as Pembroke (still called little England beyond Wales) forsook their allegiance when all other Welch counties stood loyall to his Majestie; so Cornwall (which is little Wales beyond England) proved them-selves true Brittaines, when no English county stood intirely for his Majestie'.[77] Birkenhead might well have been amused to learn that 'the British dimension' in wartime allegiance patterns which he identified here had yet another local twist. Stratton hundred—little England in Cornwall—was the one part of that county which came out wholeheartedly for Parliament.

In Wales and Cornwall the presence of a Celtic population really does seem to have led to popular Royalism. That this was so owed much to the linguistic factors already explored above, yet there was surely a racial dimension as well. In Scotland and Ireland attachment to non-Anglican faiths was, at least in part, an expression of national independence, of resistance to the military, political and cultural hegemony of England. When these faiths were perceived to be under serious threat, as in Scotland in 1637 and Ireland in 1641, religious and racial tensions combined together to form a molotov cocktail of hate. It seems probable that in Wales and Cornwall, too, a particular brand of religious faith—in this case conservative anglicanism—was seen as an integral part of national identity, and that, when this faith was threatened by Parliament, racial anxieties combined with religious ones to ensure that the bulk of the population fell in behind the King. Deep-seated sentiments like these seem a much more plaus-ible explanation of Welsh and Cornish Royalism than the defer-ence model—let alone the still popular theory that Henry VII's Welsh origins had somehow made the people of the principality feel especially well-disposed towards his Stuart successors![78]

The Welsh Borders

Popular Royalism was very strong in Wales and Cornwall but it would be quite wrong to conclude, as several historians have done, that such sentiments were restricted to the Celtic fringe alone.[79] The counties of the Welsh Marches provide a major stumbling block to this theory. Herefordshire, in particular, was an area in which popular Royalism was strong, one Roundhead pamphleteer describing it as 'a malignant county and frontier to a malignanter Wales'.[80] In 1642 the Parliamentarian Earl of Stamford complained that the people of Herefordshire 'are so base and malignant that although the roguish army of the Welsh papists ... do plunder, kill, murder and destroy men and women, take away all their goods and cattle, yet such is their hatred to our condition that they would rather be so used than be rescued by us'.[81] As Jacqueline Eales has shown, the strength of support for the King in Herefordshire was a reflection of the county's religious conservatism. The Harley family were 'the only leading Herefordshire gentry who were puritans' and their local supporters were few.[82] One of Brilliana Harley's servants was told in July 1642 'that theare was but a feawe puretaines in this cuntry, and 40 men would cut them all off'.[83]

Clarendon described Hereford itself as 'a town very well-affected' to the King and there can be little doubt that he was right.[84] The Roundhead sergeant Nehemiah Wharton commented that 'the city were all malignants, save three', observing that, when the Parliamentary forces finally got into the city, they found 'the doors shut [and] many of the people with their children fled'.[85] Walking around Hereford afterwards Wharton noted the familiar symptoms of popular Royalism, commenting that 'the inhabitants are totally ignorant of the ways of God, and are much addicted to drunkeness and other vices'. In a subsequent letter to his master he advocated the usual remedy, a supply of 'faithful and painful ministers.[86] Wharton's disdainful remark that 'many here speak Welsh' is a reminder that the substantial Welsh-speaking population of Herefordshire may well have contributed to that county's fervent Royalism.[87]

The same was probably true of Shropshire. Here too the population contained a strong Welsh element and here too popular Royalism was strong. Clarendon termed Shropshire 'that good county', while a Roundhead officer complained that 'the whole county of Salop is rotten'.[88] In this 'heartland of Royalism' local people manifested support for the King on numerous occasions.[89] At Ludlow in June 1642 the townsfolk 'set up a Maypole and a thing like a head upon it ... and gathered a great many about it, and shot at it in derision of Roundheads'.[90] A few months later multitudes poured in to swell the King's army from Shropshire and Wales, including twenty from Myddle parish alone.[91] Malcolm Wanklyn has concluded that Parliament's cause was 'not popular with the common people of Shropshire' and that only in Shrewsbury was there a substantial Roundhead group.[92] So great was the assistance which Shropshire lent the Royal cause that it was later feared the Parliamentarians would take their revenge. Writing to his parents from London in 1644 a Shropshire-born apprentice warned them that a Roundhead army was setting out for the Marches, adding 'God knows what will become of you all, for I do much feel that our county will be punished sorely'.[93]

Worcestershire was another strongly Royalist county. Clarendon described it as 'well-affected to the King', while Symonds observed that 'this county ... hath given several ample testimonies of their affection to his Majestie's cause', adding that nine regiments 'have beene raysed out of this county *pro Rege*, which consists onely of 150 od parish[es]'.[94] When Parliamentary forces marched into east Worcestershire in 1642 local people refused to supply them until Essex threatened that 'he would fire their towns'.[95] Parliamentarian pamphleteers regarded Worcestershire, 'that malignant county', with intense dislike.[96] One diurnalist informed his readers that the chief products of Worcestershire were 'apples, pears and malignancie'.[97] Worcester itself was strongly Royalist.[98] Clarendon speaks of 'the loyalty of that good town', while *Mercurius Aulicus* heaped praise upon 'the loyall citizens'.[99] On the Parliamentarian side Nehemiah Wharton bitterly reported how the inhabitants had assisted the Royalists in 1642, 'the treacherous citizens attending them in multitudes'.[100] Wharton later informed his master, 'Sir ... Worcester ... is so vile, and the country so base, papistical and atheistical and abominable, that it resembles Sodom and is the very emblem of Gomorrah'.[101]

In Cheshire majority opinion was on the other side.[102] Nantwich, Stockport and Macclesfield were all pro-Parliamentary towns while Royalist officers acknowledged the hostility of the populace at large.[103] Yet in Cheshire, as in Devon, there were variations in the pattern of allegiance. The trained bands of Broxton and Wirral hundreds turned out for the King in 1643 and there were many Royalists in Chester.[104] Chester's political stance is a hotly disputed question. Clarendon claimed that 'the city ... was firm to the King, by the virtue of the inhabitants', and this view was long accepted by historians.[105] During the 1970s, however, attempts were made to overturn this orthodoxy. John Morrill stressed the deep divisions which had existed within the city, while A.M. Johnson suggested that the citizens of Chester had not, in fact, been particularly loyal, but had rather been tricked into supporting the Crown by a small group of Royalist aldermen.[106] This argument has been convincingly refuted by Norman Dore, who reaffirms the picture of Chester as a 'Loyal City' and observes that the citizens showed 'a marked disinclination to abandon [the Royalist] cause even when it was facing defeat'.[107] In Cheshire, as elsewhere, religion was the most important factor in determining allegiances, with one Royalist officer specifically attributing local disaffection to 'the factious and seditious preachers' who had been active in the county before the war.[108]

Gloucestershire, at the other end of the Marches, was more strongly Parliamentarian still. Popular risings against the Royalists took place in many parts of the county—at Cirencester, at Stow-on-the-Wold and in the villages near Berkeley Castle—while the countryside near Bath was regarded as particularly disaffected.[109] Only in the extreme north-eastern corner of the county were the Royalists able to count on any genuine popular support.[110] Gloucester's stout resistance to the King is famous. During the epic siege of 1643 (which many commentators saw as the turning point of the entire Civil War) only three common soldiers deserted Parliament's cause.[111] The people of the surrounding countryside supported Gloucester's stand, hiding food from the King's army but assisting the beleaguered garrison.[112] Popular resistance to the King was also apparent in the far west of the county. *Mercurius Aulicus* fulminated against the inhabitants of the Forest of Dean, terming them 'most notorious rebels' and 'the rebel foresters'.[113]

Popular Parliamentarianism in Gloucestershire had both a religious and a racial dimension. Puritanism was strong in the county, especially at Gloucester and in the nearby clothing district, while local hatred of the King's Welsh supporters was intense.[114] John Corbet reported the existence of an 'inveterate hatred, derived from fabulous tradition ... betweene the Welch-men and the citizens of Gloucester', adding that 'such slight and irrationall passages prevaile much with the common people, in whom opinion beares rule'. Corbet's own references to the 'stink-ing', 'miserable Welch' demonstrate that it was not amongst the common people alone that such racial hatreds were felt.[115] As late as the 1920s a deep fear of the Welsh lingered on in rural Glouces-tershire. Laurie Lee, who grew up here, described his 'eight year old world' thus: 'first ... comes England, the home country, the limit of what is familiar ... [but beyond] lies a country of ... mortal danger, where live the Welsh, the terror of these valleys. I am not a Welshman and when I hear [their] singing I have been taught to fly. Otherwise I hide in bushes and watch them as they pass, feeling my scalp tickle at their strangeness'.[116] That the Welsh were regarded as peculiarly alien and 'other' in Gloucester-shire may well reflect the fact that the western border of this county marked a true racial frontier, as the western borders of Herefordshire and Shropshire did not. Gloucestershire possessed no large admixture of Welsh population, and was physically sep-arated from Wales by the River Wye. It may be significant that, as soon as the Welsh Royalists crossed this frontier in 1643, 'a rabble of country people' opposed them.[117]

The West

Each of the five mid-western counties can be confidently assigned to one camp or the other but this is not to say that they were unanimous. Wherever wartime allegiance has been examined in depth, clear regional patterns have emerged. This is true of Devon and Cornwall, and it is also true of Wiltshire, Dorset and Somer-set. David Underdown's pioneering study has shown that, while the inhabitants of West Dorset, North Wiltshire, North Somerset and the Somerset levels were broadly for Parliament, the inhabit-ants of the Dorset and South Wiltshire downlands, Blackmore Vale and the adjoining parts of South Somerset were mainly for the King.[118] Underdown attributes these contrasting regional loyalties chiefly to the relative strength or weakness of puritanism in each district, and his argument receives strong support from a recent study of North Somerset.[119] Local towns also favoured different sides, and for the same reasons. Thus Royalism was strong in religiously conservative Sherborne and Wells, while in puritan Dorchester, Lyme and Poole majority opinion was on the other side.[120] Underdown's conclusions have been challenged by some historians, but evidence which he himself does not use repeatedly serves to confirm his case.[121] Thus Shepton Mallet—which Underdown identifies as Royalist on statistical grounds alone—was expressly commended for its loyalty by the Royalist officer Richard Symonds, who noted in 1644 that 'this towne hath furnished the King with 300 men'.[122] Many similar instances could be cited.

There is only one area of the three western counties in which Underdown's identification of allegiances seems seriously awry. This is West Somerset, which Underdown describes as Royalist, chiefly on the evidence of a Cavalier gentleman's boast that he would be able to raise his tenants in this region.[123] In fact, Royalist recruitment was never very successful here and most local communities were strongly in favour of Parliament. Hopton noted 'the malitious activity of the country' at Dunster and Minehead, and Clarendon confirmed this, observing that, when the Royalists arrived at Minehead in 1642 they 'found the people both of the town and country ... disaffected'.[124] Pro-Parliamentary Clubmen were active near Dulverton in 1645, while Goring plundered Watchet and Minehead in order to punish the inhabitants for supporting Parliament.[125] Wellington was a strongly Parliamentarian town, as was Taunton, which Clarendon described as 'very strong against the King in the natural disaffection of the inhabitants', adding that 'all the places adjacent [were] of the same ill principles'.[126] That so few Royalist suspects were later recorded from West Somerset surely reflects the region's basic allegiance, rather than any discrepancy in the statistics.[127]

Lancashire

In the five counties of South-west England the contrasting pattern of popular allegiances can be delineated and mapped out at the regional, and even at the sub-regional, level. This is also true of Lancashire. As early as 1904 Ernest Broxap observed that, while the two south-east Lancashire hundreds of Salford and Blackburn had supported Parliament, the other four hundreds had supported the King. Broxap found that Royalism had been particularly strong in the Fylde region, on Lancashire's western coast. The inhabitants of the Fylde had frequently assisted the King's forces, sometimes even rising *en masse* to serve as irregular Royalist Clubmen, and Broxap concluded that the entire area had been 'Royalist in sympathy'.[128] Turning away from the rural areas, he found that the towns, too, had exhibited clear-cut preferences for one side or the other. Thus Manchester and Bolton had been 'strongholds of the Parliament's cause', while Preston, Salford, Warrington and Wigan had favoured the King.[129]

Certain aspects of Broxap's thesis have been attacked by Ronald Hutton, who claims that the Parliamentarianism of Manchester in particular was more apparent than real.[130] This argument is unconvincing. As B.G. Blackwood observes, the fact that Manchester contained some Royalists does not alter the fact that majority opinion in the town was on the other side.[131] Drawing on his own detailed research, Blackwood notes that 'in Lancashire, no town seems to have been neutral in the Civil War and only one, Bury, appears to have been deeply divided'.[132] Both Blackwood and Broxap agree that religion was the chief explanation for the sharply contrasting pattern of local allegiance. Thus the west coast and the Fylde—both catholic strongholds—were strongly Royalist, while Salford hundred—'the most puritanical part of Lancashire'—was strongly Parliamentarian.[133] Nowhere else in England did such a large number of catholic and puritan communities exist so closely cheek by jowl, and it is this which explains why patterns of Civil War allegiance in Lancashire are so unusually clear. Yet it is only in the clarity of its internal divisions that Lancashire is unique. In every other respect the situation in this county mirrors that which existed in Devon, Somerset, Dorset and Wiltshire. Popular allegiances elsewhere in England have not yet been examined in similar depth, but at the national level, there has been, over the last twenty-five years, a major shift in the way in which historians perceive the geographical pattern of wartime division. This trend is most apparent in recent reassessments of the situation in London, the North and the South-East.

The North

Northern England used to be regarded as a stronghold of support for the King. Yet more recently 'the Royalist North' has been dismissed as a myth.[134] Many historians now portray the five northern counties as inert and uncommitted, their eventual passage into the Royalist camp owing more to the activities of a handful of gentry extremists than to any real enthusiasm for the King's cause.[135] Particularly influential in this respect has been the work of Roger Howell. In his subtle study of Newcastle-on-Tyne Howell demonstrated that this major north-eastern city, far from being unanimously Royalist, had contained a substantial puritan/Parliamentarian element.[136] C.B. Phillips has made similar claims for Cumberland and Westmoreland, asserting that the Roundheads were wrong to see these two counties as intrinsically hostile to their cause. Instead Cumberland and Westmoreland were 'essentially a neutral area in which the Royalists, rather than the Parliamentarians tried to recruit support'.[137] That the two counties were initially secured for the King owed more to the influence of the local gentry than anything else, Phillips claims, adding that the subsequent 'militarily insignificant fumbling of the unopposed Cumberland and Westmoreland Royalists makes it nonsense to call the counties Royalist'.[138]

Scepticism about the Royalist North is clearly justified as far as Yorkshire is concerned. Popular Parliamentarianism was strong here, especially at Hull and in the West Riding. Margaret Cavendish, wife of the Royalist Earl of Newcastle, noted that the people of Sheffield were 'most of them rebelliously affected', while, around Bradford, 'the whole country was of their party [so] that my Lord could not possibly have any constant intelligence'.[139] Clarendon claimed that Leeds, Halifax and Bradford were 'wholly at ... [Parliament's] disposition', and his assessment was echoed by Fairfax, who noted that Parliament's local forces were dependent upon the support of 'Leeds, Halifax and Bradford, and some other small clothing towns adjacent, [these] being the only well affected people of the county'.[140] Yet, as the latter part of this statement makes clear, revisionism concerning Northern allegiances should not be taken too far. Margaret Cavendish—whose biography of her husband continually stressed the extent of opposition to him in order to magnify his achievements—nevertheless admitted that some parts of Yorkshire had been 'willing to embrace' the Earl's protection. She also noted that when Newcastle entered York in 1642 it was to 'the general satisfaction of most of the inhabitants'.[141] Clarendon agreed, speaking of 'the good affection of the inhabitants' of York, while the most recent study of the city has concluded that 'a sizeable number of the ordinary inhabitants were Royalist in sympathy'.[142] North Yorkshire was much more pro-Royalist than the southern parts of the county, in fact, while in the four northernmost shires of England it seems perverse to deny that majority opinion was on the King's side. Howell himself agrees that Northumberland was 'a cavalier county' and that Newcastle was 'the one safe place' for the Northern Roundheads.[143]

Phillip's comment that it would be nonsense to describe Westmoreland and Cumberland as Royalist has already been noted. Yet what else can one term an area which the Roundheads themselves described as rotten, an area in which the Royalist gentry went unopposed by an equivalent Parliamentarian group, in which large numbers of men were raised for the King's armies and in which an armed riot which 'had all the hallmarks of a rising for the King' occurred as late as August 1646?[144] The fact that, after the King's most determined local supporters had marched south with Newcastle, the Cumberland Royalists were able to defeat a Parliamentarian attempt on Carlisle 'with a tenant levy rather than organised soldiery' seems to argue for the strength of local Royalism rather than its weakness.[145] Nor was the collapse of the Royalist position in Cumberland and Westmoreland following the Scottish invasion of September 1644 as suprising as has often been claimed. After Marston Moor it is hard to see how these two small counties could possibly have resisted the combined might of the victorious Scots and Parliamentarian armies. Local people submitted to the inevitable, but their loyalties remained unchanged. During the subsequent siege of Carlisle the Scots forced the country to assist them against the Royalist garrison, but as Isaac Tullie observed, the people 'were in their harts friends to the towne and would have revolted to them upon any faire opportunity'.[146] During their incursions into the countryside the Cavaliers were assisted by 'divers of the country', the inhabitants of Cargo running joyfully after a Royalist raiding party on one occasion, 'beseeching them to baste the basterly Scots'.[147] Tullie described Carlisle itself as 'little in circuite but great and memorable for loyalty' and he clearly felt the same way about Cumberland too.[148] Significantly Tullie ascribed Cumberland's loyalty to its religious traditionalism, stating that the county was 'a place ... generally free from schisme, and therefore untainted with the present rebellion'.[149]

Even in Newcastle, where a substantial Parliamentarian element clearly did exist, the extent of popular support for the King has surely been understated in recent years. Clarendon, always keen to stress the disaffection of the common people, nevertheless observed that the townsfolk of Newcastle had possessed 'general good inclinations', while Margaret Cavendish likewise admitted that, at Newcastle, the Earl had had 'the assistance of the townsmen'.[150] It is surely significant that, even after Newcastle's army—which presumably included the most fervent local Royalists in its ranks—had marched south, Sir John Marley was able to persuade 2,300 Newcastle men to enlist themselves for the King.[151] It is hard to think of any other town in which the Royalists managed to raise so many citizen-soldiers. The section of the populace which most strongly supported Parliament, moreover, was precisely that group which was least unrepresentative of the population as a whole, the labourers in the coal trade, most of whom were Scots![152] At Newcastle, as at Chester, the old picture of a 'Loyal City' may not be so wildly inaccurate as some historians have claimed.

Popular royalism in Newcastle was chiefly explicable in terms of religious conservatism. Howell observes that 'Newcastle had never contained more than a pocket of puritanism', and many of the townsfolk were violently opposed to such beliefs.[153] The hostility which one puritan woman exhibited towards established church practice in 1640 'set the malignant superstitous people in such a fire as men and women fell upon ... [her] like wild beasts, tore her clothes and gave her at least an hundred blowes, and had slain her if the Mayor had not ... [rescued] her, he and his officers [being] both well beaten for their paines, such was the people's madness after their idols'.[154] This episode hardly breathes the spirit of indifference. If passionate concern for the established church could have moved local people to such violence in 1640, could it not equally well have led them to rally to the King in 1642?

It may be conceded that the North was less solidly Royalist than Wales and West Cornwall, where the racial imperative lent a special intensity to popular support for the King. But these areas aside, the North demonstrated as much enthusiasm for King Charles I as any other part of England. To write the Royalist North out of the history books is to ignore the fact that here, just as in Wales and the West, large numbers of ordinary people were prepared to come out in support of the King, and that many of them fought for his cause with great tenacity. Margaret Cavendish noted that Newcastle's army contained '3,000 of such valiant, stout and faithful men (whereof many were bred in the Moorish grounds of the Northern parts) that they were ready to die at my Lord's feet'.[155] As always, she implied that it was loyalty to the Earl himself rather than any other consideration which had brought these men into the King's service. Yet after Newcastle had fled from the field at Marston Moor the White Coats fought on without him, most of them dying where they stood. Survivors then made their way to Carlisle where they later endured a nine-month siege.[156] Such actions cannot be attributed to deference alone and surely bear witness to much deeper loyalties, which were founded primarily on religious belief and local patriotism.

The South-East and the Midlands

Over the past twenty years the traditional concept of a Parliamentary South-East has come under the same sort of sustained attack as the Royalist North. Particularly influential has been Clive Holmes's study of the Eastern Association. Published in 1975, this work demonstrated that East Anglia, like Newcastle, had been divided in its allegiance. Holmes showed that currents of Royalist opinion had existed throughout East Anglia and, like Howell, he laid great stress on the extent of popular apathy and indifference.[157] Holmes's discoveries, combined with the realization that there had been many Royalists in London and Kent, seemed to many to have relegated the Parliamentary South-East to the historiographical dustbin.[158] It became fashionable to suggest that the pattern of national allegiance had been accidental, that the behaviour of each town and county had owed more to the physical proximity of the rival armies than to the inhabitants' own political preferences.[159] Had London been where Birmingham is, Peter Young argued in 1979, then Kent would have been Royalist.[160]

This particular assessment was probably correct. Kent produced 'the most celebrated of the county manifestos' in support of Charles I and eventually had to be secured for Parliament by Roundhead soldiers.[161] Significantly, the arrest or flight of the leading Royalist activists did not bring anti-Parliamentarian activity to a halt. In 1643 and again in 1645 major Royalist insurrections took place in Kent.[162] Tonbridge was regarded by the Parliamentarians as especially disaffected, and in 1642 'almost the whole town' were said to be 'malignants'.[163] The behaviour of Kent is now routinely cited by historians in order to discredit the view of a 'Parliamentarian South-East',[164] yet it should not be forgotten that this county, too, was deeply divided. Kent contained Parliamentarian areas as well as Royalist ones, and the people of Tonbridge feared that they would be attacked and destroyed by their enemies 'the Cranbrook Roundheads'.[165] Moreover, the strength of Kentish Royalism was quite atypical. With the possible exceptions of Huntingdonshire and Rutland, there is no other county in south-east England in which it seems plausible to suggest that majority opinion might have been on the King's side.

London contained some Royalist districts—Clarendon stated that 'the inhabitants of Westminster, St Martins and Covent Garden ... always underwent the imputation of being well-affected to the King'—but the huge majority of the capital's inhabitants were clearly on the other side.[166] Norwich, like London and Exeter, contained both Royalist and Parliamentarian parishes, but here too majority opinion was probably against the King.[167] In Essex and Suffolk popular Royalism was almost non-existent. Bedfordshire, Buckinghamshire and Northamptonshire were all notoriously Roundhead counties. This was true of much of Norfolk, Hertfordshire and Leicestershire as well. Throughout the whole of East Anglia, in fact, there is only one district in which popular Royalism is known to have been genuinely strong. Suprisingly, this was the Fenland. Here, Crowland, King's Lynn, Wisbech and the Isle of Ely were all regarded as strongholds of malignancy. Parliament had many enemies in Rutland, Huntingdonshire and Cambridgeshire too.[168] Yet despite the existence of this Royalist pocket in East Anglia, 'the fact remains that the region as a whole was the heartland of the Parliamentary cause'.[169]

Most of the counties which bordered this Parliamentarian heartland were deeply divided. Warwickshire was split into a Parliamentarian north and east, and a more Royalist south and west.[170] In Sussex the divisions were even more clear-cut with the River Adur serving as a frontier between the 'incipiently Royalist countryside' of West Sussex and the four pro-Parliamentarian rapes of East Sussex.[171] In both counties it was clearly Parliament which possessed the greatest amount of popular support. This was probably true of Oxfordshire and Berkshire as well, although patterns of allegiance in these two counties remain unclear. In Staffordshire and Derbyshire the parties may have been more evenly balanced. Opinion in north Staffordshire favoured Parliament, but in the south there were several Royalist communities, including Dudley, Walsall and Wolverhampton.[172] In Derbyshire it was in 'the north, west and centre of the county that Parliament found most support', while the south was more Royalist.[173] In Hampshire there was considerable enthusiasm for the King in the countryside east of Winchester, but Parliamentarianism was deeply entrenched along the coast.[174] Only in Nottinghamshire—where Parliamentarianism was confined 'to the southwestern corner of the county'—were the King's supporters clearly in the majority.[175]

This cursory examination suggests that, in the twenty-three English counties to the south of Yorkshire and the east of Worcestershire, majority opinion was indeed on Parliament's side. The undoubted existence of one or two strongly Royalist counties in this area—and of many strongly Royalist pockets within otherwise Parliamentarian counties—cannot be allowed to obscure this basic truth.

The picture from across the country as a whole supports the conclusion which emerged from an examination of Devon alone: that popular allegiance was a fixed, not a constantly shifting, condition. Devon was not the only county in which certain regions, towns and villages were more Royalist or Parliamentarian than others. Nor was Devon the only county in which evenly-divided communities—let alone genuinely neutral ones—were rare. What is suggestive is that, both in Devon and elsewhere, those communities which were badly split tended to be those which contained more than one parish. One thinks of Exeter, of London, of Norwich and Bristol. In all these communities the different parties were based in different parishes. This again suggests that religion was the prime determinant of wartime allegiance.

Surveying the national picture has also confirmed that 'it is just not true that all towns were Parliamentarian'.[176] The crucial contrast, as Morrill observes, was rather the one which existed between inland towns and maritime communities. It is hard to think of a single English port (aside from large cities like Chester, which were not exclusively seafaring communities) in which majority opinion was on the King's side. Even 'Loyal Scarborough' turns out to have been much less loyal than was previously thought.[177] That the Cornish ports behaved differently is intriguing and again suggests that, in this small corner of the kingdom, racial loyalties cut across other ties. If the ports really were as Parliamentarian as has always been claimed, the old myth that popular Royalism was confined to the Celtic fringe and the catholic areas alone can surely now be laid to rest. As this survey has shown, enthusiasm for the King was visible throughout the North and West, and in many parts of the South-East as well. The Chagford farmer who swore that 'he would fight the Round headed Rogues as long as he had a bone in his back', the Dartmouth yeoman who vowed that he would 'live and dy a Cavaleir', both these men spoke for many thousands of their fellow Englishmen.[178] Richard Gough's account of Thomas Ash—'a proper comely person, [of] ... an honest and religious disposition' who 'listed himself a soldier in the King's service ... and continued a soldier untill the King's forces were utterly dispersed ... never attain[ing] to any higher post than a corporall of foot'—shows that not all the men who set off to join the Royal army from Myddle were disreputable, marginal or uncommitted.[179] There may well have been many like Ash in the King's armies. A Roundhead pamphleteer described the 4,000 Royalist infantrymen captured at Naseby as 'Pure Royall' and confessed that, should any of these men escape, 'they will certainly returne to help recruit his Majestie's Army again'.[180]

The King did have committed supporters amongst the common folk—but it is tempting to suggest that Parliament had more. As Margaret Cavendish knew well, there was a direct connection between 'populous' and 'rebellious' places.[181] The counties in which the King was strongest were those in which population was most thinly spread. Thus the three Royalist counties of Herefordshire, Shropshire and Worcestershire possessed only half as many militiamen as the single Parliamentarian county of Essex.[182] The same rule applied within counties. Throughout much of southern England, popular Royalism was concentrated in the poorer, more sparsely populated regions, the western rapes of Sussex, for example, and the Fenland and the skirts of Dartmoor. One Royalist clergyman exulted in 1642–43 that Charles I had managed to raise an army 'out of the dust of the earth'.[183] That the King had managed to perform this feat was indeed a notable success. But that he had been forced to attempt it at all is surely sufficient explanation for his eventual failure.

Why were the geographical patterns of support for King and Parliament as they were? It has been the whole argument of this book that Civil War allegiance was based primarily on religious sentiment. The areas which came out most fervently for Parliament were those which had been most exposed to advanced protestant ideas during the century which preceded the Civil War. The areas which came out most strongly for the King were those in which such ideas had enjoyed least circulation, Christopher Hill's 'Dark Corners of the Land'.[184] Certain districts—those which were especially remote from London, those in which English was a minority language, and those in which catholicism remained strong—possessed a built-in resistance to puritanism, and it was in precisely these districts that popular Royalism was most intense. Beneath the all-embracing religious anxieties lurked racial antagonisms. Although little research has yet been carried out into this subject, it is clear that dislike of the Scots helped to push many Englishmen into the King's camp.[185] This book has suggested that in the West of England too, racial hostility had a considerable bearing on popular allegiance. As far as the common people of England and Wales were concerned the Civil War was primarily a conflict about religion, but in some parts of the country it was about race as well.

★ ★ ★

During the 1970s the traditional map of Civil War allegiance was rolled up and discarded. The patterns which it appeared to show were irrelevant to the agenda of the neutralist school of historians, who pointed out—with much justification—that many of the areas labelled Royalist or Parliamentarian had, in fact, been nothing of the sort. A good example is the supposedly loyal county of Devon, which still makes regular appearances in general studies of the Civil War today.[186] As this book has shown, Devon was categorically not a loyal county, and the old picture of national allegiance patterns contained many similar flaws. But was it fundamentally wrong? This chapter has suggested that it was not, that the view of a broadly (though not unanimously) Royalist North and West pitted against a broadly (though not unanimously) Parliamentarian South and East is indeed reflected by the pattern of popular allegiance on the ground. It is time to start looking at the old map again. It is time, dare one say it, to return to the old canvas, to revise it, to correct it and to bring it up to date. Only thus will the complicated patterns of national allegiance, the undoubted correlations between loyalty and locality, be finally and fully revealed.

Notes

Preface

1. E. Hyde, Earl of Clarendon, *The History of the Rebellion and Civil Wars in England*, (W. Dunn Macray (ed.), six vols, Oxford, 1888), II, p. 408.
2. DRO, 3248/A/3/3, Okehampton Sessions Book, 1634–39, (unpaginated), entries of 19 and 20 December 1643.

Part I

Introduction

1. See D. Underdown, 'The Chalk and the Cheese: Contrasts among the English Clubmen', *P&P*, 85, (1979), pp. 25–48; D. Underdown, 'The Problem of Popular Allegiance in the English Civil War', *TRHS*, 5th Series, 31, (1981), pp. 69–94; and D. Underdown, *Revel, Riot and Rebellion*, (Oxford, 1985), *passim*.
2. Underdown, *Revel, Riot and Rebellion*, *passim*, especially pp. 4, 18, 40. The suggestion that popular allegiances in the South-West reflected patterns of local settlement was first hinted at by Brian Little in *The Monmouth Episode*, (1956), pp. 34, 68.
3. J. Morrill (ed.), *Reactions to the English Civil War* (1982), p. 11; K. Wrightson, *English Society, 1580–1680*, (1982), p. 172.
4. See, for example, G.E. Aylmer, *Rebellion or Revolution?*, (Oxford, 1986), p. 43; and A. Hughes, *The Causes of the English Civil War*, (Oxford, 1991), p. 147.
5. K. Sharpe, *Politics and Ideas in Early Stuart England*, (1989), pp. 301–02; J. Morrill, 'The Ecology of Allegiance in the English Revolution', *JBS*, 26, no. 4, (1987), pp. 456–67; M. Wanklyn, 'The People go to War', *Local Historian*, 17, no. 8, (1987), pp. 497–98.
6. A. Hughes, 'Local History and the Origins of the English Civil War', in R. Cust and A. Hughes (eds), *Conflict in Early Stuart England*, (1989), p. 242; Sharpe, *Politics and Ideas*, pp. 301–02.
7. M. Ingram, *Church Courts, Sex and Marriage in England, 1570–1640*, (Cambridge, 1987), pp. 101–02; and Morrill, 'Ecology of Allegiance', pp. 457–62.

8. Sharpe, *Politics and Ideas*, p. 301.
9. Cf. Hughes's comment that 'the complexity of the connections between religious and cultural attitudes on the one hand and the religious patterns of social and economic change on the other' might well encourage an erroneous conclusion 'that there were no connections at all and that patterns of belief and allegiance were entirely random', (*The Causes of the English Civil War*, p. 147).
10. On neutralism, see G.E. Aylmer, 'Collective Mentalities in Mid-seventeenth-century England: IV. Cross Currents: Neutrals, Trimmers and Others', *TRHS*, 5th Series, 39, (1989), pp. 1-22. On popular Parliamentarianism, see J.L. Malcolm, *Caesar's Due*, (1983), *passim*.
11. For the paucity of work on this subject, see Morrill, *Reactions*, p. 14.
12. Sharpe, *Politics and Ideas*, p. 302; Wanklyn, 'The People go to War', p. 497.
13. I use the term 'Devonians' advisedly. Although the use of this word to designate the county's inhabitants is frowned upon by some modern authorities, the term was employed by contemporaries (see, for example, E.100 (10)) and this must surely justify its present use.

Chapter 1

1. E.322 (3).
2. *CSPD*, 1628-29, p. 88; and *CSPD*, 1641-43, p. 404.
3. See W.B. Stephens, *Seventeenth-Century Exeter*, (Exeter, 1958), p. 133; and T. Moore, *The History of Devonshire*, (three vols, 1829), I, p. 426.
4. T. Westcote, *A View of Devonshire in 1630*, (G. Oliver and P. Jones, eds, Exeter, 1845), p. 33.
5. See, for example, *CSPD*, 1629-31, pp. 44, 50, 52; *CSPD*, 1635, p. 389; *CSPD*, 1636-37, pp. 71-72. For the impact of piracy on the fishing industry, see T. Gray, 'Devon's Coastal and Overseas Fisheries and New England Migration, 1597-1642', (unpublished Ph.D. thesis, Exeter, 1988), ch. 6.
6. C. Torre, *Small Talk at Wreyland*, (J. Simmonds (ed.), two vols, Cambridge, 1970), II, p. 7.
7. S.K. Roberts, *Recovery and Restoration in an English County*, (Exeter, 1985), p. xiv; and C. Vancouver, *General View of the Agriculture of the County of Devon*, (reprinted Newton Abbot, 1969), *passim*.
8. Writers have always divided Devon into regions for ease of reference. Unfortunately, most have had slightly different ideas as to precisely where the boundaries between the various districts should be fixed. As a result the terms which are most commonly used in descriptions of the shire—North, South, East and West Devon—have no universally accepted meaning. This book demands that clear lines of demarcation be drawn. Accordingly, I have divided the county into four precisely defined regions; North, South, East and Central Devon. (A similar geographic scheme is adopted in P. Slack, *Plagues and Peoples*, (1985).) Each of the county's 465 parishes has been assigned to one or another of these regions (see appendix 1). The lines which have been drawn between the various districts are fairly arbitrary, of course. Nevertheless I am confident that the boundaries employed here give a better impression of the 'countries' into which early modern Devon was divided

than would the utilization of any other scheme. To split the county up on a
hundredal basis, or by farming regions, is simply too complicated and, in
general discussion, tends rather to obscure than to illuminate.

9. W.G. Hoskins, *Devon*, (1954), p. 16; and Roberts, *Recovery and Restoration*, p. xiv.
10. T. Risdon, *The Chorographical Description or Survey of the County of Devon*, (1811), pp. 4–5.
11. Risdon, *Survey*, p. 103.
12. This figure, and all others relevant to population which follow it, are based on A.J. Howard (ed.), *Devon Protestation Returns*, (privately printed, 1973).
13. Risdon, *Survey*, p. 103.
14. Ibid., p. 132.
15. H. Tapley–Soper, 'Parochiales Bridfordii: A Devonshire Village in Olden Times', *TDA*, 68, (1936), p. 334.
16. Risdon, *Survey*, p. 6.
17. It was noted in 1794 that 'in the skirts of … [Dartmoor] there are vast numbers of little farms', see R. Fraser, *A General View of the County of Devon*, (1794), p. 63.
18. Risdon, *Survey*, p. 6.
19. *CSPD*, 1603–10, p. 640.
20. For Crediton, see Risdon, *Survey*, p. 98; and Westcote, *View*, p. 121. For Tavistock, see H.P.R. Finberg, *West-Country Historical Studies*, (New York, 1969), p. 105.
21. My definition of the South Hams broadly corresponds with that given by Fraser (*General View*, p. 19). The generally accepted limits of the South Hams have contracted in recent years. See Moore, *History of Devonshire*, I, p. 11; and M. Willy, *The South Hams*, (1955), p. 5.
22. Risdon, *Survey*, pp. 150–54, 186–87 and *passim*.
23. On Dartmouth, see Gray, 'Devon's Coastal Fisheries', pp. 14, 58, 92–93; and T. Gray, 'Fishing and the Commercial World of Early Stuart Dartmouth', in T. Gray (ed.), *Tudor and Stuart Devon*, (Exeter, 1992), pp. 173–99.
24. Risdon, *Survey*, pp. 5, 288.
25. E.36 (1).
26. Risdon, *Survey*, p. 272.
27. *CSPD*, 1631–33, p. 176.
28. *CSPD*, 1627–28, p. 288.
29. T. Gray (ed.), *Early Stuart Mariners and Shipping*, (DCRS, New Series, 33, 1990), pp. xvii, xix.
30. This figure is almost certainly an underestimate, moreover, for as Gray observes, the survey 'did not … list all the men engaged in seafaring occupations' (*Early Stuart Mariners*, p. xiv).
31. *CSPD*, 1636–37, p. 110.
32. For the relative density of seamen in the different parts of Devon, see Gray, 'Devon's Coastal Fisheries', pp. 57ff.
33. Gray, *Early Stuart Mariners*, p. xix.
34. See *CSPD*, 1627–28, p. 92; Risdon, *Survey*, pp. 177, 351; and Westcote, *View*, pp. 67–68.
35. Risdon, *Survey*, p. 34.

36. Westcote, *View*, pp. 59–60.
37. Ibid., p. 61.
38. Stephens, *Seventeenth-Century Exeter*, p. 3.
39. *CSPD*, 1627–28, p. 576; and *CSPD*, 1631–33, p. 135.
40. Westcote, *View*, pp. 61–62.
41. G. Roberts (ed.), *The Diary of Walter Yonge*, (Camden Society, Old Series, 41, 1848), p. 53.
42. See A. Fleming, 'Prehistoric Tin Extraction on Dartmoor', *TDA*, 119 (1987), pp. 117–22.
43. On the Stannaries see Lady Radford, 'Notes on the Tinners of Devon and their Laws', *TDA*, 62 (1930), pp. 225–47; H.P.R. Finberg, 'The Stannary of Tavistock', *TDA*, 81 (1949), pp. 167–69; T. Greeves, 'The Devon Tin Industry, 1450–1750', (unpublished Ph.D. thesis, Exeter, 1981), *passim*; and R.R. Pennington, *Stannary Law*, (Newton Abbot, 1973), *passim*.
44. Westcote, *View*, p. 11.
45. Anon, *The Proposal for Raising the Price of Tin*, (c. 1693, unpaginated).
46. Ibid.
47. C. Gill, *Dartmoor: A New Study*, (Newton Abbot 1970), p. 115.
48. T. Greeves, 'The Great Courts or Parliaments of Devon Tinners', *TDA*, 119 (1987), pp. 145–67.
49. Radford, 'Notes on the Tinners', p. 233.
50. DRO, Moger 867, (Consistory Court Depositions Book, 1613–19, unpaginated), deposition of 11 January 1614.
51. R.E. St Leger-Gordon, *The Witchcraft and Folklore of Dartmoor*, (1965), p. 45.
52. Ibid.
53. A.L. Rowse, *Tudor Cornwall*, (1969), p. 62. I am most grateful to Tom Greeves for discussion of the tinners.
54. *CSPD*, 1595–97, p. 70.
55. W.J. Blake, 'Hooker's Synopsis Chorographical of Devonshire', *TDA*, 47 (1915), pp. 347–48.
56. Greeves, 'Devon Tin Industry', pp. 34–37. See also T. Greeves, 'Four Devon Stannaries', in Gray, *Tudor and Stuart Devon*, p. 63, table 2.
57. The Tinners' militia regiment continued to be mustered throughout the 1630s, while individual tinners and Stannary officials are frequently referred to in the quarter sessions records for the same decade. See, for example, QSB, Box 43, (1639/40), 'examination of Thomas Nicholas, tinner'.
58. For the Duchy of Cornwall, see N.J. Pounds, *The Parliamentary Survey of the Duchy of Cornwall: Part I*, (DCRS, New Series, 25, 1982), pp. xiii–xxii; and N.J. Pounds, *The Parliamentary Survey of the Duchy of Cornwall: Part II*, (DCRS, New Series, 27, 1984), pp. 217–43. For the Duchy of Lancaster, see J. Pearson, 'On an Estate formerly belonging to the Duchy of Lancaster', *TDA*, 32 (1900), pp. 407–11, and J.A.S. Castlehow, 'The Duchy of Lancaster in the County of Devon', TDA, 80 (1948), pp. 193–209. For the Duchy constables, see QSOB 2, 1600–07, (Entry of Michaelmas 1601) and *CCAM*, III, p. 1,412.
59. B. Cherry and N. Pevsner, *The Buildings of England: Devon*, (1989), p. 791.
60. J. Youings (ed.), *Devon Monastic Lands*, (DCRS, New Series, 1, 1955), pp. 4–7.

61. *CSPD*, 1627–28, p. 288; and H. Walrond, *Historical Records of the First Devonshire Militia*, (1897), pp. 19–20.

62. For a tinners' muster certificate of 1629, see PRO, SP 16/153/113–14. For the Duchy tenants, see *APC*, 25, pp. 342–43; and *HMC*, Hatfield, 6, pp. 153–54.

63. Walrond, *First Devonshire Militia*, pp. 19–20.

64. For a much less favourable assessment of Bath, see J. Roberts, 'The Armada Lord Lieutenant, parts 1 and 2', *TDA*, 102–03, (1970–71), pp. 71–85, and pp. 103–22. While it is obviously true that the Earl made an inauspicious start in county society, I would argue that he learnt from his earlier mistakes.

65. See *APC*, 30, p. 367.

66. For an account of Henry Bourchier's movements between 1638 and 1644, see KAO, U269/A.515/5. I am most grateful to Todd Gray for lending me a microfilm of this document.

67. For a discussion of the term 'country', see A. Hughes, *Politics, Society and Civil War in Warwickshire*, (Cambridge, 1987), pp. 111–12.

68. A.M. Wolffe's recent Ph.D. thesis, ('The Gentry Government of Devon, 1625–40', Exeter, 1992), supersedes all previous accounts of the pre-war Devon gentry. See especially pp. 5, 8–9, 18–38.

69. Devon possessed fifty-five JPs in 1615, sixty-four in 1630 and fifty-six in 1643. See A.H.A. Hamilton, 'The Justices of the Peace for the County of Devon under Charles I and Cromwell', *TDA*, 10 (1878), pp. 309–10; DRO, Commissions of the Peace, (Commissions of May 1643 and September 1643); and R.L. Taverner, 'The Administrative Work of the Devon Justices in the Seventeenth Century', *TDA*, 100 (1968), p. 59.

70. Wolffe, 'Gentry Goverment', pp. 5–9.

71. Westcote, *View*, p. 49. See Roberts, *Restoration and Recovery*, pp. 67–94, for a discussion of Devon juries and their composition.

72. See W.T. MacCaffrey, *Exeter 1540–1640*, (1978), *passim*.

73. Okehampton's powers were more restricted than those of the other corporate towns. I owe this point to Mary Wolffe.

74. Westcote, *View*, p. 70.

75. Ralph Brownrigg, presented to the bishopric of Exeter in 1642, never managed to visit his diocese.

76. For a discussion of these three men, see J. Boggis, *History of the Diocese of Exeter*, (Exeter, 1922), pp. 388–404. See also K. Fincham, *Prelate as Pastor*, (1990), pp. 43, 310.

77. QSOB, 2, ff.1–109.

78. Howard, *Protestation Returns*, p. v and *passim*.

79. They were; Alwington, Arlington, Modbury, Ottery, Parkham, Pinhoe, Rewe, Sherwill, Thorverton and Zeale Monachorum.

80. For the Bassets, see *HMC*, Salisbury, 18, pp. 252–53; and H. Trevor-Roper, *Catholics, Anglicans and Puritans*, (1987), pp. 19–28. For the Careys, see Howard, *Protestation Returns*, p. 285; and PRO, SP 23/152/124–25. For the Chichesters, see Howard, *Protestation Returns*, p. 404 and QSOB, 2, f.108r. For the Courtenays, see *CSPD*, 1611–18, p. 254. For the Giffords, see *CSPD*, 1603–10, p. 413 and QSOB 2, ff.108r–09.

81. For Lyme and Exeter, see Roberts, *Diary of Walter Yonge*, pp. 18, 46, 83.

For North Devon, see *CSPD*, 1603–10, p. 564 and QSOB, 2, f.96r. For Plymouth, see *CSPD*, 1633–34, pp. 274–75.

82. EQSOB, 62, (1621–30), f.356r.

83. Such flurries of activity occurred in 1601–02, 1605–06, 1610–11, 1613, 1621–22, 1625, 1628 and 1640–42. See Roberts, *Diary of Walter Yonge*, p. 6; QSOB, 2, *passim*; QSOB, 3, f.247; QSOB, 8 (unpaginated); and EQSOB, 62, ff.34–45, 253–53v and 356v–58. The hiatus which occurs between 1628 and 1640 is significant.

84. For Cotton's assault upon the puritans see I. Cassidy, 'The Episcopate of William Cotton, Bishop of Exeter: 1598–1621', (unpublished D.Phil. thesis, Oxford, 1963), *passim*.

85. J.T. Cliffe, *The Puritan Gentry*, (1984), pp. 237–41, lists ten prominent Devon families who were puritan sympathizers. All belonged to the county elite. These families and others are discussed in more detail in I.W. Gowers, 'Puritanism in the County of Devon between 1570 and 1640', (unpublished MA thesis, Exeter, 1970).

86. Roberts, *Restoration and Recovery*, p. xix; and p. xxiii, note 40.

87. Cliffe, *Puritan Gentry*, p. 92.

88. Fraser, *General View*, p. 16.

89. This was true of the minor gentry, let alone the commons, see Wolffe, 'Gentry Government', p. 307.

Part II

Introduction

1. See R.W. Cotton, *Barnstaple and the Northern Part of Devonshire in the Great Civil War*, (1889); E.A. Andriette, *Devon and Exeter in the Civil War*, (Newton Abbot, 1971); R.N. Worth, 'The Siege of Plymouth', *RTPI*, 5, (1875–76); M.J. Stoyle, 'The Civil War Defences of Exeter and the Great Parliamentary Siege', (Exeter Museum, 1990); M.J. Stoyle, 'Documentary Evidence for the Civil War Defences of Exeter, 1642–43', (Exeter Museum, 1992); I.R. Palfrey, 'Devon and the Outbreak of the Civil War', *Southern History*, 10, (1988); and I.R. Palfrey, 'The Royalist War Effort Revisited: Sir Edward Seymour and the Royalist Garrison of Dartmouth, 1643–44', *TDA*, 123, (1991).

Chapter 2

1. J. Quick, 'Icones Sacrae Anglicanae', (n.d., manuscript copy kept at Dr Williams' Library, London), p. 368.

2. E.302 (24). For the scholarly consensus that Devon was a broadly 'Parliamentarian' county, see D. and S. Lysons, *Magna Brittania, Volume VI*, (1822), p. x; R.W. Cotton, *Barnstaple and the Northern Part of Devonshire in the Great Civil War*, (1889), p. 91; W.G. Hoskins, *Devon*, (1954), p. 195; and E.A. Andriette, *Devon and Exeter in the Civil War*, (Newton Abbot, 1971), p. 69.

3. E.115 (21).

4. DRO, Book 73/15 (James White's Chronicle).
5. E.242 (29).
6. E.245 (6).
7. E.246 (37).
8. Ibid.; and E.246 (19).
9. E.246 (20); and E.246 (25).
10. E. Rhys (ed.), *Life of the Duke of Newcastle*, (1915), p. 13.
11. J. Stucley, *Sir Bevill Grenville and his Times*, (Southampton, 1983) pp. 125–27.
12. E.246 (41).
13. DRO; DD.62701, (Disbursements by the inhabitants of Dartmouth for the Parliament), ff.10, 24; and M. Coate, 'An Original Diary of Colonel Robert Bennet of Hexworthy (1642–43)', *DCNQ*, 18, (1935), p. 257.
14. For Somerset, see D. Underdown, *Somerset in the Civil War and Interregnum*, (Newton Abbot, 1973), pp. 34–38; and J.L. Malcolm, *Caesar's Due*, (1983), p. 68.
15. For the truce of 1643, see B. Manning, 'Neutrals and Neutralism in the English Civil War', (Oxford D.Phil. thesis, 1957), pp. 126–42; and I.R. Palfrey, 'Devon and the Outbreak of the English Civil War, 1642–43', *Southern History*, 10, (1988), pp. 39–41.
16. E.105 (13).
17. E.59 (17).
18. I.R. Palfrey, 'The Royalist War Effort in Devon: 1642–6', (Birmingham MA thesis, 1985), pp. 41–45.
19. SRO, Wolesely MSS, 56/6.
20. QSB, Box 47, examination of Thomas Harford, Easter 1643.
21. E.257 (10).
22. DRO, Seymour MSS, '*A True Narration of the … Siege of Plymouth*' (1644).
23. E.80 (10).
24. E.49 (18).
25. E.262 (40).
26. E.307 (27).
27. T. Carte (ed.), *A Collection of Original Letters and Papers*, (1739), p. 135.
28. For local men blockading the Royalist garrisons, see; E.313 (3); E.320 (13); E.322 (29); E.322 (36); and E.323 (9).
29. J. Watkins, *An Essay towards a History of Bideford in the County of Devon*, (Exeter, 1792), p. 38.
30. E. Hyde, Earl of Clarendon, *The History of the Rebellion and Civil War in England*, (W. Dunn-Macray, (ed.), six vols, Oxford, 1888), III, p. 126; and J. Sprigg, *Anglia Rediviva: England's Recovery*, (reprinted Oxford, 1854) p. 198.
31. For the reading of the Commission at Barnstaple, see DRO, Book 73/15.
32. Cotton, *Barnstaple*, p. 70; and E.244 (34).
33. QSB, Box 48, presentation of Mich. 1643.
34. See E.84 (36), and Cotton, *Barnstaple*, pp. 125, 146, 149, 167, 191, 193 and 195.
35. Cotton, *Barnstaple*, pp. 238–39.
36. Ibid., p. 255; and Bod, J. Walker MSS, 4, f.338.

37. Cotton, *Barnstaple*, pp. 254–273.
38. See PRO, SP 28/128, Part 18 (account of Charles Peard, 1644).
39. Cotton, *Barnstaple*, p. 346.
40. This particular judgement on the townsmen was made by Sir John Grenville. Other Royalists made similarly caustic remarks. Thus Sir John
Berkenhead described Barnstaple as a 'perfidious towne' while Sir Edward
Walker termed it a 'rebellious Town'. For these verbal bouquets, see
Cotton, *Barnstaple*, p. 346; E.3 (19); and E. Walker, *Historical Discourses
Upon Several Occasions*, (1705), p. 81.
41. E.260 (6); and E.302 (21).
42. J. Walker MSS, 4, f.358.
43. E.84 (36); and Cotton, *Barnstaple*, pp. 126, 135, 146, 149 and 195–96.
44. E.311 (21).
45. See E.84 (36); HMC, Portland MSS, I, p. 703; and J. Walker MSS, 4,
f.392.
46. E.119 (11).
47. QSB, Box 48, presentment of Epiph. 1643. Using the (hitherto unnoted)
presentments of persons who had failed to appear on the posse as evidence
for the relative strength of anti-Royalist feeling in the various Devon
parishes is obviously risky. Many of those named in the presentments must
have had genuine reasons for failing to attend: illness, enemy activity and
bad weather could all have played their part in preventing even fervent
Royalists from appearing. Yet with this said, it is evident that some communities produced far more absentees than others. It seems fair to suggest
that the unusually high number of defaulters recorded from these particular
communities was a reflection of their underlying anti-Royalism. For the
record, the seventeen communities which produced twenty or more defaulters at any one muster between 1643 and 1645 were: Awliscombe (with 58),
Culmstock (53), Moretonhampstead (46), Tiverton (43), East Down (35),
Cleyhidon (34), Cornwood (32), Halberton (30), Hemyock (29), Crediton (29), Sandford (28), West Down (26), Pinhoe (26), Buckerell (24),
Bishops Nympton (21), Sampford Peverill (21), and South Brent (20). For
the presentments from which these statistics are derived, see QSB, Boxes
47–50, *passim*.
48. QSOB, 8 (1640–51), session of Easter 1644.
49. SP 28/139, part 16, (account of Robert Bennet), f.8.
50. Coate, 'Bennet of Hexworthy', p. 257.
51. KAO, U269/525/5 (unpaginated); see also R.W. Cotton, 'A North Devon
Cavalier's Expenses', DCNG, 3, (1890), p. 69.
52. For the attack on Ilfracombe, see Cotton, *Barnstaple*, pp. 307–10. For the
Royalist garrison there, see DRO 1148 MA/18/2 (Charles Constable's
Accounts) and M. Oppenheim, *The Maritime History of Devon*, (Exeter,
1968), p. 64.
53. See Coate, 'Bennet of Hexworthy', p. 256; BL, Add.MSS 35297, ff.30r and
67r; and E.325 (26).
54. See E.266 (39); and E.325 (1).
55. T. Moore, *The History and Topography of Devonshire*, (two vols, 1829), II,
p. 574.
56. E.121 (4).

57. See QSB, Boxes 48–50, presentments of Epiph. 1643/4, Easter 1644, Mich. 1644, and Easter 1645.
58. PRO, SP 28/128, Part 18; and Coate, 'Bennet of Hexworthy', p. 259.
59. *HMC*, De La Warre MSS, p. 308.
60. E.266 (39).
61. E.323 (7).
62. See PRO, SP 28/128, Parts 19–20, especially f.8r (Plymouth Garrison Accounts, 1642–43); WDRO, W/169, (Plymouth Garrison Accounts, 1645–46); and R.N. Worth, *Calendar of the Plymouth Municipal Records*, (1893), pp. 237–38.
63. E.124 (20) and E.9 (8).
64. BL, Harleian MSS, 6804, f.17.
65. E.250 (8).
66. DRO, DD.62701, *passim*, especially ff.12, 18v, 24. See also, DD.62703, ('Account of severall disbursements ... made against the violence of the [Royalist] Sheriffe'), f.11.
67. *HMC*, Portland MSS, I, p. 77.
68. E.130 (25).
69. *HMC*, Portland MSS, I, p. 78.
70. E.60 (17).
71. E.70 (13).
72. E.81 (17); and DRO, 1392 L/1644/34 (Seymour MSS).
73. *CSPD*, 1645–47, p. 41; and Sprigge, *Anglia Rediviva*, p. 180.
74. J. Walker, *An Attempt towards Recovering an Account of the ... Sufferings of the Clergy [in the] Great Rebellion*, (F.C. Hingeston-Randolph (ed.), Plymouth, 1908), p. 49.
75. J. Walker MSS, 3, f.305.
76. R.W. Cotton, 'Naval Attack on Topsham', *DCNG*, 1, (1888), p. 154; DRO, 1579A/17/26 (Totnes Accounts).
77. Add MSS.35297, ff.35, 65, 78r, and 94.
78. See, for example, E.37 (4).
79. DRO, 1392 L/1644/38.
80. DRO, 1392 L/1644/34.
81. *HMC*, Somerset MSS, p. 74.
82. Add MSS.35297, f.36r.
83. Ibid.; and *HMC*, Somerset MSS, p. 81.
84. *HMC*, Somerset MSS, p. 78.
85. DRO; 1392 M L/1644/55.
86. *HMC*, Somerset MSS, p. 79; and DRO, 1392 L/1644/52.
87. *HMC*, Somerset MSS, p. 80.
88. SP 19/156, f.283. For a brief discussion of the South Hams rising, see I.R. Palfrey, 'The Royalist War Effort Revisited', *TDA*, 123, (1991), pp. 52–53.
89. For Roope, Swete and Upton, see *HMC*, Somerset MSS, p. 81; DRO, 1392 L/1644/52; J.L.E. Hooppell, 'Old Traine in Modbury: The House and its Early Owners', *TDA*, 61, (1927), pp. 268–69.
90. Palfrey, 'War Effort', p. 147.
91. DRO; 1392 L/1644/59.
92. E.320 (11).
93. Ibid.

94. P.Q. Karkeek, 'Sir Edmund Fortescue and the siege of Fort Charles', *TDA*, 9, (1877), p. 346.
95. Ibid., p. 347.
96. E.114 (24).
97. E.105 (27).
98. QSB, Box 47, presentment of Bapt. 1643.
99. *CSPD*, 1644, pp. 350–52; and Walker, *Historical Discourses*, p. 41.
100. M. Dunsford, *Historical Memoirs of the Town and Parish of Tiverton*, (Exeter, 1790), p. 183. Dunsford incorrectly dates this incident to 1643.
101. E.300 (11); and E.300 (16).
102. E.320 (11).
103. E.114 (24).
104. E.21 (34).
105. *CSPD*, 1644, pp. 303–04.
106. E.21 (34).
107. PRO, SP 19/157/28; E.114 (24).
108. QSOB, 8, session of 1 August 1643.
109. QSB, Box 47, presentment of Bapt. 1643.
110. Ibid.
111. *CCAM*, III, p. 1353.
112. E.21 (34).
113. For the abortive rebellion at Hemyock, see *Mercurius Aulicus*, 10–16 March 1644; E.21 (34); QSB, Box 51, petition of Joan Illery, Mich. 1645; and Wolesely MSS, 56/6.
114. PRO, SP 19/136/133.
115. It has been claimed, on the strength of a document contained amongst the Wolesely MSS, that a rebellion took place in the East Devon village of Venn Ottery in April 1644. Examination of the document in question reveals that it was the insurrection at Hemyock which was actually being referred to. See Palfrey, 'War Effort', p. 82; and Wolesely MSS, 56/6.
116. For Crediton, see E.84 (36); P.Q. Karkeek, 'Extracts from a Memorandum Book belonging to Thomas Roberts … of Stockleigh Pomeroy', *TDA*, 10, (1878), p. 325; and QSB, Box 47, presentment of Epiph. 1642. For Fulford House, see QSOB, 8, session of Mich. 1643. For the townsmen's failure to appear on the posse, see QSB, Box 48, presentment of Epiph. 1643.
117. As the war dragged on, wholesale demolition increasingly came to be seen as a fitting punishment for ill-affected communities. In 1644 one Parliamentary commander advocated the complete destruction of Wareham, observing that 'there can be no argument against the demolishing of it … the inhabitants being almost all dreadful delinquents'. He added with glee that 'destroying it will undo knaves'. See W.D. Christie, *A Life of Anthony Ashley Cooper, 1st Earl of Shaftsbury*, (two vols, 1871), I, pp. 69–70.
118. For Fulford House, see QSOB, 8, session of Mich. 1643; For the failure of local men to appear on the posse, see QSB, Boxes 48–50, presentments of Epiph. 1643, Easter 1644, Bapt. 1644 and Epiph. 1644/45. For the Plymouth scouts, see WDRO, W/169, (unpaginated), entry of 1 November 1645.
119. See, for example, R. Hutton, 'The Royalist War Effort', in J. Morrill (ed.), *Reactions to the English Civil War, 1642–49*, (1982), p. 51; and P. Tennant, *Edgehill and Beyond*, (Stroud, 1992), *passim*.

Chapter 3

1. For a discussion of the approach adopted by the Royalist journals, see J. Malcolm, *Caesar's Due*, (1983), pp. 140–45.
2. See Malcolm, *Caesar's Due*; and B. Manning, *The English People and the English Revolution*, (1976), *passim*.
3. J. Morrill, *The Nature of the English Revolution*, (1993), pp. 215–20.
4. Recruitment of infantry regiments is particularly relevant to the study of popular allegiance, because such units were raised almost exclusively from amongst the lower classes. Cavalrymen tended to be of a rather higher social status.
5. E.244 (30).
6. E.250 (11).
7. E.84 (36)
8. Bod., Hope Adds, 1129, *A Continuation of Certain Special and Remarkable Passages*, 29 February to 7 March 1644; and E.250 (11).
9. E.84 (36).
10. Ibid.
11. Not all of those who attended the muster at Torrington were North Devonians, however. See QSB, Box 48, (Bundle of Michaelmas 1643) for evidence that the inhabitants of North Tawton Hundred had also been ordered to appear.
12. E.84 (36).
13. R. Jeffs et al. (eds), *Oxford Royalist Newsbooks: Volume I*, (1971), pp. 486–87.
14. G. Doe, *A Few Pages of Great Torrington History*, (1896), p. 21.
15. See R.W. Cotton, 'A North Devon Cavalier's Expenses', *DCNG*, 3, 1890, p. 69.
16. J. Stucley, *Sir Bevill Grenvile and his Times*, (Chichester, 1983), p. 132; E.250 (8).
17. Bod., J. Walker MSS, 4, ff.391–92r.
18. Malcolm, *Caesar's Due, passim*.
19. E.240 (18).
20. Cotton, 'North Devon Cavalier's Expenses', p. 68; and E. Hyde, Earl of Clarendon, *The History of the Rebellion and Civil War in England*, (W. Dunn Macray (ed.), six vols, Oxford, 1888), III, p. 162.
21. John Digby, commander of the Royalist forces, possessed 6–700 footmen when he first entered North Devon, but had increased this number to 3,000 by the time he left. See Clarendon, *History*, III, pp. 160–62.
22. Of the 3,000 men whom Digby had raised in North Devon and Cornwall during September 1643, only 600 were left by early 1644, and one suspects that most of these were Cornishmen.
23. R.W. Cotton, *Barnstaple and the Northern Part of Devonshire during the Great Civil War*, (1889), pp. 362–63.
24. Ibid., pp. 427, 445.
25. See, C.E.H. Chadwyck-Healey (ed.), *Bellum Civile*, (Somerset Record Society, 1902), p. 25; E.130 (16); and E.130 (25).
26. See E.84 (4); E.130 (20); DRO, 2178 A/PW 1; and Cotton, 'North Devon Cavalier's Expenses', p. 68.

27. E.83 (43).
28. DRO, 1579 A/17/30.
29. See DRO, 1579 A/10/34 and A/10/37 (three copies).
30. DRO, 1579 A/17/33 and A/17/36.
31. See DRO; Seymour MSS, 1392, *passim*; C.E. Long (ed.), *Diary of the Marches of the Royal Army During the Great Civil War*, (Camden Society, 1859), pp. 150–51; and BL., Harleian MSS, 6804, f.145 and 6851, f.228.
32. See Seymour MSS, 1392, *passim*; *HMC*, Somerset MSS, p. 75; PRO, SP 23/152/107–09; SP 23/185/503; and DRO, QS/128 (Maimed Soldiers' Petitions).
33. E.75 (11).
34. T. Carte (ed.), *A Collection of Original Letters and Papers*, (1739), p. 138.
35. Carte, *Collection*, p. 124.
36. I.R. Palfrey, 'The Royalist War Effort in Devon, 1642–46', (unpublished Birmingham MA thesis, 1985), p. 18.
37. CRO, Civil War Letters, 1/1051.
38. DRO, 2178 A/PW 1 (Tedburn St Mary Constable's Accounts, 1642/43).
39. Ibid.
40. J. Walker MSS, 2, f.235.
41. H. Walrond, *Historical Records of the First Devon Militia*, (1897), p. 21.
42. DRO, 2178 A/PW 1.
43. J. Walker MSS, 2, f.235; and Walrond, *Devon Militia*, p. 21.
44. EQSOB, 64 (1642–60), f.25.
45. Ibid.
46. Ibid.
47. Ibid.
48. J. Walker MSS, 2, f.235; and E.245 (16).
49. EQSOB, 64, f.28.
50. Ibid., f.27.
51. Hopton's forces were still in Totnes at this time. Thus the only villages near Exeter which could possibly have given them 'entertainment' were those on the west of the city.
52. EQSOB, 64, f.28.
53. DRO, 2178 A/PW 1.
54. E.86 (22). For the dismissal of the constables, see QSOB, 8 (1641–50), (unpaginated), entry of Epiphany 1642/43.
55. DRO, 'Calendar of Deeds and Documents in the Exeter City Library', I, p. 148.
56. For the looting of Fulford house, see QSOB, 8, entry of Michaelmas 1643.
57. M. Bray, *A Description of the Part of Devonshire Bordering on the Tamar and the Tavy*, (three volumes, 1836), III, pp. 62–64.
58. T. Larkham, *The Wedding Supper*, (1652), p. 125.
59. S.K. Roberts, *Recovery and Restoration in an English County*, (Exeter, 1985), p. 34.
60. Ibid.
61. J. Walker MSS, 2, f.256.
62. E.313 (3); E.313 (8); and E.320 (11).
63. DRO, 2178 A/PW 1.
64. DRO, Moger Papers, CC. 181/128.

65. QSB, Box 49, (Bundle of Easter 1644).
66. PRO, SP 28/128, part 17, f.78.
67. For July 1643, see E.60 (18) and E.63 (2). Also, J. Walker MSS, 4, ff.385–85r. For June 1645, see Carte, *Collection*, pp. 100–01.
68. CRO, Civil War Letters, 1/1051; and Bod, Clarendon MSS, 23/1738.
69. E.65 (2); and DRO, QS/128, 17/2, 94/1, 121/10.
70. See Long, *Diary*, p. 54; and E.6 (25).
71. BL, Harleian MSS, 6804, ff.31, 32, 74.
72. DRO, petitions of Robert Spray and Lawrence Eliot of Lustleigh; and E.6 (25).
73. Bod., Rawlinson MSS, Classis C. 125, f.110.
74. DRO, QS/128, 28/2 and 28/3.
75. E.244 (30).
76. E.84 (36).
77. QSB, Box 47, bundle of Bapt. 1643.
78. E.64 (7). The pamphlet's claim that the countrymen had been duped into thinking that Warwick's men were 'forraigne enemies' can probably be disregarded.
79. QSOB, 8, entry of Bapt. 1643.
80. Seymour MSS, 1392 L/43/12.
81. PRO, SP 23/152/339 ff.
82. J. Davidson, *Axminster in the Civil War*, (Axminster, 1851), p. 14.
83. R. Polwhele, *The History of Devon: Volume I*, (reprinted Dorking, 1977), p. 307.
84. J. Walker MSS, 2, f.246r.
85. Ibid., f.247.
86. E.95 (4); J. Walker MSS, f.429.
87. Carte, *Collection*, p. 99.
88. Ibid.
89. Ibid. See also ch. 6.
90. E.320 (21).
91. E.319 (8).
92. E.320 (15).
93. E.320 (21).
94. For the recruitment 'orbits' of these four regiments, see DRO, QS/128; and O.M. Moger (ed.), 'Devon Quarter Sessions Petitions, 1642–85', (two typescript volumes, WCSL), *passim*.

Chapter 4

1. P.F.S. Amery, 'Fourteenth Report on Devonshire Folklore', *TDA*, 28, (1896), p. 102.
2. G.W.G. Hughes, 'Moretonhampstead', *TDA*, 86, (1954), p. 82.
3. I am grateful to David Price-Hughes for this information.
4. S.K. Roberts, *Recovery and Restoration in an English County*, (Exeter, 1985), p. xx.
5. For the delinquents' names, see *CCAM*, *passim*. For the chief sources used to identify social status, see BL; Add.MSS, 34,012 (Desborough's List of Suspects); A.J. Howard (ed.), *Devon Protestation Returns*, (two vols,

privately printed, 1973), *passim*; PRO, SP 19/136, SP 23/83, SP 23/152, SP 23/182, SP 23/183–86, SP 23/178, SP 23/214, SP 28/128; and T.L. Stoate (ed.), *Devon Taxes*, (privately printed, 1988), pp. 111–69.

6. Add.MSS 34,012.

7. J. Morrill, 'The Ecology of Allegiance in the English Revolution', *JBS*, 26, (October 1987), p. 466.

8. The chief sources which have been used to identify Devon and Exeter Royalists are; BL, Thomason Tracts; *CCAM*; *CCC*; DRO, QS/128, 1–147; DRO, quarter sessions records for Devon and Exeter, 1642–46; PRO, SP 19; PRO, SP 23; and Anon, *A List of Officers Claiming to the Sixty Thousand Pounds*, (1663).

9. Historians working on other parts of the country have come to the same conclusion, see D. Underdown, 'A Reply to John Morrill', *JBS*, 26, (October 1987), pp. 477–78; and B.G. Blackwood, 'Parties and Issues in the Civil War in Lancashire and East Anglia', *Northern History*, 29, (1993), p. 115.

10. I am grateful to David Underdown for discussion of this point.

11. DRO, 'Calendar of Deeds and Documents in the Exeter City Library', I, p. 148.

12. DRO, QS/128, 94/1, (petition of Andrew Heywood).

13. See D. Underdown, *Revel, Riot and Rebellion*, (Oxford, 1985), pp. 191–98.

14. See especially Morrill, 'Ecology of Allegiance', pp. 465–66 and M. Wanklyn, 'The People go to War', *The Local Historian*, 17, 8, (1987), pp. 497–98.

15. O.M. Moger (ed.), 'Devonshire Quarter Sessions Petitions, 1642–85', (two typescript vols in WCSL).

16. See J. Malcolm, *Caesar's Due*, (1983), p. 90. Senior officers have been defined as those holding the rank of lieutenant or above.

17. Wanklyn, 'The People go to War', pp. 497–98; Morrill, 'Ecology of Allegiance', p. 239.

18. DRO, QS/128, (Maimed Soldiers' Petitions), 1–147.

19. These 234 individuals were not described as gentlemen and did not appear on pre-war pension lists.

20. For the names on which these figures are based, see M.J. Stoyle, 'Divisions within the Devonshire "County Community", 1600–46', (unpublished D.Phil. thesis, Oxford, 1992), Appendix II, Part I.

21. Wanklyn, 'The People go to War', p. 498.

22. Howard, *Protestation Returns*, p. v.

23. There is one notable exception. Torrington—the only North Devon community to display even the slightest degree of popular Royalism—produced just one petitioner for every 258 adult males. This meagre figure suggests that Torrington's Royalism was luke-warm at best, and that the town only appeared a hotbed of 'malignancy' in comparison with its fervently Parliamentarian neighbours.

24. Underdown, *Revel, Riot and Rebellion*, p. 191.

25. R.N. Worth, 'The Siege of Plymouth', *RTPI*, 5 (1875/76), p. 299.

26. With this said, Parliamentary raids into South Devon became increasingly wide-ranging as the war progressed, see Add.MSS, 35,297, ff.36r, 72r, 90r, 93r, 95–96.

27. See PRO, SP 28/128, part 31 (Lyme Regis garrison accounts, 1644–45); and E.200 (28).

28. Roberts, *Restoration and Recovery*, p. xx.

29. Morrill, 'Ecology of Allegiance', p. 466.

30. See Morrill, 'Ecology of Allegiance', p. 466; Wanklyn, 'The People go to War', p. 498; and Underdown 'Reply', pp. 477–78.

31. See E.100 (20); PRO, SP 28/128, part 18, (Charles Peard's account for Barnstaple, 1644); SP 28/128, parts 19 and 20 (Plymouth garrison accounts, 1642–43); DRO, DD.62701, (account of monies disbursed at Dartmouth, 1642–43).

32. See, for example, A. Hughes, *The Causes of the English Civil War*, (1991), pp. 123–24; Roberts, *Restoration and Recovery*, p. xx; and D. Underdown, *Somerset in the Civil War and Interregnum*, (Newton Abbot, 1973), pp. 39–40.

33. The many peers, gentlemen, merchants and yeomen who appear on Desborough's list have not been included in this figure.

34. Underdown, 'Reply', p. 478.

35. See J. Morrill, *The Revolt of the Provinces*, (1976), p. 39; and Underdown, *Revel, Riot and Rebellion*, p. 204.

36. See DRO, DD. 35539 (Petition of Warwick Hawkey); and Bod, Rawlinson MSS, A.57, f.141.

37. See T.A.P. Greeves, 'The Devon Tin Industry, 1450–1750', (unpublished Ph.D. thesis, Exeter, 1981), pp. 38–39.

Chapter 5

1. See M.J. Stoyle, 'Documentary Evidence for the Civil War Defences of Exeter, 1642–43', (Exeter Museum, report no. 88.12, 1992), p. iv.

2. For an overview of the war's events, see M. Coate, 'Exeter in the Civil War and Interregnum', *DCNQ*, 18, (1934–35), pp. 338–52.

3. E.128 (11).

4. E.242 (37).

5. E.67 (14).

6. E.252 (38).

7. E.52 (22).

8. E.302 (6).

9. E.322 (22).

10. E.242 (27).

11. E.244 (33).

12. E.245 (11); E.84 (36).

13. E.105 (15).

14. E.65 (2).

15. E.250 (13).

16. See, for example, BL, Burney, *The Moderate Intelligencer*, 30 October to 6 November 1645.

17. E.332 (23).

18. Ibid.

19. E.332 (2).

20. Fears of imminent conflict were expressed in the city as early as October 1641. See EQSOB, 64, (1642–60), ff.380–80v.

21. I hope to examine the outbreak of the Civil War in Exeter in a future paper.

22. For the names of the city counsellors see ECAB, 8 (1634–47), ff.136–44. For their ultimate allegiance see M.J. Stoyle, 'Divisions within the Devonshire "County Community", c. 1600–46', (Unpublished D.Phil. thesis, Oxford, 1992), appendices IV and V.
23. EQSOB, 63 (1630–42), f.397v.
24. EQSOB, 64, f.1.
25. Ibid., f.2.
26. Ibid., f.5.
27. Ibid., f.17.
28. For Bath and his mission, see I.R. Palfrey, 'Devon and the Outbreak of the English Civil War, 1642–43', *Southern History*, 10, (1988), pp. 29–35.
29. ECAB, 8, f.138.
30. EQSOB, 64, f.6.
31. EQSOB, 64, f.7.
32. Ibid.
33. E.112 (14).
34. J.S. Cockburn, *Western Circuit Assize Orders, 1629–48*, (Camden Society, 4th Series, 17, 1976), p. 234.
35. See ECAB, 8, ff.138–44.
36. See EQSOB, 64, ff.8–17; and ECAB, 8, f.139.
37. ECL, Act Book of the Dean and Chapter, 1635–43, (unpaginated), entry of 13 August 1642.
38. ECAB, 8, f.139r.
39. E.239 (17).
40. *JHL*, 5, p. 398.
41. E.116 (10).
42. The city freemen were entitled to choose one of the two mayoral candidates put forward by the Chamber, see W.T. MacCaffrey, *Exeter, 1540–1640*, (Harvard, 1978), p. 30.
43. EQSOB, 64, ff.8, 11, 12.
44. E.242 (17).
45. EQSOB, 64, f.18.
46. For the rioting of 2 November, see EQSOB, 64, ff.18, 21, 25; and ECAB, 8, f.143.
47. EQSOB, 64, f.20.
48. Ibid., f.22.
49. E.244 (16).
50. E.244 (30).
51. E.86 (22); and F.C. Hingeston-Randolph (ed.), *Dr Walker's 'Sufferings of the Clergy in the Diocese of Exeter During the Great Rebellion'*, (Plymouth, 1908), pp. 30, 49.
52. E.245 (11).
53. E.84 (36). See also E.66 (22).
54. Hingeston-Randolph, *Sufferings*, p. 30.
55. Ibid., p. 49.
56. E.A. Andriette, *Devon and Exeter in the Civil War*, (Newton Abbot, 1971), p. 82; Palfrey, 'Outbreak', p. 39.
57. CRO, Tremaine Papers, DDT/1617/A.
58. Ibid.; and E.94 (21).

59. Tremaine Papers, DDT/1617/A.
60. *HMC*, Portland MSS, I, p. 102.
61. See DRO, Letter Book 60F, DD.391.12–43.
62. Hingeston-Randolph, *Sufferings*, pp. 54–55.
63. E.105 (15); and E.65 (2).
64. EQSOB, 64, f.45.
65. E.67 (27).
66. E. Hyde, Earl of Clarendon, *The History of the Rebellion and Civil Wars in England*, (W.D. Macray (ed.), six vols, Oxford, 1888), III, p. 163.
67. See DD. 391.44–45.
68. See BL, Pamphlet C.71, D.35, *(Colonel Joseph Bamfield's Apologie)*.
69. Andriette, *Devon*, p. 95.
70. See Bod., Tanner MS, 62, 2/B, f.557.
71. EQSOB, 64, f.52.
72. See for example, EQSOB, 64, ff.48, 50, 52.
73. J. Bond, *Occasus Occidentalis*, (1645), p. 37.
74. See PRO, SP 23/184/746; SP 23/185/488; and EQSOB, 64, f.97.
75. Coate, 'Exeter', pp. 339, 345, 349; and Andriette, *Devon*, pp. 66, 83, 95.
76. A. Jenkins, *The History and Description of the City of Exeter*, (1806), p. 161; P.Q. Karkeek, 'Fairfax in the West, 1645–46', *TDA*, 8, (1876), p. 117.
77. See Stoyle, 'Divisions', appendix IV. The names of five more Royalists who do not appear in this list have since been recovered from DRO, Y5 (petitions to the Chamber for relief).
78. See DD.391.12–20, DD.391.27–29v and DRO, Misc. Papers, Box 6 (account of money paid to Captain Gandy's soldiers).
79. See EQSOB, 64, f.20.
80. For these individuals, see DD.391.35–43v.
81. EQSOB, 64, f.20.
82. The workmen were paid. See DD.391.35–43v.
83. For the names of these individuals, see Stoyle, 'Divisions', appendix V. The names of three more Parliamentarians who do not appear on this list have since been recovered from DRO, Y5; and S. Lawrence, 'A Population Study of St Sidwell's Parish ... 1642–46' (1993, typescript kept at the Devon and Exeter Institute, Exeter), p. 5.
84. See Stoyle, 'Divisions', appendix IV, table 1.
85. Ibid., appendix V, table 1.
86. Cf. L. Stone 'The Bourgeois Revolution of Seventeenth Century England Revisited', *P&P*, 109, (1985), pp. 44–45.
87. E.84 (36).
88. Bod., Hope Adds, 1133, *Mercurius Rusticus*, 21, 16 March 1643.
89. See Stoyle, 'Divisions', appendix IV, table 2.
90. Ibid., appendix V, table 2.
91. Ibid., appendix IV, table 2.
92. Ibid., appendices IV and V, table 2.
93. DRO, Y5, (petition of Richard Cooke).
94. Stoyle, 'Divisions', appendices IV and V, table 2.
95. See J.T. Evans, *Seventeenth-Century Norwich*, (Oxford, 1979), pp. 133–44; and K. Lindley, 'London's Citizenry in the English Revolution' , in R.C.

Richardson (ed.), *Town and Countryside in the English Revolution*, (Manchester, 1992), pp. 19–45.

96. W.G. Hoskins, *Industry, Trade and People in Exeter, 1688–1800*, (Manchester, 1935), pp. 111–23.

97. DRO, Book 73/15, (James White's Chronicle), f.134. Why these particular names were chosen remains unclear.

98. J. Cossins, *Reminiscences of Exeter Fifty Years Since*, (Exeter, 1878), p. 11.

Chapter 6

1. See B. Manning, 'Neutrals and Neutralism in the English Civil War', (Oxford D.Phil. thesis, 1957), *passim*; J.S. Morrill, *Cheshire 1630–60*, (Oxford, 1974), *passim*; J.S. Morrill, *The Revolt of the Provinces*, (1976), *passim*, especially pp. 36–39, 46, 89; G.E. Aylmer, 'Collective Mentalities in Mid Seventeenth Century England: IV. Cross Currents: Neutrals, Trimmers and Others', *TRHS*, 5th series, 39, (1989), pp. 1–22.

2. R.N. Worth, *The Buller Papers*, (privately printed, 1895), pp. 33–34.

3. E.37 (10).

4. Most notably in early 1643, see note 12.

5. See below, ch. 7.

6. E. Hyde, Earl of Clarendon, *The History of the Rebellion and the Civil Wars in England*, (W. Dunn Macray (ed.), six vols, Oxford, 1888), III, pp. 73–75.

7. *CCAM*, III, p. 1379; *CCAM*, II, p. 1055; BL, Add.MSS, 35297, (John Syms' Daybook), f.61.

8. PRO, SP 23/152/31.

9. See A.C. Miller, *Sir Richard Grenville of the Civil War*, (1979), p. 69; E.70 (13); and Add.MSS, 35297, f.25r.

10. See R.W. Cotton, *Barnstaple and the Northern Parts of Devon during the Great Civil War*, (1889), pp. 273–76; J. Sprigg, *Anglia Rediviva*, (1645), pp. 155–56; and Add.MSS, 35297, ff.23r, 61.

11. E.67 (27).

12. For these negotiations, see Manning, 'Neutrals', pp. 126–42; E.A. Andriette, *Devon and Exeter in the English Civil War*, (Newton Abbot, 1971), pp. 80–84; and I.R. Palfrey, Devon and the Outbreak of the English Civil War, 1642–43', *Southern History*, 10, (1988), pp. 39–41.

13. For the Clubmen in general, see P. Gladwish, 'The Herefordshire Clubmen: A Reassessment', *Midland History*, 10, (1985), pp. 62–71; R. Hutton, 'The Worcestershire Clubmen in the English Civil War', *Midland History*, 5, (1979–80), pp. 39–49; Morrill, *Revolt of the Provinces*, pp. 97–111; and D. Underdown, 'The Chalk and the Cheese: Contrasts among the English Clubmen', *P&P*, 85, (1979), pp. 25–48.

14. D. Underdown, *Somerset in the Civil War and Interregnum*, (Newton Abbot, 1973), pp. 98–99; and Clarendon, *History*, IV, p. 54.

15. G.M. Trevelyan, *England Under the Stuarts*, (1904), p. 269.

16. Underdown, 'Chalk and the Cheese', *passim*.

17. Ibid., p. 28.

18. T. Carte (ed.), *A Collection of Original Letters and Papers... found among the Duke of Ormonde's Papers* (1739), p. 99.

19. Ibid.
20. See above, ch. 3, pp. 71–72.
21. Underdown, 'Chalk and the Cheese', pp. 30, 48.
22. Carte, *Letters*, pp. 100–01.
23. As happened with the 'Peaceable Army' in South Wales. See R. Hutton, *The Royalist War Effort 1642–46*, (1982), pp. 183–84.
24. Miller, *Grenville*, pp. 119–20.
25. Underdown, *Somerset*, p. 106.
26. E.293 (17); and E.293 (20).
27. E.294 (26).
28. E.262 (36).
29. Ibid.; and E.262 (29).
30. E.262 (29).
31. Ibid.
32. E.262 (34); and E.262 (36).
33. E.262 (36).
34. Ibid.
35. Ibid.
36. Ibid.
37. E.295 (6).
38. E.262 (44).
39. Clarendon, *History*, IV, p. 63.
40. See R. Hutton, 'Clarendon's History of the Rebellion', *EHR*, 97, (1982), pp. 79–88.
41. DRO, 1597/748/A (Totnes Mayoral Accounts, 1645–46).
42. DRO, ECAB, 8, f.169r.
43. Miller, *Grenville*, p. 127.
44. DRO, 1148 MA/18/2 (Charles Constable's accounts).
45. WCSL, B.F. Cresswell and A.J. Skinner (eds), 'Crediton Parish Registers, Volume 7', (DCRS, n.d.), p. 69.
46. WCSL, E. Searle (ed.), 'Moretonhampstead Parish Registers, Volume 2', (DCRS, 1936), p. 56.
47. PRO, SP 23/183/158.
48. PRO, SP 23/184/746.
49. PRO, SP 23/185/502–03 and 545
50. As late as 1671 a group of plunderers could still be termed a 'Goring's Crew' by a disapproving Devonian. This shows how deeply the troopers' excesses had etched themselves upon the popular memory. See J. Hickes, *A True and Faithful Narrative of the ... Illegal Sufferings of Many Christians ... injudiciously call'd Fanaticks*', (1671), p. 14. During the Commonwealth the Royalist privateers which preyed upon local shipping were known as 'Gorings', again demonstrating that Goring's name had become synonymous with robbery and rapine. See S.K. Roberts, *Recovery and Restoration in an English County*, (Exeter, 1985), p. 15.
51. E.262 (42).
52. E.296 (31); E.262 (48); and E.262 (51).
53. E.262 (48); and E.262 (51).
54. E.262 (51); and E.298 (15).
55. DRO, 1148 MA/18/2.

56. E.298 (15).
57. E.298 (17).
58. E.299 (8).
59. E.300 (10); and E.300 (11).
60. E.300 (11); and E.300 (16).
61. E.302 (21).
62. Ibid.
63. E.302 (6); and E.302 (9).
64. Though the error is perpetuated in I. Gentles, *The New Model Army in England, Scotland, and Ireland*, (Oxford, 1992), p. 64, where Apsley is mistakenly titled 'Sir Leven Ashley'.
65. E.303 (3).
66. NDRO, 1677A/PW 1 (Braunton churchwardens' accounts).
67. E.304 (1); and E.264 (21).
68. E.262 (51).
69. *CSPD*, 1645–47, p. 153.
70. Cotton, *Barnstaple*, pp. 404–05.
71. *CSPD*, 1645–47, p. 153.
72. E.264 (21); E.304 (8); and E.304 (18).
73. E.304 (8).
74. E.304 (18).
75. DRO, 1392/L/1645/19 (Seymour MSS).
76. DRO, 1597/748/A.
77. Sprigg, *Anglia Rediviva*, pp. 157–58.
78. WDRO, W/169 (Plymouth Siege Accounts, 1644/45).
79. E.308 (11).
80. Cotton, *Barnstaple*, pp. 432–34.
81. Add.MSS, 35297, f.94.
82. E.266 (27).
83. Sprigg, *Anglia Rediviva*, pp. 78–79.
84. E.320 (13).
85. Cotton, *Barnstaple*, p. 459.
86. DRO, 1201 A/ MFK 12/ B1, (Hartland Borough Accounts).
87. Cotton, *Barnstaple*, p. 459.
88. R. Pearse-Chope, *Farthest from Railways*, (privately printed, 1934), p. 22.
89. Cotton, *Barnstaple*, p. 459.
90. Underdown, 'Chalk and the Cheese', pp. 36–37.
91. Ibid., p. 32.
92. Hutton, *War Effort*, p. 164.
93. Underdown, *Somerset*, p. 98.
94. E.262 (51).
95. Bod., J.Walker MSS, II, f.305.
96. Carey was serving as a JP in 1644, see QSOB, 1/8, epiphany 1644. I owe this reference to Mary Wolffe.
97. Squire Courtenay is first mentioned in connection with North Molton, so it is reasonable to assume that he dwelt nearby. John Courtenay not only lived in neighbouring Molland but was invariably termed an 'esquire'.
98. Only one, brief, reference to the 'Ashburne' incident survives. See E.262 (51).

99. See E.262 (38); E.262 (36); E.262 (29); E.264 (21); E.300 (11); and E.300 (16).
100. The South Hams rising is referred to in five different sources. See E.308 (11); DRO, 1392/L/1645/19; WDRO, W/169; DRO, 1597/748/A; and Add.MSS, 35297, ff.90r, 94.
101. The fifteen North Devon communities either known or suspected to have participated in the risings are; Ashford, Ashreigney, Barnstaple, Bideford, Braunton, Charles, Clovelly, Hartland, Martinhoe, Molland, North Molton, South Molton, Parkham, Welcombe, and Woolfardisworthy.
102. Bod., Clarendon MSS, 1911/93.
103. See E.91 (8); and Hickes, *True and Faithful Narrative*, p. 31.
104. For a reference to those who rose in support of Parliament in 1643 as 'Clubmen', see E.91 (8).

Part III

Chapter 7

1. Clarendon was a particularly influential exponent of this theory, see R. Hutton, 'Clarendon's History of the Rebellion', *EHR*, 97, (1982), pp. 70–76.
2. P.Q. Karkeek, 'Fairfax in the West', *TDA*, 8, (1876), p. 118.
3. K. Wrightson, *English Society, 1580–1680*, (1982), p. 172. For other statements of this point of view, see B. Manning, *The English People and the English Revolution*, (1976); J. Malcolm, *Caesar's Due*, (1983); and D. Underdown, *Revel, Riot and Rebellion*, (Oxford, 1985).
4. J. Morrill (ed.), *Reactions to the English Civil War*, (1982), p. 11.
5. See A.J. Howard, *Devon Protestation Returns*, (privately printed, 1973), *passim*.
6. See M. Wolffe, 'The Gentry Government of Devon, 1625–40', (unpublished Ph.D. thesis, Exeter, 1992), p. 8.
7. D. MacCulloch, *Suffolk and the Tudors*, (Oxford, 1986), p. 287.
8. There are parallels here with the situation in Lancashire. See B.G. Blackwood, *The Lancashire Gentry and the Great Rebellion*, (Manchester, 1978), p. 6.
9. BM, Add.MSS, 9427, (Lysons' Correspondence), f.210.
10. For Davy, Drewe and Prideaux, see *CCAM*, II, p. 1127; E.8 (6); and E.10 (11).
11. I am grateful to Mary Wolffe for confirming this point.
12. For Seymour and Southcott, see P.R. Newman, *Royalist Officers in England and Wales, 1642–60*, (1981), pp. 337–38, 353.
13. Limitations of space—and the fact that this book is concerned primarily with non-gentry allegiance—mean that the names on which this statement is based cannot be given here. I hope to publish full lists of those Devon gentlemen who supported King or Parliament elsewhere.
14. I am grateful to Mary Wolffe for discussion of this point.
15. See note 13.
16. E.114 (24).

17. See E.114 (24), E.115 (21), E.119 (5), E.119 (24), and E.121 (4); *HMC*, Portland MSS, I, p. 76; and EQSOB, 64, (1642–60), f.11.
18. E. Chadwyck-Healey (ed.), *Bellum Civile*, (Somerset Record Society, 18, 1902), p. 24.
19. E.83 (43).
20. See E.84 (4), E.245 (16), E.86 (22), and E.245 (17).
21. Chadwyck-Healey, *Bellum Civile*, p. 38.
22. E. Hyde, Earl of Clarendon, *The History of the Rebellion and Civil Wars in England*, (W. Dunn MacCray (ed.), six vols, Oxford, 1888), III, p. 233.
23. E. Walker, *Historical Discourses Upon Several Occasions*, (1705), p. 41.
24. E.318 (6).
25. E.63 (2).
26. Clarendon, *History*, III, p. 329.
27. Chadwyck-Healey, *Bellum Civile*, p. 24.
28. *HMC*, Portland, I, p. 77.
29. The records of the Committees for Compounding and Advance of Money are not particularly reliable for this purpose. See ch. 4, p. 76.
30. Newman, *Royalist Officers, passim*.
31. See note 13.
32. Malcolm, *Caesar's Due*, pp. 89–90.
33. See note 13.
34. These figures are not as trustworthy as those for the field officers alone. It has proved impossible to ascribe a parish of origin to almost a fifth of the total number of officers identified and as a result considerable distortion may have occurred.
35. A. Hughes, *The Causes of the English Civil War*, (1991), p. 145.
36. See note 13.
37. E.121 (4).
38. See C.B. Phillips, 'Landlord–Tenant Relationships, 1642–60', in R.C. Richardson (ed.), *Town and Countryside in the English Revolution*, (Manchester, 1992), p. 230.
39. QSB, Box 47, Examination of William Beare, 13 November 1642.
40. EQSOB, 64, f.21.
41. Ibid., f.18.
42. For an audacious coup of this sort, see A.C. Miller, *Sir Richard Grenville of the Civil War*, (1979), p. 67.
43. *CCAM*, III, p. 1,400.
44. E.257 (10); E.258 (13); and E.67 (3).
45. R.W. Cotton, *Barnstaple and the Northern Part of Devonshire during the Great Civil War*, (1889), p. 346.
46. Clarendon, *History*, III, p. 329.
47. Chadwyck-Healey, *Bellum Civile*, pp. 26–27.
48. M.Coate, *Cornwall in the Great Civil War and Interregnum*, (Oxford, 1933), p. 139.
49. See E.81 (8).
50. G. Chapman, *The Siege of Lyme*, (Lyme Regis, 1982), p. 41.
51. See J. Morrill and J. Walter, 'Order and Disorder in the English Revolution', reprinted in J. Morrill (ed.), *The Nature of the English Revolution*, (1993).
52. QSB, Box 46, examination of Robert Moxham, 7 September 1642.

53. E.127 (6).
54. CRO, Tremaine Papers, DDT. 1767.
54. M. Coate, 'The Duchy of Cornwall: Its History and Administration, 1640–60, *TRHS*, 4th series, 10, (1927), p. 169. See also, Malcolm, *Caesar's Due*, pp. 78–79.
55. E.A. Andriette, *Devon and Exeter in the Civil War*, (Newton Abbot, 1971), p. 60.
56. E.21 (34).
57. T. Carte (ed.), *A Collection of Original Letters and Papers concerning the Affairs of England*, (1793), p. 101. See also ch. 9, p. 169.
58. O.M. Moger (ed.), 'Devon Quarter Sessions Petitions, 1642–85, (two vols, 1985, typescript in WCSL), II, p. 270.
59. See, for example, DRO, QS/128, 17/2.
60. Morrill, *Reactions*, p. 10.
61. Wrightson, *English Society*, p. 172.
62. T. Risdon, *The Chorographical Description or Survey of the County of Devon*, (1811 edition), p. 186.
63. PRO, SP 23/152/483.

Chapter 8

1. Although there were many persons of Flemish descent sprinkled along the South-east Devon coast, see ch. 10, pp. 200–202.
2. A.L. Rowse, *Tudor Cornwall*, (1941), p. 20.
3. Such migrants frequently appear in the Devon sessions records, see, for example, QSB, Box 40, examination of Alice Treferron, 1 August 1637.
4. J.E. Gover, A. Mawer and F.M. Stenton (eds), *The Place Names of Devon: Part I*, (Cambridge, 1969), p. xxi.
5. W.G. Hoskins, *Devon*, (1964), p. 43. See also, M.F. Wakelin, *Language and History in Cornwall*, (Leicester, 1985), pp. 55, 58, 64.
6. E. Hyde, Earl of Clarendon, *The History of the Rebellion and Civil Wars in England*, (W.D. Macray (ed.), six vols, Oxford, 1888), III, p. 69.
7. E.266 (27).
8. See ch. 6, pp. 126–27.
9. E.T. MacDermott, *The History of the Forest of Exmoor*, (Newton Abbot, 1973), ch. 8, *passim*.
10. F. Rose-Troup, *The Western Rebellion of 1549*, (1913), pp. 131–36.
11. Cf. A. Everitt, *Landscape and Community in England*, (1985), p. 3; A. Hughes, *Politics, Society and Civil War in Warwickshire, 1620–60*, (Cambridge, 1987), preface; and D. MacCulloch, *Suffolk and the Tudors*, (Oxford, 1986), p. 2.
12. Cf. MacCulloch, *Suffolk*, p. 42; and Hughes, *Politics, Society and Civil War*, p. 20.
13. C. Morris (ed.), *The Illustrated Journeys of Celia Fiennes*, (1982), p. 207.
14. See Hoskins, *Devon*, p. 121.
15. See R.C. Richardson, 'Introduction', in R.C. Richardson (ed.), *Town and Countryside in the English Revolution*, (Manchester, 1992), p. 5.
16. Devon possessed some forty-five market towns in 1640. See J. Chartres (ed.), *Agriculture, Markets and Trade, 1500–1750*, (Cambridge, 1990), p. 20.

17. J. Thirsk, 'Seventeenth Century Agriculture and Social Change', in P.S. Seaver (ed.), *Seventeenth Century England*, (1976), p. 71.
18. C. Hill, *The World Turned Upside Down*, (1972), pp. 46–47, 57; and D. Underdown, *Revel, Riot and Rebellion*, (Oxford, 1985), *passim*. Guarded support for these views is also expressed in Hughes, *Politics, Society and Civil War*, p. 151.
19. Underdown, *Revel, Riot and Rebellion*, p. 176. I am most grateful to David Underdown for discussing these matters with me during his stay in Oxford in 1992.
20. A. Hughes, 'Local History and the Origins of the English Civil War' in R. Cust and A. Hughes (eds), *Conflict in Early Stuart England*, (1989), p. 242; K. Sharpe, *Politics and Ideas in Early Stuart England*, (1989), pp. 301–02.
21. B. Sharp, 'Rural Discontents and the English Revolution', in Richardson, *Town and Countryside*, pp. 251–72, especially pp. 254–57.
22. M. Ingram, *Church Courts, Sex and Marriage in England, 1570–1640*, (Cambridge, 1987), pp. 101–02; and J. Morrill, 'The Ecology of Allegiance in the English Revolution', *JBS*, 26, no. 4, (1987), pp. 457–62.
23. W. Marshall, *The Rural Economy of the West of England*, (two vols, 1796), p. 5.
24. For the importance of arable farming in this area, see S.H. Burton, *Devon Villages*, (1982), p. 61; J. Thirsk (ed.), *The Agrarian History of England and Wales, IV: 1500–1640*, (Cambridge, 1967), p. 72; and W.G. Hoskins, *Old Devon*, (Newton Abbot, 1966), p. 159.
25. Thirsk, *Agrarian History, IV*, p. 72.
26. For the wealth of the Taw-Torridge basin in the medieval period, see Hoskins, *Old Devon*, p. 159.
27. R. Fraser, *A General View of the County of Devon*, (reprinted Barnstaple, 1970), p. 20.
28. Burton, *Devon Villages*, p. 96.
29. For agrarian practice around Torbay, see Thirsk, *Agrarian History, IV*, p. 72.
30. See A. Hughes, *The Causes of the English Civil War*, (1991), p. 143.
31. See Morrill, 'Ecology of Allegiance', p. 458 for a suggestion that the alleged field/pasture divide might be better expressed as an arable/non-arable one.
32. Underdown, *Revel, Riot and Rebellion*, pp. 8, 96, 99, 103–04, 165, 176.
33. Only Exeter and Tavistock contained appreciable numbers of Royalists.
34. S.K. Roberts, *Recovery and Restoration in an English County*, (Exeter, 1985), p. xvi.
35. C. Gill, *Dartmoor: A New Study*, (Newton Abbot, 1970), p. 116.
36. Ibid.
37. For evidence of such clashes during the 1590s, see QSOB, 1, (1592–1600), ff.45, 67–68, 134.
38. Lady Radford, 'Notes on the Tinners of Devon and their Laws', *TDA*, 62, (1930), pp. 233–34.
39. *CSPD*, 1635–36, p. 550.
40. See, for example, H.C.B. Rogers, *Battles and Generals of the English Civil War*, (1968), p. 17.
41. B. Reay (ed.), *Popular Culture in Seventeenth Century England*, (1988), p. 62.

42. For the disturbances at Plymouth and the appalling conditions which had prompted them, see *CSPD*, 1628–29, pp. 28, 33, 35–38; and T. Gray, 'Devon's Coastal and Overseas Fisheries and New England Migration, 1597–1642', (unpublished Exeter University Ph.D. thesis, 1988), p. 256.
43. See *CSPD*, 1628–29, pp. 68, 97, 121.
44. Gray, 'Devon Fisheries', p. 267.
45. See *CSPD*, 1629–31, pp. 44, 50, 52, 80, 232, 296, 333.
46. *CSPD*, 1633–34, p. 532; and *CSPD*, 1631–33, p. 412–13.
47. K. Wrightson, *English Society, 1580–1680*, (1982), p. 194; K. Wrightson and D. Levine, *Poverty and Piety in an English Village*, (1979), p. 146.
48. See MacCulloch, *Suffolk*, p. 176.
49. R.H. Tawney and E. Power (eds), *Tudor Economic Documents*, (three vols, 1924), II, p. 45; and A. Powell, *John Aubrey and his Friends*, (1988), pp. 116–17. See also, B.E. Supple, *Commercial Crisis and Change in England, 1600–42*, (Cambridge, 1970), p. 234.
50. For the clothworkers' radicalism, see B. Manning, *The English People and the English Revolution*, (1976), pp. 202, 209–10, 215.
51. See G. Roberts (ed.), *The Diary of Walter Yonge*, (Camden Society, Old Series, 41, 1848), pp. 52–53.
52. I am most grateful to Marjorie McIntosh for discussion of this subject.
53. See P. Collinson, *Godly People*, (1983), p. 401; and Gray, 'Devon Fisheries', pp. 149–54.
54. H. Johnson and H. Tapley-Soper (eds), 'Lustleigh Parish Registers', (DCRS, Exeter, 1927).
55. E.C. Wood and H. Tapley-Soper (eds), 'Widecombe-in-the-Moor Parish Registers', (DCRS, Exeter, 1938).
56. Wrightson, *English Society*, p. 41.
57. A force of tin-miners from this area served in the Parliamentary garrison of Plymouth. See BM, Add.MSS, 34297, (John Syms' Diary), ff.30–30r.
58. Underdown, *Revel, Riot and Rebellion*, p. 204.

Chapter 9

1. E.A. Andriette, *Devon and Exeter in the Civil War*, (Newton Abbot, 1971), p. 24.
2. For the cost of billeting, see R.P. Cust, 'The Forced Loan and English Politics', (Ph.D. thesis, London, 1984), p. 172. For a full discussion of the local governors' response to Crown policies, see A.M. Wolffe, 'The Gentry Government of Devon 1625–40', (unpublished Ph.D. thesis, Exeter, 1992), pp. 66–102 and 123–238.
3. See, for example, *CSPD*, 1625–26, pp. 38, 70, 77, 83, 93, 95, 120, 184, 214, 227, 291, 319, 350, 370, 375, 410.
4. *HMC*, Cowper, I, p. 275.
5. Ibid.
6. Andriette, *Devon*, p. 28. I am grateful to Mary Wolffe for information on billeting.
7. Cust, 'Forced Loan', pp. 172–73; see also Wolffe, 'Gentry Government', p. 140.
8. BM, Sloane MSS, 1775, f.72.

9. Cust, 'Forced Loan', p. 114.
10. L.J. Reeve, *Charles I and the Road to Personal Rule*, (Cambridge, 1989), pp. 134–35.
11. Wolffe, 'Gentry Government', p. 164.
12. E.S. Cope, *Politics Without Parliaments 1629–40*, (1987), p. 181; and *JHC*, 2, 14.
13. When the mutineers were finally apprehended, the Deputies asked to be excused from taking part in their trial, see *CSPD*, 1640, pp. 645–46.
14. This petition is referred to in BM, Add.MSS, 35331, f.76, a point I owe to Mary Wolffe.
15. R.N. Worth, *The Buller Papers*, (1895), pp. 135–37.
16. PRO, SP 16/469/54.
17. *CSPD*, 1627–28, p. 488; Reeve, *Road to Personal Rule*, p. 135; Cust, 'Forced Loan', pp. 401–03; *CSPD*, 1639, p. 62; *CSPD*, 1640, pp. 203–04, 438.
18. Andriette, *Devon*, p. 195, note 4.
19. See M.J. Stoyle, 'Divisions within the Devonshire "County Community"', 1600–46', (D.Phil. thesis, Oxford, 1992), ch. 9, note 20.
20. See Stoyle, 'Divisions', ch. 9, note 21.
21. E.84 (36).
22. Worth, *Buller Papers*, p. viii.
23. J.S. Morrill, 'William Davenport and the "Silent Majority" of early Stuart England', *Journal of the Chester Archaeological Society*, (1974).
24. See J. Morrill, *The Revolt of the Provinces*, (1976), p. 13; and J. Morrill, *Cheshire 1630–60*, (Oxford, 1974), pp. 30, 34.
25. EQSOB, 61 (1618–21), f.13.
26. See F. Nicolls, *The Life and Death of Mr Ignatius Jurdain*, (1654), *passim*; *CSPD*, 1639, p. 160; D. Underdown et al. (eds), *William Whiteway of Dorchester, His Diary*, (Dorset Record Society, 12, 1990), p. 135. I am currently writing a paper on Jurdain.
27. This supports the view that, whatever the fears of contemporaries, Charles I's regime was by no means a ruthless engine of repression. See G.E. Aylmer, *Rebellion or Revolution?*, (Oxford, 1986), p. 7.
28. See G. Roberts (ed.), *The Diary of Walter Yonge*, (Camden Society, Old Series 41, 1848), *passim*; and BM, Add.MSS, 35,331.
29. DRO, Book 73/15 (James White's Chronicle), ff.101–18.
30. Underdown, *Whiteway Diary*, pp. 12–13.
31. DRO, Book 73/15, ff.101–02, 105.
32. Ibid., f.106.
33. DRO, Book 73/15, ff.107–12.
34. DRO, Letter Book 60F, DD.391.34.
35. R. Cust, *The Forced Loan and English Politics*, (Oxford, 1987), ch. 5, *passim*.
36. *CSPD*, 1640, pp. 476, 494–95.
37. PRO, SP 16/463/88.
38. Ibid.
39. *CSPD*, 1640, p. 496.
40. Ibid., p. 494.
41. PRO, SP 16/463/88.
42. For Wellington, see D. Underdown, *Revel, Riot and Rebellion*, (Oxford, 1985), pp. 133–34, 191; D. Underdown, *Somerset in the Civil War and*

Interregnum, (Newton Abbot, 1973), pp. 54, 117; and *CSPD*, 1640, p. 476.

43. *CSPD*, 1640, p. 509; J.F. Larkin, *Stuart Royal Proclamations, II*, (Oxford, 1983), pp. 722–24.

44. B. Manning, *The English People and the English Revolution*, (1976), pp. 119, 123. See also B. Sharp, *In Contempt of All Authority*, (Berkley, 1980), *passim*.

45. E.T. MacDermot, *A History of the Forest of Exmoor*, (Newton Abbot, 1973), p. 7.

46. Ibid., pp. 257, 265–67, 272–73, 279 and 283–84.

47. Ibid., pp. 277–85.

48. Ibid., pp. 271–72 and 284–93.

49. Ibid., p. 296.

50. At Banbury and Dorchester, for example. See Cope, *Politics Without Parliaments*, p. 220.

51. I owe this point to Mary Wolffe.

52. *CSPD*, 1631–33, p. 27; and *CSPD*, 1634–35, p. 424.

53. PRO, SP 16/55/88; SP 16/72/35; and SP 16/76/14.

54. PRO, SP 16/55/88.

55. Although it should not be forgotten that at least 25 per cent of the 'refractory persons' recorded were gentlemen or esquires.

56. For a discussion of Ship Money in its national context, see K. Sharpe, *The Personal Rule of Charles I*, (1992), pp. 545–96. For a detailed account of the collection of the levy in Devon, see Wolffe, 'Gentry Government', pp. 158–91.

57. See, for example, *CSPD*, 1635, pp. 477–78; and *CSPD*, 1636–37, p. 526. For the rate of 1639–40, see PRO, SP 16/463/107.

58. *CSPD*, 1635–36, p. 546; and *CSPD*, 1637, p. 552.

59. *CSPD*, 1639–40, p. 299.

60. Ibid., p. 420.

61. The situation was similar in Cornwall, see A. Duffin, 'The Political Allegiances of the Cornish Gentry, 1600–42', (unpublished Ph.D. thesis, Exeter, 1989), pp. 266–67.

62. *CSPD*, 1636–37, p. 526.

63. *CSPD*, 1635, p. 556; and *CSPD*, 1639–40, p. 498.

64. *CSPD*, 1635, p. 556; and *CSPD*, 1636–37, p. 434.

65. *CSPD*, 1638–39, p. 306; and *CSPD*, 1639, p. 94.

66. *CSPD*, 1636–37, p. 388; and PRO, SP 16/444/73.

67. *CSPD*, 1636–37, p. 287; and *CSPD*, 1639, pp. 428–29.

68. *CSPD*, 1634–35, p. 424; and Sharpe, *Personal Rule*, pp. 717–18.

69. *CSPD*, 1635–36, p. 10.

70. Ibid.

71. Wolffe, 'Gentry Government', pp. 165–66.

72. See *CSPD*, 1636–37, p. 244; and *CSPD*, 1637–38, p. 93.

73. J.R. Chanter and T. Wainwright, *Reprint of the Barnstaple Records*, (two vols, 1900), I, pp. 102–03.

74. Barnstaple's experiences between 1600 and 1646 are strikingly paralleled by those of Gloucester, see P. Clark, '"The Ramoth Gilead of the Good": Urban Change and Radicalism at Gloucester, 1540–1640', in P. Clark et al. (eds), *The English Commonwealth, 1547–1640*, (Leicester, 1979).

75. *CSPD*, 1638–39, p. 232.
76. *CSPD*, 1635, p. 605.
77. PRO, SP 16/435/33.
78. Ibid.
79. Ibid.
80. BM, Add.MSS, 35,331, f.77; and *CSPD*, 1640, p. 494.
81. Catholics may well have been more heavily rated than everybody else. I owe this point to Mary Wolffe.
82. *HMC*, Salisbury MSS, 11, p. 443.
83. Morrill, *Revolt of the Provinces*, p. 24.
84. PRO, SP 16/435/33.
85. QSB, Box 46, deposition of Thomas Rosemond, June 1642.
86. On the perceived link between puritanism and Ship Money, see Sharpe, *Personal Rule*, p. 731. William Gould and Sir Richard Strode are two prominent Devon puritans who appear on Wise's list. For Gould's puritanism, see E.48 (9).
87. Worth, *Buller Papers*, p. 33.
88. W. Hunt, *The Puritan Moment*, (1983), pp. 271–72.
89. Cope, *Politics Without Parliaments*, pp. 108, 112; K. Sharpe, *Politics and Ideas in Early Stuart England*, (1989), p. 117.
90. For Strode, see *CSPD*, 1639, pp. 439–41.
91. J. Quick, 'Icones Sacrae Anglicanae', ff.203 ff.
92. E.250 (11).
93. E.21 (34).
94. J. Brown, *Abstracts of Somerset Wills: III*, (1889), p. 73.
95. See, for example, Hunt, *Puritan Moment*, pp. 196, 202, 259, 273; P. Lake, 'Anti-Popery, the Structure of a Prejudice', in R. Cust and A. Hughes (eds), *Conflict in Early Stuart England*, (1989), p. 90; Reeve, *Road to Personal Rule*, p. 75; and J. Somerville, 'Ideology, Property and Constitution', in Cust and Hughes, *Conflict*, p. 65.
96. Quick, 'Icones', ff.403, 414.
97. F.R. Troup, 'An Exeter Worthy and his Biographer', *TDA*, 29, (1897), pp. 352–54; J.F. Chanter, *The Life and Times of Martin Blake*, (1910), p. 22; R.N. Worth (ed.), *Calendar of the Plymouth Municipal Records*, (Plymouth, 1893), p. 23.

Chapter 10

1. *CSPD*, 1636–37, p. 229, cited in K. Sharpe, *The Personal Rule of Charles I*, (1992), p. 737.
2. See J. Abbott, *The Story of Charles I, King of England*, (1912); G.M. Trevelyan, *England Under the Stuarts*, (1904), pp. 166–80; N. Tyacke, *Anti-Calvinists*, (Oxford, 1987); and J. Davies, *The Caroline Captivity of the Church*, (Oxford, 1992).
3. K. Sharpe, 'Archbishop Laud', *History Today*, 33, (1983); G.W. Bernard, 'The Church of England, c. 1529–1642', *History*, 75, no. 244, (June, 1990); Sharpe, *Personal Rule*, especially pp. 275–84.
4. J. Brown, *Abstracts of Somersetshire Wills*, (six vols, 1889), III, p. 75.
5. See J. Malcolm, *Caesar's Due*, (1983), p. 144; and N. Tyacke, 'Puritanism,

Arminianism and Counter-Revolution' in C. Russell (ed.), *The Origins of the English Civil War*, (1973), p. 143.

6. SRO, Wolesely MSS, 56/6.
7. The phrase is Sibthorpe's. See E.S. Cope, *Politics Without Parliaments*, (1987), p. 176.
8. BL, Add.MSS 35297, (Day-book of John Syms), ff.22–22v.
9. EQSOB, 64, (1642–60), f.21.
10. QSB, Box 46, information of Thomas Rosemond, 23 June 1642.
11. EQSOB, 64, f.1.
12. J. Eales, *Puritans and Roundheads*, (Cambridge, 1990), pp. 143–44.
13. Thomas Larkham, *The Attributes of God*, (1656), p. 135.
14. This was true of nine out of the ten local puritan families identified by J.T. Cliffe in *The Puritan Gentry*, (1984), pp. 237–41.
15. For these men's adherence to Parliament see J. Quick, 'Icones Sacrae Anglicanae', (MSS held at Dr Williams's Library, London), pp. 506–07, 513; W.J. Harte, *Ecclesiastical and Religious Affairs in Exeter, 1640–62*, (Exeter, 1937), p. 7; and W. Lewis (ed.), *Diary of the Reverend Thomas Larkham*, (Bristol, 1888), p. 1.
16. Wolesely MSS, 56/6, (Acland to Willoughby, 24 April 1644).
17. The puritan preacher William Yeo served as chaplain to Colonel William Gould's horse, for example. See PRO, SP 28/128, part 17 (Richard Clapp's account, 1643–49), f.52.
18. In 1645 an indignant pamphleteer reported that the Royalists had forbidden the inhabitants of Barnstaple to 'have any conference with godly ministers'. See E.260 (6).
19. J. Bond, *Occasus Occidentalis*, (1645), p. 56.
20. A.R. Bayley, *The Great Civil War in Dorset*, (Taunton, 1910), p. 205.
21. W. Hunt, *The Puritan Moment*, (1983), p. 279.
22. P. Collinson, *English Puritanism*, (Historical Association Pamphlet no. 106, 1983), p. 6.
23. See D. Underdown, *Fire from Heaven*, (1992), pp. 21–22; A. Hughes, *The Causes of the English Civil War*, (1991), p. 103.
24. See, for example, P. Collinson, *The Religion of Protestants*, (Oxford, 1982).
25. Sharpe, *Personal Rule*, pp. 731–38, especially p. 735. See also C. Hill, *Society and Puritanism in Pre-Revolutionary England*, (1964).
26. M. Spufford, *Contrasting Communities*, (Cambridge, 1974), p. 297.
27. N. Orme, 'The Later Middle Ages and the Reformation', in N. Orme (ed.), *Unity and Variety*, (Exeter, 1991), p. 70.
28. R. Whiting, *The Blind Devotion of the People*, (Cambridge, 1989), *passim*.
29. Whiting attempts to play down the significance of the Prayer Book Rebellion, (*Blind Devotion, passim*, especially pp. 34–38). I do not find his arguments convincing, see Stoyle, 'Divisions', pp. 279–80.
30. Whiting, *Blind Devotion, passim*.
31. Quick, 'Icones', pp. 58–59.
32. See I.W. Gowers, 'Puritanism in the County of Devon between 1570 and 1641', (unpublished MA thesis, Exeter, 1970).
33. BM, Lansdowne MSS, 24, f.34v.
34. I. Cassidy, 'The Episcopate of William Cotton, Bishop of Exeter 1598–1621', (unpublished D.Phil. thesis, Oxford, 1963), pp. 48–49. For brief

accounts of puritanism in Devon between 1600 and 1642 see J. Barry, 'The Seventeenth and Eighteenth Centuries', in Orme (ed.), *Unity and Variety*, pp. 81–108; and T. Gray, 'Devon's Coastal and Overseas Fisheries and New England Migration, 1597–1642', (unpublished Exeter Ph.D. thesis, 1988), pp. 158–68.

35. Quick, 'Icones', p. 500.
36. Anon, *Winthrop Papers, III*, (Massachussets Historical Society, Boston, 1943), pp. 395–96.
37. W.T. MacCaffrey, *Exeter, 1540–1640*, (1978), pp. 188–89.
38. For these events, see MacCaffrey, *Exeter*, pp. 197–98; P. Collinson, *The Elizabethan Puritan Movement*, (Oxford, 1990), pp. 442–43.
39. MacCaffrey, *Exeter*, p. 199.
40. For a short account of Jurdain, see F.R. Troup, 'An Exeter Worthy and his Biographer', *TDA*, 29, (1897), pp. 350–77. See also Collinson, *English Puritanism*, pp. 29, 33, 35, 37.
41. F. Nicolls, *The Life and Death of Mr Ignatius Jurdain*, (1654), pp. 20, 64–65, 76.
42. PRO, STAC 8/161/10.
43. Ibid. For Jewell, see Gowers, 'Puritanism', pp. 48–103.
44. PRO, STAC 8/161/10.
45. For Tyrling, see Quick, 'Icones', p. 505; for Painter, see *CSPD*, 1639, p. 69.
46. Gowers, 'Puritanism', p. 59; and A.J. Howard, *Devon Protestation Returns*, (privately printed, 1973), pp. 321, 326, 334.
47. H. Peskett, 'Heresy in Axminster in 1535', *DCNQ*, 33, (1974–77), pp. 68–70.
48. Gowers, 'Puritanism', p. 182.
49. Ibid., p. 54.
50. Cliffe, *Puritan Gentry*, p. 181.
51. Ibid. For Laud's suspicions of Erle, see R.N. Worth, *The Buller Papers*, (privately printed, 1895), p. 136.
52. Gowers, 'Puritanism', pp. 185–89.
53. Ibid., pp. 183–86.
54. Ibid., p. 182.
55. Bod., Tanner MSS, 141, f.120.
56. Howard, *Protestation Returns*, p. 155.
57. Gowers, 'Puritanism', p. 161.
58. QSOB, 5, (1618–25), f.120.
59. D. Underdown et al. (eds), *William Whiteway of Dorchester, His Diary*, (Dorset Record Society, 12, 1990), p. 114; see also Underdown, *Fire from Heaven*, p. 109; and DRO, Chanter 866 (Consistory Court Depositions Book, 1634–41, unpaginated), entry of 26 September 1636.
60. DRO, Chanter 867, (Consistory Court Depositions Book, 1613–19, unpaginated), entries of 15 January 1617 and 7 July 1618; see also Wolesely MSS, 53/4.
61. Gowers, 'Puritanism', pp. 187–90.
62. Cliffe, *Puritan Gentry*, p. 167; *CSPD*, 1639/40, p. 403.
63. Bod., J. Walker MSS, 2, f.311v.
64. QSB, Box 26, recognisance of 15 May 1622.
65. DRO, CC 198, f.233, cited in Gray, 'Coastal Fisheries', p. 163.

66. QSOB, 5, ff.475, 484, 488; and QSOB, 6, (1625–33), f.140. Significantly, Berry had previously attempted to set up a lecture in Tiverton. See E.S. Chalk, *A History of the Church of St Peter, Tiverton*, (Tiverton, 1905), p. ix.
67. Ibid, pp. 203–04; Gowers, 'Puritanism', pp. 193–94, Gray, 'Coastal Fisheries', p. 163.
68. CSPD, 1640, pp. 385, 399. See also Howard, *Protestation Returns*, p. 50.
69. Chalk, *History of the Church of St Peter*, p. 62.
70. Gowers suggests that Richard Peck, 'Preacher of God's Word', was lecturing in Cullompton by 1615, ('Puritanism', p. 165).
71. Gowers, 'Puritanism', pp. 161–62, 185; QSB, Box 46, examination of T. Rosemond. Edmund Snape had been active at Budleigh during the early 1600s, see Collinson, *Elizabethan Puritan Movement*, p. 442.
72. Gowers, 'Puritanism', pp. 26, 36, 37, 39, 125, 163.
73. Ibid., p. 54.
74. Bod., Walker MSS, 5, f.146v.; Lewis, *Diary of Larkham*, p. 3.
75. QSOB, 2, (1600–07), (unpaginated), entry of pasch 1605.
76. QSOB, 5, f.277.
77. CSPD, 1639–40, p. 20.
78. Ibid., p. 151.
79. Lansdowne MSS, 377, f.11.
80. Collinson, *Elizabethan Puritan Movement*, pp. 143, 151.
81. Gowers, 'Puritanism', pp. 28–29, 39, 275.
82. J.R. Chanter, *Sketches of some Striking Incidents in the History of Barnstaple*, (Barnstaple, 1865), p. 92; J.R. Chanter and T. Wainwright, *Reprint of the Barnstaple Records*, (two vols, 1900), II, p. 99.
83. Chanter, *Sketches*, p. 104.
84. Ibid., p. 106.
85. N. Tyacke, 'Popular Puritan Mentality in Late Elizabethan England' in P. Clark, A.G.R. Smith and N. Tyacke (eds), *The English Commonwealth, 1547–1640*, (Leicester, 1979). I am grateful to Dr Tyacke for discussing this point with me.
86. Chanter, *Sketches*, p. 109.
87. HMC, Salisbury, 11, p. 443.
88. J.F. Chanter, *The Life and Times of Martin Blake*, (1910), pp. 37–38.
89. For Coxe see Chanter and Wainwright, *Reprint of the Barnstaple Records*, I, p. 201; and CSPD, 1639–40, p. 20.
90. For Crumpton, see Quick, 'Icones', pp. 187–224.
91. Blake left an invaluable account of his experiences in Barnstaple (Bod., J. Walker MSS, 5, ff.141–76). For a biography of Blake which draws very heavily upon this source, see Chanter, *Life and Times of Martin Blake*.
92. Bod., J. Walker MSS, 5, f.146v. For Cann's previous activities in London, see *DNB*.
93. Bod., J. Walker MSS, 5, ff.146v–47.
94. Ibid., ff.147–48v.
95. Bod., J. Walker MSS, 4, ff.183–84.
96. Ibid., f.185.
97. CSPD, 1634–35, pp. 371–72.
98. I am currently writing a paper on religious affairs in Barnstaple.

99. *Winthrop Papers, III*, p. 357.
100. Gowers, 'Puritanism', p. 277.
101. Gowers, 'Puritanism', pp. 38, 162–63; W.I. Leeson-Day (ed.), 'Holsworthy Parish Register, II', (DCRS, 1932, unpaginated). The Royalists later accused Saunders of sparking off the rising at Hemyock. See Wolesely MSS, 56/6.
102. QSOB, 4, (1614–18), (unpaginated), entry of michaelmas 1617.
103. Hunt, *Puritan Moment*, p. 263; C.E. Long, *Diary of the Marches of the Royal Army During the Great Civil War*, (Camden Society, Old Series, 74, 1859), p. 67.
104. See Gowers, 'Puritanism', p. 192 and Hill, *Society and Puritanism*, p. 91.
105. For Bideford, see Gowers, 'Puritanism', pp. 165, 181, 255.
106. For Sandford, see Venn, 'Crediton', (two vols, n.d., typescript housed in WCSL), II, pp. 142–43 and *CSPD*, 1639–40, p. 20.
107. Bod., J. Walker MSS, 4, ff.390–90v.
108. For Plymouth's early protestants, see Whiting, *Blind Devotion*, pp. 156–62.
109. Quick, 'Icones', pp. 51, 69, 76; and *DNB*.
110. Quick, 'Icones', p. 85.
111. Ibid., p. 402.
112. For Wallis, see R.N. Worth (ed.), *Calendar of the Plymouth Municipal Records*, (Plymouth, 1893), pp. 199, 250; Gowers, 'Puritanism', p. 54.
113. Quick, 'Icones', p. 74.
114. Worth, *Plymouth Records*, pp. 250–51.
115. Quick, 'Icones', p. 657.
116. Ibid., pp. 655–57; *CSPD*, 1631–33, p. 146.
117. Ibid., pp. 404–06; Worth, *Plymouth Records*, p. 251; *CSPD*, 1633–34, p. 73.
118. *CSPD*, 1635, pp. 514–15.
119. Ibid. For further disputes between Wilson and the corporation, see *CSPD*, 1636–37, p. 441; *CSPD*, 1637, p. 89; and Worth, *Plymouth Records*, p. 252.
120. Worth, *Plymouth Records*, p. 252.
121. Quick, 'Icones', p. 513.
122. I am grateful to Todd Gray for discussion of religious affairs in early Stuart Dartmouth.
123. DRO, DD.62500.
124. J. Walker, *An Attempt Towards Recovering an Account of the … Sufferings of the Clergy*, (F.C. Hingeston-Randolph, (ed.), Plymouth, 1908), p. 49; and E.71 (8). See also E.71 (28).
125. Quick, 'Icones', pp. 231–34.
126. Ibid., p. 234; Gowers, 'Puritanism', pp. 54, 161.
127. For Dodding, see Gowers, 'Puritanism', pp. 54, 180; and Quick, 'Icones', pp. 70, 227.
128. Gowers, 'Puritanism', p. 159; Quick, 'Icones', p. 228.
129. Quick, 'Icones', pp. 67, 76–77.
130. For Crediton, see Whiting, *Blind Devotion*, p. 160; Collinson, *Elizabethan Puritan Movement*, p. 442; Gowers, 'Puritanism', p. 54. That two Kirtonians buried in the late 1620s were described as 'old professours for Jesus Christ' shows that at least some of the townsmen were puritanically inclined, see WCSL, B.F. Cresswell and A.J.P. Skinner (eds), 'Crediton Parish Register, VII', (DCRS, nd.), part 2, pp. 25–26.

131. G. Friend, *Memories of Moreton*, (Exeter, 1989), p. 22.
132. Southmead's activities can occasionally be traced in the records of the Devon Sessions Court. See, for example, QSOB, 5, f.261.
133. J.A. Benton, *The Parish Church of Saint Andrew, Moretonhampstead*, (privately printed, 1986), p. 19.
134. J.S. Cockburn, *Western Circuit Assize Orders, 1629–48*, (Camden Society, 4th Series, 17, 1976), p. 234.
135. F. Whiddon, *A Golden Topaze or Heart Jewell*, (Oxford, 1656). pp. 2–3. In a valedictory note in the parish register, Whiddon described his father-in-law as 'an eminent and faithful servant of Jesus Christ', see E. Searle (ed.), 'Moretonhampstead Parish Registers, II', (DCRS, 1936, typescript in WCSL), p. 62.
136. Gowers, 'Puritanism', p. 163.
137. For Randall and Stevens, see Gowers, 'Puritanism', pp. 23–24, 33–34.
138. Cliffe, *Puritan Gentry*, p. 92. Only one Devon town bucked the trend. This was Axminster which had a long radical tradition, but nevertheless showed clear signs of Royalism in 1642–46. The town's ancient rivalry with neighbouring (and strongly Parliamentarian) Lyme Regis may help to explain this anomaly.
139. Lansdowne MSS, 22/37. For the association of heresy with shoemaking in early modern Europe, see D. MacCulloch, *Suffolk and the Tudors*, (Oxford, 1986), p. 172.
140. BL, Add.MSS 9426, (Lysons Correspondence), f.253.
141. Gowers, 'Puritanism', pp. 90–91, 216–20; MacCulloch, *Suffolk*, p. 158.
142. Sharpe, *Personal Rule*, pp. 745–46.
143. P.S. Seaver, *Wallington's World*, (Stanford, 1985), *passim*.
144. Quick, 'Icones', pp. 77, 200, 225–28, 402.
145. Ibid., p. 235.
146. Ibid, p. 503.

Chapter 11

1. R.N. Worth, *The Buller Papers*, (privately printed, 1895), pp. 41–48, 84.
2. See J.S. Morrill, *Cheshire, 1630–60*, (Oxford, 1974), pp. 46–50; and W. Hunt, *The Puritan Moment*, (1983), p. 289.
3. For the names of the Catholic officers, see M.J. Stoyle, 'Divisions within the Devonshire "County Community", 1600–46', (D.Phil. thesis, Oxford, 1992), p. 347, notes 3–4.
4. G.E. Aylmer, 'Collective Mentalities in Seventeenth Century England: II. Royalist Attitudes', *TRHS*, 5th Series, 37, (1987), p. 11.
5. See PRO, SP 28/128, part 27 (Charles Vaughan's account, 1642–43) for Parliamentarian anxiety concerning the Ottery recusants in 1643.
6. 'Icones', p. 382.
7. EQSOB, 63, (1630–42), ff.351r–52r.
8. Bod., J. Walker MSS, 4, f.156.
9. Ibid., f.159.
10. J. Walker MSS, 4, f.155.
11. Hunt, *Puritan Moment*, p. 297.

12. J. Walker MSS, 2, f.252r.
13. J. Bond, *Occasus Occidentalis*, (1645), p. 54.
14. QSB, Box 46, examination of Thomas Rosemond.
15. Bond, *Occasus Occidentalis*, pp. 30–31.
16. Bod., Gough, Devon, 20 (3), *A Compleat History of Devonshire*, (n.d.), p. 471; and Bod., MSS.Top.Devon.D1, f.7r.
17. MSS.Top.Devon.D1, f.7r.
18. P.F.S. Amery, 'Eleventh Report of the Committee for Devonshire Folk Lore', *TDA*, 24, (1892), p. 49.
19. E.35 (24).
20. O.L. Dick (ed.), *Aubrey's Brief Lives*, (1987), p. 25.
21. For the tinners' addiction to games, see F.E. Halliday (ed.), *Richard Carew of Anthony*, (1953), p. 92. For evidence that, in the nineteenth century at least, Devon tin-miners were particularly superstitious, see Mrs Bray, *A Description of the Parts of Devon bordering on the Tamar and the Tavy*, (1836), pp. 225–26.
22. Bod., Wood Pamphlets 622, *A Full Answer to a Scandalous Pamphlet Intituled 'A Character of a London Diurnal'*, p. 13.
23. J. Morrill, 'The Ecology of Allegiance in the English Revolution', *JBS*, 26, 4, (1987), p. 465.
24. I. Gowers, 'The Clergy in Devon, 1641–62, in T. Gray (ed.), *Tudor and Stuart Devon*, (Exeter, 1992), pp. 202–03.
25. A.G. Matthews, *Walker Revised*, (Oxford, 1948).
26. 'Icones', p. 67.
27. Ibid, p. 410.
28. Ibid., pp. 498–500.
29. Ibid, pp. 506–07.
30. T. Larkham, *The Attributes of God*, (1656), p. 217.
31. T. Larkham, *The Wedding Supper*, (1652), p. 72.
32. Ibid, p. 52; and Larkham, *Attributes*, pp. 182, 233.
33. I.W. Gowers, 'Puritanism in the County of Devon between 1570 and 1641', (unpublished MA thesis, Exeter, 1970), p. 248.
34. Ibid, p. 163; and DRO, 3248/A/3/3, (Okehampton Quarter Sessions Records, 1634–49), entry of 25 September 1637.
35. EQSOB, 63, ff.380–80r.
36. Hunt, *Puritan Moment*, p. 291.
37. E.140 (17).
38. Bod., Hope Adds, 1133, *Mercurius Rusticus*, 21, 16 March 1643; Bray, *Description*, p. 61; J. Walker MSS, 2, f.246; and MSS.Top.Devon.D1, f.138.
39. J. Walker MSS, 2, f.235; and MSS.Top.Devon.D1, f.138.
40. B.F. Cresswell, *Notes on the Churches of the Deanery of Kenn*, (Exeter, 1912), p. 54.
41. Devon and Exeter Institution, Exeter; 'Stone's Cuttings', 26, p. 52, 'The Death of Vaughan the Puritan at Dunsford', by W.P.S., (n.d.).
42. D. Underdown, *Revel, Riot and Rebellion*, (Oxford, 1985), *passim*, especially pp. 176–81.
43. Ibid., pp. 49, 88–91.
44. M. Ingram, *Church Courts, Sex and Marriage in England*, (Cambridge, 1990), pp. 101–02.

45. Morrill, 'Ecology of Allegiance', p. 460; A. Fletcher, 'New Light on Religion and the English Civil War', *JEH*, 38, (1987), p. 101.
46. Ingram, *Church Courts*, pp. 101–02; see also Fletcher, 'New Light', p. 101. I am most grateful to Martin Ingram for discussing the subject of church ales with me.
47. For church ales in general see; T.G. Barnes, 'County Politics and a Puritan Cause Celebre: Somerset Church Ales 1633', *TRHS*, 5th Series, 9, (1959), pp. 103–22; L.S. Marcus, *The Politics of Mirth*, (Chigaco, 1986); and Underdown, *Revel, Riot and Rebellion*, pp. 45–48, 60–63, and 90–99.
48. Neither of the two surviving church court depositions books for the pre-Civil War period [DRO, CC. 867 (1613–19) and CC. 866 (1634–41)] contains a single reference to church ales. I am grateful to Todd Gray for confirming that the other local church court records are similarly unhelpful.
49. The relevant accounts are those for Awliscombe, Bere Ferrers, Bishop's Tawton*, Braunton*, Brixham, Buckland in the Moor, Buckland Monachorum†, Chagford, Chudleigh, Clawton, Clyst St George, Coldridge, Colebrooke, Crediton, Cullompton, Dartington, Dawlish, Dean Prior, Exeter St John, Exeter St Kerrian, Exeter St Petrock, Farway, St Giles in the Wood*, Halberton, Hartland*, Honiton, Kilmington, Kingsbridge, Lapford, Littleham, Modbury, Molland, Morebath, Northam*, North Molton*, North Tawton, Paignton, Poughill, Shobrooke, South Tawton, Stoke Gabriel, Tavistock, Tiverton, Uplyme, Washfield, Whitchurch†, Winkleigh*, Wolborough, Woodbury, Woodland, Yealmpton† and Zeale Monachorum. Most of these documents are kept in the DRO. The chief exceptions are those marked *, which are held by the NDRO, and those marked †, which are held by the WDRO. The Tiverton wardens' accounts are kept at Mr Newte's Library, in Tiverton Church.
50. The parishes in which ales were held were; Braunton, Chagford, Chudleigh, Coldridge, Dartington, Dean Prior, Farway, Halberton, Honiton, Kilmington, Molland, Morebath, Northam, North Molton, Shobrooke, Washfield, Winkleigh, Woodbury and Woodland. The parishes in which ales had been abandoned were Barnstaple and Tavistock.
51. J. Chanter and W. Wainwright, *Reprint of the Barnstaple Records*, (two vols, Barnstaple, 1900), I, pp. 209–13.
52. This was the case in twenty-one of the twenty-eight parishes for which relevant accounts survive.
53. R. Cornish (ed.), *Kilmington Wardens' Accounts*, (Exeter, 1901), *passim*.
54. C.A.T. Fursdon (ed.), 'Halberton Churchwardens' Accounts' (DCRS, 1930), pp. 17–263.
55. In Chudleigh for example. See DRO; Chudleigh PW 1.
56. This was the case in Somerset too where, by 1634, ales had been 'most left off or put down', *CSPD*, 1633–34, p. 275.
57. DRO, Tavistock CWA, 482/A, PW/24.
58. QSOB, 6 (1625–33), f.356.
59. For the four sessions orders issued between 1595 and 1615, see Underdown, *Revel, Riot and Rebellion*, p. 49. For evidence that the first order against the ales had been issued well before 1595, see QSOB, 1 (1592–1600), ff.125–26; and DRO, Brixham, PW2.
60. QSOB, 1, f.126.

61. QSOB, 4 (1614–18), entry of 24 July 1615.
62. M. McIntosh, 'Order and Social Control', paper given at the Institute of Historical Research, June 1992. See also, M. Spufford, 'Puritanism and Social Control', in A. Fletcher and J. Stevenson (eds), *Order and Disorder in Early Modern England*, (Cambridge, 1985).
63. Halliday, *Richard Carew of Anthony*, pp. 141–44.
64. T. Westcote, *A View of Devonshire in 1630*, (G. Oliver and P. Jones, eds, Exeter, 1845), p. 54.
65. QSOB, 1, ff.125–26.
66. QSOB, 4, entry of 24 July 1615.
67. QSOB, 5 (1618–25), f.323.
68. Barnes, 'County Politics', p. 109.
69. See, for example, QSOB, 2, ff.97, 188, 234.
70. Morrill, 'Ecology of Allegiance', p. 460.
71. F. Nicolls, *The Life and Death of Mr Ignatius Jurdain*, (1654), p. 50.
72. F. Whiddon, *A Golden Topaze or Heart-Jewell*, (Oxford, 1656), p. 2.
73. Nicolls, *Jurdain*, p. 50.
74. EQSOB, 61, (1618–21), f.269.
75. Ibid.
76. Ibid., f.405.
77. EQSOB, 62, (1621–30), f.103r.
78. W.T. MacCaffrey, *Exeter, 1540–1640*, (1975), p. 288.
79. EQSOB, 62, f.208r.
80. EQSOB, 63, (1630–42), f.104r.
81. E.258 (11).
82. E.52 (12).
83. Ibid.
84. Bond, *Occasus Occidentalis*, pp. 30–32.
85. QSOB, 6, ff.103, 181; and QSOB, Box 40, examination of Jacob Beare, 4 June 1637.
86. QSOB, 2, entry of 16 April 1607; J. Scanes (ed.), 'Dartington Church-wardens' Accounts', (DCRS), pp. 392, 400, 412, 682, 705, 716; DRO, 1981/A/PW1, (Stoke Gabriel CWA).
87. H. Burton, *A Divine Tragedie Lately Acted*, (1641), C.2.
88. QSOB, 5, ff.323, 383; F. Osborne (ed.), *The Churchwardens' Accounts of St Michael's Church Chagford*, (1979), *passim*; DRO, Chudleigh, PW1; DRO, Coldridge, MFK1; F. Nesbitt (ed.), 'Colebrooke CWA' (DCRS, 1933), p. 182; DRO, Dawlish PW1-A; DRO, Wolborough, PF6/30, and E.C. Wood (ed.), *Widecombe in the Moor Parish Registers*, (Exeter, 1938), p. v.
89. W.H.K. Wright, *Some Account of the Barony and Town of Okehampton*, (Tiverton, 1889), p. 93.
90. QSOB, 2, ff.188, 233–33r.
91. QSB, Box 20, recognisance of Richard Halfeyeard; QSOB, 5, f.333; and DRO, 1301/F/A1, (Accounts of the Eight Men of Broadclyst).
92. QSB, Box 12, recognisance of J. Godfrey; DRO, 3147A/PW5, (Clyst St George CWA); QSB, Box 13, case of 29 June 1607; QSOB, 2, ff.97, 234; and DRO, Woodbury, PW1.
93. QSB, Box 10, examination of M. Turner; and QSOB, 5, f.177.

94. BM, Add.MSS, 35331, (Walter Yonge's diary), f.59r.
95. DRO, 2404/A/PW1, (Cullompton CWA); and QSOB, 4, entry of epiph. 1616.
96. QSOB, 6, f.356.
97. See Fursdon, 'Halberton Churchwardens' Accounts', pp. 196, 204, 209.
98. E.89 (4).

Part IV

Introduction

1. PRO, SP.19/142/126r.
2. G. Orwell, *Homage to Catalonia*, (1984 edition), p. 126.
3. PRO, SP.19/157/27–28.

Chapter 12

1. R. Hutton, 'Review', *Midland History*, 18, (1993), p. 150.
2. C. Russell, *The Causes of the English Civil War*, (Oxford, 1990), p. 3; G.E. Aylmer, *Rebellion or Revolution?*, (Oxford, 1986), p. 50; R.C. Richardson (ed.), *Town and Countryside in the English Revolution* (Manchester, 1992), 'Introduction', p. 6. It is only fair to acknowledge that many earlier historians made the same point, see, for example, A.R. Bayley, *Dorset in the Great Civil War*, (Taunton, 1910), p. 2; and E. Broxap, *The Great Civil War in Lancashire*, (1910, reprinted Manchester 1973), p. 35.
3. Aylmer, *Rebellion or Revolution*, p. 43.
4. R. Hutton, 'The Royalist War Effort', in J. Morrill (ed.), *Reactions to the English Civil War*, (1982), pp. 52–53. See also R. Hutton, *The Royalist War Effort, 1642–46*, (1982). The suggestion that popular Royalism was uniquely strong in Herefordshire is effectively rebutted in J. Eales, *Puritans and Roundheads*, (1990), p. 127.
5. Hutton, 'Royalist War Effort', p. 53.
6. C. Holmes, *The Eastern Association in the English Civil War*, (Cambridge, 1974); R. Howell, *Newcastle-on-Tyne and the Puritan Revolution*, (Oxford, 1967); R. Howell, 'The Structure of Urban Politics in the English Civil War', *Albion*, 11, (1979); B. Manning, 'Neutrals and Neutralism in the English Civil War, 1642–46', (unpublished Oxford D.Phil. thesis, 1957); J.S. Morrill, *Cheshire 1630–60*, (1974); J. Morrill, *The Revolt of the Provinces* (1976).
7. Richardson, 'Introduction', p. 6. See also R.E. Sherwood, *Civil Strife in the Midlands*, (Chichester, 1974), p. 42.
8. D. Underdown, *Somerset in the Civil War and Interregnum*, (Newton Abbot, 1973), p. 79; D. Underdown, 'The Problem of Popular Allegiance in the English Civil War', *TRHS*, 5th Series, 21, (1981); D. Underdown, *Revel, Riot and Rebellion*, (Oxford, 1985), especially p. 4; A. Hughes, *Politics, Society and Civil War in Warwickshire, 1620–60*, (Cambridge, 1987); A. Hughes, 'Local History and the Origins of the English Civil War', in R. Cust and A. Hughes (eds), *Conflict in Early Stuart England*, (1989); A. Hughes, 'Coventry and the English Revolution' in Richardson (ed.), *Town and Countryside*, pp. 69–99.

9. Underdown, *Revel, Riot and Rebellion*, p. ix.
10. See, for example, P.Q. Karkeek, 'Jacobite Days in the West', *TDA*, 28, (1896), p. 257. I am most grateful to Anne Duffin—whose major new study of the pre-war Cornish gentry is soon to be published—for discussing the situation in Cornwall with me.
11. M. Coate, *Cornwall in the Great Civil War and Interregnum*, (1933), pp. 32-33.
12. Ibid., p. 35.
13. See Hutton, *Royalist War Effort*, pp. 31-32; and J.L. Malcolm, *Caesar's Due*, (1983), pp. 75-77.
14. BM, Add.MSS, 11,314, f.13.
15. E.65 (24).
16. E.4 (30).
17. E. Walker, *Historical Discourses upon Several Occasions*, p. 49.
18. E. Long (ed.), *Diary of the Marches of the Royal Army during the Great Civil War*, (Camden Society, Old Series, 74, 1859), p. 49.
19. W. Dunn-Macray (ed.), *The History of the Rebellion and Civil Wars in England, by E. Hyde, Earl of Clarendon*, (six vols, Oxford, 1888), III, p. 387.
20. Walker, *Historical Discourses*, p. 50.
21. Long, *Diary*, p. 47.
22. Walker, *Historical Discourses*, p. 51.
23. Coate, *Cornwall*, p. 147.
24. Walker, *Historical Discourses*, p. 79.
25. Long, *Diary*, p. 67.
26. BM, Add.MSS, 35,331, f.241.
27. Clarendon, *History*, III, p. 405.
28. Walker, *Historical Discourses*, p. 80.
29. J. Sprigg, *Anglia Rediviva*, (Oxford, 1854), p. xi.
30. R. Bell (ed.), *Memorials of the Civil War: Volume I (1642-49)*, (1849), p. 284; and P.Q. Karkeek, 'Fairfax in the West, 1645-46', *TDA*, 8, (1876), pp. 127, 133-34.
31. Karkeek, 'Fairfax', pp. 144-45.
32. Clarendon, *History*, II, p. 448.
33. C.E.H. Chadwyck-Healey (ed.), *Bellum Civile*, (Somerset Record Society, 18, 1902), pp. 19-22.
34. DRO, Tremayne MSS, 1499/M/4/3.
35. Chadwyck-Healey, *Bellum Civile*, pp. 20-21.
36. E.266 (37).
37. Chadwyck-Healey, *Bellum Civile*, p. 44.
38. Coate, *Cornwall*, p. 43, note 1.
39. W. Hals, *The Compleat History of Cornwall, II*, (Exeter, 1750), p. 29.
40. Walker, *Historical Discourses*, pp. 50-51.
41. Ibid., p. 73.
42. Clarendon, *History*, III, p. 69.
43. Walker, *Historical Discourses*, p. 50.
44. Malcolm, *Caesar's Due*, pp. 78-79.
45. For Walker's conviction that the true design of the 'rebels' was 'to destroy the King, nobility and gentry', see *Historical Discourses*, p. 50.

46. Coate, *Cornwall*, p. 32.
47. Hals, *Compleat History of Cornwall*, p. 29.
48. See A. Duffin, 'The Political Allegiance of the Cornish Gentry, 1600–42, (unpublished Ph.D. thesis, Exeter, 1989), p. 292.
49. A.C. Miller, 'Joseph Jane's Account of Cornwall During the Civil War', *EHR*, 90, (1975), p. 98.
50. Karkeek, 'Fairfax', p. 144.
51. E.35 (24); E.86 (3) and Bod., Ashm. 1027 (3), (*Mercurius Britannicus*, 30 September to 7 October 1644).
52. BM, Lansdowne MS, 24, no. 16, f. 34.
53. Duffin ('Political Allegiance', *passim*, especially chs V–VI) shows that, by 1642, puritanism was relatively widespread amongst the gentry of eastern Cornwall and was even beginning to have a limited impact on their brethren to the west. The gentry were the standard bearers of local puritanism, however. Amongst those of a less exalted social status, the puritan advance was much slower.
54. See R. Cust 'News and Politics in Early Seventeenth Century England, *P&P*, 111, (1986), pp. 66–69; and A. Bellany, 'Raylinge Rymes and Vaunting Verse': Libellous Politics in Early Stuart England, 1603–1628', in P. Lake and K. Sharpe (eds), *Culture and Politics in Early Stuart England* (1994), pp. 285–310.
55. See Hutton, 'Royalist War Effort', p. 52; Malcolm, *Caesar's Due*, p. 87; and P. Gaunt, *A Nation Under Siege*, (1991), p. 17 (although Gaunt advances much more convincing explanations on p. 12 of this excellent book).
56. J. Corbet, *A True and Impartiall History of the Military Government of Gloucester*, (1645), p. 10.
57. Clarendon, *History*, III, p. 113; and R. Jeffs et al. (eds), *Oxford Royalist Newsbooks: Volume III*, (1971), p. 96.
58. Gaunt, *Nation Under Siege*, p. 30.
59. J.R. Phillips, *Memoirs of the Civil War in Wales and the Marches*, (two vols, 1874), II, p. 211.
60. Malcolm, *Caesar's Due*, p. 197.
61. Phillips, *Memoirs*, II, p. 155.
62. Bell, *Memorials*, I, pp. 316–17.
63. Phillips, *Memoirs*, II, p. 361.
64. R.N. Dore, *The Letter Books of Sir William Brereton: II*, (RSLC, 128, 1990), pp. 21, 23.
65. Ibid., p. 228.
66. S. Roberts, 'Welsh Puritanism in the Interregnum', *History Today*, 41, (March 1991), p. 36.
67. E.37 (2).
68. E.10 (19) and E.12 (23).
69. E.33 (27).
70. E.32 (12).
71. Phillips, *Memoirs*, II, p. 309.
72. Gaunt, *Nation Under Siege*, p. 39.
73. Phillips, *Memoirs*, II, p. 111.
74. Roberts, 'Welsh Puritanism', pp. 36, 38. See also Eales, *Puritans and Roundheads*, pp. 9–10.

75. See Gaunt, *Nation Under Siege*, p. 22, 40–42; Hutton, *Royalist War Effort*, p. 34, 68–75.
76. Jeffs, *Oxford Royalist Newsbooks: III*, p. 181.
77. Ibid., p. 189.
78. Hutton, *Royalist War Effort*, p. 17.
79. See Malcolm, *Caesar's Due*; and B. Manning, *The English People and the English Revolution*, (1976).
80. E.67 (27).
81. Sherwood, *Civil Strife*, p. 44.
82. Eales, *Puritans and Roundheads*, pp. 11–12, 66–61.
83. T.T. Lewis (ed.), *Letters of the Lady Brilliana Harley*, (Camden Society, Old Series, 58, 1854), p. 181.
84. Clarendon, *History*, III, p. 17.
85. S. Peachey (ed.), *The Edgehill Campaign and the Letters of Nehemiah Wharton*, (Leigh-on-Sea, 1989), p. 25.
86. Ibid, p. 26.
87. Ibid.
88. Clarendon, *History*, II, p. 469; and M.D.G. Wanklyn, 'Landed Society and Allegiance in Cheshire and Shropshire in the First Civil War', (unpublished Ph.D. thesis, Manchester, 1976), p. 263.
89. A. Fletcher, *The Outbreak of the English Civil War*, (1981), pp. 330–31.
90. Lewis, *Harley*, p. 167.
91. D. Hey (ed.), *The History of Myddle*, (1981), p. 71.
92. Wanklyn, 'Landed Society', p. 263, and pp. 174, 256.
93. Ibid., p. 262.
94. Clarendon, *History*, II, p. 349; and Long, *Diary*, p. 11.
95. Peachey, *Edgehill Campaign*, p. 19.
96. E.27 (8).
97. E.23 (26).
98. See Clarendon, *History*, III, p. 357; Jeffs, *Oxford Royalist Newsbooks: III*, p. 296; C.V. Wedgwood, *The King's War*, (1958), p. 113. P. Styles— 'The Royalist Government of Worcestershire during the Civil War', (*Transactions of the Worcestershire Archaeological Society*, Third Series, 5, 1976)—stresses the divisions which existed within the city, but does not overturn the view of Worcester as essentially pro-Royalist.
99. Jeffs, *Oxford Royalist Newsbooks: III*, p. 296.
100. Peachey, *Edgehill Campaign*, p. 21.
101. Ibid, p. 22.
102. Morrill, *Cheshire*, p. 78; see also R.N. Dore, *The Civil Wars in Cheshire*, (1966), pp. 12, 19, 97; Dore, *Letter Books of Sir William Brereton: II*, p. 53.
103. Dore, *Cheshire*, pp. 18–19.
104. Dore, *Cheshire*, p. 26; Morrill, *Cheshire*, pp. 75, 132.
105. Clarendon, *History*, II, p. 469.
106. Morrill, *Cheshire*; and A.M. Johnson, 'Politics in Chester During the Civil War and Interregnum, 1640–42', in P. Clark and P. Slack (eds), *Crisis and Order in English Towns*, (1972).
107. Dore, *Letter Books of Sir William Brereton: II*, pp. 95, 282, 457, 551, 555, and especially pp. 585–93.

108. Dore, *Cheshire*, p. 19. For the strength of pre-war puritanism in the county, see Dore, *Cheshire*, pp. 5–8 and Morrill, *Cheshire*, pp. 19–20.
109. M. Atkin and W. Laughin, *Gloucester and the Civil War*, (Stroud, 1992), pp. 13, 17, 24; and Clarendon, *History*, III, p. 94.
110. See E.90 (7) for the rising of 'a strong malignant party' near Sudeley Castle in January 1643.
111. Ibid., p. 167.
112. See discussion in Atkin and Laughin, *Gloucester*, p. 14.
113. Jeffs, *Oxford Royalist Newsbooks: III*, p. 379.
114. For the strength of puritanism, both in Gloucester and amongst the county gentry, see P. Clark, 'The Ramoth Gilead of the Good": Urban Change and Political Radicalism at Gloucester, 1540–1640', reprinted in J. Barry (ed.), *The Tudor and Stuart Town*, (1990), pp. 245, 265–269.
115. Corbet, *True and Impartial History*, p. 27.
116. L. Lee, *I Can't Stay Long*, (1975), pp. 24–25.
117. Clarendon, *History*, II, p. 482.
118. Underdown, *Revel, Riot and Rebellion*, p. 165.
119. J. Wroughton, *A Community at War*, (Bath, 1992), especially pp. 87–90.
120. Underdown, *Revel, Riot and Rebellion*, pp. 165–168.
121. See, for example, B. Sharp, 'Rural Discontents and the English Revolution', in Richardson (ed.), *Town and Countryside*, pp. 261–62.
122. Underdown, *Revel, Riot and Rebellion*, p. 204; and Long, *Diary*, p. 32.
123. Underdown, *Revel, Riot and Rebellion*, pp. 172–73.
124. Clarendon, *History*, II, p. 316; and Chadwyck-Healey, *Bellum Civile*, p. 18.
125. E.304 (5); and E.304 (8).
126. Clarendon, *History*, III, p. 449.
127. Underdown, *Revel, Riot and Rebellion*, pp. 199, 203.
128. Broxap, *Civil War in Lancashire*, pp. 3, 68, 74.
129. Ibid., pp. 314, 16, 39, 58, 65, 76.
130. R. Hutton, 'The Failure of the Lancashire Cavaliers', *THSLC*, 129, (1980).
131. B.G. Blackwood, 'Parties and Issues in the Civil War in Lancashire', in J.J. Kermode and C.B. Phillips (eds), *Seventeenth Century Lancashire*, (1982), p. 111.
132. Ibid., p. 109.
133. Broxap, *Civil War in Lancashire*, pp. 3, 65; Blackwood, 'Parties and Issues', p. 106.
134. C.B. Phillips, 'The Royalist North: The Cumberland and Westmoreland Gentry, 1642–60', *Northern History*, 14, (1978), p. 192.
135. See, for example, Malcolm, *Caesar's Due*, pp. 57–65 and Hutton, *War Effort*, pp. 17–18.
136. Howell, *Newcastle-on-Tyne*, especially p. 336.
137. Phillips, 'The Royalist North', especially pp. 169, 172–73.
138. Ibid., p. 192.
139. E. Rhys (ed.), *The Life of the Duke of Newcastle*, (1915), pp. 42, 44.
140. Clarendon, *History*, II, p. 464; and Manning, *English People*, pp. 299–300.
141. Rhys, *Life of the Duke of Newcastle*, pp. 37 and 34.
142. Clarendon, *History*, II, p. 464; D. Scott, 'Politics and Government in York', in Richardson (ed.), *Town and Country*, pp. 49, 57.

143. Howell, *Newcastle-on-Tyne*, pp. 197–98.
144. Phillips, 'Royalist North', p. 192; Rhys, *Life of the Duke of Newcastle*, pp. 32–33; P.R. Newman, 'The Royalist North: A Rejoinder', *Northern History*, 17, (1981), p. 254; C.B. Phillips, 'County Committees in Cumberland and Westmoreland', *Northern History*, 5, (1970), p. 45.
145. Phillips, 'County Committees', p. 38.
146. S. Jefferson (ed.), *A Narrative of the Siege of Carlisle, by I. Tullie*, (1840, reprinted Whitehaven, 1988), p. 12.
147. Ibid., pp. 27, 30–31.
148. Ibid., p. 48.
149. Ibid., p. 1.
150. Clarendon, *History*, II, p. 227; and Rhys, *Life of the Duke of Newcastle*, p. 30.
151. Howell, *Newcastle-on-Tyne*, p. 146.
152. Ibid., pp. 98, 123–24, 145.
153. Ibid., p. 218.
154. Ibid., p. 142.
155. Rhys, *Life of the Duke of Newcastle*, p. 108.
156. Jefferson, *Narrative*, p. 8.
157. C. Holmes, *The Eastern Association in the English Civil War*, (Cambridge, 1975).
158. For Royalism in the capital, see V. Pearl, *London and the Outbreak of the Puritan Revolution*, (London 1961); and K. Lindley, 'London's citizenry in the English Revolution', in Richardson, *Town and Country*, pp. 19–45.
159. See, for example, J. Morrill, 'Introduction', in Morrill (ed.), *Reactions*, p. 12.
160. Ibid., p. 13.
161. Fletcher, *Outbreak*, p. 307. See also Clarendon, *History*, III, p. 330.
162. E. Melling (ed.), *Kentish Sources II: Kent and the Civil War*, (Maidstone, 1960), pp. x, 24–25.
163. R. Almack (ed.), 'Papers Relating to Proceedings in the County of Kent', *Camden Miscellany III*, (Camden Society, Old Series, 61, 1855), p. 5.
164. See, for example, C. Russell, *The Crisis of Parliaments*, (1971), p. 343.
165. Almack, 'Papers Relating to Kent', pp. 31–32.
166. Clarendon, *History*, II, p. 430.
167. J.T. Evans, *Seventeenth-Century Norwich*, (Oxford, 1979), especially pp. 105, 133–35, 143–44.
168. For popular Royalism in East Anglia, see Holmes, *Eastern Association*, pp. 54–56, 67, 72, 73, 95.
169. A. Fletcher, 'The Coming of War', in Morrill (ed.), *Reactions*, p. 32.
170. Hughes, *Politics, Society and Civil War*, pp. 150–51.
171. A. Fletcher, *A County Community in Peace and War*, (1975), p. 267. See also pp. 239, 255–58, 262, 271–73.
172. On Staffordshire, see Sherwood, *Civil Strife*, pp. 31, 62, 67, 101; Hughes, *Causes*, p. 145; Malcolm, *Caesar's Due*, p. 89.
173. See J.R. Dias, 'Lead, Society and Politics in Derbyshire Before the Civil War', *Midland History*, 6, (1981), pp. 52–53.
174. For Royalism in Winchester and eastern Hampshire, see G.N. Godwin, *The Civil War in Hampshire*, (1904), pp. 43, 45, 123; and D. Underdown,

'The Chalk and the Cheese: Contrasts Among the English Clubmen', *P&P*, 85, (1979), p. 41.

175. See A.C. Wood, *Nottinghamshire in the Civil War*, (Oxford, 1937), pp. 12, 16, 18, 20, 30, 36, 129, 135–36.
176. Morrill, 'Introduction', p. 14.
177. Ibid.; and J. Binns, 'Scarborough and the Civil Wars, 1642–51', *Northern History*, 22, (1986), pp. 104–05.
178. *CCAM*, II, p. 1160; SP 23/152, f.376.
179. Hey, *History of Myddle*, pp. 226–27.
180. BM, Burney Collection, *The Moderate Intelligencer*, 19–26 June, 1645.
181. Rhys, *Life of the Duke of Newcastle*, p. 40.
182. See Malcolm, *Caesar's Due*, Appendix 2, pp. 234–35.
183. C. Holmes (ed.), *The Suffolk Committees for Scandalous Ministers*, (Suffolk Record Society, 13, 1970), p. 58.
184. C. Hill, 'Puritans and the "Dark Corners of the Land"', *TRHS*, 1963, pp. 77–102.
185. Cf. Russell, *Causes of the English Civil War*, pp. 15–16.
186. See, for example, J. Kenyon, *The Civil Wars of England*, (1988), p. 38.

Appendix

This appendix sets out the names of all the Devon parishes in 1642 and specifies which region each parish has been assigned to for the purposes of this book. The appended figures show adult male population in 1642 ('x' indicates no figures available)

Part I—Central Devon

Alphington	196	Coryton	x
Ashburton	x	Crediton	1059
Ashbury	17	Dawlish	365
Ashcombe	61	Denbury	112
Ashton	79	Doddiscombsleigh	102
Beaworthy	51	Down St Mary	75
Belstone	34	Drewsteignton	182
Bickington	99	Dunchideock	50
Bishopsteignton	144	Dunsford	148
Bondleigh	64	Dunterton	33
Bovey, North	146	Exbourne	107
Bovey Tracey	353	Exminster	182
Bow (Nymet Tracey)	129	Germansweek	61
Bradstone	57	Gidleigh	38
Bratton Clovelly	129	Halwill	54
Brentor	36	Hennock	150
Bridestowe	110	Highweek	128
Bridford	97	Hittesleigh	25
Broad Nymet	7	Holcombe Burnell	39
Broadwoodwidger	156	Holne	88
Buckland in the Moor	49	Honeychurch	17
Chagford	293	Ide	163
Cheriton Bishop	154	Ideford	65
Christow	131	Ilsington	179
Chudleigh	220	Inwardleigh	95
Clannaborough	21	Jacobstowe	55
Coldridge	108	Kelly	53
Colebrooke	184	Kenn	223

Kenton	260	Sampford Spiney	75
Kingsteignton	169	Shillingford	32
Lamerton	266	Sourton	108
Lewtrenchard	60	Spreyton	74
Lifton	200	Stowford	65
Luffincott	26	Sydenham Damarel	64
Lustleigh	53	Tavistock	750
Lydford	39	Tawton, North	217
Mamhead	46	Tawton, South	228
Manaton	77	Tedburn St Mary	144
Marystow	68	Teigngrace	20
Mary Tavy	89	Teignmouth	167
Milton Abbot	241	Throwleigh	67
Moretonhampstead	411	Thrushelton	72
Newton Abbot & Wolboro	270	Trusham	32
Northlew	146	Virginstow	31
Okehampton	318	Walkhampton	136
Peter Tavy	98	Werrington	110
Petherwin, North	198	Whitchurch	138
Powderham	68	Whitestone	90
St Giles in the Heath	62	Widecombe in the Moor	147
Sampford Courtenay	254	Zeal Monachorum	110

Number of parishes = 100.   Total number of adult males = 13,269.

Part II—East Devon

Awliscombe	142	Clayhanger	69
Axminster	x	Clayhidon	161
Axmouth	116	Clyst Honiton	x
Aylesbeare	x	Clyst Hydon	x
Bampton	328	Clyst St George	x
Beer	x	Clyst St Lawrence	x
Bickleigh	83	Clyst St Mary	x
Bicton	x	Colaton Raleigh	x
Bradninch	370	Colyton	575
Brampford Speke	56	Combepyne	x
Branscombe	x	Combe Raleigh	x
Broad Clyst	443	Cotleigh	x
Broadhembury	240	Cullompton	725
Buckerell	86	Culmstock	336
Budleigh, East	x	Dunkeswell	86
Burlescombe	234	Farringdon	x
Butterleigh	35	Farway	x
Cadbury	53	Feniton	87
Cadleigh	102	Gittisham	x
Calverleigh	44	Halberton	442
Cheriton Fitzpaine	200	Harpford	x

Heavitree	185	Salcombe Regis	x
Hemyock	256	Sampford Peverell	210
Hockworthy	57	Seaton	x
Holcombe Rogus	195	Sheldon	51
Honiton	x	Shobrooke	168
Huntsham	41	Shute	x
Huxham	33	Sidbury	x
Kentisbeare	281	Sidmouth	x
Kilmington	x	Silverton	310
Littleham	x	Southleigh	x
Loxbeare	37	Sowton	86
Luppitt	x	Stockleigh Pomeroy	56
Lympstone	x	Stoke Canon	78
Membury	x	Talaton	111
Monkton	x	Thorncombe	x
Morebath	102	Thorverton	258
Musbury	x	Tiverton	1767
Nether Exe	83	Topsham	293
Newton Poppleford	x	Uffculme	428
Newton St Cyres	227	Uplowman	133
Northleigh	x	Uplyme	x
Offwell	x	Upottery	x
Otterton	x	Upton Pyne	84
Ottery St Mary	x	Venn Ottery	x
Payhembury	69	Washfield	157
Pinhoe	124	Whimple	x
Plymtree	146	Widworthy	x
Poltimore	75	Willand	91
Rewe	69	Woodbury	x
Rockbeare	x	Yarcombe	x
Rousdon	x		

Calculating East Devon's population is difficult because the Protestation Returns for forty-eight of the region's 103 parishes have not survived. Nevertheless, an approximate figure can be reached. Howard estimated that the adult male population of the missing parishes was around 8,000, and this figure, combined with the 11,274 names which do survive, gives a total of c. 19,000.

Part III—Exeter

All Hallows, Goldsmith St	65	St Kerrian	50
All Hallows on the Walls	116	St Lawrence	115
Cathedral Close	30	St Leonard	345
St Davids	194	St Martin	66
St Edmunds	157	St Mary Arches	122
St George	140	St Mary Major	396
St John	135	St Mary Steps	149

St Olave	65	St Sidwells	474
St Pancras	39	St Stephens	61
St Paul	152	St Thomas	x
St Petrock	102	Trinity	289

Total number of parishes = 22. Total number of adult males recorded in 1642 = 3262.

Part IV—North Devon

Abbot's Bickington	18	Chulmleigh	264
Abbotsham	179	Clawton	112
Alverdiscott	76	Clovelly	83
Alwington	90	Combe Martin	246
Anstey, East	39	Cookbury	62
Anstey, West	60	Countisbury	41
Arlington	30	Creacombe	6
Ashford	35	Cruwys Morchard	135
Ashreigney	154	Dolton	113
Ashwater	167	Dowland	66
Atherington	132	Down, East	81
Barnstaple	731	Down, West	20
Beaford	82	Eggesford	32
Berrynarbor	162	Filleigh	51
Bideford	662	Fremington	292
Bishop's Nympton	191	Frithelstock	162
Bishop's Tawton	271	George Nympton	59
Bittadon	x	Georgeham	217
Black Torrington	165	Goodleigh	92
Bradford	68	Great Torrington	568
Bradworthy	166	Hartland	453
Bratton Fleming	129	Hatherleigh	207
Braunton	383	Heanton Punchardon	142
Brendon	49	High Bickington	158
Bridgerule	53	Highampton	52
Broadwood Kelly	76	Hollacombe	15
Brushford	31	Holsworthy	238
Buckland, East	42	Horwood	24
Buckland, West	45	Huish	43
Buckland Brewer	215	Huntshaw	66
Buckland Filleigh	67	Iddesleigh	92
Bulkworthy	23	Ilfracombe	322
Burrington	161	Instow	138
Challacombe	38	Kennerleigh	29
Charles	63	Kentisbury	54
Chawleigh	195	King's Nympton	155
Cheldon	39	Knowstone	88
Chittlehampton	342	Landcross	12

Landkey	150	Rackenford	92
Langtree	133	Roborough	96
Lapford	123	Romansleigh	45
Little Torrington	116	Roseash	92
Littleham	80	St Giles in the Wood	120
Loxhore	48	Sandford	383
Lynton	117	Satterleigh	23
Mariansleigh	62	Shebbear	142
Martinhoe	46	Sheepwash	74
Marwood	185	Shirwell	95
Meeth	78	Stockleigh English	41
Merton	133	Stoke Rivers	80
Meshaw	18	Stoodleigh	77
Milton Damarel	97	Sutcombe	85
Molland	112	Swimbridge	289
Molton, North	341	Tawstock	331
Molton, South	608	Templeton	42
Monkleigh	100	Tetcott	51
Monk Okehampton	43	Thelbridge	38
Morchard Bishop	253	Thornbury	78
Mortehoe	88	Trentishoe	16
Newton St Petrock	64	Twitchen	52
Newton Tracey	22	Upton Hellions	40
Northam	617	Warkleigh	71
Nymet Rowland	25	Washford Pyne	24
Oakford	102	Weare Gifford	87
Pancrasweek	87	Welcombe	71
Parkham	170	Wembworthy	74
Parracombe	82	Westleigh	92
Peters Marland	65	Winkleigh	274
Petrockstow	146	Witheridge	150
Pilton	294	Woolfardisworthy	27
Poughill	83	Woolfardisworthy	117
Puddington	45	Worlington, East	51
Putford, East	36	Worlington, West	25
Putford, West	81	Yarnscombe	142
Pyworthy	137		

Total number of parishes = 150. Total number of adult males recorded in 1642 = 18,743.

Part V—South Devon

Abbotskerswell	74	Berry Pomeroy	309
Allington, East	120	Bickleigh	65
Alvington, West	174	Bigbury	149
Ashprington	141	Blackawton	283
Aveton Gifford	150	Brent, South	267
Bere Ferrers	248	Brixham	264

Brixton	x	Milton, South	79
Broadhempston	225	Modbury	468
Buckfastleigh	331	Moreleigh	46
Buckland Monachorm	290	Newton Ferrers	124
Buckland Tout Saints	x	Ogwell, East	81
Charleton	151	Ogwell, West	23
Chivelstone	116	Paignton	344
Churchstow	67	Plymouth	1440
Churston Ferrers	207	Plympton Earl	159
Cockington	115	Plympton St Mary	374
Coffinswell	86	Plymstock	311
Combeinteignhead	122	Portlemouth, East	70
Cornwood	228	Rattery	154
Cornworthy	155	Revelstoke	72
Dartington	185	Ringmore	72
Dartmouth	808	Roborough	96
Dean Prior	145	St Budeaux	x
Diptford	157	St Marychurch	139
Dittisham	144	Shaugh Prior	123
Dodbrooke	130	Sheepstor	57
Egg Buckland	136	Sheldon	51
Ermington	232	Sherford	120
Haccombe	7	Slapton	159
Halwell	102	South Pool	96
Harberton	306	Staverton	396
Harford	64	Stoke Fleming	153
Holbeton	254	Stoke Gabriel	144
Huish, North	100	Stokeinteignhead	159
Huish, South	114	Stokenham	393
Ipplepen	199	Tamerton Foliot	166
Kingsbridge	151	Thurlestone	102
Kingskerswell	124	Torbryan	99
Kingston	x	Torquay [Tormoham]	67
Kingswear	157	Totnes	550
Littlehempston	108	Ugborough	314
Loddiswell	145	Wembury	109
Malborough	304	Woodland	187
Marldon	116	Woodleigh	72
Meavy	78	Yealmpton	195

Total number of parishes = 90. Total number of adult males recorded in 1642 = 16,217.

Part VI—Summation

1. Total number of Devon parishes in 1642 = 465. Of which 22 were situated in Exeter, 90 in South Devon, 100 in Mid-Devon, 103 in East Devon and 150 in North Devon.

2. Total adult male population of Devon in 1642 = *c.* 72,000.
   Of whom:
      c. 3,500 (5 per cent of county total) were residents of Exeter.
      c. 13,500 (19 per cent of county total) were residents of Mid-Devon.
      c. 16,000 (22 per cent of county total) were residents of South Devon.
      c. 19,000 (27 per cent of county total) were residents of North Devon.
      c. 19,500 (27 per cent of county total) were residents of East Devon.

The statistics in this appendix are all taken from A.J. Howard (ed.), *Devon Protestation Returns*, (two vols, privately printed, 1973).

Bibliography

Primary Sources

I. Manuscripts

PUBLIC RECORD OFFICE

SP. 16, State Papers, Domestic, Charles I.
SP. 19, Records of the Committee for Advance of Money.
SP. 23, Records of the Committee for Compounding.
SP. 28, Commonwealth Exchequer Papers.
STAC 8, Star Chamber Cases, James I.

BRITISH LIBRARY

Additional MSS 9426–27, Lysons correspondence.
Additional MSS 11314, Letters relating to Devon and Cornwall.
Additional MSS 18980–82, Prince Rupert's correspondence.
Additional MSS 24984, Letters and petitions to the King.
Additional MSS 34012, Desborough's list of suspects.
Additional MSS 35297, John Syms's day-book.
Additional MSS 35331, Walter Yonge's diary.
Additional MSS 44058, Savery papers.
Burney Collection, News pamphlets, 1642–46.
Harleian MSS 6804–51, Papers of the Royalist Council of War.
Lansdowne MSS 22, 24, Letters from Devonshire, 1576.
Lansdowne MSS 377, The 'Epistle to the Moltonians'.
Sloane MSS 1775, Letter from the Devon JPs.
Thomason Tracts, News pamphlets, 1642–46.

BODLEIAN LIBRARY

Clarendon MSS, Sir Edward Hyde's papers.
Hope Adds, News pamphlets, 1642–46.
Rawlinson MSS, Papers relating to the Civil War.
Tanner MSS, The Clerk of Parliament's papers.
Top. Devon MSS, Topographical accounts of Devon.
J. Walker MSS, Dr Walker's papers.
Wood Pamphlets, News pamphlets, 1642–46.

CORNISH RECORD OFFICE

DD. T. 1610–22, Tremaine MSS.
DD. V. BO/20–21, Vyvyan MSS.
DD. R. 1051–1112, Civil War letters.

DEVON RECORD OFFICE

Book 73/15, James White's chronicle.
CC. 181, Moger papers.
CC. 198, Consistory Court papers.
CC. 866, Consistory Court depositions book, 1634–41.
CC. 867, Consistory Court depositions book, 1613–19.
DD. 35,539, Petition of Warwick Hawkey.
DD. 36,765–75, St John's, Exeter, churchwardens' accounts.
DD. 62,500, Anthony Harford's book of receipt.
DD. 62,701–13, Dartmouth financial accounts, 1642–46.
ECAB, 8, Exeter Chamber act book, 1634–47.
EQSOB, 61–64, Exeter Quarter Sessions order books, 1618–60.
EQSR, Exeter Quarter Sessions rolls, 1642–46.
QSOB, 1–8, Devon Quarter Sessions order books, 1592–1647.
QSR, Devon Quarter Sessions rolls, boxes 10–15 (1601–08), 20 (1615–16), 26–27 (1622–24), 30 (1627), 40–51 (1637–46).
QS/128, Maimed soldiers' petitions.
Y5, Miscellaneous petitions.
Z/19/36/14, John Hayne's account book.
67 A/PO 17, Farway churchwardens' accounts.
269 A/PW 8, Modbury churchwardens' accounts.
272 A/MFK 1–3, Coldridge churchwardens' accounts.
272 A/PW 6, Coldridge church rate.
347 A/PW 1–3, Dartington churchwardens' accounts.
356 A/PW 1, Poughill churchwardens' accounts.
482 A/PW 21–48, Tavistock churchwardens' accounts.
540 A/PW 1, Colebrooke churchwardens/constables' accounts.
971 A/PW 1A, Dawlish churchwardens' accounts.
1048 A/PW 1–78, Shobrooke churchwardens' accounts.
1095 A/PW 1, Zeal Monachorum churchwardens' accounts.
1146 A/PW 1, Washfield churchwardens' accounts.
1148 MA/18/2, Charles constable's accounts.
1201 A/MFK 12/B1, Hartland borough accounts.
1237 A/PW 1–56, Bere Ferrers churchwardens' accounts/rates.
1301 F/A.16, Act book of the Eight Men of Broadclyst.
1392 L, Seymour papers.
1429 A/PW 1–3, Chagford churchwardens' accounts.
1499 M/4/3–5, Tremayne MSS.
1579 A, Totnes borough records.
1639 A/PW 1, Honiton churchwardens' accounts.
1660 A/13–100, Crediton governors' accounts.
1700 M/CP 6–25, Miscellaneous letters and documents.
1815 Z PZ 1, Transcript of Bere churchwardens' accounts.

1981 A/PW 1–2, Stoke Gabriel churchwardens' accounts.
2021 A/PW 1, Lapford churchwardens' accounts.
2105 A/PW 1, Buckland-in-the Moor churchwardens' accounts.
2178 A/PW 1, Tedburn St Mary constables' accounts.
2203 A/PW 1–3, Brixham churchwardens' accounts.
2404 A/PW 1, Cullompton churchwardens' accounts.
2518 A/PF 1–30, Wolborough feoffees' accounts.
2530 M, James Huish's legacy.
2660 A/PW 1–2, Woodland churchwardens' accounts.
2715 Z/Z 1, Kingsbridge churchwardens' accounts.
2785 A/PW 1, Woodbury churchwardens' accounts.
2785 A/PX 1, Miscellaneous accounts for Woodbury.
2914 A/PW 1, North Tawton churchwardens' accounts.
2932 A/PW 7, Littleham churchwardens' accounts.
2983 A/PW 1–2, Morebath churchwardens' accounts.
3020 A/PW 1–7, Awliscombe churchwardens' accounts.
3030 A/PW 1, Uplyme churchwardens' accounts.
3047 A/PW 1–2, Kilmington churchwardens' accounts.
3134 A/P 25, Paignton churchwardens' accounts.
3147 A/PW 5, Clyst St George churchwardens' accounts.
3248 A/3/3, Okehampton sessions book, 1634–49.
3577 A/PW 1, Clawton churchwardens' accounts.
3944 A/PW 1, Chudleigh churchwardens' accounts.
4074 A/PW 1–2, Halberton churchwardens' accounts.
Letter Book 60F, Exeter siege accounts, 1642–43.
Misc. Papers, 6, Captain Gandy's accounts, 1643.

NORTH DEVON RECORD OFFICE
914/Z, North Molton churchwardens' accounts.
1469/A, Bishops Tawton churchwardens' accounts.
1677/A/PW 1, Braunton churchwardens' accounts.
1843/A/PW 1, Northam churchwardens' accounts.
3788/A/PW 1, Frithelstock churchwardens' accounts.

WEST DEVON RECORD OFFICE
W/132, Widey Court book.
W/169, Plymouth garrison accounts, 1645–46.
600/58, Buckland Monachorum churchwardens' accounts.
731/34, Yealmpton churchwardens' accounts.
796/22, Whitchurch churchwardens' accounts.
890/84, Marystow sidesmen's accounts.

EXETER CATHEDRAL LIBRARY
Act Book of the Dean and Chapter, 1635–43.

KENT ARCHIVES OFFICE
U269/A.515–25, Accounts of the Fifth Earl of Bath, 1638–46.

MR NEWTE'S LIBRARY, TIVERTON
Tiverton churchwardens' accounts, 1600–60.

SOMERSET RECORD OFFICE
DD/WO, Boxes 52–53, 56, Woleseley MSS.

DR WILLIAMS'S LIBRARY, LONDON
J. Quick, 'Icones Sacrae Anglicanea'.

WEST COUNTRY STUDIES LIBRARY, EXETER
B.F. Cresswell (ed.), 'Crediton Parish Registers', (DCRS, n.d.).
M.C.S. Cruwys (ed.), 'Clawton Churchwardens' Accounts', (DCRS, 1937).
C.A.T. Fursdon (ed.), 'Halberton Churchwardens' Accounts', (DCRS, 1930).
C.A.T. Fursdon (ed.), 'Woodbury Wardens' Accounts', (DCRS n.d.).
W.J. Harte, 'Ecclesiastical and Religious Affairs in Exeter, 1640–62', (unpublished lecture notes, 1937).
H. Johnson (ed.), 'Lustleigh Parish Registers', (DCRS, Exeter, 1927).
W.I. Leeson-Day (ed.), 'Holsworthy Registers', (DCRS, 1932).
O.M. Moger (ed.), 'Devonshire Quarter Sessions Petitions, 1642–85', (two typescript vols, 1983).
F. Nesbitt (ed.), 'Colebrooke Churchwardens' Accounts', (DCRS, 1933).
F. Nesbitt (ed.), 'Winkleigh Churchwardens' Accounts', (DCRS, n.d.).
F. Pearce (ed.), 'Modbury Churchwardens' Accounts), (DCRS, 1936).
J. Scanes (ed.), 'Dartington Churchwardens' Accounts', (DCRS, 1936), II, part 2.
E. Searle (ed.), 'Moretonhampstead Parish Registers', II, (DCRS, 1936).
Venn, 'Crediton', (two typescript vols, n.d.).
E.C. Wood (ed.), 'Widecombe-in-the-Moor Parish Registers', (DCRS, Exeter, 1938).

II. Reports of the Historical Manuscripts Commission
Cowper MSS.
De La Warre MSS.
Hatfield MSS.
Portland MSS.
Somerset MSS.
Welbeck MSS.

III. Books
Anon, *The Proposal for Raising the Price of Tin*, (c. 1693).
J. Bamfield, *Colonel Joseph Bamfield's Apologie*, (The Hague, 1685).
J. Barlow, *Hieron's Last Farewell*, (1618).
J. Barlow, *The Good Man's Glory in Affliction*, (1618).
J. Barlow, *A True Guide to Glory: A Sermon Preached at Plympton-Mary in Devon*, (1619).
J. Bond, *Occasus Occidentalis, or Job in the West*, (1645).
H. Burton, *A Divine Tragedie lately Acted*, (1641).
J. Carpenter, *Contemplations for the Institution of Children in the Christian Religion*, (1601).
T. Fuller, *The History of the Worthies of England*, (three vols, 1840 edition).
F. Glanville, *The Tavistock Naboth Proved Nabal*, (1658).
J. Hickes, *A True and Faithfull Narrative of the Unjust and Illegal Sufferings ... of many Christians ... injudiciously call'd Fanaticks*, (1671).

G. Hughes, *The Art of Embalming Dead Saints*, (1642).

E. Hyde, *The History of the Rebellion and Civil Wars in England*, (W. Dunn-Macray (ed.), six vols, Oxford, 1888).

S. Isacke, *Remarkable Antiquities of the City of Exeter*, (1677).

T. Larkham, *The Wedding-Supper*, (1652).

T. Larkham, *The Attributes of God*, (1656).

J. Mico, *A Pill to Purge out Poperie*, (1624).

F. Nicolls, *The Life and Death of Mr Ignatius Jurdain*, (2nd edn, 1655).

T. Risdon, *The Chorographical Description or Survey of the County of Devon*, (1811 edition).

J. Sprigge, *Anglia Rediviva: England's Recovery*, (1647, reprinted Oxford 1854).

J. Vicars, *The Burning Bush Not Consumed*, (1646).

J. Vicars, *England's Parliamentary Chronicle*, (1646).

E. Walker, *Historical Discourses Upon Several Occasions*, (1705).

T. Westcote, *A View of Devonshire in 1630*, (G. Oliver and P. Jones (eds), Exeter, 1845).

F. Whiddon, *A Golden Topaze or Heart-Jewell*, (Oxford, 1656).

IV. Editions of Documents

Anon, *Winthrop Papers, III*, (Massachussets Historical Society, Boston, 1943).

R. Almack (ed.), 'Papers Relating to Proceedings in the County of Kent', *Camden Miscellany III*, (Camden Society, Old Series, 61, 1855).

R. Bell (ed.), *Memorials of the Civil War: Comprising the Correspondence of the Fairfax Family*, (1849).

J. Brown, *Abstracts of Somersetshire Wills*, (six vols, 1889).

T.E. Carte (ed.), *A Collection of Original Letters and Papers ... Found among the Duke of Ormonde's Papers*, (1739).

J. Cockburn (ed.), *Western Circuit Assize Orders, 1629–48*, (Camden Society, 4th Series, 17, 1976).

R. Cornish (ed.), *Kilmington Wardens' Accounts*, (Exeter, 1901).

O.L. Dick (ed.), *Aubrey's Brief Lives*, (1987 edition).

R.N. Dore (ed.), *The Letter Books of Sir William Brereton, II, 1645–46*, (Record Society of Lancashire and Cheshire, 128, 1990).

T. Gray (ed.), *Early Stuart Mariners and Shipping: The Maritime Surveys of Devon and Cornwall, 1619–35*, (DCRS, New Series, 33, 1990).

M.A.E. Green (ed.), *Calendar of the Committee for Advance of Money, 1643–56*, (three vols, 1881).

M.A.E. Green (ed.), *Calendar of the Committee for Compounding with Delinquents, 1643–60*, (five vols, 1882–92).

I.L. Gregory (ed.), *Hartland Church Accounts*, (1950).

W.D. Hamilton (ed.), *Calendar of State Papers, Domestic Series*, (1887).

A. Hanham (ed.), *Ashburton Wardens' Accounts, 1497–1580*, (DCRS, New Series, 15, Torquay, 1970).

C. Healey (ed.), *Bellum Civile: Hopton's Narrative of his Campaign in the West*, (Somerset Record Society, 18, 1902).

D. Hey (ed.), *The History of Myddle*, (1981 edition).

F.C. H. Randolph, *Dr Walker's Sufferings of the Clergy in the Diocese of Exeter*, (Plymouth, 1908).

W.G. Hoskins (ed.), *Exeter in the Seventeenth Century: Tax and Rate Assessments, 1602–99*, (DCRS, New Series, 2, Torquay, 1957).

C. Holmes (ed.), *The Suffolk Committees for Scandalous Ministers, 1644–46*, (Suffolk Records Society, 13, 1970).

A.J. Howard (ed.), *Devon Protestation Returns*, (privately printed, 1973).

S. Jefferson (ed.), *A Narrative of the Siege of Carlisle in 1644 and 1645*, (1840, reprinted Whitehaven, 1988).

R. Jeffs et al. (eds), *Oxford Royalist Newsbooks: Volumes I–III*, (1971).

Journals of the House of Commons, vols 2–4.

Journals of the House of Lords, vols 4–8.

J. Larkin (ed.), *Stuart Royal Proclamations II: Royal Proclamations of King Charles I, 1625–46*, (1983).

T.T. Lewis (ed.), *Letters of the Lady Brilliana Harley*, (Camden Society, Old Series, 58, 1854).

W. Lewis (ed.), *Diary of the Rev Thomas Larkham*, (Bristol, 1888).

C.E. Long (ed.), *Diary of the Marches of the Royal Army During the Great Civil War*, (Camden Society, Old Series, 74, 1859).

A.G. Matthews, *Walker Revised*, (Oxford, 1948).

C. Morris (ed.), *The Illustrated Journeys of Celia Fiennes*, (1982).

F. Osborne (ed.), *The Churchwarden's Accounts of St Michael's Church, Chagford*, (1979).

N.J. Pounds (ed.), *The Parliamentary Survey of the Duchy of Cornwall: Parts I and II*, (DCRS, New Series, 25 and 27, 1982 and 1984).

E. Rhys (ed.), *Memoirs of the Life of Colonel Hutchinson, written by his Widow, Lucy*, (1913).

E. Rhys (ed.), *The Life of the Most Illustrious Duke of Newcastle*, (1915).

G. Roberts (ed.), *The Diary of Walter Yonge, Esquire*, (Camden Society, Old Series, 41, 1848).

J. Rushworth (ed.), *Historical Collections*, (eight vols, 1721–22).

T.L. Stoate (ed.), *Devon Taxes*, (privately printed, 1988).

M.J. Stoyle (ed.), 'Documentary Evidence for the Civil War Defences of Exeter, 1642–43', (Exeter Museum, 1992).

C. Trevelyan (ed.), *Trevelyan Papers, Volume III*, (Camden Society, Old Series, 105, 1872).

D. Underdown (ed.), *William Whiteway of Dorchester, His Diary*, (Dorset Record Society, 12, 1990).

R.N. Worth (ed.), *Calendar of the Plymouth Municipal Records*, (Plymouth, 1893).

R.N. Worth (ed.), *The Buller Papers*, (privately printed, 1895).

J. and J. Wylie, *Report on the Records of the City of Exeter*, (1916).

J. Youings (ed.), *Devon Monastic Lands*, (DCRS, New Series, 1, 1955).

Secondary Sources

I. Books

E.A. Andriette, *Devon and Exeter in the Civil War*, (Newton Abbot, 1971).

Anon, *A Compleat History of Devonshire*, (nd.), copy kept at Bod., Gough, Devon 20 (3).

M. Atkin, *Gloucester and the Civil War*, (Stroud, 1992).

G.E. Aylmer, *Rebellion or Revolution?: England From Civil War to Restoration*, (Oxford, 1986).

S. Baring-Gould, *Devon*, (1983 edition).

T.G. Barnes, *Somerset 1624–40: A County's Government during the Personal Rule*, (Cambridge, Massachusetts, 1961).

J. Barry (ed.), *The Tudor and Stuart Town, 1530–1688*, (1990).

A.R. Bayley, *The Great Civil War in Dorset*, (Taunton, 1910).

B.G. Blackwood, *The Lancashire Gentry and the Great Rebellion*, (Chetham Society, 3rd Series, 25, Manchester, 1978).

J.E. Boggis, *History of the Diocese of Exeter*, (Exeter, 1922).

M. Bray, *A Description of the Part of Devonshire Bordering on the Tamar and the Tavy*, (three vols, 1836).

E. Broxap, *The Great Civil War in Lancashire*, (1910, reprinted Manchester, 1973).

E.S. Chalk, *A History of the Church of St Peter, Tiverton*, (Tiverton, 1905).

J.F. Chanter, *The Life and Times of Martin Blake*, (1910).

J.R. Chanter, *Sketches of some Striking Incidents in the History of Barnstaple*, (Barnstaple, 1865).

J.R. Chanter, *Reprint of the Barnstaple Records*, (two vols, 1900).

G. Chapman, *The Siege of Lyme Regis*, (Lyme Regis, 1982).

W.D. Christie, *A Life of Anthony Ashley Cooper, 1st Earl of Shaftesbury, 1621–83*, (two vols, 1871).

J.T. Cliffe, *The Puritan Gentry: The Great Puritan Families of Early Stuart England*, (1984).

M. Coate, *Cornwall in the Great Civil War and Interregnum. A Social and Political Study*, (Oxford, 1933).

P. Collinson, *The Elizabethan Puritan Movement*, (Oxford, 1967).

P. Collinson, *The Religion of Protestants*, (Oxford, 1982).

P. Collinson, *English Puritanism*, (Historical Association pamphlet, 106, 1983).

P. Collinson, *Godly People: Essays on English Protestantism and Puritanism*, (1983).

E.S. Cope, *Politics Without Parliaments, 1629–40*, (1987).

J. Cossins, *Reminiscences of Exeter Fifty Years Since*, (Exeter, 1878).

R.W. Cotton, *Barnstaple and the Northern Part of Devonshire during the Great Civil War*, (1889).

W. Cotton (ed.), *Gleanings from the Municipal and Cathedral Records Relative to the History of the City of Exeter*, (Exeter, 1877).

B.F. Cresswell, *Notes on the Churches of the Deanery of Kenn*, (Exeter, 1912).

D. Cressy, *Literacy and the Social Order: Reading and Writing in Tudor and Stuart England*, (Cambridge, 1980).

R. Cust and A. Hughes (eds), *Conflict in Early Stuart England*, (1989).

R.P. Cust, *The Forced Loan and English Politics, 1626–28*, (Oxford, 1987).

J. Davidson, *Axminster in the Civil War*, (Axminster, 1851).

J. Davies, *The Caroline Captivity of the Church: Charles I and the Remoulding of Anglicanism*, (Oxford, 1992).

A.G. Dickens, *The Reformation*, (1967).

G. Doe, *A Few Pages of Great Torrington History*, (1896).

R.N. Dore, *The Civil Wars in Cheshire*, (Chester, 1966).

M. Dunsford, *Historical Memoirs of the Town and Parish of Tiverton*, (Exeter, 1790).

R. Dymond, *Widecombe in the Moor and its Neighbourhood*, (Torquay, 1876).

J. Eales, *Puritans and Roundheads: The Harleys of Brampton Bryan and the Outbreak of the English Civil War*, (Cambridge, 1990).

J.T. Evans, *Seventeenth-Century Norwich: Politics, Religion and Government, 1620–90*, (Oxford, 1979).

A. Everitt, *The Community of Kent and the Great Rebellion*, (1966).

A. Everitt, *Landscape and Community in England*, (1985).

H.P.R. Finberg, *West-Country Historical Studies*, (New York, 1969).

A.J. Fletcher, *A County Community in Peace and War: Sussex 1600–60*, (London, 1975).

A.J. Fletcher, *The Outbreak of the English Civil War*, (1981).

R. Fraser, *A General View of the County of Devon*, (1794).

G. Friend, *Memories of Moretonhampstead*, (Exeter, 1989).

S.R. Gardiner, *History of the Civil War*, (three vols, 1886–91).

P. Gaunt, *A Nation under Siege: The Civil War in Wales, 1642–48*, (1991).

I. Gentles, *The New Model Army*, (Oxford, 1992).

C. Gill, *Dartmoor: A New Study*, (Newton Abbot, 1970).

J. Gover et al. (eds), *The Place Names of Devon: I*, (Cambridge, 1969).

R. Granville, *The King's General in the West: The Life of Sir Richard Granville, 1600–59*, (1908).

T. Gray et al. (eds), *Tudor and Stuart Devon*, (Exeter, 1992).

J.B. Gribble, *Memorials of Barnstaple*, (Barnstaple, 1830).

F. Halliday (ed.), *Richard Carew of Anthony: The Survey of Cornwall*, (1953).

W. Hals, *The Compleat History of Cornwall*, (Exeter, 1750).

A.H.A. Hamilton, *Quarter Sessions from Queen Elizabeth to Queen Anne*, (1878).

C. Hill, *Society and Puritanism in Pre-Revolutionary England*, (1986).

C. Hill, *The World Turned Upside Down*, (1984).

C. Holmes, *The Eastern Association in the English Civil War*, (Cambridge, 1974).

W.G. Hoskins, *Industry, Trade and People in Exeter, 1688–1800*, (Manchester, 1935),

W.G. Hoskins, *Devon*, (1954).

W.G. Hoskins, *Old Devon*, (Newton Abbot, 1966).

W.G. Hoskins, *Two Thousand Years in Exeter*, (Exeter, 1960).

R. Howell, *Newcastle-on-Tyne and the Puritan Revolution*, (Oxford, 1967).

A. Hughes, *Politics, Society and Civil War in Warwickshire, 1620–60*, (Cambridge, 1987).

A. Hughes, *The Causes of the English Civil War*, (1991).

W. Hunt, *The Puritan Moment: The Coming of Revolution in an English County*, (1983).

R. Hutton, *The Royalist War Effort, 1642–46*, (1982).

M. Ingram, *Church Courts, Sex and Marriage in England, 1570–1640*, (Cambridge, 1987).

A. Jenkins, *The History ... of the City of Exeter*, (1806).

P. Lake and K. Sharpe (eds), *Culture and Politics in Early Stuart England*, (1994).

G.R. Lewis, *The Stannaries: A Study of the English Tin-miner*, (1908).

B. Little, *The Monmouth Episode*, (1956).

D. and S. Lysons, *Magna Brittania; being a concise Topographical Account of the several Counties of Great Britain, Volume 6*, (1822).

W.T. MacCaffrey, *Exeter, 1540–1640: The Growth of an English County Town*, (Cambridge, 1958).

E.T. MacDermot, *A History of the Forest of Exmoor*, (Newton Abbot, 1973).

D. MacCulloch, *Suffolk and the Tudors: Politics and Religion in an English County, 1500–1600*, (Oxford, 1986).

J.L. Malcolm, *Caesar's Due: Loyalty and King Charles, 1642–46*, (RHS Studies in History, 38, 1983).

B. Manning, *The English People and the English Revolution*, (1976).

W. Marshall, *The Rural Economy of the West of England*, (two vols, 1796).

A.C. Miller, *Sir Richard Grenville of the Civil War*, (1979).

T. Moore, *The History and Topography of Devonshire*, (three vols, 1829).

J. Morrill, *Cheshire 1630–60: County Government and Society During the English Revolution*, (Oxford, 1974).

J. Morrill, *The Revolt of the Provinces: Conservatives and Radicals in the English Civil War*, (1976).

J. Morrill (ed.), *Reactions to the English Civil War*, (1982).

J. Morrill (ed.), *The Impact of the English Civil War*, (1991).

J. Morrill, *The Nature of the English Revolution*, (1993).

P.R. Newman, *Royalist Officers of England and Wales, 1642–60: A Biographical Dictionary*, (New York, 1981).

N. Orme (ed.), *Unity and Variety: A History of the Church in Devon and Cornwall*, (Exeter, 1991).

V. Pearl, *London and the Outbreak of the Puritan Revolution*, (Oxford, 1961).

R. Pearse-Chope, *Farthest from Railways: An Unknown Corner of Devon*, (1934).

R.R. Pennington, *Stannary Law*, (Newton Abbot, 1973).

J.R. Phillips, *Memoirs of the Civil Wars in Wales and the Marches*, (two volumes, 1874).

R. Polwhele, *The History of Devonshire*, (1797).

A. Powell, *John Aubrey and his Friends*, (1988).

B. Reay (ed.), *Popular Culture in Seventeenth Century England*, (1988).

L.J. Reeve, *Charles I and the Road to Personal Rule*, (Cambridge, 1989).

R.C. Richardson (ed.), *Town and Countryside in the English Revolution*, (Manchester, 1992).

S.K. Roberts, *Recovery and Restoration in an English County: Devon Local Administration, 1646–70*, (Exeter, 1985).

H.C.B. Rogers, *Battles and Generals of the English Civil Wars*, (1968).

I. Roots, *The Great Rebellion, 1642–60*, (1966).

A.L. Rowse, *Tudor Cornwall*, (1941).

C. Russell (ed.), *The Origins of the English Civil War*, (1973).

C. Russell, *The Causes of the English Civil War*, (Oxford, 1990).

R.E. St Leger-Gordon, *The Witchcraft and Folklore of Dartmoor*, (1965).

P. Seaver, *The Puritan Lectureships: The Politics of Religious Dissent, 1560–1662*, (1970).

P. Seaver (ed.), *Seventeenth Century England: Society in an Age of Revolution*, (1976).

P. Seaver, *Wallington's World: A Puritan Artisan in Seventeenth Century London*, (Stanford, 1985).

B. Sharp, *In Contempt of All Authority: Rural Artisans and Riot in the West of England, 1586–1660*, (Berkley, 1980).

K. Sharpe, *Politics and Ideas in Early Stuart England*, (1989).

K. Sharpe, *The Personal Rule of Charles I*, (1992).

R.E. Sherwood, *Civil Strife in the Midlands, 1642–51*, (Chichester, 1974).

P. Slack (ed.), *Rebellion, Popular Protest and the Social Order in Early Modern England*, (Cambridge, 1968).

P. Slack, *Plagues and Peoples*, (1985).

M. Spufford, *Contrasting Communities*, (Cambridge, 1974).

M. Spufford, *Small Books and Pleasant Histories*, (1981).

W.B. Stephens, *Seventeenth Century Exeter: A Study of Industrial and Commercial Development*, (Exeter, 1958).

J. Stucley, *Sir Bevill Grenville*, (Southampton, 1983).

B.E. Supple, *Commercial Crisis and Change in England, 1600–42*, (Cambridge, 1970).

P. Tennant, *Edgehill and Beyond: The People's War in the South Midlands, 1642–45*, (Stroud, 1992).

J. Thirsk (ed.), *The Agrarian History of England and Wales, IV: 1500–1640*, (Cambridge, 1967).

J. Thirsk (ed.), *The Agrarian History of England and Wales, V.1: Regional Farming Systems, 1640–1750*, (Cambridge, 1984).

C. Torre, *Small Talk at Wreyland*, (J. Simmonds (ed.), Cambridge, 1970).

G.M. Trevelyan, *England Under the Stuarts*, (1904).

H.R. Trevor-Roper, *Catholics, Anglicans and Puritans*, (1987).

N. Tyacke, *Anti-Calvinists: The Rise of English Arminianism*, (Oxford, 1987).

D. Underdown, *Somerset in the Civil War and Interregnum*, (Newton Abbot, 1973).

D. Underdown, *Revel, Riot and Rebellion*, (Oxford, 1985).

D. Underdown, *Fire from Heaven*, (1992).

C. Vancouver, *General View of the Agriculture of the County of Devon*, (1808; reprinted Newton Abbot 1969).

M.F. Wakelin, *Language and History in Cornwall*, (Leicester, 1985).

H. Walrond, *Historical Records of the First Devonshire Militia*, (1897).

J. Watkins, *An Essay towards a History of Bideford in the County of Devon*, (Exeter, 1792).

C.V. Wedgwood, *The King's War*, (1958).

R. Whiting, *The Blind Devotion of the People: Popular Religion and the English Reformation*, (Cambridge, 1989).

A.C. Wood, *Nottinghamshire in the Civil War*, (Oxford, 1937).

W. Wright (ed.), *Some Account of the Barony and Town of Okehampton*, (Tiverton, 1889).

K. Wrightson and D. Levine, *Poverty and Piety in an English Village: Terling 1525–1700*, (1979).

K. Wrightson, *English Society, 1580–1680*, (1982).

J. Wroughton, *A Community at War*, (Bath, 1992).

II. Articles

P.F.S. Amery, 'Eleventh Report on Devonshire Folklore', *TDA*, 24, (1892), pp. 49–54.

G.E. Aylmer, 'Collective Mentalities in Mid-Seventeenth Century England', *TRHS*, 5th series, 36, (1986), pp. 1–25; *TRHS*, 5th series, 37, (1987), pp. 1–30; *TRHS*, 5th series, 38, (1988), pp. 1–25; *TRHS*, 5th series, 39, (1989), pp. 1–22.

T.G. Barnes, 'County Politics and a Puritan Cause Celebre: Somerset Churchales, 1633', *TRHS*, pp. 103–22.

G.W. Bernard, 'The Church of England, 1529–1642', *History*, 75, no. 244, (June 1990).

W.J. Blake, 'Hooker's Synopsis Chorographical of Devonshire', *TDA*, 47, (1915), pp. 334–48.

R.J.E. Bush, 'The Civil War and Interregnum in Exeter, 1642–60', *DCNQ*, 29, (1962), pp. 80–87, 102–09, 132–38, 171–76.

J. Castlehow, 'The Duchy of Lancaster in the County of Devon', *TDA*, 80, (1948), pp. 193–209.

P. Clark, 'Thomas Scott and the Growth of Urban Opposition to the Stuart Regime', *HJ*, 21, (1978), pp. 1–26.

M. Coate, 'An Original Diary of Colonel Robert Bennet of Hexworthy' (1642–43), *DCNQ*, 18, (1935), pp. 251–59.

M. Coate, 'The Duchy of Cornwall: Its History and Administration, 1640–60', *TRHS*, 4th Series, 10, (1927), pp. 135–69.

M. Coate, 'Exeter in the Civil War and Interregnum', *DCNQ*, 18, (1935), pp. 338–52.

R.W. Cotton, 'Naval Attack on Topsham', *DCNG*, 1, (1888), pp. 153–54.

R.W. Cotton, 'A North Devon Cavalier's Expenses', *DCNG*, 3, (1890), pp. 68–71.

R. Cust, 'News and Politics in Early Seventeenth-Century England', *P&P*, 112, (August 1986), pp. 60–90.

J.R. Dias, 'Lead, Society and Politics in Derbyshire before the Civil War, *Midland History*, 6, (1981).

H.P. Finberg, 'The Stannary of Tavistock', *TDA*, 81, (1949), pp. 155–84.

A. Fisher, 'The Apologie, Relation and Petition of Colonel John Were', *DCNQ*, 4, (1906–07), pp. 153–74.

A. Fletcher, 'New Light on Religion and the English Civil War', *Journal of Ecclesiastical History*, 38, (1987), pp. 95–106.

P. Gladwish, 'The Herefordshire Clubmen: A Reassessment', *Midland History*, 10, (1985), pp. 62–71.

T. Greeves, 'The Great Courts or Parliaments of Devon Tinners', *TDA*, 119, (1987), pp. 145–67.

A.H. Hamilton, 'The Justices of the Peace for the County of Devon under Charles I and Cromwell', *TDA*, 10 (1878), pp. 309–14.

C. Hill, 'Puritans and "The Dark Corners of the Land"', *TRHS*, 5th Series, 13, (1963), pp. 77–102.

G.W. Hughes, 'Moretonhampstead', *TDA*, 86, (1954), pp. 75–88.

R. Hutton, 'The Worcestershire Clubmen in the Civil War', *Midland History*, 5, (1979–80), pp. 40–49.

R. Hutton, 'The Failure of the Lancashire Cavaliers', *Transactions of the Lancashire and Cheshire Historic Society*, 129, (1980), pp. 47–69.

R. Hutton, 'Clarendon's History of the Rebellion', *EHR*, 97, (1982), pp. 70–88.

P.Q. Karkeek, 'Fairfax in the West, 1645–46', *TDA*, 8, (1876), pp. 117–47.

P.Q. Karkeek, 'Sir Edmund Fortescue and the Siege of Fort Charles', *TDA*, 9, (1877), pp. 336–50.

P.Q. Karkeek, 'Extracts from a Memorandum Book belonging to Thomas Roberts and Family of Stockleigh Pomeroy, 1621–44', *TDA*, 10, (1878), pp. 315–29.

P.Q. Karkeek, 'Jacobite Days in the West', *TDA*, 28, (1896).

E. Lega-Weeks, 'The Churchwardens' Accounts of South Tawton', *TDA*, pp. 39–41, (1907–09).

J. Malcolm, 'A King in Search of Soldiers: Charles I in 1642', *HJ*, 21, (1978), pp. 251–74.

A.C. Miller, 'The Impact of the Civil War on Devon and the Decline of the Royalist Cause in the West of England, 1644–45', *TDA*, 104, (1972), pp. 149–74.

A.C. Miller, 'Joseph Jane's Account of Cornwall During the Civil War', *EHR*, 90, (1975), pp. 94–102.

J.S. Morrill, 'Provincial Squires and "Middling Sorts" in the Great Rebellion', *HJ*, 20, (1977), pp. 229–36.

J.S. Morrill, 'The Religious Context of the English Civil War', *TRHS*, 5th Series, 34, (1984), pp. 155–78.

J.S. Morrill, 'The Ecology of Allegiance in the English Revolution', *JBS*, 26, no. 4, (1987), pp. 451–67.

I.R. Palfrey, 'Devon and the Outbreak of the English Civil War, 1642–43', *Southern History*, 10, (1988), pp. 29–46.

I.R. Palfrey, 'The Royalist War Effort Revisited: Edward Seymour and the Royalist Garrison at Dartmouth, 1643–44', *TDA*, 123, (1991), pp. 41–55.

J. Pearson, 'On an Estate formerly belonging to the Duchy of Lancaster', *TDA*, 32, (1900), pp. 407–11.

H. Peskett, 'Heresy in Axminster in 1535', *DCNQ*, 33, (1977), pp. 68–70.

J.B. Phear, 'Molland Accounts', *TDA*, 35, (1903), pp. 198–238.

C.B. Phillips, 'County Committees in Cumberland and Westmoreland', *Northern History*, 5, (1970), pp. 37–56.

C.B. Phillips, 'The Royalist North: The Cumberland and Westmoreland Gentry, 1642–60', *Northern History*, 14, (1978), pp. 170–89.

Lady Radford, 'Notes on the Tinners of Devon and their Laws', *TDA*, 62, (1930), pp. 225–47.

J. Roberts, 'The Armada Lord Lieutenant, parts 1 and 2', *TDA*, 102–03, (1970–71), pp. 71–85 and pp. 103–22.

F. Snell, 'A Devonshire Yeoman's Diary', in G. Apperson (ed.), *Gleanings After Time*, (1907), pp. 160–75.

J. Somerville, 'Ideology, Property and Constitution', in Cust and Hughes (eds), *Conflict in Early Stuart England*, pp. 47–71.

P. Styles, 'The Royalist Government of Worcestershire During the Civil War', *Transactions of the Worcestershire Archaeological Society*, 3rd Series, 5, (1976), pp. 23–40.

R.L. Taverner, 'The Administrative Work of the Devon JPs in the Seventeenth Century', *TDA*, 100, (1968), pp. 55–84.

J. Thirsk, 'Seventeenth Century Agriculture and Social Change', in Seaver (ed.), *Seventeenth Century England*, pp. 71–110.

F.B. Troup, 'An Exeter Worthy', *TDA*, 29, (1897), pp. 350–77.

N. Tyacke, 'Puritanism, Arminianism and Counter-Revolution' in C. Russell (ed.), *The Origins of the English Civil War*, (1973), pp. 119–43.

N. Tyacke, 'Popular Puritan Mentality in Late Elizabethan England' in P. Clark, et al. (eds), *The English Commonwealth*, (Leicester, 1979), pp. 77–92.

D. Underdown, 'The Chalk and the Cheese: Contrasts among the English Clubmen', *P&P*, 85, (1979), pp. 25–48.

D. Underdown, 'The Problem of Popular Allegiance in the English Civil War', *TRHS*, 5th Series, 31, (1980), pp. 69–94.

D. Underdown, 'A Reply to John Morrill', *JBS*, 26, 4 (1987), pp. 468–79.

M.D.G. Wanklyn, 'The People Go to War', *The Local Historian*, 17, 8 (1987), pp. 497–98.

R.N. Worth, 'The Siege of Plymouth', *RTPI*, 5, (1875–76), pp. 250–311.

E.H. Young, 'Okehampton during the Civil War', *TDA*, 60, (1928), pp. 277–98.

III. Theses

I. Cassidy, 'The Episcopate of William Cotton Bishop of Exeter 1598–1621', (upublished D.Phil. thesis, Oxford, 1963).

R.P. Cust, 'The Forced Loan and English Politics, 1626–28', (Ph.D. thesis, London, 1984).

A. Duffin, 'The Political Allegiances of the Cornish Gentry, 1600–42', (unpublished Ph.D. thesis, Exeter, 1989).

I.W. Gowers, 'Puritanism in the County of Devon between 1570 and 1641', (unpublished MA thesis, Exeter, 1970).

T. Gray, 'Devon's Coastal and Overseas Fisheries and New England Migration, 1593–1642', (unpublished Ph.D. thesis, Exeter, 1992).

T.A. Greeves, 'The Devon Tin Industry 1450–1750, (unpublished Ph.D. thesis, Exeter, 1981).

A. Kittermaster, 'Politics and Religion in Exeter: 1635–60', (unpublished Ph.D. thesis, Exeter, 1985).

B. Manning, 'Neutrals and Neutralism in the English Civil War', (unpublished D.Phil. thesis, Oxford, 1957).

I.R. Palfrey, 'The Royalist War Effort in Devon, 1642–46', (unpublished MA thesis, Birmingham, 1985).

S. Porter, 'The Destruction of Urban Property in the English Civil Wars, 1642–51', (Ph.D. thesis, London, 1983).

I. Roy, 'The Royalist Army in the First Civil War', (unpublished D.Phil. thesis, Oxford, 1963).

M.J. Stoyle, 'Divisions within the Devonshire "County Community" *c.* 1600–46', (D.Phil. thesis, Oxford, 1992).

M.D.G. Wanklyn, 'Landed Society and Allegiance in Cheshire and Shropshire in the First Civil War, (unpublished Ph.D. thesis, Manchester, 1976).

A.M. Wolffe, 'The Gentry Government of Devon, 1625–40', (unpublished Ph.D. thesis, Exeter, 1992).

Index

Clayhidon 51, 87.
Cliffe, J.T., 22.
Close, George, minister 191.
cloth industry and clothworkers 9, 13–16,
90–91, 105–16, 149, 155–57, 160–61, 172,
176, 188, 190–91, 199–200, 202.
Clovelly 127–28, 137.
clubmen, 29, 111–32, *passim*, 150–52,
246–47.
Clyst Hydon 118.
Clyst St George 225.
Clyst St Lawrence 225.
Coate, Mary, 232, 237.
Coldridge 225.
Cole, John, separatist 194.
Colebrooke 225.
Coles, Richard, minister 199.
Collinson, Patrick, 185.
Collyer, Richard, glovemaker xvi.
Colyford 146.
Colyton 176, 179, 189–91.
Comb Pine 190.
Commission of Array, 31, 40, 139–41, 143,
164–65, 169.
Committee for Advance of Money 76.
Committee for Compounding 76.
common prayer, book of, 98, 183–84,
190, 196, 198–99, 207, 239.
consistory court 216.
constables 18, 20, 40–41, 50–51, 63–64,
66–67, 119, 121, 183, 219.
Cookbury 195.
Cooke, Richard, weaver 109.
Cooke, William, minister 199.
Corbet, John, 244–45.
Cornish, James, 64.
Cornwall and the Cornish xv, 7–8, 16–17,
21, 28–29, 31–32, 36–37, 47, 55, 68,
100, 119, 126–27, 140, 145–47, 149–52,
164–65, 206, 208–09, 218, 232–38 *passim*,
239, 241.
Cornwall, duchy of, 18–19, 237.
Coryton, William, member of parliament,
165.
Cottington, Francis, chancellor 170.
Cottington, George, tithe-farmer 170–71.
Cotton, William, bishop 21–22, 186–87.
Cotton, W.G., 125.
Courtenay family 21.
Courtenay, John, esquire 121, 129.
Courtenay, Sir William, 204–05, 212.
Covent Garden 252.
Coxe, Benjamin, minister 192–93, 195.

Coxe, William, doctor 102.
Cranbrook, co. Kent 252.
Crediton 12, 15, 52, 66–68, 77, 86, 104,
115–16, 120, 147, 157, 176, 198–99.
Cresswell, B.F., 213.
Crowland, Lincolnshire 252.
Crumpton, William, preacher 193–94,
203.
cudgel-playing 219.
Cullompton 9, 15, 50, 87, 146, 157, 172,
176, 178, 180, 182, 191, 225–26.
Culme, Richard, sheriff 140.
Culmstock 51, 87, 230.
Cumberland 248–49.
Cust, Richard, 163, 167, 178.

Dart, River, 8.
Dartmoor 11–12, 16–18, 65, 82, 154, 157,
161, 199, 208–09, 211, 254.
Dartmouth 12, 19–20, 27–29, 35, 45–48,
62, 68, 84, 89, 124, 140–41, 197–98, 200,
224–25, 231, 254.
Dartington 224.
Davenport, William, 165.
Davey, John, of Burrington 120.
Davy, Sir John, 138.
Dawlish 14, 225.
Dean, Forest of, 244.
Dedham, co. Essex 194–95.
Delbridge, John, merchant 178, 180–81,
193, 199, 202.
Derbyshire 252–53.
Desborough, John, major-general 76–77,
91–92, 104.
Digby, Lord George, 167.
Dintch, John, soldier 112.
Diptford 112.
disease 27, 35, 159.
Dodding, William, minister 198.
Doddiscombsleigh 82.
Dorchester, co. Dorset 51, 190, 246.
Dore, Norman, 239, 244.
Dorset 3, 9, 14, 79, 113–14, 128, 245–46.
Down, East, 41, 176.
Down, West, 41.
Down, Richard, minister 192.
Drake, Sir Francis, 138.
Drewe, Sir Thomas, 138, 173.
Drewsteignton 82, 206.
Dudley, co. Staffordshire 253.
Duke, John, 115.
Dulverton, co. Somerset 118, 246.
Dunchideock 82.

Dunsford 63–66, 78, 206, 213–14.
Dunster, co. Somerset 246.
Dunterton 82.

Eales, Jacqueline, 242.
Eastern Association 251.
Edward VI 237.
Eggesford, 192.
Egloskerry, co. Cornwall 150.
Elizabeth I 191.
Elliot, William, cordwainer 220–21.
Ely, Isle of, 252.
Erle, Sir Walter, 189.
Ermington 198.
Essex, county of, 167, 178, 182, 194–95, 206, 252, 254.
Essex, Earl of, 29, 35–39, 42, 47–50, 66–67, 140, 145, 233–34, 243.
Evans, Richard, captain 144.
Evers, Compton, lieutenant 168–69, 178.
Exe, River, 7–9, 11, 69, 202.
Exeter 9, 11, 15, 19–22, 27–28, 31, 33, 35, 45–47, 50–51, 63, 65–66, 69, 71, 74, 76–77, 87, 93–110 passim, 112, 118, 120, 124, 137–38, 140, 142, 145, 161, 172–73, 175, 178, 183, 186–88 passim, 200, 205–06, 213, 253.
——, All Hallows Goldsmith Street parish, 107.
——, Bear Inn, 97–98.
——, Cathedral close, 21, 99–100, 106–07, 205.
——, St Davids parish, 109.
——, Dean and chapter, 99, 212.
——, St Edmunds parish, 109.
——, St George parish, 107.
——, Holy Trinity parish, 109, 220–21.
——, St Kerrian parish, 107, 188.
——, St Lawrence parish, 107.
——, St Martins parish, 102, 106–07.
——, St Mary Arches parish, 107, 188.
——, St Mary Major parish, 107.
——, St Mary Steps parish, 107.
——, St Olaves parish, 107, 109.
——, St Pancras parish, 107.
——, St Pauls parish, 107.
——, St Petrock parish, 107, 188.
——, St Sidwells parish, 109.
——, St Stephens parish, 107.
——, South Gate prison, 144.
Exmoor 13, 128, 151, 170–71, 178.
Exmouth 69.

Fairfax, Sir Thomas, 36–37, 41–42, 46, 48, 67, 70, 94–95, 117–18, 121, 124–25, 131, 140, 234, 238–39, 248.
Feniton 75, 225.
Fenland 252, 254.
Fiennes, Celia, 152.
Finch, Sir John, lord keeper 163.
fishing industry 13–14, 158, 175.
Flanders and the Flemings 199–200, 202.
Fletcher, Anthony, 215.
folklore 66–67, 75, 201, 202, 213–14.
Foord, William, colonel 123, 129.
Ford, Thomas, lecturer 197.
forced loan 163–64, 166–67, 171–72, 178.
'foreigners' 17, 59, 99. See also **Cornwall, Flanders, Holland, Ireland, Scotland, Spain, Wales.**
Fort, John, clothier 190.
Fortescue, Sir Edmund, 47, 62.
Fraser, Robert, 155.
Fulford, Sir Francis, 66, 78, 139.
Fulford House 52, 66, 78.
Fylde, co. Lancashire 246–47.

gaming 221.
Garnett, —, minister 64–65, 206.
Gaunt, Peter, 240.
Gefferyes, George, minister 198.
Germansweek 67.
Gibson, —, lieutenant colonel 168.
Gidleigh 82.
Gifford family 21.
Gittesham 144.
Gloucester 94, 244–45.
Gloucestershire 244–45.
Godolphin, Sidney, poet xv–xvi, 67.
Godolphin, William, colonel 147.
Gollopp, John, musician 97–98.
Goring, Lord George, 29, 36, 116–26, 128–29, 131, 151, 246.
'Goring's Crew' 120, 123.
Gough, Richard, 254.
Gowers, Ian, 202.
Gray, Todd, 14.
'Grecians' 109.
Grenville, Sir Bevill, 32, 147.
Grenville, Sir John, 144.
Grenville, Sir Richard, 29, 71, 112, 114–16, 119, 147, 235.
Grosse, Alexander, lecturer 197, 200, 210.

Halberton 50, 87, 118, 131, 155, 180, 216, 226.

sailors, *see* **seamen.**
Salcombe 49.
Salcombe castle 47, 49.
Salford hundred, co. Lancashire 246–47.
Salisbury, co. Wiltshire 128.
Saltash, co. Cornwall 204, 236.
Salway, John, 189.
Sampford Courtenay 82, 225.
Sampford Peverill 82.
Sandford 41, 66, 192, 195–96.
Satterlie, —, minister 65, 207.
Saunders, Humphrey, minister 195.
Saunders, Richard, major 101.
Scarborough, co. Yorkshire 253.
schoolmasters 193, 195.
Scotland and the Scots 163–64, 166–67, 169, 182, 241, 249–50, 255.
seamen 14, 33, 41, 89–91, 156–61 *passim*, 169.
Searell, Edward, 220.
Searle, John, of Buckerell 50.
Seaton 146, 190.
seminary priests 22.
Seymour, Edward, colonel 46–48, 62.
Seymour, Sir Edward, 139.
Shaugh Prior 198.
Sharp, Buchanan, 153.
Sharpe, Kevin, 202.
Shebbear, manor of, 18.
Sheepstor 183.
Sheffield, co. Yorks 248.
Shepton Mallet, co. Somerset 246.
Sherborne, co. Dorset 31, 45, 49–50, 99, 143, 245.
Sherwill, Thomas, magistrate 180–81, 196, 202.
Ship Money 160, 163–64, 166, 172–76 *passim*, 178–79, 181–82, 191.
Shirwell 192–93.
Short, Anthony, minister 206.
Short Parliament, the, 163–64.
Shrewsbury, co. Shropshire 243.
Shropshire 242–43, 245, 254.
Shute 190.
Sidbury 87, 190–91.
Sidmouth 14, 183, 207.
Silverton 82, 120, 154.
Slanning, Nicholas, colonel 147.
Slapton 48.—
Snape, Edmund, preacher 187, 199.
Somerset 3, 13, 32–33, 79, 113–14, 116–18, 122–24, 128, 151, 156, 168–69, 215, 218, 222, 245–46.

Sourton Down, battle of, 27.
South Pool 198.
Southcombe, Humfrey, 64.
Southcote, Sir Popham, 139.
Southmead, John, gentleman 199, 202, 206, 219.
Spain 158, 229.
Speccot, Sir John, 138.
Spie, The, 221–22.
Sports, book of, 166, 182, 217.
Spreyton 67, 82, 200.
Squire, Roger, minister 192.
Staffordshire 252–53.
Stamford, Earl of, 31, 33–34, 101–02, 112, 242.
Stanborough, hundred of, 151.
stannaries 16–17, 19, 68, 157–58, 237. *See also* **tin-miners.**
'star of the west', *see* **Hieron, Samuel.**
Staverton 12.
Stevens, —, minister 200.
Stockport, co. Cheshire 243.
Stoke Gabriel 82, 224.
Stokenham 48.
Stow-on-the-Wold, co. Gloucestershire, 244.
Stratton, co. Cornwall 126, 150–52, 236, 241.
Stratton, battle of, 28, 33–34, 37–38, 40, 45, 93, 95, 112, 140.
Strode, Sir Richard, 138, 179–80.
Suffolk 161, 252.
Survey of Cornwall 218.
Sussex 252.
Swete, Mr Adrian, 48.
Swimbridge 169.
Sydenham, Sir Ralph, 139.
Symonds, Richard, captain 234, 243, 246.
Syms, John, minister 183.

Tamar, River, 8, 119, 126, 149–50, 233–34, 236.
Tapp, James, anabaptist 190.
Taunton, co. Somerset 40, 50, 78, 246.
Tavistock 12, 15–16, 18, 62–63, 66–68, 82, 161, 200, 210–11, 213–14, 217.
Taw, River, 8, 13.
Tawstock 18, 38, 59.
Tawton, South, 82.
Tedburn St Mary 63–65, 67, 206.
Teign, River, 11.
Teign, South, manor of, 18.
Teign valley 213–14.